VISUAL QUICKSTART GUIDE

InDesign cs3

FOR MACINTOSH AND WINDOWS

SANDEE COHEN

Peachpit Press

Visual QuickStart Guide

InDesign cs3 for Macintosh and Windows

Copyright © 2008 by Sandee Cohen

Peachpit Press

1249 Eighth Street
Berkeley, CA 94710
510 524 2178
510 524 2221 (fax)

Find us on the Web at www.peachpit.com.
To report errors, please send a note to errata@peachpit.com.

Peachpit Press is a division of Pearson Education.

Editor: Becky Morgan
Production Editor: Becky Winter
Compositor & Interior Design: Sandee Cohen
Cover Design: Peachpit Press
Copy Editor: Dave Awl
Proofreader: Dave Awl
Indexer: Steve Rath

ISBN-13: 978-0-321-50306-0
ISBN-10: 0-321-50306-6
0 9 8 7 6 5 4 3 2 1

Printed and bound in the United States of America

Dedicated to

MY STUDENTS

You ask all the right questions, so I have to figure out the right answers.

Thanks to

Nancy Ruenzel, publisher of Peachpit Press.

Becky Morgan, my editor at Peachpit Press. Thanks for being so patient with me.

Becky Winter, for her eagle production eye.

The staff of Peachpit Press, all of whom make me proud to be a Peachpit author.

Steve Rath, the best indexer I've ever had. Steve proves the point that indexing is an art, and no program can ever automate the decision making involved in creating an elegant index.

Dave Awl, my new right hand, who dissected all the new features, marked up the previous edition, took screen shots, and then copyedited the whole damn thing! He even wrote one of the jokes in a sidebar. "It's only funny till someone loses an icon!"

Robert Levine, of the User-to-User forum, who figured out how I could still use the new numbering system for all the exercises in the book. His one suggestion helped me save many hours of manual labor.

Barry Anderson and **David Blatner** of the InDesign Conference and Creative Suite Conference. Speaking at those events helps me write better.

Peter Truskier of Premedia Systems (www.premediasystems.com) who created the script that automated my screen shot spotlights.

Dave Saunders who created my script to find all overset text boxes. Dave is a terrific scripter who can write custom scripts to order. Reach him at www.pdsassoc.com.

Hemera™ Technologies which gave me the use of its extensive Photo-Objects 50,000 collection of photographs. The DVDs and search engine made looking for artwork a real pleasure.

The **InDesign team** in Seattle, who continue to make InDesign my favorite program to use and to write about. In fact, cs3 is so good, I broke my own rule and moved the book from the previous version over to the new one in the middle of production.

The **InDesign Talk List** of the Yahoo listserve. You all have given me great insight as to what subjects I need to cover. You have also given me great tips in working with InDesign.

The **InDesign User to User forum**. We may not always agree, but we've created a great community of questions, comments, advice, complaints, and silly threads.

And a very special thanks to **David Lerner** of **Tekserve,** who once again helped me keep my computers running in the middle of the book crunch. Tekserve (www.tekserve.com) is the best place to buy, fix, or enhance Macintosh computers.

Colophon

This book was created using InDesign cs3. The computers used were a MacBook Pro and a Sony Vaio. Screen shots were taken using Snapz Pro X (Macintosh) and Snaggit (Windows). Fonts used were Minion Pro and Myriad Pro from Adobe.

TABLE OF CONTENTS

INTRODUCTION

Welcome to the *InDesign* cs3 *Visual QuickStart Guide*, my sixth version of the book. It's hard to believe how quickly InDesign has become a major force in desktop publishing and page layout. I feel very lucky to have been working with and teaching InDesign since its very first version. In fact, this is the only third-party book that has had editions for all four versions of InDesign.

Rarely has an application caused as much excitement as InDesign. The first version, released in April 2000, was hailed for its innovative typographic features. Version 1.5, which came out in December of 2000, added more tools and text controls. With version 2, InDesign created great excitement by adding transparency effects, drop shadows, feather effects, and support for transparency in files imported from Photoshop and Illustrator.

When InDesign became part of the Creative Suite packages, things really took off. Now, with InDesign cs3, Adobe has added more sophisticated effects, text variables, and better integration with the other cs3 applications. My favorite new feature is the automatic numbered lists which you will see throughout this book. Just that feature alone has saved me hours and hours of work.

Using This Book

If you have used any of the other Visual QuickStart Guides, you will find this book to be similar. Each chapter is divided into different sections that deal with a specific topic — usually a tool or command. For instance, the chapter on text has sections on creating text frames, typing text, selecting text, and so on.

Each of the sections contains numbered exercises that show you how to perform a specific technique. As you work through the steps, you gain an understanding of the technique or feature. The illustrations help you judge if you are following the steps correctly.

I've also sprinkled sidebars, printed in gray boxes, throughout the chapters. Some of these sidebars give you a bit of history or background for a specific feature. Other times, I've written out humorous stories about desktop publishing. These sidebars are the same as the little stories and anecdotes I tell my students in the classes I teach.

Instructions

You will find it easier to use this book once you understand the terms I am using. This is especially important since some other computer books use terms differently. Therefore, here are the terms I use in the book and explanations of what they mean.

Click refers to pressing down and releasing the mouse button on the Macintosh, or the left mouse button on Windows. You must release the mouse button or it is not a click.

Press means to hold down the mouse button, or a keyboard key.

Press and drag means to hold the mouse button down and then move the mouse. I also use the shorthand term **drag**. Just remember that you have to press and hold as you drag the mouse.

Menu Commands

InDesign has menu commands that you follow to open dialog boxes, change artwork, and initiate certain actions. These menu commands are listed in bold type. The typical direction to choose a menu command might be written as **Object > Arrange > Bring to Front**. This means that you should first choose the Object menu, then choose the Arrange submenu, and then choose the Bring to Front command.

Keyboard Shortcuts

Most of the menu commands for InDesign have keyboard shortcuts that help you work faster. For instance, instead of choosing New from the File menu, it is faster and easier to use the keyboard shortcut (Cmd-N on the Macintosh and Ctrl-N on Windows). Often these shortcuts use multiple keystroke combinations.

The modifier keys used in keyboard shortcuts are sometimes listed in different orders by different software companies or authors. The order that you press those modifier keys is not important. However, it is very important that you always add the last key (the letter or number key) after you press the other keys.

Learning Keyboard Shortcuts

While keyboard shortcuts help you work faster, you really do not have to start using them right away. In fact, you will most likely learn more about InDesign by using the menus. As you look for one command, you may see another feature that you would like to explore.

Once you feel comfortable working with InDesign, you can start adding keyboard shortcuts to your repertoire. My suggestion is to look at which menu commands you use most often. Then each day choose to use one of those shortcuts. For instance, if you import a lot of art from other programs, you might decide to learn the shortcut for the Place command (Cmd-D on the Mac; Ctrl-D on Windows). For the rest of that day use the shortcut every time you import text or art. Even if you have to look at the menu to refresh your memory, use the keyboard shortcut to actually open the Place dialog box. By the end of the day you will have memorized the Place shortcut. The next day you can learn a new one.

Cross-Platform Issues

One of the great strengths of InDesign is that it is almost identical on both the Macintosh and Windows platforms. In fact, at first glance it is hard to tell which platform you are working on. However, because there are some differences between the platforms, there are some things you should keep in mind.

Modifier Keys

Modifier keys are always listed with the Macintosh key first and then the Windows key second. So the instruction "Hold the Cmd/Ctrl key" means hold the Cmd key on the Macintosh platform or the Ctrl key on the Windows platform. When the key is the same on both computers, such as the Shift key, only one key is listed.

Generally the Cmd key on the Macintosh (sometimes called the Apple key) corresponds to the Ctrl key on Windows. The Opt key on the Macintosh corresponds to the Alt key on Windows. The Control key on the Macintosh does not have an equivalent on Windows. Notice that the Control key for the Macintosh is always spelled out while the Ctrl key for Windows is not.

Platform-Specific Features

A few times in the book, I have written separate exercises or instructions for the Macintosh and Windows platforms. These exercises are indicated by (Mac) and (Win).

Most of the time this is because the procedures are so different that they need to be written separately. Some features exist only on one platform. Those features are then labeled as to their platform.

Whether you're learning InDesign in a class or on your own, I hope this book helps you master the program. Just don't forget to have fun!

Sandee Cohen

(Sandee@vectorbabe.com)
September, 2007

GETTING STARTED 1

One of the reasons why InDesign has become so popular is that it uses many of the same tools, panels, and onscreen elements that are found in Adobe Photoshop and Adobe Illustrator. With the cs3 version of InDesign, all the programs have undergone a significant change from their previous interface elements.

So, although you may feel you have a strong foundation in previous versions of the Adobe products, most likely you will still need to take a look at the pages in this chapter. In it, you will discover some hidden features in the new interface.

And if you haven't looked at the other cs3 products, this chapter will serve as an excellent introduction to the interface changes in all the Creative Suite 3 applications.

Choosing Panels

Most of the commands and features that control InDesign are found in the onscreen panels. Each of the panels covers special features. The panels are similar to those found in other Adobe applications. Although they first appear on your screen the way Adobe arranges them, we'll tackle them in alphabetical order.

Align panel

The Align panel ① (**Window > Object & Layout > Align**) aligns and distributes objects on a page (*see Chapter 4, "Working with Objects"*).

Assignments panel

The Assignments panel ② (**Window > Assignments**) lets you control the editorial revisions of InCopy stories.

Attributes panel

The Attributes panel ③ (**Window > Attributes**) allows you to set fills and strokes to overprint (*see Chapter 5, "Working in Color"*). It also lets you create non-printing objects (*see Chapter 19, "Output"*).

Book panel

The Book panel ④ (**File > New > Book**) is created by the user and contains documents that can be managed and synchronized using the Book features (*see Chapter 10, "Pages and Books"*).

Bookmarks panel

The Bookmarks panel ⑤ (**Window > Interactive > Bookmarks**) allows you to define pages as bookmarks. These bookmarks are then used as navigation aids in PDF documents (*see the online Chapter 18, "Interactive PDF Elements"*).

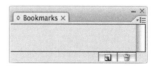

① *Use the **Align panel** to align objects or distribute the space between objects.*

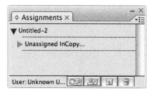

② *The **Assignments panel** lets you check stories in and out of an InDesign/InCopy workflow.*

③ *The **Attributes panel** lets you set the overprinting controls for fills and strokes or set objects to not print.*

④ *The **Book panel** is created by the user. It synchronizes document styles and manages page numbering.*

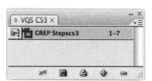

⑤ *The **Bookmarks panel** lets you create navigation bookmarks that are used in Adobe PDF documents.*

Choosing Panels

6 *The **Cell Styles panel** is used to format the appearance of cells in tables.*

7 *Use the **Character panel** to format the appearance of text characters.*

8 *Use the **Character Styles panel** to automate the formatting of text characters.*

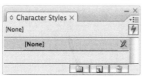

9 *The **Color panel** is used to mix colors to apply to text and objects.*

10 *The **Command Bar panel** contains common commands such as Open, Save, and Print. (Only a portion is shown here.)*

Cell Styles panel

The Cell Styles panel **6** (**Window > Type & Tables > Cell Styles**) allows you to coordinate the appearance of cells in tables *(see Chapter 13, "Tabs and Tables")*.

Character panel

The Character panel **7** (**Window > Type & Tables > Character** or **Type > Character**) controls character-level attributes such as the typeface and point size *(see Chapter 3, "Basic Text")*.

Character Styles panel

The Character Styles panel **8** (**Window > Type & Tables > Character Styles** or **Type > Character Styles**) lets you define and work with character styles *(see Chapter 14, "Automating Your Work")*.

Color panel

The Color panel **9** (**Window > Color**) allows you to mix or apply colors *(see Chapter 5, "Working in Color")*.

Command Bar panel

The Command Bar panel **10** (**Window > Object & Layout > Command Bar**) allows you to click an icon to apply commonly used commands *(see Chapter 2, "Document Setup")*.

Choosing Panels

Choosing Panels

Control panel

The Control panel (**Window > Control**) changes its layout depending on the object selected on the page. If you are working with text, the Control panel shows a combination of the Paragraph and Character panels. If you are working with objects, the panel shows a combination of the Transform and Stroke panels. The Control panel is covered in Chapters 3, 4, and 13.

11 *The* **Control panel** *changes its options depending on the selected object. (Only a portion is shown here.)*

Data Merge panel

The Data Merge panel **12** (**Window > Automation > Data Merge**) gives you the controls for merging information from databases into InDesign documents.

12 *The* **Data Merge panel** *lets you integrate data from spreadsheets into your layouts.*

Effects panel

The Effects panel **13** (**Window > Effects**) contains the special opacity, blend mode, and other effects you can apply to elements in the layout *(see Chapter 6, "Styling Objects").*

13 *The* **Effects panel** *lets you apply opacity and other effects to elements in a layout.*

Flattener Preview panel

The Flattener Preview panel **14** (**Window > Output > Flattener Preview**) lets you display the page as it would look after flattening has been applied during the printing process *(see Chapter 19, "Output").*

14 *The* **Flattener Preview panel** *shows how effects will affect objects and images.*

Glyphs panel

The Glyphs panel **15** (**Window > Type & Tables > Glyphs** or **Type > Glyphs**) lets you insert or replace characters from a font *(see Chapter 3, "Basic Text").* The Glyphs panel also helps you work with OpenType features *(see Chapter 16, "Typography Controls").*

15 *The* **Glyphs panel** *lets you insert characters from a font.*

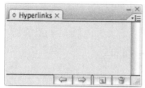

16 The **Gradient panel** *lets you create color blends.*

17 Use the **Hyperlinks panel** *to create and store links to other pages in a PDF document or on the Web.*

18 The **Index panel** *lets you create and manage index entries for a document or book.*

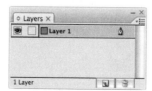

19 The **Info panel** *shows the attributes of objects. These attributes change depending on the object chosen.*

Gradient panel

The Gradient panel **16** (**Window > Gradient**) lets you define and control the appearance of gradients or color blends *(see Chapter 5, "Working in Color").*

Hyperlinks panel

The Hyperlinks panel **17** (**Window > Interactive > Hyperlinks**) is used to create links that let you easily navigate around PDF and HTML documents *(see Chapter 18, "Interactive PDF Elements").*

Index panel

The Index panel **18** (**Window > Type & Tables > Index**) lets you create cross-referenced index entries for a document or book *(see Chapter 10, "Pages and Books").*

Info panel

The Info panel **19** (**Window > Info**) gives you feedback on the type of object selected, and the action taken on that object *(see Chapter 4, "Working with Objects").*

Layers panel

The Layers panel **20** (**Window > Layers**) controls the stacking order, editability, and visibility of different layers *(see Chapter 11, "Layers").*

Choosing Panels

Even More Panels?

Your copy of InDesign may display even more panels. These may be part of third-party plug-ins that give you features not found in the basic InDesign program.

Third-party panels are not available in the ordinary installation. You need to install the plug-ins for those features.

20 Use the **Layers panel** *to add layers and change their display.*

Links panel

The Links panel (**Window > Links**) controls the status of placed images *(see Chapter 8, "Imported Graphics")*.

21 *The **Links panel** displays a list of all the imported graphics and text files.*

Navigator panel

The Navigator panel 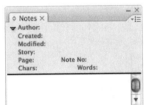 (**Window > Object & Layout > Navigator**) lets you see the layout of pages as well as zoom in to a portion of a page or spread *(see Chapter 2, "Document Setup")*.

22 *Use the **Navigator panel** to see a preview of your document and move around the pages.*

Notes panel

The Notes panel 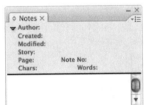 (**Window > Notes**) is used to insert queries and comments into text as part of an InDesign/InCopy workflow.

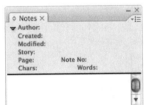

23 *Use the **Notes panel** to insert comments into text stories.*

Object Styles panel

The Object Styles panel 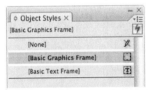 (**Window > Object Styles**) lets you quickly apply complex formatting to text and graphic frames *(see Chapter 14, "Automating Your Work")*.

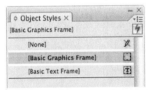

24 *The **Object Styles panel** lets you create and apply object styles for frames.*

Pages panel

The Pages panel (**Window > Pages**) lets you add and control pages and master pages, as well as move from one page to another *(see Chapter 10, "Pages and Books")*.

25 *The **Pages panel** lets you add and delete pages, apply master pages, and move through the document.*

26 *The* **Paragraph panel** *contains all the formatting controls for text paragraphs.*

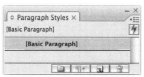

27 *The* **Paragraph Styles panel** *makes it easy to apply complex formatting to paragraphs.*

28 *The* **Pathfinder panel** *allows you to easily change the shape of objects.*

29 *The* **Script Label panel** *allows you to edit the labels applied to objects in a script.*

30 *The* **Scripts panel** *allows you to run scripts directly within InDesign.*

Paragraph panel

The Paragraph panel **26** (**Window** > **Type & Tables** > **Paragraph**) controls paragraph-level attributes such as the alignment and margin indents *(see Chapter 3, "Basic Text")*.

Paragraph Styles panel

The Paragraph Styles panel **27** (**Window** > **Type & Tables** > **Paragraph Styles**) lets you define and apply paragraph styles *(see Chapter 14, "Automating Your Work")*.

Pathfinder panel

The Pathfinder panel **28** (**Window** > **Object & Layout** > **Pathfinder**) allows you to apply the Pathfinder and Convert Shape commands that change the shapes of objects *(see Chapter 4, "Working with Objects")*.

Script Label panel

The Script Label panel **29** (**Window** > **Automation** > **Script Label**) lets you edit labels that are applied to objects as part of scripts.

Scripts panel

The Scripts panel **30** (**Window** > **Automation** > **Scripts**) displays the scripts that have been placed inside the Scripts folder. These scripts can be run directly from within InDesign *(see Chapter 14, "Automating Your Work")*.

Choosing Panels

Choosing Panels

Separations Preview panel

The Separations Preview panel (**Window > Output > Separations Preview**) lets you change the display for the color plates in the document. This lets you see the individual color separations (*see Chapter 19, "Output"*).

31 *The **Separations Preview panel** lets you see the color plates that are in a document.*

Story panel

The Story panel (**Window > Type & Tables > Story**) lets you change the automatic margin alignment to an optical margin alignment that adjusts the position of punctuation and serifs (*see Chapter 14, "Automating Your Work"*).

32 *Use the **Story panel** to control the optical margin alignment for hanging punctuation.*

Stroke panel

The Stroke panel (**Window > Stroke**) controls attributes such as stroke width, dashes, and end arrows and symbols (*see Chapter 6, "Styling Objects"*).

Swatches panel

The Swatches panel (**Window > Swatches**) stores the colors and gradients used in a document (*see Chapter 5, "Working in Color"*).

33 *The **Stroke panel** controls the appearance of rules and lines around objects.*

34 *The **Swatches panel** stores colors and gradients.*

35 *Use the **Table panel** to format tables and table cells.*

36 *Use the **Table Styles panel** to modify the appearance of tables.*

37 *The **Tabs panel** lets you position and format tabs within text.*

38 *Use the **Tags panel** to control tags in a document.*

Table panel

The Table panel **35** (**Window > Type & Tables > Table**) contains the formatting controls for creating tables within text frames *(see Chapter 13, "Tabs and Tables").*

Table Styles panel

The Table Styles panel **36** (**Window > Type & Tables > Table Styles**) allows you to easily apply and modify the appearance of tables *(see Chapter 13, "Tabs and Tables").*

Tabs panel

The Tabs panel **37** (**Type > Tabs**) controls the position of the tab stops for text *(see Chapter 13, "Tabs and Tables").*

Tags panel

The Tags panel **38** (**Window > Tags**) lets you apply and control XML (extensible markup language) tags in a document. Working with tags is beyond the scope of this book. For more information on using XML tags, see *Real World InDesign CS3*, by Olav Martin Kvern and David Blatner, published by Peachpit Press in association with Adobe Press.

Screen Real Estate

Your workspace may feel cramped with so many panels on your screen. One way I solved the problem was to invest in a large second monitor.

I have set up InDesign so that the panels are displayed on my laptop screen while the Tools panel and the document window are displayed on the larger monitor.

This gives me much more room to work on my documents.

Choosing Panels

Text Wrap panel

The Text Wrap panel **39** (**Window > Text Wrap**) controls how text wraps around objects and placed images *(see Chapter 9, "Text Effects").*

Transform panel

The Transform panel **40** (**Window > Object & Layout > Transform**) lets you see the size and position of objects. You can also use the Transform panel to apply transformations such as scaling and rotation *(see Chapter 4, "Working with Objects").*

Trap Presets panel

The Trap Presets panel **41** (**Window > Output > Trap Presets**) is used to store different settings for how colors are trapped between one object and another. Setting traps is not covered in this book. Talk to the print shop that will output your file before you attempt to set traps in InDesign.

39 *Use the* **Text Wrap** *panel to control how text wraps around objects and images.*

40 *The* **Transform panel** *lets you control the position and size of objects.*

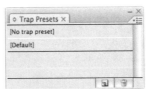

41 *The* **Trap Presets panel** *lets you store and apply trapping settings.*

Panel menu   Minimize   Close

42   *The* **controls** *for panels.*

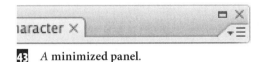

43   *A minimized panel.*

Working with Panels

If you don't see a panel onscreen, you can open it by choosing the command in the Window menu.

To open a panel:

◆ Choose the name of the panel from the Window menu or submenu.

To close a panel:

◆ Click the close control in the panel's title bar **42**.

You can also shrink a panel so that it only displays the panel tab.

To shrink a panel display:

◆ Click the minimize icon **42** to collapse the panel.

To expand a panel display:

◆ If the panel is collapsed, click the minimize icon to expand the panel **43**.

In addition to the panel buttons and fields, most panels contain a menu with additional commands.

To display the panel menus:

1. Click the panel menu icon to open the panel menu.

2. Choose a command from the menu.

To hide panels:

1. Make sure the insertion point is not within a text frame to avoid inserting a tab character into your text.

2. Press the Tab key. This hides all the panels including the Tools panel.

   or

   Press Shift+Tab key. This hides all the panels except the Tools panel.

Working with Panels

Another way to save screen space is to move one panel so that it is located within the boundaries of another. This is called *nesting*.

To nest panels:

1. Position the cursor over the panel tab.

2. Drag the tab so that the outline is inside another panel. A black rectangle around the inside perimeter of the panel indicates that the two panels will be nested **44**.

3. Release the mouse button. The panel appears next to the other item.

44 *Drag the panel tab into another panel area to **nest panels**.*

To unnest panels:

1. Drag the panel tab so that the outline is completely outside the other panel.

2. Release the mouse button. The panel appears as a separate onscreen item.

Another way to arrange panels is to dock the panel to the sides of your screen.

To dock a panel:

1. Drag the panel tab to the left or right side of the screen. A vertical outline of the tab appears at the edge of the screen **45**.

2. Release the mouse. This adheres the panel to the side of the screen.

TIP Click the double-arrows at the top of a docked panel to expand or collapse the panel.

45 *Drag a panel to the left or right side of the screen to **dock the panel**.*

To undock panels:

1. Drag the panel title bar so that the outline is completely outside the dock area.

2. Release the mouse button. The docked panel appears as a separate panel **46**.

46 *Drag a panel away from the left or right dock area to **undock the panel**.*

47 *The* **Save Workspace dialog box** *lets you name the custom workspace configuration.*

48 *The* **Delete Workspace dialog box** *lets you choose the workspace you want to delete.*

Suggestions for Using Workspaces

Workspaces save all the attributes, appearances, and positions of the panels. This means that you can have a workspace that closes all the panels except one or two that you want to use.

You can have workspaces that show just the panels that apply colors, gradients, and other object attributes. You can have other workspaces that show only the panels that you use for text. You can even have a workspace that puts all the panels on the left for left-handed users.

You can apply workspaces at any time as you are working — even with a document open. It's very soothing to see all your panels rearrange into orderly groups.

Using Workspaces

I don't know any two InDesign users who agree as to how to arrange their panels. Although my panels may start out neatly arranged, within a short time I've got them scattered all over my screen — especially if I am demonstrating in front of a class.

Fortunately, you can arrange and save your panel arrangements into workspaces that you can call up at any time.

TIP InDesign ships with a workspace labeled Default. This is the workspace that the panels revert to if you delete the InDesign preferences.

To save a custom workspace:

1. Arrange your panels as you want them to appear on the screen.
2. Choose Window > Workspace > Save Workspace. The Save Workspace dialog box appears **47**.
3. Enter a name for the workspace.
4. Click the OK button. The name of the workspace appears in the Workspace menu.

To apply a workspace:

◆ Choose the custom workspace from the **Window > Workspace** menu.

To delete a workspace:

1. Choose Window > Workspace > Delete. The Delete Workspace dialog box appears **48**.
2. Use the pop-up menu to choose the workspace you want to delete.
3. Click the Delete button to delete the workspace.

TIP You cannot delete the Default workspace.

Using the Tools Panel

The Tools panel contains the tools for working in InDesign, as well as controls for applying the colors of fills and strokes **49**. Some of the tools have fly-out panels that let you access the other tools in the category **50**. *(See the exercise on the next page for how to access the fly-out panels.)*

To choose a tool:

◆ Click the tool in the Tools panel.

or

Tap the individual keyboard shortcuts for each of the tools.

TIP You can change the arrangement of the Tools panel from single column to double column or horizontal column using the preferences.

or

Double-click the title bar on the Tools panel to change the arrangement.

Title bar

Selection tool	Direct Selection tool
Pen tool	Type tool
Pencil tool	Line tool
Rectangle frame tool	Rectangle tool
Button tool	Scissors tool
Rotate tool	Scale tool
Gradient tool	Free Transform tool
Notes tool	Eyedropper tool
Hand tool	Zoom tool

Swap fill and stroke

Fill control

Default fill and stroke — Stroke control

Format container — Format text

Apply color — Apply gradient

Apply none

Normal view — Preview mode

49 *The **Tools panel** at its default tool display.*

50 *The **fly-out panels** in the Tools panel.*

Using the Tools Panel

51 *A **fly-out panel** displays the additional tools for that slot in the Tools panel.*

52 *Pause over a tool to see the **tool tip** with the tool name and keyboard shortcut.*

Tools and controls in the Tools panel that have a small triangle in their slot have other tools hidden in a fly-out panel.

To open the other tools in the Tools panel:

1. Press the fly-out triangle on the tool slot. The fly-out panel appears **51**.

2. Choose one of the tools listed in the fly-out panel.

To see the tool keyboard shortcuts:

◆ Move the cursor over the tool and pause. A tool tip appears with the name of the tool and the keyboard shortcut **52**.

TIP If you don't see the tool tip after pausing for a moment, make sure the Tool Tips control is turned on in the application preferences *(see Chapter 21, "Customizing InDesign")*.

TIP You can change or add keyboard shortcuts for tools using the keyboard shortcut controls *(see Chapter 21, "Customizing InDesign")*.

Using the Tools Panel

Using Contextual Menus

Contextual menus are menus that change depending on the type of object selected or where the mouse is positioned 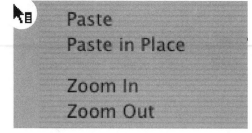. The benefit of contextual menus is that you don't have to move all the way up to the menu bar to invoke a command. Also, the menu changes to provide you commands that are appropriate for the type of object chosen.

To display contextual menus:

- ◆ (Mac) Hold the Control key and click the mouse button.

  or

  (Win) Click the right mouse button.

- **TIP** Watch for the Macintosh contextual menu cursor, which appears next to the arrow as you press the Control key.

Contextual cursor

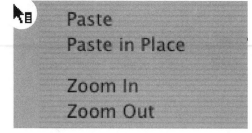

Paste
Paste in Place

Zoom In
Zoom Out

53 *The* **contextual menu** *changes depending on what type of object is selected.*

DOCUMENT SETUP 2

Billions of years ago, when dinosaurs ruled the earth — or about 22 years ago, before the start of desktop publishing — people prepared documents for printing using pieces of stiff board. They marked up the boards with special blue pencils to indicate the edges of the pages. They drew marks that specified where the margins and columns should be and how the pages should be trimmed. This board, called a *mechanical,* was used as the layout for the document.

Unlike the board mechanicals of the past, InDesign documents are electronic layouts. Just as with the board mechanicals, you need to set the page sizes, margins, and column widths. However, since you are not using a pencil but a computer, you have additional controls for how the document is laid out.

Of course, changing an electronic layout takes far less time than it did with the board mechanicals that old dinosaurs like me used to use.

The Welcome Screen

How nice of InDesign to welcome you when you first launch the application. Rather than just close the Welcome screen, take a look at its features as there are things that may be useful.

Using the Welcome Screen:

1. The Welcome Screen automatically appears when you first launch InDesign.

2. You can click the close button to hide the screen.

   or

   Click one of the Welcome Screen features.

TIP You can click the Don't Show Again checkbox to keep the Welcome Screen from opening.

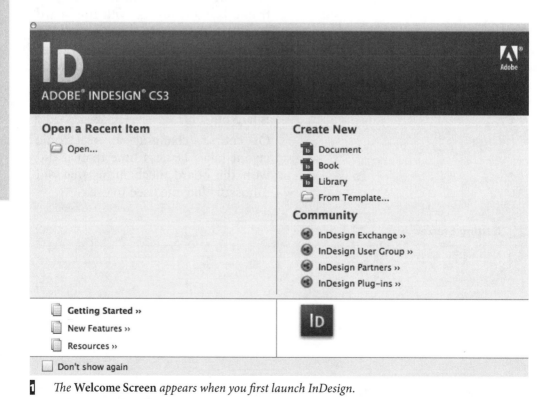

1 *The* **Welcome Screen** *appears when you first launch InDesign.*

Create New

 Document

Book

Library

From Template...

 The **Create New** *commands in the Welcome Screen.*

Open a Recent Item

Open...

 The **Open a Recent Item** *lists InDesign documents you have recently opened and saved.*

Community

 InDesign Exchange »

InDesign User Group »

InDesign Partners »

InDesign Plug-ins »

 The **Community area** *sends you to Web sites where you can get more information on InDesign.*

Getting Started »

New Features »

Resources »

 The **Help area** *opens the tutorials, help files, and other resources that are installed with InDesign.*

Choosing the Welcome Screen commands:

◆ To create new documents or open sample templates, click one of the Create New commands .

or

Use the Recent Items area to open InDesign documents that you have recently opened and saved .

or

Click one of the choices in the Community area to open a Web browser where you can get more information or support for working with InDesign .

or

Click one of the Help area links to open tutorials, help files, and other resources for working with InDesign .

Most people I know click the Don't Show Again box and never look at the Welcome Screen again. However, one day you may decide that you would like to investigate the Welcome Screen resources. Here's how to get the Welcome Screen back

To reopen the Welcome Screen:

◆ Choose **Help** > **Welcome Screen**. The Welcome Screen opens.

Setting up Documents

When you create a new document, you have the opportunity to set many options in the New Document dialog box.

To set the basic options for a new document:

1. Choose **File > New > Document**. This opens the New Document dialog box .

2. Type the number of pages in your document in the Number of Pages field.

3. Check Facing Pages to set your document with left-hand and right-hand pages.

4. Check Master Text Frame to make it easy to flow text onto pages. *(See Chapter 10, "Pages and Books," for more information on master text frames.)*

5. Use the Page Size pop-up list to set the size of your page.

6. Set the Orientation to portrait or landscape.

7. Enter the size of the margins in the Margins fields.

8. Set the number of columns and the gutter width in the Columns Number and Gutter fields.

9. Click OK. The document appears in the window .

TIP The pages are surrounded by an area called the pasteboard. Like a drawing table, you can set items there for later use. Items on the pasteboard do not print.

6 *The New Document dialog box set for the basic layout options.*

Pasteboard area   Document page

7 *Each document page is surrounded by the non-printing pasteboard area where you can store objects for later use.*

Setting up Documents

8 The **New Document dialog box** *set for the advanced layout options.*

— **Document trim**

— **Bleed area**

— **Slug area**

9 *A document with* **bleed and slug areas.**

10 *The* **Make Same Size icon** *forces all the fields to the same amount.*

You can also set the advanced options for a document. The first is the area around the page, called a *bleed*. When you set a bleed, you define an area outside the trim of the page where objects will still print. The second area is called a *slug*. This is an area outside the page that may or may not print. Slugs are often used by advertising agencies to list insertion dates and the name of the product, manufacturer, and ad agency.

To set the advanced options for a new document:

1. Click the More Options button in the New Document dialog box. The advanced options for Bleed and Slug dimensions appear at the bottom of the dialog box.

2. Set the amounts for the size of the bleed area around the document **8**.

3. Set the amounts for the size of the slug area around the document. The slug area is displayed outside the document trim **9**.

TIP Click the Make Same Size icon **10** for the Bleed or Slug to automatically set all the dimensions to the same size.

Setting up Documents

Choosing Layout Options

Facing pages refers to documents such as a book where pages on one side of its spine face the pages on the other side. (This is also called a *spread*.) Single pages, such as advertisements, have facing pages turned off.

To set facing pages:

◆ With the Document Setup dialog box open, click Facing Pages. This changes the document from single page to facing pages and ⓬.

TIP When a document is set for facing pages, the names in the dialog box for the Left and Right margins change to Inside and Outside margins ⓬.

The page size is the size of the individual pages of the document.

To set the size of the page:

◆ Choose one of the following 11 choices from the Page Size menu ⓭:
  - **Letter**, 8½ by 11 inches.
  - **Legal**, 8½ by 14 inches.
  - **Tabloid**, 11 by 17 inches.
  - **Letter–Half**, 8½ by 5½ inches.
  - **Legal–Half**, 8½ by 7 inches.
  - **A4**, 21 by 29.7 centimeters.
  - **A3**, 29.7 by 42 centimeters.
  - **A5**, 14.8 by 21 centimeters.
  - **B5**, 17.6 by 25 centimeters.
  - **Compact Disc**, 4.7222 by 4.75 inches.
  - **Custom**, which allows you to enter your own specific values.

TIP The A4, A3, A5, and B5 sizes are used primarily outside of the United States.

TIP If you change the values in the Width or the Height field, the Page Size automatically switches to the Custom setting.

Left margin   **Right margin**

⓫ *The* **left and right margins** *on nonfacing pages.*

Outside margin   **Inside margins**   **Outside margin**

⓬ *The* **outside and inside margins** *on facing pages.*

⓭ *The* **Page Size menu** *offers standard U.S. and international paper sizes, as well as customization controls.*

Choosing Layout Options

Portrait   Landscape

14 *The* **Orientation controls** *let you set the position of the page.*

15 *The margin settings for a document with* **facing pages**.

16 *The margin settings for a document with* **nonfacing pages**.

17 *Click the* **Make Same Size icon** *to automatically enter the same amount for all four margins.*

The term *orientation* refers to how the page is positioned, either up and down or sideways.

To set the orientation:

◆   Click the Portrait orientation to create a document where the width is always less than the height **14**.

or

Click the Landscape orientation to create a document where the width is always greater than the height **14**.

To set the margins:

1.   Click the field arrows or enter an amount for the Top and Bottom fields **15**.

2.   If the document is set for facing pages, click the field arrows or enter an amount for the Inside and Outside fields.

or

If the document is not set for facing pages, click the field arrows or enter an amount for the Left and Right margins **16**.

TIP When you finish typing in one of the fields, press the Tab key to jump to the next field.

TIP Click the Make Same Size icon in the Margins area to control how the margins are created **17**. When the icon displays a link, all the margins will be the same size. (This saves you typing in the same number four times.) When the icon displays a broken link, you can enter different sizes for each margin.

Choosing Layout Options

You can also set visible guides for columns and the *gutters* (or spaces) between the columns.

To set the columns and gutters:

1. Click the field arrows or enter an amount for the number of columns .

2. Click the field arrows or enter an amount for the gutter.

TIP The columns and gutters act as guidelines on your page **19**. You can still place text or graphics across or outside the columns or gutters.

Wouldn't it be nice if the New Document dialog box remembered your favorite setup so you wouldn't have to change the settings each time you start a new document? It can, and that's called setting the *defaults*.

To set the document defaults:

1. Close all InDesign documents, leaving just the application open.

2. Choose **File > Document Setup**. The Document Setup dialog box appears.

3. Make whatever changes you want to the options in the Document Setup dialog box.

4. Click OK. The settings you have chosen become the default for any new documents.

TIP You can also specify a Document Preset *(covered later in this chapter)* to use as the document default.

18 *The* **column settings** *let you set the number of columns and the amount of space for the gutter between the columns.*

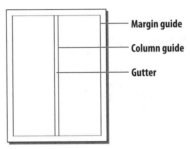

19 *A* **two-column document** *with margin, column, and gutter guidelines.*

Setting Other Defaults

As you work in InDesign, you will discover other areas where you would like to set defaults. Perhaps you'd like certain colors to appear (or not appear) in each new document. Or you would like certain text options to appear automatically.

Just as you can set the Document Setup options with no document open, you can also set other defaults.

With no document open, choose File > Document Setup and in the dialog box choose those options you would like to set as a default. Whatever is available for you to choose can then be set as a default.

Choosing Layout Options

20 *The* **Document Setup dialog box** *for an existing document.*

21 *The* **Margins and Columns dialog box** *for an existing document.*

Changing Layout Options

You may discover that you need to change some of the settings of an existing document. When you start a new document, all the settings appear in one dialog box. However, after you begin working on the document you must use two separate controls to make changes to the document.

To change the document setup:

1. Choose **File > Document Setup** to open the Document Setup dialog box **20**.

2. Make whatever changes you want to the following settings:
   - **Number of Pages**
   - **Facing Pages**
   - **Page Size**
   - **Orientation**
   - **Bleed and Slug**

3. Click OK to apply the changes to the document.

To change the margins and columns:

1. Choose Layout > Margins and Columns to open the Margins and Columns dialog box **21**.

2. Make whatever changes you want to the following settings:
   - **Margins**
   - **Number of columns**
   - **Gutter** (the width of the space between the columns)

3. Click OK to apply the changes to the document.

TIP Changing the margins and columns while on a page or spread changes the settings only for that page or spread. To change the settings for all the pages, you need to work with the Master Page. *(See Chapter 10, "Pages and Books," for more information on master pages.)*

Changing Layout Options

Using the Document Presets

You may want to save all the settings for certain types of documents so they can easily be applied when you start new documents. For instance, my Visual QuickStart books require different settings than the handouts I use when teaching. Document presets make it easy to apply the different settings when I create new documents.

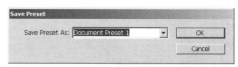

22 *Click the Save Preset button in the New Document dialog box to save the current settings as a preset.*

To save the document settings as document preset:

1. Choose **File** > **New** > **Document** and set the options in the New Document dialog box.

2. Click the Save Preset button **22**. This opens the Save Preset dialog box **23**.

3. Enter a name for the preset in the Save Preset As field and click OK. This adds the preset to the Document Preset menu in the New Document dialog box.

23 *Enter a name for a document preset in the* **Save Preset As field**.

To apply a document preset:

- Choose the document preset from the Document Preset menu in the New Document dialog box **24**.

  or

  Choose **File** > **Document Presets** and then choose one of the presets listed in the menu. This opens the New Document dialog box with that preset chosen.

24 *You can apply presets using the* **Document Preset menu** *in the New Document dialog box.*

To edit a document preset:

1. Choose **File** > **Document Presets** > **Define**. This opens the Document Presets dialog box.

2. Choose the document preset in the Document Presets dialog box, and click the Edit button **25**. This opens the Edit Document Preset dialog box **26**.

3. Make whatever changes you want. Click OK to save the changes in the preset.

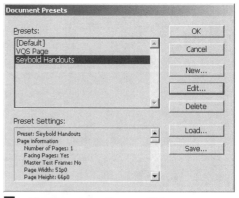

25 *The* **Document Presets dialog box** *lets you edit, delete, and create new document presets.*

26 *Use the* **Edit Document Preset** *dialog box to make changes to existing document presets.*

You can also use the Document Presets dialog box to create document presets without going through the New Document dialog box.

To create a new document preset:

1. Choose **File** > **Document Presets** > **Define**. This opens the Document Presets dialog box.

2. Click the New button to open the New Document Presets dialog box.

TIP This dialog box is similar to the Edit Document Preset dialog box.

3. Use the dialog box to name and set the options for the new preset.

4. Click OK to save the preset.

To delete a document preset:

◆ Choose the document preset, and click the Delete button.

TIP You can't delete the [Default] preset.

You can also export document presets into a file that can be shared with others.

To export document presets:

1. Click the Save button in the Document Presets dialog box.

2. Name and save the document preset file.

You can also import document presets from others.

To import document presets:

1. Click the Load button in the Document Presets dialog box.

2. Navigate to find the document preset file.

3. Click the Open button. The document presets are imported into InDesign.

Using the Document Presets

Using Document Rulers

Designers need to measure things on pages. Rather than hold a ruler up to your monitor, you can use InDesign's electronic rulers.

To show and hide the document rulers:

◆ To see the rulers along the top and left edges of the document window, choose **View > Show Rulers** 27.

or

To hide the rulers, choose **View > Hide Rulers.**

You can change the rulers to display different units of measurement. This is helpful if you receive instructions written in measurements with which you are not familiar.

To change the unit of measurement:

1. Choose **Edit > Preferences > Units & Increments** (Win) or **InDesign > Preferences > Units & Increments** (Mac). This opens the Units & Increments dialog box.

2. For the Horizontal and Vertical settings, choose one of the measurements from the pop-up lists 28.

TIP You can have different units for the horizontal and the vertical rulers. For instance, the vertical ruler can match the document's leading so that each unit equals each line of copy. The horizontal unit can be in inches or picas.

3. If you choose Custom, enter the number of points for each unit on the ruler.

TIP You can also change the units with the ruler contextual menus 29.

TIP The Units & Increments preferences also let you set your own value for the number of points per inch.

Vertical ruler   **Horizontal ruler**

27 *The* **horizontal and vertical rulers.**

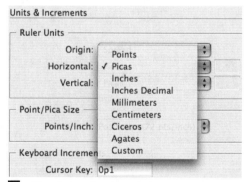

28 *The choices for the ruler's* **units of measurement.**

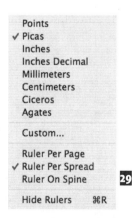

29 *The* **contextual** menu *when you click over a ruler.*

30 *The zero point indicator of the rulers.*

The rulers start numbering at the top-left corner of the page. You may want to move this point, called a *zero point,* to a different position. This can help you judge how much space you have from one spot of the page to another.

To reposition the zero point:

1. Position the cursor over the zero point crosshairs at the upper-left corner of the rulers **30**.

2. Drag the zero point to the new position on the page **31**.

3. Release the mouse button to position the zero point.

TIP Double-click the zero point crosshairs in the corner of the rulers to reset the zero point to the upper-left corner.

31 *You set the ruler's **zero point** by dragging the zero point indicator to a new position on the page.*

If you are working on a project such as an advertising spread, it may be easier to position objects if the rulers continue across the *spine* of the pages. (The spine is where the pages of a book, magazine, or other multipage document are bound together.) InDesign lets you customize the origin of the rulers.

To set the origin of the rulers:

1. Choose **Edit > Preferences > Units & Increments** (Win) or **InDesign > Preferences > Units & Increments** (Mac).

2. Set the Ruler Units Origin menu to Page, Spread, or Spine **32**.

   or

   Choose a setting from the ruler contextual menu **29**.

TIP There is no difference between the page or spine settings unless there are more than two pages to the spread.

Spine

Page

Spread

32 *You can control whether the rulers reset for each spine or each page. They can also be set to stay across a spread.*

Working with Guides

Guides are nonprinting lines that help you position objects. InDesign has many different types of guides that you can work with 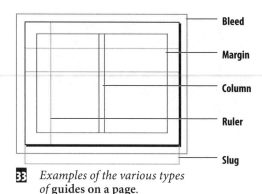.

- **Ruler guides** can be positioned anywhere on the page or pasteboard.

- **Margin guides** show the settings of the margins for the document.

- **Column guides** show the column settings for a page or master page.

- **Bleed guides** show the bleed area for the document.

- **Slug guides** show the slug area for the document.

InDesign gives you options for how to work with guides.

To change the guide preferences:

1. Choose **Edit** > **Preferences** > **Guides & Pasteboard** (Win) or **InDesign** > **Preferences** > **Guides & Pasteboard** (Mac) to open the Guides & Pasteboard Preferences .

2. Use each of the menus to set the colors of the guides.

3. Check Guides in Back to position the guides behind text and graphics on the page .

4. Enter an amount in the Snap to Zone field. This is the distance, in pixels, for how close an object must be before it will snap or jump to align with a guide.

To show or hide guides:

- To see the margin, column, and ruler guides, choose **View** > **Grids & Guides** > **Show Guides**.

    or

    To hide the guides, choose **View** > **Grids & Guides** > **Hide Guides**.

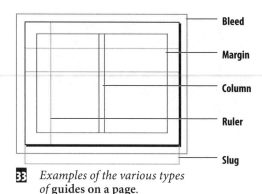

33 *Examples of the various types of* **guides on a page**.

34 *The dialog box for the* **guides preferences**.

Bleed
Margin
Column
Ruler
Slug

Guides in Back turned on

Guides in Back turned off

35 *The* **Guides in Back command** *changes how guides are displayed as they pass through text and artwork.*

36 *The* **two-headed arrow** *indicates that a column guide can be moved.*

37 *You can* **drag ruler guides** *out from the horizontal ruler or vertical ruler.*

Objects can be set to automatically snap to guides as you move them. This makes it easier to align objects to guides.

To make objects snap to guides:

◆ Choose View > **Grids & Guides** > **Snap to Guides.**

TIP Choose the command again to turn off the feature.

There may be times when you want to move a column guide manually. This results in a custom guide setting.

To unlock and move column guides:

1. If **View** > **Grids & Guides** > **Lock Column Guides** is checked, choose the command to unlock the column guides.

2. Position the cursor over the guide you want to move.

3. Press the mouse button. The cursor turns into a two-headed arrow that indicates that the column has been selected **36**.

4. Drag the column guide to the new position.

TIP You cannot change the width of the gutter space between the columns by moving a column guide. But you can change it in the Margins and Columns dialog box.

Ruler guides are more flexible than margin or column guides and can be positioned anywhere on the page to help with object placement.

To create ruler guides:

1. Position the cursor over the horizontal or vertical ruler.

2. Press the mouse button. The cursor turns into a two-headed arrow.

3. Drag to pull the guide out onto the page **37**.

Working with Guides

Rather than pulling guides out one at a time, you can also create a series of ruler guides in rows and columns.

To create rows and columns using guides:

1. Choose **Layout** > **Create Guides**. This opens the Create Guides dialog box .

2. Enter the number of rows (horizontal guides) in the Rows Number field.

3. Enter the amount for the space between the rows in the Rows Gutter field.

4. Enter the number of columns (vertical guides) in the Columns Number field.

5. Enter the amount for the space between the columns in the Columns Gutter field.

6. Choose between Fit Guides to Margins or Fit Guides to Page **39**.

7. Check Remove Existing Ruler Guides to delete all the ruler guides that were previously on the page. This includes ruler guides that were manually added to the page.

8. Click OK to apply the guides.

TIP Check Preview to see the guides on the page change as you enter the values within the dialog box.

TIP If you set the Number fields to zero for both the Rows and Columns, the Remove Existing Ruler Guides option will delete all the ruler guides on the page.

To reposition ruler guides:

1. Position the cursor over the guide you want to move.

2. Press the mouse button. The cursor turns into a two-headed arrow and the guide changes color. This indicates that the guide has been selected.

3. Drag the ruler guide to a new position.

38 *The* **Create Guides dialog box** *lets you automatically add many guides on a page.*

Fit to margins

Fit to page

39 *Fit Guides to Margin spaces the guides equally inside the page margins. Fit Guides to Page spaces the guides equally inside the page trim.*

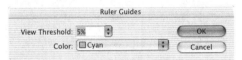

40 *Use* **either of the Selection tools** *to select a ruler guide.*

41 *Use the* **Ruler Guides dialog box** *to change the color of the ruler guides. You can also set the threshold to determine at what magnification the guides are visible.*

42 *A view threshold of 200% means the guides are visible only when the magnification is 200% or higher.*

You can also manually move or delete ruler guides.

To move existing ruler guides:

◆ Use either of the Selection tools to drag the ruler guide to a new position **40**.

To delete ruler guides:

1. Click the ruler guide with one of the Selection tools. The ruler guide turns a darker color, indicating it is selected.

2. Press the Delete/Backspace key. This deletes the ruler guide.

You may want to lock your ruler guides so they don't move inadvertently.

To lock guides:

◆ Choose **View** > **Grids & Guides** > **Lock Guides.**

TIP Choose the command again to unlock the guides.

You can change the color of ruler guides. You can also set the magnification at which the guides are not visible.

To change the appearance of ruler guides:

1. Choose Layout > Ruler Guides to open the dialog box **41**.

2. Use the Color pop-up list to pick the color for the ruler guides.

3. Set a percentage for the View Threshold. This sets the amount of magnification below which the ruler guides are not displayed **42**.

TIP Increase the View Threshold if you have many guides on the page. This hides the guides at low magnifications and shows them at higher ones.

Working with Guides

Working with Document Grids

Ruler guides aren't the only way to align objects. The document grid can also be used as a structure for designing pages. The baseline grid is used to keep lines of text even.

To display the grids:

◆ Choose **View** > **Grids & Guides** > **Show Document Grid** or **View** > **Grids & Guides** > **Show Baseline Grid.**

To hide the grids:

◆ Choose **View** > **Grids & Guides** > **Hide Document Grid** or > **Hide Baseline Grid.**

To change the grid appearance:

1. Choose **Edit** > **Preferences** > **Grids** (Win) or **InDesign** > **Preferences** > **Grids** (Mac) to open the preferences dialog box **44**.

2. Use the Color list to change the grid color.

3. Enter an amount in the Horizontal and Vertical Gridline Every fields to set the distance between the main gridlines.

4. Enter an amount in the Subdivisions field to create lighter gridlines between the main gridlines.

5. Enter an amount in the Start field to set where the baseline grid should start.

6. Use the Relative To list to position the start of the grid relative to the top of the page or the top margin.

7. Enter a percentage in the View Threshold field. This sets the lowest magnification at which the grid is visible.

8. Check Grids in Back to position the gridlines behind objects on the page.

To turn on Snap to Grid:

◆ Choose **View** > **Grids & Guides** > **Snap to Document Grid.** If Snap to Document Grid is checked, the feature is already turned on.

43 *Choose* **Show Document Grid** *to see the horizontal and vertical gridlines.*

44 *The* **Grids Preferences dialog box** *lets you control the display and arrangement of the document grid.*

Working with Document Grids

45 *The* **Entire Pasteboard command** *shows the page as well as the pasteboard.*

InDesign's "Smart" View Commands

If you have not used other page layout programs, you may not realize how smart some of InDesign's View commands are. These are the commands Fit Page in Window, Fit Spread in Window, and Entire Pasteboard.

In most other programs, if you choose the Fit Page in Window command, the magnification changes to show the entire page. If you then change the size of the window, the magnification is no longer the correct size to show the entire page.

InDesign, however, is much smarter. When you choose those three View commands, InDesign continues to display the entire page, spread, or pasteboard even if you resize the window. The magnification dynamically changes as you change the size of the window.

The command will stay active until you choose a new view or manually change the magnification. That's pretty smart!

Changing the Magnification

Magnification refers to the size of the document as it appears on your screen. InDesign gives you many ways to change the magnification setting. Some of the quickest and easiest ways to change the magnification settings are to use View commands.

To zoom with the View commands:

1. To increase the magnification, choose **View > Zoom In.**

2. To decrease the magnification, choose **View > Zoom Out.**

3. To see all of the current page, choose **View > Fit Page In Window.** This changes the magnification setting to whatever amount is necessary to see the entire page.

TIP A small monitor forces you to use small magnifications to see the entire page. A larger monitor allows you to set its resolution so that it shows the entire page at magnifications that are easier to read.

4. To see all of the current spread, choose **View > Fit Spread in Window.**

5. To see the document at 100% magnification, choose **View > Actual Size.**

6. To see the entire pasteboard area, choose View > Entire Pasteboard **45**.

InDesign lets you view the page with a wide range of magnification settings. You can select a specific magnification amount from the magnification list.

To use the magnification list:

1. Click the control at the bottom-left corner of the document window to display the magnification list .

2. Choose one of the magnifications in the list.

You can also view specific magnifications not in the list.

To enter a specific magnification amount:

1. Double-click or drag across the magnification shown in the bottom-left corner of the document window.

2. Type a number between 5 and 4000.

TIP It is not necessary to type the % sign.

3. Press Return or Enter to apply the setting.

46 *The* **magnification list** *at the bottom of the document window.*

Magnification Shortcuts

Because the View commands are used so often, the keyboard shortcuts are listed here. You can also find these shortcuts displayed on the View menu.

Mac Commands

Zoom In	Cmd-=
Zoom Out	Cmd-hyphen
Fit Page in Window	Cmd-0
Fit Spread in Window	Cmd-Opt-0
Actual Size	Cmd-1

Windows Commands

Zoom In	Ctrl-=
Zoom Out	Ctrl-hyphen
Fit Page in Window	Ctrl-0
Fit Spread in Window	Ctrl-Alt-0
Actual Size	Ctrl-1

Changing the Magnification

47 *Click the* **Normal View Mode icon** *to see all the elements of the document.*

48 *The* **Normal View Mode** *shows all the elements of the document.*

49 *Choose* **one of the view modes** *to see specific areas in a Preview Mode.*

50 *The* **Preview Mode** *shows only the printing elements and hides the pasteboard.*

51 *The* **Bleed Mode** *shows only the printing elements and the bleed area.*

52 *The* **Slug Mode** *shows only the printing elements and the slug area.*

View and Pasteboard Controls

As you work, you may want to view your document in different ways. The four View modes provide different ways of looking at your document.

To choose the four View modes:

◆ Click the Normal View Mode icon at the bottom of the Toolbox **47**.

- **Normal View Mode** is the default view and shows you all the guides in the document as well as the pasteboard, bleed, and slug areas **48**.

or

Choose one of the view modes from the fly-out panel at the bottom of the Toolbox **49**.

- **Preview Mode** shows only the area inside the page boundaries. All guides are automatically hidden **50**.
- **Bleed Mode** adds the area inside the bleed to the Preview Mode **51**.
- **Slug Mode** adds the area inside the slug to the Preview Mode **52**.

When you switch to the Preview Mode the pasteboard is replaced by a colored background. The default color is gray; but you can change that to any color you like.

To change the Preview Background color:

1. Choose **Edit** > **Preferences** > **Guides & Pasteboard** (Win) or **InDesign** > **Preferences** > **Guides & Pasteboard** (Mac) to open the Guides & Pasteboard Preferences.

2. Use the Preview Background list to set the color for the background . This changes the color shown in the Preview Mode .

TIP Restrain yourself from changing the color to something extremely intense. A vivid color around a document can change how colors on the page appear.

The area above and below the document is controlled by the Minimum Vertical Offset. You can make that area larger.

To change the Minimum Vertical Offset:

1. Choose **Edit** > **Preferences** > **Guides & Pasteboard** (Win) or **InDesign** > **Preferences** > **Guides & Pasteboard** (Mac) to open the Guides & Pasteboard Preferences.

2. Enter an amount in the Minimum Vertical Offset field . This increases the pasteboard above and below the page .

53 *Use the **Preview Background List** to change the color of the pasteboard area shown in the Preview Mode.*

54 *A black background in the pasteboard area presents your work with a more dramatic appearance.*

55 *Use the **Minimum Vertical Offset** field to increase the size of the pasteboard above and below the document.*

56 *The effects of increasing the size of the Minimum Vertical Offset.*

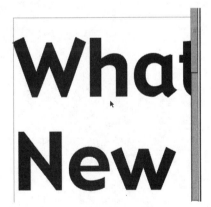

57 *Use the **Zoom tool** to change the magnification of the page.*

Using the Zoom and Hand Tools

The Zoom tool lets you jump to a specific magnification and position on the page. The Hand tool moves the view to a new position.

To use the Zoom tool:

1. Click the Zoom tool in the Toolbox **57**. The cursor turns into a magnifying glass.

2. Click the Zoom tool on the area you want to zoom in on. Click as many times as is necessary to change the magnification.

TIP Press Cmd/Ctrl and Spacebar to access the Zoom tool without leaving the tool that is currently selected.

TIP Each click of the Zoom tool changes the magnification to the next setting in the magnification list.

TIP Press the Opt/Alt key while in the Zoom tool to decrease magnification. The icon changes from a plus sign (+) to a minus sign (–).

TIP Double-click the Zoom tool in the Toolbox to set the view to the actual size (100%).

A *marquee zoom* allows you to zoom quickly to a certain magnification and position.

To create a marquee zoom:

- Drag the Zoom tool diagonally across the area you want to see. Release the mouse button to zoom in **58** and **59**.

58 **Drag the Zoom tool diagonally** *to magnify a specific area. The marquee indicates the area to be selected.*

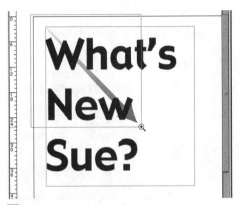

59 *The selected area fills the window after you release the mouse button.*

You can also use the Hand tool (sometimes called the *Grabber* tool) to move around within the area of the document. This is more flexible than using the scrollbars, which only go up and down or left and right.

*Use the **Hand tool** to move the page around the window.*

To use the Hand tool:

1. Click the Hand tool in the Toolbox **60**.

2. Drag the Hand tool to move around the page.

TIP Double-click the Hand tool in the Toolbox to fit the entire page in the window.

If you want to become a true InDesign power user, you need to use keyboard shortcuts. One of the primary shortcuts you should learn is how to temporarily access the Hand tool without leaving the current tool. This lets you scroll around a document very quickly.

To temporarily access the Hand tool:

♦ Press the Opt/Alt plus Spacebar keys. This gives you the Hand tool in all situations.

TIP You can also access the Hand tool by pressing just the Opt/Alt key if you are working in a text frame.

Playing the Keyboard "Bass Notes"

I confess! I haven't chosen the Zoom or Hand tools in years. Rather than move the mouse all the way over to the toolbox, I use the keyboard shortcuts.

On the Mac, I keep my fingers lightly resting on the Cmd, Opt, and Spacebar keys. By changing which keys are pressed, I alternate between the Zoom In, Zoom Out, and Hand tools.

On Windows, I do the same thing with the Ctrl, Alt, and Spacebar keys.

So, as my right hand moves the mouse around and taps other keys on the keyboard, my left hand is always playing the three bass notes of the keyboard.

Using the Zoom and Hand Tools

61 *The elements of the* **Navigator panel***.*

62 *When* **View All Spreads** *is chosen, the Navigator displays all the spreads in the document.*

Using the Navigator Panel

The Navigator panel combines the functions of both the Zoom and Hand tools. As you change the views in the Navigator, you change the views in your document.

TIP Enlarge the size of the Navigator panel to see more details in your document.

To use the Navigator zoom buttons:

1. If the Navigator panel is not already open, choose **Window** > **Object & Layout** > **Navigator**. This opens the Navigator panel **61**.

2. Click the Zoom In button to increase the magnification.

3. Click the Zoom Out button to decrease the magnification.

To set a specific magnification:

1. Highlight the value in the Magnification field and enter the specific magnification.

2. Press Return or Enter.

To use the Zoom slider:

◆ Drag the Zoom slider to the right to increase the magnification.

   or

   Drag the slider to the left to decrease the magnification.

To change the view spread options:

◆ Choose View All Spreads from the Navigator panel menu. This displays all the spreads in the document **62**.

TIP When you choose View All Spreads, the menu choice changes to View Active Spread. This displays only the currently selected spread.

The Preview area within the Navigator panel can also be used to move around the document window.

To move using the Navigator Preview area:

1. Position the cursor inside the Preview area of the Navigator panel. The cursor changes into a hand .

2. Drag the Hand cursor around the Preview area. The Preview Box moves to change the area displayed within the document window.

TIP Notice how the Hand cursor turns into an animated fist as it grabs the page to move around the document. *Cute!*

The View Box is the rectangle that shows the size of the area displayed in the document window. You can change the color of that rectangle so that it is more easily seen against the color of your document pages.

To change the color of the View Box:

1. Choose Panel Options from the Navigator menu. This opens the Panel Options dialog box .

2. Use the Color list to pick a new color.

63 *The* **Hand cursor** *inside the Preview area of the Navigator panel.*

64 *The* **Panel Options** *let you change the color of the View Box inside the Navigator panel.*

> ## Too Many Navigation Choices
>
> Between the document scrollbars, the Hand tool, the Navigator panel, and the Pages panel controls, you may feel a little overwhelmed by all your choices for moving around a document. Here are some guidelines for when to use what:
>
> - Use the Hand tool when you want to move short distances.
>
> - Use the Navigator panel if you need some visible clues as to where you are moving.
>
> - Use the page controls such as the Pages panel if you need to jump across many pages in a document.

Using the Navigator Panel

65 *Two views of the same document set to* **Tile Vertically.**

66 *Two views of the same document set to* **Tile Horizontally.**

Controlling Windows

The window commands let you view one document in two windows and control the display of multiple windows.

To see a document in two windows:

1. Choose **Window > Arrange > New Window**. This creates a second window containing the document.

2. Choose **Window > Arrange > Tile Vertically** 65 or **Window > Arrange > Tile Horizontally** 66. This changes the size of the windows and positions them so that all the documents are visible.

   or

   Choose **Window > Arrange > Cascade**. This stacks all the open windows so that their title bars are visible.

In the Macintosh OS X operating system, some of the windows for InDesign documents may be obscured by other application windows. Fortunately there is a command that lets you move all the InDesign windows to be seen at the front of the screen.

To control the order of documents (Mac):

◆ Choose **Window > Arrange > Bring All To Front**. This moves all the InDesign documents to the front of the stacking order of all other applications.

Controlling Windows

File Maintenance

After you work on a document for even a little while, you must save your work to a hard drive or disk. This is vital so that you don't lose important information should your computer crash in a power blackout or you do something stupid.

TIP You have a choice to save files as an InDesign document (.indd) or template (indt). The template format saves the file so that each time it is opened, it opens as an untitled document. This protects the document from inadvertent changes.

67 *The Save As dialog box (Win).*

To save and name a file (Win):

1. Choose **File > Save** or **File > Save As.** This opens the Save As dialog box **67**.

2. Use the Save In field to choose a destination disk and folder for the file.

3. Use the File Name field to name the file.

4. Use the Save As Type field to choose between an InDesign document and an InDesign template.

5. Click Save to save the file and close the dialog box.

68 *The Save As dialog box (Mac).*

To save and name a file (Mac):

1. Choose **File > Save** or **File > Save As.** This opens the Save As dialog box **68**.

2. Use the Macintosh navigational elements to choose a destination disk and folder for the file.

3. Use the Name field to name the file.

4. Use the Format pop-up list to choose between an InDesign document and an InDesign template.

5. Click Save to save the file and close the dialog box.

> ## OS or Adobe Dialog Box?
>
> There's an option in the Save and Open dialog boxes to use the Adobe dialog box or the OS (operating system) dialog box. The Adobe dialog box is another way of displaying the information in your computer. You should also choose the Adobe dialog box if you are using Version Cue.
>
> However, for this book I will use the OS dialog boxes.

The Three Different Save Commands

The first time you look under the File menu you may be a little confused by the three different commands for saving documents. What are the differences between Save, Save As, and Save a Copy?

The first time you save an untitled document, there is no difference between choosing **File > Save** and **File > Save As**. Both commands bring up the Save As dialog box.

Once you have named a file, the Save command adds new work to the file without changing the file's name. The Save As command will always open the dialog box where you can change the file's name or location.

I use the Save command almost all the time. That way I only have to remember one keystroke combination: Cmd/Ctrl-S. The only time I use the Save As command is if I want to change the name of a document or save it somewhere else.

The **File > Save A Copy** command is different. When you save a copy, you can save the file under a new name. However, unlike the Save As command, you continue to work on the file you were working on.

I use the Save a Copy command when I am about to do something strange or bizarre to my work. The Save a Copy command lets me create a version of the file that I know I can fall back on.

As you work, you may want to spin off a copy of your document under another name. The Save a Copy command makes this easy to do.

To create a copy of a document:

1. Choose **File > Save a Copy**. This opens the Save As dialog box.

2. Use the same steps as described in the two previous exercises to save the file.

3. Click Save. The copy of the document is saved while you can continue to work on your current file.

There may be times when you want to revert to the previously saved version of a document without saving any changes.

To go back to the saved version of a document:

◆ Choose **File > Revert**. The file closes and then reopens to where it was when last saved.

To undo the steps you have done:

◆ Choose **Edit > Undo [Action]**.

TIP Repeat this command as often as necessary.

To redo the steps you have done:

◆ Choose **Edit > Redo [Action]**.

To close a document:

◆ Choose **File > Close**.

or

Click the Close box or button in the document window.

File Maintenance

It happens — someday, somehow your computer will crash, a blackout will hit your city, or you will be forced to restart the computer without saving your work. Fortunately, InDesign has an automatic recovery option that can save your work.

To recover a file:

1. Restart the computer after the crash or data loss.

2. Start InDesign. Any files that were open when the crash occurred will be automatically opened.

3. Choose **File > Save As** to save the file with a new name and destination.

TIP The restored data is a temporary version of the file and must be saved in order to ensure the integrity of the data.

InDesign gives you options for opening and closing files.

To open a file within InDesign:

1. Choose **File > Open**.

2. Use the navigation controls to select the file you want to open.

TIP You can also open a document by double-clicking its icon.

To open recently saved documents:

♦ Choose **File > Open Recent** and then choose one of the files listed in the submenu.

TIP InDesign lists the ten last-opened documents in the submenu.

Opening QuarkXPress or PageMaker Files

InDesign can convert documents and templates from QuarkXPress 3.3 or 4.0, and Adobe PageMaker 6.5 (or later). Simply choose **File > Open** and choose the file. InDesign converts the file into a new InDesign document.

How good is the conversion? It's great for templates that consist of the layout without any text. All the master pages are converted along with the style sheets and colors. This lets you use your old templates to produce new work in InDesign.

Graphics that were pasted via the clipboard into QuarkXPress or PageMaker — and not placed using the Place or Get Picture commands — are not converted.

The conversion may change documents with lots of text. For instance, InDesign arranges type with a very sophisticated composition engine. This means that text could move to new lines when it appears in the InDesign document.

If you need to make just one or two small changes to an old document, you're better off opening the file in QuarkXPress or PageMaker and making the changes to the original files.

However, if you need to completely redo a document, export the text from the file, and then use InDesign to convert the template into an InDesign file. You can then use that template for all new documents.

What if you need to open QuarkXPress 5.0, 6.0, 6.5, or 7.0 files in InDesign? I suggest you investigate the product *Q2ID* from Markzware. It provides a conversion for those versions of QuarkXPress files.

BASIC TEXT 3

When I started in advertising, back in the late seventies, setting type was a complicated process. First, the writer typed out the text on paper. The art director or typographer then marked up the copy with a red pencil to indicate the typeface, point size, leading, and so on.

Then, the copy was sent to a typesetting house where a typesetter retyped the text into a special typesetting machine. The text was printed onto special photographic paper and sent back the next morning. The copywriter then had to proof the text to make sure that there were no errors.

She might also have to cut some lines of text to fit the layout. Depending on how much text had to be cut, the art director would use a razor blade to delete the text, or the copy would be sent back to the typesetter.

That's why I am amazed every time I use a program such as InDesign to set text. I don't type the copy onto a piece of paper; I type to fit right onto my actual layout. I don't have to send the copy out overnight; it's right there on my computer screen. And I know that the only mistakes are the ones I make myself!

Creating Text Frames

InDesign holds text in objects called *frames*. Before you can start typing text, you need to create a text frame. The easiest way to do this is with the Type tool.

TIP You can resize or reshape text frames like you can other objects. *(See Chapter 4, "Working with Objects," for more details on creating and working with objects.)*

*Choose the **Type tool** in the Tools panel to work with text.*

To create a text frame with the Type tool:

1. Click the Type tool in the Tools panel .
2. Move the cursor to the page. The cursor changes to the Type tool cursor.
3. Drag diagonally to create the frame.

TIP The frame starts from the horizontal line that intersects the text frame cursor.

4. Release the mouse button. The text frame appears with an insertion point that indicates you can type in the frame.

The cursor set to create a text frame.

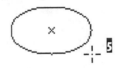

Drag diagonally with the Type tool to create a text frame.

The Type tool will always create rectangular frames. However, you can use the frame tools to create other geometric shapes such as ellipses and polygons to hold text.

TIP The frame tools also let you use numerical settings to specify the exact dimensions of a frame.

The Ellipse tool in the Tools panel.

To draw an elliptical frame:

1. Click the Ellipse tool in the Tools panel.
2. Drag diagonally to create the ellipse.
3. Release the mouse button when the ellipse is the correct size.
4. Click the Type tool inside the frame to convert it to a text frame.

Drag diagonally to create an ellipse.

The **Polygon tool** *in the Tools panel.*

7 *Use the* **Polygon Settings dialog box** *to change the shape and the number of sides of a polygon.*

8 *Drag diagonally to create polygons or stars.*

Unassigned Frames

The Ellipse, Polygon, and Rectangle tools create frames that are unassigned. This means they hold neither text nor graphics. But don't let the unassigned designation mislead you. It doesn't really matter if a frame is unassigned or not.

You can convert unassigned frames to hold text or you can convert unassigned frames to hold graphics.

The Polygon tool also lets you draw stars as well as ordinary polygons.

To draw a polygon frame:

1. Double-click the Polygon tool in the Tools panel **6**. This opens the Polygon Settings dialog box **7**.

2. Enter a number in the field for the number of sides.

3. Leave the Star Inset amount as 0%. If you increase the star inset, you create a star. (See the next exercise.)

4. Drag across the page to create the polygon **8**.

TIP Press the up or down arrow keys as you drag to increase or decrease the number of sides of the polygon.

5. Release the mouse button when the polygon or star is the correct size.

6. Click the Type tool inside the frame to convert it to a text frame.

To create a star frame:

1. Double-click the Polygon tool in the Tools panel to open the Polygon Settings dialog box **7**.

2. Enter a number in the Number of Sides field for the number of outer points.

3. Enter a value for the Star Inset amount. The greater the amount, the sharper the points will be.

4. Drag to create the star **8**.

TIP Press the up or down arrow keys as you drag to increase or decrease the number of points of the star.

TIP Press the left or right arrow keys as you drag to increase or decrease the star inset.

5. Release the mouse button when the star is the correct size.

6. Click the Type tool inside the frame to convert it to a text frame.

Creating Text Frames

You can also create rectangular frames using the Rectangle tool.

To draw a rectangular frame:

1. Click the Rectangle tool in the Tools panel .
2. Drag diagonally to create the rectangle .
3. Release the mouse button when the rectangle is the correct size.
4. Click the Type tool inside the frame to convert it to a text frame.

The Elliptical and Rectangular frame tools let you numerically specify the frame size.

To set the size of a frame numerically:

1. Choose the Ellipse or Rectangle tool from the Tools panel.
2. Position the cursor where you want to create the frame.
3. Click. A dialog box appears **11**.
4. Set the Width and Height of the frame.
5. Click OK. The frame appears with its upper-left point where you first clicked.

TIP Hold the Opt/Alt key as you click to position the centerpoint of the frame at that point.

Frames created with the Ellipse, Polygon, and Rectangle tools must be converted before they can be used as text frames.

To convert unassigned frames:

1. Select the frame you want to convert.
2. Choose the Type tool and click inside the frame.

   or

   Choose **Object > Content > Text.** An insertion point appears indicating that you can begin typing.

9 *The **Rectangle tool** in the Tools panel.*

10 *Drag diagonally to create a rectangle.*

11 *The **Ellipse and Rectangle dialog boxes** let you specify the width and height of a frame.*

Tips for Drawing Frames

There are several keyboard shortcuts you can press as you draw frames:

- Hold the **Shift key** to constrain the frame to a square, circle, or uniform polygon.
- Hold the **Opt/Alt key** to draw the frame from the center outward.
- Hold the **Spacebar** to reposition the frame as you draw.

---

ightened to see the Witch
away like brown sugar
eyes.
now water would be the

12 *The* **overset symbol** *indicates that there is more text than will fit in the frame.*

"See what you have done
screamed. "In a minute I sh
"I'm very sorry, indeed,"

13 *The* **blinking insertion point** *indicates where text will be added.*

Typing Text

The two most important parts of working with text are typing the text and then selecting it to make changes.

To type text:

1. Click with the Type tool in a frame.

2. Begin typing.

3. Press Return to begin a new paragraph.

   or

   Press Shift-Return to begin a new line without starting a new paragraph. InDesign calls this a *Forced Line Break.* Others call it a *soft return.*

TIP InDesign automatically wraps text within the text frame.

TIP If the text frame is too small to display all the text, an overset symbol appears **12**. You can reshape the frame or flow the text into a new frame to eliminate the overset text.

To add text into a passage you have already typed, you move the *insertion point* to where you want to place the new material. The point blinks to help you find it **13**.

To move the insertion point:

1. Position the Type tool cursor where you want the insertion point.

2. Click to set the insertion point.

To move the point using the keyboard:

1. Use the arrow keys to move the insertion point left or right one character at a time or up and down one line at a time.

2. Use the Cmd/Ctrl key with the arrow keys to move the insertion point one word or one paragraph at a time.

Typing Text

Selecting Text

The simplest way to select text is to use the mouse.

To select text using the mouse:

◆ Press and drag across the text. The highlight indicates which text is being selected.

TIP You don't have to drag from left to right to select multiple lines. Simply drag down.

Like other programs, InDesign has special techniques to select words, lines, and paragraphs with the mouse.

To select a single word:

◆ Double-click within a word to select it **14**.

TIP Although only the word is selected, if you hit the Delete key, the word and the space after it will be deleted.

To select a single line:

◆ Triple-click within the line **15**.

TIP Turn on **Triple Click to Select a Line** in the Type preferences.

To select a paragraph:

◆ If **Triple Click to Select a Line** is turned off, triple-click within the paragraph **16**.

or

If **Triple Click to Select a Line** is turned on, quadruple-click in the paragraph.

To select all the text in a frame or story:

◆ If **Triple Click to Select a Line** is turned off, quadruple-click within any paragraph.

or

If **Triple Click to Select a Line** is turned on, quintuple-click in any paragraph.

Dorothy began to sob for she felt lonely among all these strange people. The kind-hearted Munchkins immediately took out their handkerchiefs and began to weep also.

14 Double-click to select a single word, *which is then highlighted.*

Dorothy began to sob for she felt lonely among all these strange people. The kind-hearted Munchkins immediately took out their handkerchiefs and began to weep also.

15 *A triple-click selects a single line in a paragraph.*

Dorothy began to sob for she felt lonely among all these strange people. The kind-hearted Munchkins immediately took out their handkerchiefs and began to weep also.

16 *An example of how a* **triple-click** *or* **quadruple-click can select a paragraph.**

Keyboard, Mouse, or Menu?

One of the hot topics in working with software is the keyboard-versus-mouse debate. If you are a fast typist, you will work faster using keyboard shortcuts. There are times when you may consider using a mouse.

If my hands are already on the keyboard, I try to keep them there to select text or apply a formatting change.

But if my hands are on the mouse, I try to use it. So if I've just finished moving a text frame to a new position, I can easily highlight the text with the mouse.

Menu commands are another matter entirely. I try whenever possible to learn the keyboard shortcuts for menu commands.

That way I don't have to move the mouse all the way up to the top of the page to choose a command such as Cut, Copy, or Paste.

Quick Guide to the Shortcuts

Here are some easy ways to understand the selection shortcuts:

- The up, down, left, and right arrow keys all jump around the text.
- Add the Cmd/Ctrl keys to make the bigger jumps. Instead of a character, you jump a word. Instead of a line, you jump a paragraph. (Remember: you have more power when you take *Command* or *Control*!)
- Adding the Shift key lets you select the text. The *S* in *Shift* stands for *Select*.

If you spend a lot of time typing and modifying text, you should learn the following techniques for selecting text.

To select text using keyboard shortcuts:

1. Use the following keyboard commands to select text using the keyboard:

Keystroke	Selects
Shift key and tap the left or right arrow key	Single character.
Shift key and tap the up or down arrow key	One line of text. Repeat to select additional lines.
Cmd/Ctrl+Shift keys and tap the left or right arrow key	One word and the space following it.
Cmd/Ctrl+Shift keys and tap the up or down arrow key	Paragraph.
Shift key and tap the Home or End key	All the text to the beginning or end of a line.
Cmd/Ctrl+Shift keys and tap the Home or End key	All the text to the beginning or end of a text frame or story.
Cmd/Ctrl+A	All the text within an entire text frame or story.

2. Repeat any of the above commands to select additional text.

TIP You can switch commands to first select a line and then the following word.

TIP You can quickly edit text by double-clicking a text frame with either selection tool. This switches to the Type tool and places an insertion point where you double-clicked.

TIP Press the Escape (esc) key to switch out of the text editing mode and then select the frame as an object.

Moving and Deleting Text

You can copy or move text from one place and then paste it into another. Text that is copied or cut is stored on the computer clipboard. *(See the sidebar on this page for an explanation of how the clipboard works.)*

To copy and paste text:

1. Select the text or text frame **17**.

2. Choose **Edit > Copy** or **Cut**.

TIP If you choose Cut, the highlighted text disappears and the remaining text reflows.

3. Position the insertion point where you want to put the copied or cut text **18**.

4. Choose **Edit > Paste**. The text is inserted into the new position **19**.

    or

    Choose **Edit > Paste Without Formatting** to paste the text so that its formatting (point size, typeface, style, etc.) matches the text it is being pasted into.

TIP The Paste Without Formatting command is very helpful if you want the text from one place to be pasted into a paragraph that has different formatting.

TIP You can select text before pasting to replace the selected text with the copied text.

17 *Select text in order to copy or cut it from one position to another.*

18 *Click to put the insertion point where you want to insert the copied or cut text.*

19 *The **Paste command** inserts the copied or cut text at the insertion point.*

What Is the Computer Clipboard?

The Copy command places the copied objects into an area of the computer memory called the clipboard. The contents of the clipboard stay within the memory until a new copy or cut command is executed or until the computer is turned off.

The clipboard can hold only one set of information at a time. So if you copy one sentence, you will lose it from the clipboard if you copy or cut something else later on.

Moving and Deleting Text

The·Cyclone¶
The·Wonderful·Wizard·
Chapter·One·-·#

20 *Press on the highlighted text to display the* **Drag-and-Drop Text cursor.**

The·Cyclone¶
The·Wonderful·Wizard·
Chapter·One·-·#

21 *Drag to display the* **destination insertion point** *for drag-and-drop text.*

onderful·Wizard·of·Oz¶
er·One·-·The·Cyclone#

22 *Release the mouse button to drop the text into its new position.*

You can also use the mouse to drag text from one place to another.

TIP Use the Preferences to set the options for drag-and-drop text to be active in the Story Editor and/or the Layout View.

To drag text from one place to another:

1. Select the text so that it is highlighted within the frame.

2. Position the cursor inside the highlighted text. The cursor changes to a curved arrow with the letter T next to it **20**.

3. Press with the mouse and drag to the new position. An insertion point appears at the new location **21**.

4. Release the mouse to move the text to the new position **22**.

TIP Hold the Opt/Alt key as you drag text to create a copy of the original text in the new location.

TIP Hold the Shift key as you drag text to force the text to inherit the formatting of the destination. This works for text dragged within InDesign as well as from external applications.

The Duplicate command copies and pastes in one step. It also leaves the contents of the clipboard untouched.

To duplicate text:

1. Select the text or text frame.

2. Choose **Edit > Duplicate**. The copied text is duplicated as follows:

   • A text frame is created slightly offset from the original object.

   • Text inside a frame is pasted immediately following the original text.

TIP The Duplicate command does not replace the contents of the clipboard.

Moving and Deleting Text

Using the Character Panel

Character formatting refers to attributes that can be applied to a single character or *glyph* in a paragraph without applying that formatting to the entire paragraph. The Character panel controls character attributes.

TIP As you work with text frames, the Control panel changes to display many of the text controls found in the Character panel. This makes it possible to style text using just the Control panel.

To work with the Character panel:

1. If the Character panel is not visible, choose **Window > Type & Tables > Character** or **Type > Character**. This opens the Character panel .

   or

   Click the Character panel tab to move it to the front of a set of nested panels.

2. Click the panel tab to reveal all the panel options.

   or

   Choose Show Options from the Character panel menu .

TIP The Character panel menu also contains additional controls for formatting text.

23 *The* **Character panel** *lets you change the character attributes.*

24 *The* **Character panel menu** *contains additional controls for formatting text.*

Setting the Text Defaults

When you first open InDesign, text frames are set with the fonts that the Adobe folks thought you'd like to work with. You don't have to live with those settings.

Deselect all objects and change the text settings to whatever you like. Those settings will become the defaults for that document. You can also set the defaults for all new documents by changing the settings with no document open.

---

25 *The* **font menu in the Character panel** *lets you choose the typeface for text. The style menu next to each font name displays the style choices.*

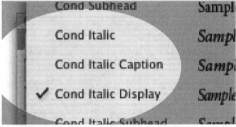

26 *The* **style menu in the Character panel** *lets you choose the proper style choices for a typeface.*

27 *The* **point size field in the Character panel** *lets you choose common point sizes or enter a specific size in the field.*

Setting the Typeface and Point Size

The design of type is called the *typeface*. The typeface you are reading now is called Minion Pro. The typeface of the subhead below is called Myriad Pro Bold Condensed.

To choose a font (typeface):

1. Choose **Type > Font** and then choose the typeface from the font menu. The font menu can be set to preview the typefaces.

   or

   In the Character panel, choose a typeface from the font menu **25**.

2. If necessary, choose the styling for the font from the style menu next to the name of the font.

   or

   Use the style list in the Character panel to choose the styling **26**.

TIP The style list changes depending on the typeface and the fonts you have installed. If you do not have the bold version of a font, for example, it will not be listed.

TIP You can use the keyboard commands to apply styling such as regular, bold, italic, and bold italic.

The size of type is measured using a system called *points*. There are 72 points per inch. The point size of this text is 10.25.

To change the point size:

◆ Choose **Type > Size** and then choose a point size from the list.

   or

   Use the point size field controls to enter a custom point size **27**.

Styling Text

InDesign also lets you apply electronic styling such as All Caps, Small Caps, Subscript, and Superscript.

To apply electronic styles:

- ◆ Choose one of the styles listed in the Character panel menu **28**. The text changes to the style chosen **29**.

  - **All Caps** converts lowercase letters to all capital letters.

  - **Small Caps** converts lowercase letters to reduced capitals.

  - **Superscript** reduces and raises the text above the baseline.

  - **Subscript** reduces and lowers the text below the baseline.

  - **Underline** draws a line under the text.

  - **Strikethrough** draws a line through the text.

  - **Ligatures** automatically substitutes the combined letterforms for characters such as fi and fl **30**.

TIP The All Caps style has no effect on text typed with the Caps Lock or Shift key held down.

TIP The sizes of the Small Caps, Subscript, and Superscript are controlled in the text preferences.

28 *The* electronic style options *in the Character panel menu.*

Dorothy and TOTC — **All caps**

L. Frank Baum — **Small caps**

Emerald City® — **Superscript**

H_2O — **Subscript**

<u>Tin</u> Woodman — **Underline**

~~Cowardly~~ Lion — **Strikethrough**

29 *Examples of the electronic styles applied to text.*

30 *Applying the* Ligatures command *to the top text replaces specific pairs of letters with combination letterforms such as those on the bottom.*

As mentioned on the previous page, you can change the appearance of the Underline and Strikethrough effects.

To customize Underline and Strikethrough Options:

1. Select the text.

2. Choose Underline Options or Strikethrough Options from the Character panel menu. The Underline Options or Strikethrough Options dialog box appears **31**.

3. Click Underline On or Strikethrough On to turn on the effect.

TIP The effect will already be on if it was applied in the Character panel menu.

4. Use the Weight controls to set the thickness of the line.

5. Use the Offset controls to move the line as follows:
   - **Positive underline numbers** move the line *below* the baseline.
   - **Positive strikethrough numbers** move the line *above* the baseline.

6. Choose one of the rules from the Type list.

7. Choose a color and tint from the Color and Tint lists.

8. If your line type has a gap, such as in a dashed line, use the Gap Color and Gap Tint lists to color the gap.

9. If desired, check the Overprint Stroke and Overprint Gap options (*See Chapter 5, "Working in Color," for more information on overprinting colors*).

31 *The* **Underline Options and Strikethrough Options dialog boxes** *let you customize the appearance of the Underline and Strikethrough effects.*

Underlines as Highlights!

One of the most exciting uses for the custom underlines and strikethrough effects is to use them as highlights for individual lines or words of text. This is something designers have wanted to do for years.

All you have to do is set the weight of the line to slightly thicker than the text point size. And use the offset to position the line around the text. You can then apply these custom underlines as highlights for text. You can also combine the underline and strikethrough lines above and below the text **32**.

The Wonderful
Wizard of OZ

32 *An example of how custom underlines and strikethrough settings can be used for highlights and other special effects.*

Setting Line and Character Spacing

Leading is the space between lines of type within a paragraph **33**. (It is pronounced *ledding,* because it refers to the lead metal formerly used to set type.) Leading is specified as an absolute point size or as auto leading. The leading of this paragraph is 12 points.

To set the leading:

1. Select the paragraph of text.

2. Use the leading controls in the Character panel to enter an amount of leading **34**.

   or

   Set the leading to Auto to have the leading automatically change to an amount based on the point size.

TIP The amount of the auto leading is set in the Paragraph panel's Justification menu.

Kerning is the space between two letters. It is applied so letters fit snugly together **35**.

To set kerning:

1. Select the text you want to kern, or place an insertion point between the letters.

2. To use the kerning pairs in the typeface, choose Metrics from the kerning list **36**.

   or

   Choose Optical to adjust the kerning using a visual representation of the text.

TIP Use optical kerning when there are no built-in font metrics (for instance, when you combine two different typefaces).

3. To apply a specific kerning amount, use the kerning controls or pop-up menu to apply a numerical amount.

TIP Positive numbers increase the space. Negative numbers decrease the space. Zero indicates no kerning is applied.

"Well in a few m
be all melted an
have the cas

"Well in a few m
be all melted an
have the castle a

33 *The 24-point leading (top) has more line space than the 16-point leading (bottom).*

34 *The* **leading controls in the Character panel** *let you change the amount of space between lines.*

Avoid
Avoid
Avoid

35 *A comparison of the different kerning settings: 0 (top), Metrics (middle), Optical (bottom).*

36 *The* **kerning controls in the Character panel** *change the space between characters.*

Setting Line and Character Spacing

The Emerald City
The Emerald City

37 *Tracking of 100 increases the space along all the letters.*

Tracking is similar to kerning; however, unlike kerning, which applies to letter pairs, tracking is applied to a range of letters **37**. Tracking is very useful, because as you increase the space between the letters, you don't lose the relative spacing that is applied by kerning.

To set tracking:

1. Select the text you want to track.

2. Use the tracking controls in the Character panel to set the amount of tracking **38**.

TIP Positive numbers increase the space between letters. Negative numbers decrease the space. Zero indicates no tracking is applied.

38 *The **tracking controls** in the Character panel change the space across a sequence of letters.*

Wonderful Wizard

39 *A negative baseline shift lowers the capital letters from the rest of the characters.*

Baseline shift moves text up or down from the *baseline*, or the imaginary line that the letters sit on. Baseline shift is often applied to shift bullets or parentheses so they sit better next to text. It can also be used for special effects in display or headline text **39**.

To set the baseline shift:

1. Select the text that you want to reposition.

2. Use the baseline shift controls in the Character panel to move the text away from the baseline **40**.

TIP Positive numbers move the text up. Negative numbers move the text down.

40 *The **baseline shift controls** in the Character panel move text above or below the line.*

Setting Line and Character Spacing

Applying Text Distortions

InDesign also lets you apply horizontal or vertical scaling to text. This distorts the text to increase its height or width **41**. This changes the type from the original design of the characters. Typographic purists (such as this author) disdain distorting text.

To apply horizontal scaling:

1. Select the text that you want to distort.
2. Use the horizontal scale field controls in the Character panel to change the width of the text **42**.

To apply vertical scaling:

1. Select the text that you want to distort.
2. Use the vertical scale field controls in the Character panel **43**.

Skewing allows you to slant or tilt text **44**. This is also called *false italic* because it resembles the slant of italic text.

To skew text:

1. Select the text that you want to skew.
2. Enter an angle in the skew field in the Character panel to specify how much the text should be slanted **45**.

TIP Positive numbers to 180 degrees tilt the text to the left. Negative numbers to 180 degrees tilt the text to the right.

Applying Text Distortions

DOROTHY Vertical scale

DOROTHY Normal

DOROTHY Horizontal scale

41 *The effects of applying either vertical scaling or horizontal scaling to text.*

42 *Use the* **horizontal scale controls** *in the Character panel to distort the width of text.*

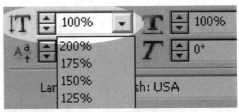

43 *The* **vertical scale controls** *in the Character panel let you distort text height.*

CYCLONE!

44 *You can apply negative and positive skew to text to create a special effect.*

45 *The* **skew controls in the Character panel** *let you create fake oblique and slanted text.*

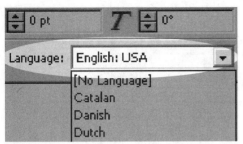

46 *The* **Language menu** *lets you set the language used for spelling checks as well as for typographer's quotes.*

Setting the Language

You can also set the language. This ensures that foreign words as well as your native language are spell-checked and hyphenated using the proper dictionary. (Sorry, but changing the language doesn't translate the text.)

TIP If you have [No Language] selected, InDesign can't substitute typographer's quotes ("curly" quotes) for the ordinary typewriter quotes ("dumb" quotes).

To set the language:

1. Select the text that you want to set the language for.

2. Choose the language from the pop-up menu in the Character panel **46**.

Electronic Styling: Myths and Realities

As you set type using programs such as InDesign, people may tell you *never* to style fonts electronically. So if you use the Roman version of a font (such as Minion), you should never press the keyboard shortcut for italic. You should only choose the actual typeface (Minion Italic) from the font menu.

This rule emerged because some typefaces do not have an italic or bold version. The styling shows on the screen, but it doesn't print. Techno or Zapf Dingbats are examples of fonts that shouldn't be styled electronically. When people see their printed samples, they're disappointed that there is no bold or italic appearance.

Fortunately, InDesign prevents you from making errors like that. If you apply the shortcut for italic, InDesign applies the actual italic version. If there is no version, InDesign does not change the font. So there is no harm styling electronically using InDesign.

I've also heard people advise to avoid all caps, subscript, small caps, and other electronic styles on type. In most cases, there is nothing wrong with applying those styles, and InDesign allows you to apply those electronic styles to text.

In some cases you'll have better results with a small-caps version of a font than with the electronic style for small caps. However, a special small-caps font offers a subtle effect that few people will recognize.

I personally hate the electronic styling for Vertical and Horizontal Scale. They distort the type horribly. The Skew command is even worse! However, I do accept that there might be times (grotesque Halloween cards?) where those distortions are acceptable.

Applying Paragraph Formatting

Paragraph formatting refers to the attributes that are applied to the paragraph as a whole. For instance, you cannot have half of the paragraph centered and the other half on the left size of the page. The alignment must be applied to the whole paragraph. InDesign paragraph formatting is applied using the Paragraph panel.

TIP As you work with text frames, the Control panel changes to display many of the text controls found in the Paragraph panel. This makes it possible to style text using just the Control panel.

To work with the Paragraph panel:

1. If the Paragraph panel is not visible, choose **Window > Type & Tables > Paragraph** or **Type > Paragraph**. This opens the Paragraph panel .

   or

   Click the Paragraph panel tab to move it to the front of a set of tabbed panels.

2. To display all the paragraph formatting controls, choose Show Options from the Paragraph panel pop-up menu.

TIP The Paragraph panel menu also contains additional controls for formatting text **48**.

TIP The following techniques are useful when applying paragraph attributes:

   • To apply attributes to a single paragraph, click to place an insertion point within the paragraph.

   • To apply attributes to more than one paragraph, select a portion of the first and last paragraphs and the paragraphs in between.

47 *The* **Paragraph panel** *controls attributes that are applied to the whole paragraph.*

48 *The* **Paragraph panel menu** *contains additional controls for paragraph attributes.*

49 *The* **Alignment buttons** *on the Paragraph panel control how the type is aligned to the frame edges.*

Setting Alignment and Indents

In addition to the common paragraph alignment controls found in page layout or word processing programs, InDesign offers some special controls for setting alignment.

To set paragraph alignment:

1. Select the paragraphs.
2. Click one of the Alignment buttons **49** to set the alignment as follows:

Alignment	Icon	Example	Description
Flush Left		I have been wicked in my day but I never thought a little girl like you would be able to melt me.	Sets the text to align at the left margin.
Centered		I have been wicked in my day but I never thought a little girl like you would be able to melt me.	Sets the text to align at the center of the paragraph.
Flush Right		I have been wicked in my day but I never thought a little girl like you would be able to melt me.	Sets the text to align at the right margin.
Justified Last Left		I have been wicked in my day but I never thought a little girl like you would be able to melt me.	Sets the text to align at both the left and right margins, but aligns the last line flush left.
Justified Last Centered		I have been wicked in my day but I never thought a little girl like you would be able to melt me.	Sets the text to align at both the left and right margins, but centers the last line.
Justified Last Right		I have been wicked in my day but I never thought a little girl like you would be able to melt me.	Sets the text to align at both the left and right margins, but aligns the last line flush right.
Justified All		I have been wicked in my day but I never thought a little girl like you would be able to melt me.	Sets the text to align at both the left and right margins.
Align Towards Spine		I have been wicked in my day but I never thought a little girl like you would be able to melt me.	Sets the text to align along the spine of the document. This flips the alignment on recto and verso pages.
Align Away From Spine		I have been wicked in my day but I never thought a little girl like you would be able to melt me.	Sets the text to align toward the outside edge of the pages. This flips the alignment on recto and verso pages.

TIP Look closely and you'll see that the lines in the alignment buttons resemble how the alignment changes the position of the text.

Setting Alignment and Indents

You might want to indent a paragraph so that it stands out or indent the first line of a paragraph to make the text easier to read. These looks are created by the margin indents.

To set the margin indents:

1. Select the paragraphs.

2. Use the margin indent controls **50** to move the text as follows **51**:

   • **Left Indent** moves the left side of the paragraph away from the left side of the text frame.

   • **First Line Left Indent** moves the first line of the paragraph away from the left edge of the rest of the paragraph.

   • **Right Indent** moves the right side of the paragraph away from the right side of the text frame.

   • **Last Line Right Indent** moves the last line of the paragraph away from the right side of the text frame.

Another look you can create is to hang elements on the first line outside the rest of the paragraph **52**.

TIP You can use these steps to create bulleted and numbered paragraphs. Or you can create those automatically *(as covered in Chapter 14)*.

To create a hanging bullet or numbered list:

1. Select the paragraphs.

2. Set the Left indent to the amount that the body of the paragraph should be indent.

3. Set the First Line indent to a negative amount.

4. Insert a tab character to separate the bullet or number from the rest of the line.

TIP The order of these steps is important because the First Line indent can't have a negative amount until the Left indent has been created.

50 *The* **margin indent fields** *control the space around a paragraph and the first and last lines.*

Left indent
　First line indent　　　　　　　　**Right indent**

Well in a few minutes I shall be all melted and you shall have the castle all to yourself. I have been wicked in my day but I never thought a little girl like you would be able to melt me and end my life.

51 *The effect of applying margin indents to text inside a text frame.*

First line indent (-1p6)
　Left indent (1p6)

•　Take balloon out of storage and inflate.

•　Wind clock and set the correct time.

52 *The* **margin indent settings for a hanging bullet***. Notice that the First Line indent has a negative value.*

Setting Alignment and Indents

The **Indent to Here character** *is indicated by the small dagger symbol. It automatically creates a hanging indent for the drop cap.*

The Pros and Cons of Using the Indent to Here Character

When should you use the Indent to Here character? When should you use the paragraph margin indents?

The Indent to Here character is an excellent solution for setting off a drop cap. Because it is not set by a measurement, it doesn't need to be adjusted if you change the drop cap letter from a wide letter such as *M* to a thin one such as *I* or *J*.

However, the Indent to Here character is not a good solution for long documents with outdented characters. Margin indents applied to style sheets are more useful for those situations. For instance, all the numbered lists, bulleted lists, and tip characters in this book have been formatted using margin indents—not the Indent to Here character.

Inserting a Manual Indent

The Indent to Here character allows you to set an indent command that is tied to the position of the character.

TIP The Indent to Here character makes it easy to set a hanging indent for a drop cap or bulleted list.

To use the Indent to Here character:

1. Click inside a text frame where you would like the indent to occur.

TIP The insertion point is placed not in the lines that you want to indent, but inside the line that serves as the model. This is usually the first line of text.

2. Type Cmd/Ctrl-\ (backslash).

   or

   Choose **Type > Insert Special Character > Other > Indent to Here**. This inserts a character that creates an indent at that point .

TIP The Indent to Here character is indicated by a cross symbol when the Show Hidden Characters command is chosen.

To remove the Indent to Here character:

1. Place the insertion point to the right of the Indent to Here character.

2. Press the Delete/Backspace key.

Setting Paragraph Effects

The paragraph effects are available when Show Options is chosen in the Paragraph panel menu. One of the paragraph effects is to add space above and below a paragraph . For instance, the space between this paragraph and the one following is controlled by adding space below.

To add space between paragraphs:

1. Select the paragraphs that you want to add space above or below.

2. Use the Space Before field controls to add space before the paragraphs .

3. Use the Space After field controls to add space after the paragraphs .

TIP Never insert paragraph returns to add space between paragraphs. That can cause problems later if text reflows!

Drop caps increase the size of the first character or characters and positions them so that they drop down into the rest of the paragraph . The opening page for each chapter of this book contains a paragraph that has a drop cap applied.

To create drop caps:

1. Select the paragraph you want to set with a drop cap.

2. Use the Drop Cap Number of Lines field to set the number of lines that the letter should occupy .

3. Use the Drop Cap Number of Characters field to set how many characters of the text should have the drop cap applied .

"At the East, not far from here," said one, "there is a great desert, and none could live to cross it."
————————————— **Paragraph space**

"It is the same at the South," said another, "for I have been there and seen it. The South is the country of the Quadlings."

"I am told," said the third man, "that it is the same at the West and that country, where the Winkies live, is ruled by the Wicked Witch of the West, who would make you her slave if you passed her way."

54 *An example of* **adding space between paragraphs**.

Space before   **Space after**

55 *Use the* **Paragraph Space controls** *to add space before or after a paragraph.*

Dorothy lived in the midst of the great Kansas prairies, with Uncle Henry, who was a farmer, and Aunt Em, who was the farmer's wife.

56 *An example of a* **drop cap** *set for one character and three lines.*

Number of Lines   **Number of Characters**

57 *Use the Drop Cap controls to change the appearance of a paragraph drop cap.*

58 *The* **Drop Caps and Nested Styles dialog box** *allows you to refine the settings for drop caps.*

B**y the time she
the flamingo a
it back, the fig**

59 *An example of how* **Align Left Edge** *forces the drop cap character to align to the left margin edge.*

B**y**the time
caught th
and broug
the fight was over, a

60 *An example of how* **Scale for Descenders** *changes the size of the drop cap so that descenders don't touch the other lines of text.*

61 *Use the* **Hyphenate checkbox** *to hyphenate words at the ends of lines.*

The Control panel contains only the basic options for drop caps. There are additional controls for refining the appearance of drop cap characters.

To set the additional drop cap attributes:

1. Choose Drop Caps and Nested Styles from the Control panel menu or the Paragraph panel menu. This opens the Drop Caps and Nested Styles dialog box **58**.

2. Check the Align Left Edge option to force the drop cap character to align flush to the left side of the paragraph **59**.

3. Check the Scale for Descenders option to reduce the size of the drop cap letters to keep character descenders from touching lines of text **60**.

4. Use the Character Style menu to apply a different typeface or other character attribute to the drop cap. *(See Chapter 15, "Text and Object Styles," for information on how to create a character style.)*

You can also control whether the text within a paragraph is hyphenated or not.

To turn on hyphenation:

1. Select the paragraphs you want to set the hyphenation for.

2. To turn on hyphenation, click the Hyphenate checkbox in the Paragraph panel **61**. Depending on what words are hyphenated, the text may reflow. *(See Chapter 16, "Typography Controls," for information on controlling the number of hyphens in a paragraph.)*

Working with Hidden Characters

Every time you tap the Spacebar, Tab key, Return key, or Enter key, you create a non-printing character in the text. These hidden characters (sometimes called *invisibles*) can be turned on to let you see where the spaces, tab characters, and paragraph returns fall in the text.

To show or hide hidden characters:

◆ Choose **Type > Show Hidden Characters.** This displays the characters in the same color as the highlight for the layer 62.

   or

   Choose **Type > Hide Hidden Characters** to hide the hidden characters.

TIP Hidden characters are also hidden when you turn on the Preview mode or Overprint Preview.

TIP You can change the color of the hidden characters by changing the color of the Layer in the Layers panel.

Hidden Characters:

The following is a chart of the various hidden characters.

62 *An* assortment of the hidden characters *displayed within text.*

⟫ **Tab**	**Right Indent Tab**	**Indent To Here**	**End Nested Style**
Non-joiner	**Em Space**	**En Space**	**Anchored Object**
Nonbreaking Space	**Nonbreaking Space (Fixed Width)**	**Hair Space**	**Sixth Space**
Thin Space	**Quarter Space**	**Third Space**	**Punctuation Space**
Figure Space	**Flush Space**	**Column Break**	**Frame Break**
Page Break	**Odd Page Break**	**Even Page Break**	¶ **Paragraph Return**
Forced Line Break	**Discretionary Line Break**	**End Of Story**	

(Side tab: Working with Hidden Characters)

Increase
preview size

Decrease
preview size

63 *Use the* **Glyphs panel** *to insert characters from fonts.*

64 **Press the triangle under the glyph** *to display the alternatives for the glyph.*

Using the Glyphs Panel

Quick — what's the keystroke for a trademark symbol? The Euro symbol or Japanese Yen symbol? If you can't remember the keystrokes for all the characters you use, then you need to open the Glyphs panel. The Glyphs panel lets you easily see all the characters in a typeface. You can also use the panel to display the alternate letterforms in OpenType fonts.

To insert characters:

1. Place the insertion point where you would like the character to be inserted.

2. Choose **Type** > **Glyphs.** This opens the Glyphs panel **63**.

3. Choose the typeface and style of the character you want to insert.

4. Scroll through the Preview area to find the character you want to insert.

TIP Use the Preview Size controls to increase or decrease the size of the preview.

5. Double-click the character you want to insert.

6. Repeat step 5 to insert any additional characters.

TIP The Glyphs panel allows you to insert characters that are not usually available for certain operating systems. For instance, Macintosh users can insert fractions and Windows users can insert ligatures.

To access alternative characters:

1. Place your insertion point where you want to insert the alternative characters.

2. Press the small triangle next to the glyph in the Glyphs panel **64**. This opens the alternative letterforms for that character.

3. Choose the alternative character. This inserts the character into the text.

Using the Glyphs Panel

As you hunt through the Glyphs panel, you may find there are too many glyphs to look through. You can access the recently used glyphs or you can create your own custom glyph sets.

To access the recently used glyphs:

1. Make sure Show Options is chosen in the Glyphs panel menu.

2. Double-click one of the glyphs in the Recently Used area. This adds the glyph to your document.

To create a custom glyph set:

1. Choose New Glyph Set from the Glyphs panel menu.

2. Name the set in the New Glyph Set dialog box **65**.

3. Choose where you want new additions to the set to appear.

4. Click OK to add the set.

TIP You can have many different glyph sets. Organize them however you want.

Once you have created a glyph set, you can add your favorite characters from any font into the glyph set.

To add characters to a glyph set:

1. Use the Glyphs panel to select the character you want to add to an existing glyph set.

2. Choose Add to Glyph Set > [Set Name] from the Glyphs panel menu. The character appears in the glyph set.

3. Choose what order you want the glyphs to appear in the set from the Insert Order list **66**.

4. Click OK to create the glyph set.

65 The **New Glyph Set dialog box** *lets you name the new glyph set.*

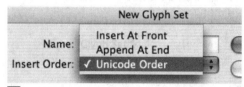

66 The **Insert Order list** *lets you control how glyphs are added to a set.*

67 *The **Edit Glyph Set** dialog box lets you delete or modify the glyphs in a custom glyph set.*

So What's a Glyph?

If you're like me, you're probably wondering about the word *glyph*. Why use that word? Why not call it the Character panel?

The answer has to do with being precise. You know what a letter is: a, b, c, X, Y, or Z. You wouldn't call things like 1, @, ? or $ letters, though. They're characters.

Well, glyphs are the proper name for everything including letters, characters, and alternative letterforms for things like ligatures and swashes.

So rather than call it the Insert Letters/Characters/Alternative Letterforms panel, Adobe calls it the Glyphs panel.

I could have sworn that the word glyph was some special Adobe typographic term; but then one of my students reminded me of Egyptian hieroglyphics. And then I remembered the Hawaiian petroglyphs.

So glyph really isn't as strange a word as I originally thought.

To insert characters in a glyph set:

1. Choose the glyph set from the Glyph Set menu in the Glyphs panel.

2. Double-click to insert the glyph.

Once you have created a glyph set, you can edit the items in the set.

To edit the characters in a glyph set:

1. Choose **Edit Glyph Set** > **[Set Name]** from the Glyphs panel menu. The Edit Glyph Set dialog box appears **67**.

2. Select the glyph item that you want to edit.

3. Use the Insert Order list to change where new glyphs are added.

4. Choose Remember Font with Glyph to set the glyph to a specific font. This means the glyph does not change to match the font in the text it's inserted into.

   or

   Deselect Remember Font with Glyph to use the Unicode value of the current font. This option lets you match a character such as the Euro symbol to the text it is inserted into.

5. If you have selected Remember Font with Glyph, you can change the typeface and style in the Edit Glyph dialog box.

6. Click the Delete from Set button to delete a glyph from a set.

7. Click OK to apply the changes to the set.

Using the Glyphs Panel

Working with Text Flow

As mentioned earlier in this chapter, if text is too long to fit in its text frame, you can link the text into another frame.

To link text between frames:

1. Click the overset text symbol. The cursor changes to the load text cursor **68**.

2. Move the cursor over to the frame you want to flow the text into. The cursor changes to the link text cursor **69**.

TIP Unlike with QuarkXPress, the second text frame does not have to be empty.

3. Click in the text frame. The link indicators show that the text in the frame flows to or from another frame **70**.

TIP You can use the same steps to link empty text frames. This makes it easy to flow text into the layout later.

To change the link between frames:

1. Click the link indicator in the frame where you want to break the link. The cursor turns into a link text cursor.

2. Click in a new text frame to flow the text into a new frame.

   or

   Click inside the text frame to keep all the text within that frame. (The overset text symbol appears.)

InDesign also displays *text threads*, which show you the links between text frames.

To show the links between frames:

1. Select the text frame that you want to see the links for.

2. Choose **View > Show Text Threads.** This displays lines that show which frames are linked together **71**.

68 *The* **load text cursor** *indicates that you can continue the overset text in another frame.*

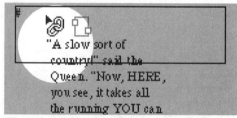

69 *The* **link text cursor** *indicates you can click to fill the next frame with text.*

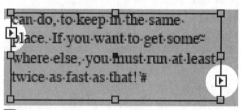

70 *The* **link indicators** *show that the text flows into and out of the text frame.*

71 *The* **text threads** *show the links between frames.*

72 *The* **Text Frame Options dialog box** *controls the flow of text within a frame.*

73 *The* **Columns settings** *for the Text Frame Options dialog box.*

Setting Text Frame General Controls

Once you create a text frame, you can still control the flow of text within the frame. This is similar to creating a mini-layout within the text frame.

To change text frame options:

1. Select the text frame.

2. Choose **Object > Text Frame Options**. This opens the Text Frame Options dialog box **72**.

3. Click the General tab.

4. Make whatever changes you want to the settings.

TIP As you modify the text frame options, click the Preview checkbox to see the effects of your changes.

You can create columns within a text frame.

To create text frame columns:

◆ Set the following options in the Columns area **73**:

- **Number** sets the number of columns.

- **Width** sets the column width.

- **Gutter** controls the space between the columns.

Setting Text Frame General Controls

InDesign also has a powerful feature that helps you maintain a fixed column width when working with a text frame. This is very helpful for magazine and newspaper layouts where all text is in the same column width.

To use Fixed Column Width:

1. Click Fixed Column Width in the Text Frame Options dialog box.

2. Drag to resize the frame width. The width automatically jumps to whatever size can accommodate an additional column .

You can also add space between the text and the frame. This is called the *inset spacing*.

To control the frame inset:

1. Select the text frame and open the Text Frame Options dialog box.

2. Enter the values in the Inset Spacing fields to control the amount of space between the top, bottom, left, and right edges of the frame .

3. Click OK to apply the changes to the column 76.

TIP If you have applied a stroke to a frame, you will most likely want to create an inset spacing so that the text does not touch the stroke.

74 *Applying* **Fixed Column Width** *ensures that the columns in a text frame are always the same size.*

75 *The Inset Spacing settings for the Text Frame Options dialog box.*

"At the East, not far from here," said one, "there is a great desert, and none could live to cross it."
"It is the same at the South," said another, "for I have been there and seen it. The South is the country of the Quadlings."
"I am told," said the third man, "that it is the same at

76 *A* **text frame with inset spacing** *has space between the text frame and the text.*

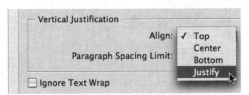

77 The **Vertical Justification Align menu** *lets you choose where text is positioned vertically.*

Top   **Center**

"The Wonderful
Wizard of Oz"
by L. Frank Baum
Chapter One, The Cyclone

"The Wonderful
Wizard of Oz"
by L. Frank Baum
Chapter One, The Cyclone

Bottom   **Justify**

"The Wonderful
Wizard of Oz"
by L. Frank Baum
Chapter One, The Cyclone

"The Wonderful
Wizard of Oz"
by L. Frank Baum
Chapter One, The Cyclone

78 *The four vertical alignment settings change the position of text within a frame.*

Center Vertical Justification for Non-Rectangular Frames?

As mentioned, the Vertical Justification controls are dimmed out if the text frame is not a rectangle. However, here's a cool tip on how to set text to center vertical justification even if the frame is not rectangular.

Set the text frame options to centered vertical justification. Then change the shape of the frame to add rounded corners or whatever non-rectangular shape you want.

Now, go back into the text frame options, and set an inset for the text. As you increase the text inset you will see the text jump from the top of the frame to the center.

Your text will now be vertically centered inside the frame.

The vertical justification of a text frame controls where the text is positioned from the top to the bottom of the frame.

To set the vertical justification:

1. Select the text frame and open the Text Frame Options dialog box.

2. Choose one of the four options in the Vertical Justification Align pop-up list **77**:

   • **Top** positions the text so that the first line sits at the top of the frame **78**.

   • **Center** positions the text so it is centered between the top and bottom of the frame **78**.

   • **Bottom** positions the text so that the last line sits at the bottom of the frame **78**.

   • **Justify** positions the text so that it fills the entire frame from top to bottom **78**.

TIP The vertical justification options are only available for rectangular text frames. If the frame is another shape or has corner effects applied, the vertical justification options are dimmed out.

Setting Text Frame General Controls

When you set the vertical alignment to Justify, you can set how the space between paragraphs is applied.

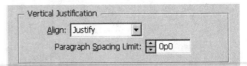

To set the paragraph spacing limit:

1. Set the Vertical Justification Align list to Justify.

2. Set an amount in the Paragraph Spacing Limit field 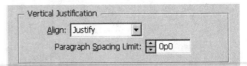. The higher the number, the more space between paragraphs and the less likely the leading between the lines will be affected by justifying the text vertically.

TIP Set an amount equal to the height of the text frame to add space only between the paragraphs, not between the lines ⑧⓪.

⑦⑨ *The **Paragraph Spacing Limit** for justified vertical alignment controls how much space will exist between paragraphs before the leading is increased.*

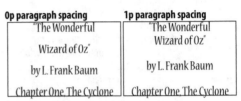

0p paragraph spacing	1p paragraph spacing
"The Wonderful Wizard of Oz" by L. Frank Baum Chapter One, The Cyclone	"The Wonderful Wizard of Oz" by L. Frank Baum Chapter One, The Cyclone

⑧⓪ *A paragraph spacing limit of 0p causes the leading to increase. A limit of 1p only adds space between the paragraphs, not the leading.*

Character icon

81 *Click the* **Character icon** *to move the character attributes to the first position in the Control panel.*

Paragraph icon

82 *Click the* **Paragraph icon** *to move the paragraph attributes to the first position in the Control panel.*

Using the Control Panel for Text

As mentioned previously, the Control panel changes its settings depending on the type of object selected. For example, when a text object is selected, the Control panel displays a combination of the Character and Paragraph panel controls.

To use the Control panel for character settings:

1. Use the Type tool to create an insertion point within a text frame. The Control panel displays the text options.

2. Click the Character icon to display the character attributes in the first position in the Control panel **81**. The paragraph attributes follow.

TIP Cmd-Opt-7 (Mac) or Ctrl-Alt-7 (Win) switches the focus between the Character and Paragraph settings in the Control panel.

To use the Control panel for paragraph settings:

1. Use the Type tool to create an insertion point within a text frame. The Control panel displays the text options.

2. Click the Paragraph icon to display the paragraph attributes in the first position in the Control panel **82**. The character attributes follow.

Using Special Text Characters

Text does not consist of just alphanumeric characters. There are special alphanumeric characters and spaces that are used as part of professional typography. InDesign lets you insert those characters into your documents.

To insert special characters:

1. Place the insertion point where you want to insert the special character.

2. Choose **Type** > **Insert Special Character**.

   or

   Control-click (Mac) or right-mouse click (Win) and choose Insert Special Character from the contextual menu.

3. Choose a character from the submenu.

You can insert white space characters, which are fixed spaces such as *em* and *en* spaces. You can also insert a nonbreaking space that forces two words to stay together.

TIP See the sidebar on the right for descriptions of the size of the white spaces.

To insert special space characters:

1. Place the insertion point where you want to insert the special character.

TIP You can highlight a regular space to replace it with a white space character.

2. Choose **Type** > **Insert White Space**.

   or

   Control-click (Mac) or right-mouse click (Win) and choose Insert White Space from the contextual menu.

3. Choose a white space character listing from the submenu.

How Wide are the Spaces?

While some of the white space character widths are obvious, others need some definition.

- An *em space* is the size of the letter M at that point size. In traditional typesetting, an em space was often used as the indent for a paragraph.

- An *en space* is one-half of an em space. An en space is often used as a fixed-width space between bullets and the next character of text.

- A *hair space* is one-twenty-fourth of an em space. A hair space is used when extremely small spaces are needed.

- A *sixth space* is one-sixth of an em space.

- A *thin space* is one-eighth of an em space. I use a thin space on either side of an em dash or the greater than (>) sign in menu commands such as **File** > **New**.

- A *quarter space* is one-quarter of an em space.

- A *third space* is one-third of an em space.

- A *punctuation space* is the width of a period or comma.

- A *figure space* is the width of a number in the same typeface. This is used to help align numbers in financial tables.

- A *flush space* is a variable space that is used with the Justify All paragraph alignment setting. When flush space is inserted, the space between the characters will automatically expand so that the line of text fills the entire column width. A flush space character ensures that the justification of the text comes from the word spacing and not letter spacing.

WORKING WITH OBJECTS 4

Back in the old days of board mechanicals, advertising agencies and design studios had a production area called the bullpen. It was the people in the bullpen — called bullpen artists — who actually created the mechanical. Most of them were kids just out of design school; the bullpen was usually their first step up the ladder in advertising or design.

The kids in the bullpen were amazing. Although not professional illustrators, they could create all sorts of artwork for the layout.

The same is true with InDesign. While InDesign is not a full-fledged drawing program such as Adobe Illustrator, you can use InDesign's tools to create a wide variety of effects by distorting, moving, resizing, duplicating, and aligning objects. It's your electronic bullpen.

Types of Frames

Frames are the containers in which you place graphics or text. Frames can also be used as graphic shapes. There are three types of frames you can create: unassigned, graphic, and text.

Unassigned frames

Unassigned frames are created with the Rectangle, Ellipse, and Polygon tools 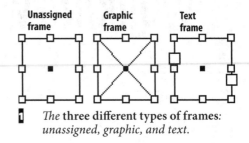. These frames are useful for adding color to your layout or a stroke around an area without inserting a graphic or text.

Graphic frames

Graphic frames are created with the Rectangle Frame, Ellipse Frame, and Polygon Frame tools. When you create a graphic frame, diagonal lines inside the frame indicate that you can insert a graphic inside the frame ❶.

TIP Although most people insert images inside graphic frames, there is nothing to prevent you from flowing text inside a graphic frame.

Text frames

Text frames are created using the Text tool or by converting frames. When you create a text frame, two link boxes appear on the sides of the frame in addition to the bounding box handles. Text frames also display a blinking insertion point when they are selected ❶.

Unassigned frame   **Graphic frame**   **Text frame**

❶ *The* **three different types of frames***: unassigned, graphic, and text.*

Diagonal Lines in Graphic Frames?

The diagonal lines inside a graphic frame come from a convention that was used in traditional pasteboard mechanicals.

When pasteboard artists drew the lines on mechanicals, they would often block off an area with diagonal lines to indicate that a picture or graphic was to go in that area.

Electronic page-layout programs such as QuarkXPress and Adobe InDesign use the same convention. The diagonal lines indicate where scanned images or graphics need to be inserted.

However, there is absolutely no rule that says you can only place images in graphic frames. You can place text in graphic frames or images in unassigned frames. The choice is yours.

The **Rectangle Frame tool in the Tools panel** *creates rectangular graphic frames.*

The **Ellipse Frame tool in the Tools panel** *creates elliptical graphic frames.*

The **Ellipse and Rectangle dialog boxes** *let you create frames with precise width and height.*

Creating Basic Shapes

You use the rectangle, ellipse, and polygon frame tools to create graphic frames into which you place images.

TIP If another tool is visible, press the corner triangle to reveal the toolset.

To create a rectangular graphic frame:

1. Click the Rectangle Frame tool in the Tools panel **2**.

2. Drag across the page to create the rectangle.

TIP Hold the Opt/Alt key to draw the object from the center.

3. Release the mouse button when the rectangle is the correct size.

TIP Hold the Shift key to constrain the rectangle into a square.

To create an elliptical graphic frame:

1. Click the Ellipse Frame tool in the Tools panel **3**.

2. Drag across the page to create the ellipse.

TIP Hold the Opt/Alt key to draw the object from the center.

3. Release the mouse button when the ellipse is the correct size.

TIP Hold the Shift key to constrain the ellipse into a circle.

You can also create rectangles and ellipses by specifying their size numerically.

To create objects numerically:

1. Click with either the Rectangle or Ellipse Frame tools. A dialog box appears **4**.

2. Enter the width and height amounts.

3. Click OK. The frame appears where the mouse was clicked.

Creating Basic Shapes

To create a polygon graphic frame:

1. Double-click the Polygon Frame tool in the Tools panel . This opens the Polygon Settings dialog box .

2. Enter a number in the field for the Number of Sides to the polygon.

3. To create a star, change the amount in the Star Inset field from 0% to a higher number.

TIP A star inset of 0% creates a basic polygon. As you increase the percentage, the points of the star become more pronounced.

4. Drag across the page to create the polygon or star.

TIP Hold the Opt/Alt key to draw the object from the center.

TIP Hold the Shift key to constrain the width and height of the object to the same amount.

5. Release the mouse button when the polygon or star is the correct size.

InDesign is definitely the program for anyone who says they can't even draw a straight line. The Line tool makes it easy.

To create straight lines:

1. Click the Line tool in the Tools panel .

2. Position the cursor where you want the line to start.

TIP Hold the Opt/Alt key to draw the line from its centerpoint.

3. Drag to create a line.

4. Release the mouse where you want the line to end.

TIP Hold the Shift key to constrain the line to 45-degree angles.

5 *Use the **Polygon Frame tool** to create polygon and star graphic frames.*

6 *The **Polygon Settings** dialog box creates either polygons or stars.*

7 *The **Line tool** in the Tools panel creates straight lines.*

Converting Shapes

So what if you've created a circle and later on realize you need a rectangle? What do you do?

Simple, you can use the Pathfinder Convert Shape commands to change an object from one shape to another. *(See Chapter 7, "Points and Paths" for more information on the Pathfinder commands.)*

Creating Basic Shapes

Selection tool   **Direct Selection tool**

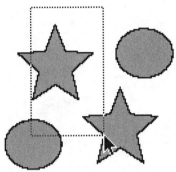

8 *The Selection tool in the Tools panel selects entire objects. The Direct Selection tool selects a point on an object or images inside objects.*

9 *Drag to create a marquee to select objects.*

What Are The Differences Between the Selection Tools?

Perhaps the most confusing part of InDesign is the difference between the Selection tool (black arrow) and the Direct Selection tool (white arrow) **8**.

If you are familiar with QuarkXPress, you can think of the Selection tool as Quark's *Object* tool. It will always select the object as a whole. Use this tool when you want to manipulate the entire object.

Think of the Direct Selection tool as Quark's *Content* tool. It selects the points that make up a frame or the image that is pasted inside a frame. Use this tool when you want to select inside a frame.

If you've ever worked with Adobe Illustrator, you'll instantly recognize the two selection tools as identical to their Illustrator cousins.

Selecting Objects

Once you've created objects, you can use different techniques to select them.

To select by clicking:

1. Choose the Selection tool (black arrow) in the Tools panel **8**.
2. Click the object you want to select.
3. Hold the Shift key to select any additional objects.

TIP Hold the Shift key and click on a selected object to deselect that object.

TIP To select objects behind others, hold the Command/Ctrl key as you click the mouse button.

TIP Double click on a graphic frame to toggle between the Selection and Direct Selection tools.

You can also select objects by dragging an area, or *selection marquee,* around the object.

To select by dragging a marquee:

1. Choose the Selection tool.
2. Drag along a diagonal angle to create a marquee around the objects you want to select **9**.

TIP You do not need to marquee the entire object to select it. Objects are selected if any portion is within the marquee.

TIP Hold the Shift key and drag around another area to add to a selection.

You can also use a menu command to select all the objects on a page.

To select all the objects on a page:

♦ Choose Edit > Select All.

TIP This command works only if you do not have an insertion point blinking inside a text frame.

Selecting Objects

Moving Objects

The simplest way to position an object on a page is to drag it to a new position, but you can also move objects by using menu and keyboard commands, or by typing specific numerical locations into a dialog box, as you'll learn later in this chapter.

To move an object by dragging:

1. Choose the Selection tool in the Tools panel.

2. Click the object you want to move. A bounding box with eight handles appears around the object. This indicates the object is selected.

3. Position the Selection tool on the edges of the bounding box (but not on the handles of the bounding box).

TIP If an object has a fill color, gradient, or image inside it, you can drag with the Selection tool directly inside the object. Otherwise, you must drag by the stroke or bounding box.

4. Drag to move the object. If you drag quickly, you will see only a bounding box preview of the object being moved **10**.

    or

    Press and pause for a moment before you drag the object. The pause gives InDesign enough time to let you see a preview of the object as you move it **11**.

10 *Quickly drag to see the bounding box of the object being moved.*

11 *Pause before you drag to see a preview of the object being moved.*

Moving Objects

12 *The* **Move dialog box** *gives you numerical controls for moving objects.*

13 *The* **double-headed arrow** *indicates that a copy is being created of the moved object.*

You can also move an object more precisely. One way to do this is with the Move command in the Transform menu.

To use the Move command:

1. Select the object or objects.

2. Choose **Object > Transform > Move.** This opens the Move dialog box **12**.

TIP This command is also available in a contextual menu or by double-clicking the Selection or Direct Selection tools.

TIP Click the Preview checkbox to see the results of your actions as you enter numbers in the dialog box.

3. Use the Horizontal and Vertical fields to move the object along those axes.

4. Use the Distance field to move the object an absolute distance.

5. Use the Angle field to set the angle along which the object moves.

6. Click OK to move the original object.

   or

   Click Copy to create a duplicate of the object in the new position.

To copy an object as you drag:

1. Hold the Opt/Alt key before you start the move.

2. Move the object as described on the opposite page. A double-headed arrow indicates that a copy is being created **13**.

3. Release the mouse button. The copy appears in the new position.

Moving Objects

Replicating Objects

There are several commands you can use to create duplicates of objects. Use the Copy command when you want to put the object on the clipboard so you can paste it somewhere else.

To copy objects:

1. Select an object to copy.

2. Choose **Edit > Copy.**

Use the Cut command to remove the object from the page so it can be pasted elsewhere.

To cut objects:

1. Select an object to cut.

2. Choose **Edit > Cut.**

Use the Paste command to see the contents of the clipboard.

To paste objects:

◆ Choose **Edit > Paste.** The contents of the clipboard appear in the center of the window area .

   or

   Choose **Edit > Paste in Place.** The contents of the clipboard appear in the same location on the page as when they were originally selected.

The Duplicate command makes a copy without changing the contents of the clipboard.

To duplicate objects:

1. Choose the object to duplicate.

2. Choose **Edit > Duplicate.** The selected object appears on the page slightly offset from the original .

Copied object

Pasted object

14 *The* **Paste command** *places the object in the center of the page.*

Original object

Duplicated object

15 *The* **Duplicate command** *places the object slightly offset from the original.*

Using Paste in Place

I always wondered just how useful the Paste in Place command is. After all, if you already have a copy of an object in one place, why would you need a second copy right over it?

That's not the point of Paste in Place. The power of the command is that you can paste an object in the same place on different pages. You can even paste in the same place in different documents.

PageMaker users will recognize this as the Powerpaste command.

Replicating Objects

16 *Use the* **Step and Repeat dialog box** *to make multiple copies of an object positioned at specific horizontal and vertical intervals.*

17 *The* **Step and Repeat command** *created five copies of the first circle.*

Objects created in step 1

Objects created in step 2

18 *An example of how to use the Step and Repeat command to create a grid of objects.*

You can also duplicate many objects at once.

To duplicate multiple objects:

1. Choose an object.

2. Choose **Edit > Step and Repeat.** The Step and Repeat dialog box appears **16**.

3. In the Repeat Count field, enter the number of duplicates that you want to create in the top row.

4. In the Horizontal Offset field, enter a distance for the horizontal space between duplicates.

5. In the Vertical Offset field, enter a distance for the vertical space between duplicates.

6. If desired, check the Preview box to see how your settings affect the objects.

TIP If you want space between the objects, make the offset at least the width or height of the object plus the amount of space between the objects.

7. Click OK. The selected object is duplicated in the desired positions **17**.

Step and Repeat can also create a grid **18**.

To create a grid of objects:

1. Set the Step and Repeat dialog box as follows:

   • In the Repeat Count field, enter the number of duplicates for the top row.

   • Enter the distance for the Horizontal Offset with the Vertical Offset as zero.

2. Click OK to duplicate the objects.

3. Select all the objects in the row, and set the Step and Repeat dialog box a second time:

   • In the Repeat Count field, enter the number for the additional rows.

   • Enter a distance for the Vertical Offset, with the Horizontal Offset as zero.

Replicating Objects

Resizing Objects

Very often things need to be made bigger or smaller. InDesign gives you several different ways to scale objects. You can also use the bounding box handles to change the dimensions of the object visually. This is the easiest way to quickly resize an object.

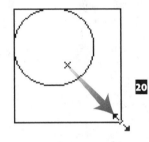

To resize using the bounding box handles:

1. Choose the Selection tool.

2. Choose which handle to drag based on the following options 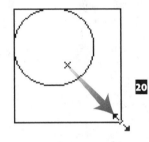:

   - Drag the corner handles to change both the width and height.

   - Drag the top or bottom handles to change the height only.

   - Drag the left or right handles to change the width only.

3. Drag the handle. If you drag quickly, you will see only the bounding box of the object **20**.

   or

   Press and hold for a moment and then drag the handle. This shows a preview of the object as you resize the bounding box **21**.

   TIP Hold down the Shift key as you drag a corner to keep the original proportions of the width and height.

   TIP Hold the Cmd/Ctrl key as you drag to scale the frame as well as any text and images inside the object.

4. Release the mouse button when the object is the correct size.

Use the **bounding box handles** *to resize an object.*

20 *If you* **drag quickly,** *you only see a box as you resize an object.*

21 *If you* **press and pause a moment,** *you see an actual preview as you resize an object.*

Resizing or Scaling?

While you and I might feel the words are the same, InDesign treats them differently. When you *resize* an object, you change its width or height. The amount of scaling stays the same in the Control panel or the Transform panel. You have to resize the object again to get it back to its original size.

When you *scale* an object, the width and height change, and the amount of scaling applied to the object is shown in the Scale fields in the Control panel or Transform panel. You can convert the object back to its original size by setting the scaling to 100%.

*(side margin: **Resizing Objects**)*

22 Objects selected with the Selection tool have both the object and its content transformed *by the transform tools.*

23 Objects selected with the Group Selection tool have only the object transformed *by the transform tools.*

24 *The indicator that the reference point can be moved to a new position.*

Using the Transform Tools

The transform tools resize and distort objects. You can transform the object itself (also called the container) or the object as well as any content. How you select objects changes the effect of the transform tools.

To control the effect of the transform tools:

◆ Select the object using the Selection tool. This type of selection causes the transform tools to affect both the container and any text or images inside it **22**.

or

Hold the Opt/Alt key as you click the frame with the Direct Selection tool. This causes the transformation to affect only the container, not any text or images contained in the frame **23**.

TIP The plus (+) sign next to the Direct Selection tool indicates that the tool is the Group Selection tool.

All the transformations take place in relation to a reference point. Each object has a default reference point, but you can change it if necessary.

To control the reference point:

1. Select the object to be transformed.

2. Choose one of the transform tools. A reference point appears inside the object.

3. Move the cursor near the reference point. A small icon appears next to the cursor that indicates you can move the reference point **24**.

4. Drag the reference point to a new position.

or

Click to position the reference point in a new position.

The Scale tool lets you increase or decrease the size of objects.

To scale objects visually using the Scale tool:

1. Select the object or objects.
2. Choose the Scale tool in the Tools panel .
3. If necessary, change the position of the reference point.
4. Move the cursor away from the reference point, and drag to scale the object .

TIP Hold down the Shift key to constrain the tool to horizontal, vertical, or proportional scaling.

TIP To see a preview of the image as you scale, press and hold the mouse button for a moment before you start to drag.

TIP Hold down the Opt/Alt key to copy the object as you scale it.

If you prefer, you can resize objects numerically using the Scale command.

To scale objects using the Scale command:

1. Select the object or objects.
2. Choose **Object > Transform > Scale.** This opens the Scale dialog box 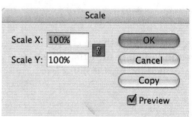.
3. Enter an amount for the Scale X (horizontal) field.
4. Enter an amount for the Scale Y (vertical) field.

TIP If the chain icon is checked, the X and Y fields scale the same amounts.

5. Check the Preview check box to see the effects of entering the amounts.
6. Click OK to scale the object.

    or

    Click Copy to create a scaled copy of the object.

The **Scale tool** *in the Tools panel is used to change the size of objects.*

The arrowhead appears while scaling an object.

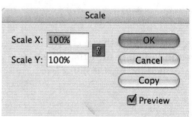

The **Scale dialog box** *lets you scale objects using numerical values.*

Making Copies as You Scale, Rotate, and Shear

As you use the Scale, Rotation, and Shear tools, you can duplicate the object as you transform it.

Drag, as usual, to start the transformation, but then add the Opt/Alt key *after* you start the drag. You will see the double-headed arrow that indicates you are duplicating the object.

Release the mouse button first, and then the Opt/Alt key to finish the transformation and duplication.

Using the Transform Tools

28 *The* **Rotate tool in the Tools panel** *is used to change the orientation of objects.*

29 *Rotating an object around its reference point.*

30 *The* **Rotate dialog box** *lets you rotate objects using numerical values.*

To scale objects numerically using the Scale tool:

1. Select the object or objects.

2. Choose the Scale tool in the Tools panel.

3. Hold the Opt/Alt key and click to designate the position of the reference point. This opens the Scale dialog box **27**.

4. Set the dialog box controls as described in the previous exercise.

The Rotation tool changes the orientation, or angle, of the object on the page.

To rotate objects visually using the Rotate tool:

1. Select the object or objects.

2. Click the Rotation tool in the Tools panel **28**.

3. If necessary, change the default reference point.

4. Move the cursor away from the reference point, and drag to rotate the object **29**.

TIP Hold down the Shift key to constrain the rotation to 45-degree increments.

To rotate objects using the Rotate command:

1. Select the object or objects.

2. Choose **Object > Transform > Rotate**. This opens the Rotate dialog box **30**.

3. Use the Angle field to set how much the object should rotate.

4. Check the Preview command to see the effects of entering the angle.

5. Click OK to rotate the object.

   or

   Click Copy to create a copy as you rotate the object.

Using the Transform Tools

Using the Transform Tools

To rotate objects numerically using the Rotate tool:

1. Select the object or objects.

2. Choose the Rotate tool in the Tools panel.

3. Hold the Opt/Alt key and click to set the position of the reference point. This opens the Rotate dialog box .

4. Set the dialog box controls as described in the previous exercise.

The Shear tool distorts the shape of objects.

To shear objects visually using the Shear tool:

1. Select the object or objects.

2. Click the Shear tool in the Tools panel 31.

3. If necessary, change the reference point by dragging it to a new position. The cursor indicates the reference point can be moved.

4. Move the cursor away from the reference point, and drag to shear the object 32.

To shear objects using the Shear command:

1. Select the object or objects.

2. Choose **Object > Transform > Shear**. This opens the Shear dialog box 33.

3. Use the Shear Angle field to set the amount of distortion.

4. Check one of the Axis options:

   • **Horizontal** shears along the horizontal axis.

   • **Vertical** shears along the vertical axis.

5. Check the Preview command to see the effects of entering the shear angle and choosing the axis.

6. Click OK to shear the object.

   or

   Click Copy to create a sheared copy of the object.

31 *Use the* **Shear tool** *in the Tools panel to distort objects.*

32 *Shearing an object around the reference point.*

33 *The* **Shear dialog box** *lets you distort objects using numerical values.*

Choose the **Free Transform tool in the Tools panel** *to scale, rotate, and shear objects.*

35 *The double-headed arrow indicates that the Free Transform tool is in the scale mode.*

36 *The curved double-headed arrow indicates that the Free Transform tool is in the rotation mode.*

To shear objects numerically using the Shear tool:

1. Select the object or objects.

2. Choose the Shear tool in the Tools panel.

3. Hold the Opt/Alt key and click to set the position of the reference point. This opens the Shear dialog box **33**.

4. Set the dialog box controls as described in the previous exercise.

Rather than switching between the Scale and Rotate tools, you can use the Free Transform tool to scale, rotate, or shear an object.

To use the Free Transform tool:

1. Select the object or objects.

2. Click the Free Transform tool in the Tools panel **34**. A bounding box appears around the object.

3. To scale the object, place the cursor over one of the handles. The cursor changes to a double-headed arrow **35**.

   or

   Place the cursor outside one of the handles of the bounding box. The cursor changes to a curved double-headed arrow **36**.

   or

   Drag one of the handles and then hold the Cmd/Ctrl key *after* you have started the drag. The cursor does not change appearance, but the object will be sheared.

4. Release the mouse button to apply the transformation.

Using the Transform Tools

Using the Transform Panel

The Transform panel allows you to move, scale, rotate, and shear objects precisely, using numerical values.

TIP When you have objects selected, the Control panel displays many of the controls that are found in the Transform panel.

To open the Transform panel:

◆ Choose **Window > Object & Layout > Transform** to open the panel .

or

If the Transform panel is behind other panels, click the Transform panel tab.

As you work with the Transform panel, it is important to know its reference point on the object. This is the same as the reference point used with the transform tools.

To set the Transform panel reference point:

1. Select the object or objects that you want to transform.

2. Click the reference point control on the Transform panel to choose the point around which the object moves **38**.

37 The **Transform panel** is a command center for positioning and transforming objects.

38 The **reference point** controls where in the object the transformation occurs.

Using the Transform Panel

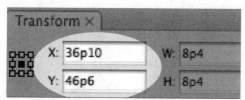

39 *The* X and Y fields in the Transform panel control *the position of an object.*

40 *The* W and H fields in the Transform panel *control the width and height of objects.*

You can use the Transform panel to move objects numerically.

To move an object with the Transform panel:

1. Select the object or objects that you want to move.

2. To move the object horizontally, enter an amount in the X field **39**.

   TIP As you increase the numbers, the object moves to the right.

3. To move the object vertically, enter an amount in the Y field **39**.

   TIP As you increase the numbers, the object moves down.

4. Press Enter or Return to apply the changes.

You can use the Transform panel to resize an object numerically.

To resize with the Transform panel:

1. Select the object or objects.

2. If necessary, change the reference point as explained on the preceding page.

3. To change the width of the object, enter an amount in the W field **40**.

4. To change the height of the object, enter an amount in the H field **40**.

5. Press Enter or Return to resize the object.

You can resize proportionally even if you know the size for only one side of the object.

To resize proportionally:

1. Select the object or objects.

2. Enter the new size in the W field or H field **40**.

3. Do not change the amount in the other field.

4. Hold Cmd/Ctrl as you press Enter or Return. The amount in both the W and H fields changes proportionally.

Using the Transform Panel

You can also scale using the Transform panel.

To scale with the Transform panel:

1. Select the object or objects.

TIP Use the Selection tool to scale the object and its contents. Use the Direct Selection tool to scale only the object.

2. If necessary, change the reference point.

3. To change the horizontal size, enter a percentage in the Scale X field .

4. To change the height of the object, enter a percentage in the Scale Y field .

TIP The Scale X and Y fields also have pop-up lists from which to choose the amount of scaling.

5. Press Enter or Return to apply the changes.

TIP You can also scale text within a text frame by dragging on the edge of the frame while holding the Cmd/Ctrl key. Hold Cmd/Ctrl-Shift and drag by a corner point to scale proportionally. This also applies to text frames in groups.

To scale proportionally with the Transform panel:

1. Select an object or objects.

2. If the Link icon is in the open state, click to close it **42**.

3. Enter an amount in either the Scale X or Scale Y fields. You do not have to enter an amount in both fields. The closed Link icon forces both fields to display the same amount.

4. Press Enter or Return to apply the changes.

TIP Hold the Cmd/Ctrl key as you press the Enter or Return key to scale proportionally even if the Link icon is in the open state.

Scale width   Scale height

41 *The* **Scale width and height fields in the Transform panel** *let you apply percentage amounts to scale objects.*

Closed state   Open state

42 *The* **Link icon in the closed state** *forces both the Scale X and the Scale Y fields to the same amount. In the open state, you can enter different amounts for the Scale X and Scale Y fields.*

Using the Transform Panel

43 *The Rotate field in the Transform panel lets you change the angle of objects.*

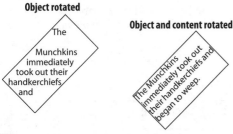

Object rotated

Object and content rotated

44 *The difference between rotating an object or rotating an object and its content.*

45 *The Shear field in the Transform panel lets you distort the shape of objects.*

Object sheared

Object and content sheared

46 *The difference between shearing an object or shearing an object and its content.*

You can also rotate objects using the Transform panel.

To rotate with the Transform panel:

1. Select the object or objects.

TIP Use the Selection tool to rotate the object and its contents. Use the Direct Selection tool to rotate only the object.

2. If necessary, change the reference point.

3. Enter the amount of rotation in the Rotation field **43**.

TIP The Rotation field also has a pop-up list from which to choose the amount of rotation.

4. Press Enter or Return to apply the changes **44**.

You can also shear objects using the Transform panel.

To shear with the Transform panel:

1. Select the object or objects.

TIP Use the Selection tool to shear the object and its contents. Use the Direct Selection tool to shear only the object.

2. If necessary, change the reference point.

3. Enter the amount of distortion in the Shear field **45**.

TIP The Shear field also has a pop-up list from which to choose the amount of shearing.

4. Press Enter or Return to apply the changes **46**.

Using the Transform Panel

Using the Transform Commands

In addition to the transform tools and transform fields, there are a whole bunch of transform commands you can use on objects. These commands make it easy to perform commonly used transformations, such as rotating and flipping objects.

To rotate with the Transform commands:

1. Select an object or objects.
2. Click to open the Transformation panel menu.

    or

    Choose **Object > Transform**.
3. Choose one of the rotation settings as follows :
    - **Rotate 180°.**
    - **Rotate 90° CW** (clockwise).
    - **Rotate 90° CCW** (counter-clockwise).

To flip objects using the Transform commands:

1. Select an object or objects.
2. Click to open the Transform panel menu.

    or

    Choose **Object > Transform**.
3. Choose one of the flip settings as follows :
    - **Flip Horizontal.**
    - **Flip Vertical.**

47 *The effects of rotating objects using the Transform submenu.*

48 *The effects of flipping objects using the Transform submenu.*

Circle moved to new position

Transform Again command applied to triangle

49 *The* **Transform Again command** *allows you to duplicate transformation commands applied to objects.*

Rotation applied to single triangle

Transform Again applied to two triangles

Transform Again Individually applied to two triangles

50 *The differences between the Transform Again command and the Transform Again Individually when applied to multiple objects.*

When you perform a transformation on an object, that transformation is stored in InDesign's memory. You can then perform the same transformation again on another object — even in another document! This is similar to Illustrator's Transform Again command.

To repeat transformations:

1. Use any of the transform commands on a selection.

2. Select a different object or objects.

3. Choose one of the following from the **Object > Transform Again** submenu.

    -   **Transform Again** applies the last single transform command to the selection as a whole **49**.

    -   **Transform Again Individually** applies the last single transform command to each object in the selection **50**.

    -   **Transform Sequence Again** applies the last set of transformation commands to the selection as a whole.

    -   **Transform Sequence Again Individually** applies the last set of transformation commands to each object in the selection.

TIP InDesign remembers all the transformation commands until you select a different object or perform a different task.

TIP InDesign can even remember an Opt/Alt-drag transformation that duplicated an object.

Using the Transform Commands

Using the Arrange Commands

Objects in InDesign are layered on top of one another in the same order they were created. (This is sometimes called the *stacking order.*) The first object created is behind the second, the second behind the third, and so on. Though you may not see the layering when objects are side by side, it is apparent when they overlap .

TIP The layering of objects is not the same as the layers of a document. *(See Chapter 11, "Layers," for more information on working with layers.)*

The Arrange commands allow you to move objects through the stacking order.

To move up or down one level in a stack:

1. Select the object you want to move.
2. Choose **Object** > **Arrange** > **Bring Forward** to move the object in front of the next object in the stacking order .

   or

   Choose **Object** > **Arrange** > **Send Backward** to move the object behind the next object in the stacking order .

To move up or down the entire stack:

1. Select an object you want to move.
2. Choose **Object** > **Arrange** > **Bring to Front** to move the object in front of all the others in its layer .

   or

   Choose **Object** > **Arrange** > **Send to Back** to move the object behind all the others in its layer .

51 *When two objects overlap, it is obvious which object is in front of the other.*

Star in back   Bring Forward applied

52 *Effects of the Bring Forward command.*

Star in front   Send Backward applied

53 *Effects of the Send Backward command.*

Star in back   Bring to Front applied

54 *Effects of the Bring to Front command.*

Star in front   Send to Back applied

55 *Effects of the Send to Back command.*

Use the **Align panel** to arrange objects in an orderly fashion.

The **alignment menu** lets you choose how the objects should be aligned.

Effects of the **vertical alignment icons**.

Effects of the **horizontal alignment icons**.

Aligning Objects

The Align panel provides commands that align objects or distribute them evenly along a horizontal or vertical axis.

To work with the Align panel:

1. Choose **Window > Object & Layout > Align.** This opens the Align panel **56**.

2. Choose Show Options from the Align panel menu to see all the commands in the panel.

To align objects:

1. Select two or more objects.

2. Use the Alignment menu to choose to what items the objects should align **57**.

   - **Align to Selection** uses the objects themselves for alignment.

   - **Align to Margins** uses the margins for alignment.

   - **Align to Page** uses the page trim for alignment.

   - **Align to Spread** uses the size of the spread for alignment.

3. Click an alignment icon as follows:

   - Click a vertical alignment icon to move the objects into left, centered, or right alignment **58**.

   - Click a horizontal alignment icon to move the objects into top, centered, or bottom alignment **59**.

TIP The align commands move objects based on the best representation of the controls. For instance, the Align Left command uses the leftmost object; Align Top uses the topmost object, and so on.

TIP You can use the Lock command (covered later in this chapter) to force one object to be the reference object for others.

Aligning Objects

You can also move objects so the spaces between certain points of the objects are equal. This is called *distributing* objects.

To distribute objects:

1. Select three or more objects.
2. Click a distribute icon as follows:
   - Click a vertical distribute icon to move the objects so that their tops, centers, or bottoms are equally distributed **60**.
   - Click a horizontal distribute icon to move the objects so that their left edges, centers, or right edges are equally distributed **61**.

You can also distribute objects based on their size. This ensures that the space between the objects is equal.

To distribute the space between objects:

1. Select three or more objects.
2. Click a distribute space icon as follows:
   - Click the vertical space icon to move objects so the vertical spaces between them are equal **62**.
   - Click the horizontal space icon to move objects so the horizontal spaces between them are equal **63**.

60 *Effects of the* **vertical distribute icons**. *Notice that the middle object changes position to create an even distribution.*

61 *Effects of the* **horizontal distribute icons**. *Notice that the middle object changes position to create an even distribution.*

62 *Effect of the* **vertical distribute space icon**.

63 *The effect of the* **horizontal distribute space command**.

Aligning Objects

64 *The* **Use Spacing** *option for* **Distribute Objects** *lets you set a specific distance between the tops, centers, bottoms, or sides of objects.*

65 *The* **Use Spacing** *option for* **Distribute Spacing** *lets you set a specific distance between objects.*

Setting the Anchor Object for Alignment

The Align to Selection option in the Align panel doesn't let you designate which object in the selection should be used as the reference object for the alignment commands. So what if you want to designate a specific object to be used as the alignment reference object?

Select the object you want to use and apply the Lock command. Then select all the objects and apply the alignment.

The locked object remains stationary and forces the other objects to align to it. Then if you need to, unlock the object to move it and the others.

The Align panel also has controls to space objects numerically. You can apply a numerical distance between the tops, centers, bottoms, or sides of objects.

To use spacing to distribute objects:

1. Select two or more objects.

2. Check Use Spacing in the Distribute Objects section of the Align panel **64**.

3. Enter the numerical distance in the Use Spacing field.

4. Click one of the Distribute Objects icons. Now the objects are separated by a specific space inserted between the tops, centers, bottoms, or sides of the objects.

TIP If a positive number moves the objects in the wrong direction, use a negative number.

You can also set a specific numerical distance between the objects themselves. This is very useful when you want the same amount of space between objects, but the objects themselves have different sizes.

To set the spacing between objects:

1. Select two or more objects.

2. Check Use Spacing in the Distribute Spacing section of the Align panel **65**.

3. Enter the numerical distance in the Use Spacing field.

4. Click one of the Distribute Spacing icons. Now a specific amount of space is added between the objects horizontally or vertically.

TIP If a positive number moves the objects in the wrong direction, use a negative number.

Aligning Objects

Grouping and Pasting Into Objects

You can group objects so you can easily select and modify them as a unit.

To group objects:

1. Select the objects you want to group.
2. Choose **Object > Group.** A dotted-line bounding box encloses all the objects .

You can also create groups within groups. This is called *nesting*.

To nest groups:

1. Select the grouped objects.
2. Hold the Shift key and select another object or group.
3. Choose **Object > Group.**

Once you have grouped objects, you can select individual objects within the group.

To select groups or objects within groups:

◆ Click once on any item in the group. The group is selected as a whole.

   or

   Double-click to select a specific item in the group 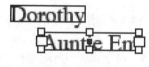.

TIP The first double-click may act like the Direct Selection tool. If so, double-click again to select the entire item.

Ungrouped items

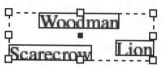

Grouped items

66 *When selected with the Selection tool,* grouped items display a bounding box around the entire group.

Group selected

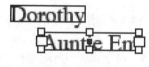

Single item selected

67 *When selected with the Direct Selection tool,* a single item in a group is displayed on its own.

Grouping and Pasting Into Objects

68 *An object to be pasted into another should be positioned over the other.*

69 *The Paste Into command displays the content only within the borders of the container.*

To use commands to select objects within groups:

1. Use the Selection tool to select the group.

2. Choose **Object > Select > Content**. This selects the topmost object in the group.

3. Choose **Object > Select > Previous Object**. This selects the object that is layered below the selected object.

   or

   Choose **Object > Select > Next Object**. This selects the object that is directly above the selected object.

To ungroup objects:

1. Select the group.

2. Choose **Object > Ungroup**.

3. If you have nested groups, continue to ungroup the objects as necessary.

You can also paste an object into a frame. This is similar to the concept of *masks* in illustration programs. InDesign refers to the object that is pasted as the *content*. It refers to the frame that holds the object as the *container*.

To paste an object into another:

1. Select the first object and position it over the second object **68**.

2. Choose **Edit > Cut** to place the first object on the computer clipboard.

3. Select the second object and choose **Edit > Paste Into**. The content appears within the borders of the container **69**.

TIP To paste multiple objects, group the objects together.

To remove pasted-in content:

1. Use the Direct Selection tool to select the pasted-in content.

2. Choose **Edit > Cut**.

TIP The pasted-in content can be placed back on the page by choosing Edit > Paste.

Grouping and Pasting Into Objects

There are some special techniques for selecting just the container or the content of pasted-in objects.

To select just the container object:

◆ Click on the frame that holds the content with the Direct Selection tool to select the container 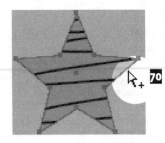.

or

Click with the Selection tool and then choose **Object > Select > Container**.

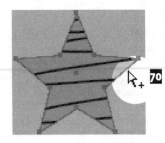
70 Click with the Direct Selection tool to select just the container.

To select just the content object:

◆ Click inside the container with the Direct Selection tool to select the content .

or

Click with the Selection tool and then choose **Object > Select > Content**.

You use special techniques to move the content inside the container.

71 Click inside the container with the Direct Selection tool to select the content.

To move only the content object:

1. Select the content object.
2. Use either the Direct Selection or the Selection tool to drag the content by its center point . The content moves within the container.

To move only the container:

1. Select the container object.
2. Use either the Direct Selection or the Selection tool to drag the container by its center point . The container moves without disturbing the content.

72 Use the center point to move just the selected content.

73 Drag the center point of the container to move it without disturbing the content.

Using the Control Panel for Objects

The Control panel is context sensitive. This means it displays different commands depending on the number of objects selected, or if the objects are grouped or pasted-in.

To use the Control panel with a single object:

◆ Select an object, grouped object, or several objects. The Control panel displays the following options :

- • Transform panel commands
- • Flip commands
- • Select container, content, next object, and previous object
- • Stroke options for width and stroke style
- • Effects
- • Text wrap
- • Object styles
- • Alignment controls

74 *The* **Control panel** *when an object is selected.*

Using the Measure Tool

There are many places where you can find the numerical sizes of items. But what if you want to measure the distance to another item? That's where the Measure tool is so helpful.

The **Measure tool** in the Tools panel.

To measure distances using the Measure tool:

1. Choose **Window** > **Info** to open the Info panel.

TIP All amounts measured by the Measure tool are displayed in the Info panel.

2. Click the Measure tool in the Tools panel 75.

3. Place the Measure tool on the start point and drag to the end point. A measuring line appears on the page 76. The Info panel displays the following attributes 77:

   • **Horizontal position** displays the X coordinate of the first point in the line or whichever point is then moved.

   • **Vertical position** displays the Y coordinate of the first point in the line or whichever point is then moved.

   • **Distance** shows the length of the line.

   • **Width** shows the width of the bounding box that would enclose the line.

   • **Height** shows the height of the bounding box that would enclose the line.

   • **Angle** shows the angle on which the line was drawn.

76 Drag the **Measure tool** *to measure the distance between two points.*

77 The **measurements displayed in the Info panel** *for the measuring line drawn with the Measure tool.*

78 *Drag the line segment of the measuring line to move it to a new position.*

79 *The **angle cursor** indicates that you are about to create a second measuring line.*

80 *Two measuring lines let you measure angles with the Measure tool.*

Distance 1 — Angle
Distance 2

81 *The **Info panel** display for two measuring lines.*

Once you have drawn a measuring line, you can move it to other areas of the page.

To move a measuring line:

1. With the Measure tool still selected, position the cursor over the measuring line.
2. Drag the line to a new position **78**.

TIP Do not position the cursor over the start or end points of the measuring line.

You can also change the start or end points of the measuring line.

To reposition the points of the measuring line:

1. With the Measure tool still selected, position the cursor over either point in the measuring line.
2. Drag the point to a new position.

You can also extend a second line out from the origin of the measuring line to create an electronic protractor to measure angles.

To measure angles:

1. Drag the first line with the Measure tool.
2. Hold the Opt/Alt key and move the Measure tool back to the origin of the first line. An angle cursor appears **79**.
3. Drag to create a second line extending out from the origin point **80**. The Info panel displays the distance of the second line, as well as the angle between the measuring lines **81**.

TIP No bounding box is displayed when two measuring lines are created.

Using the Measure Tool

Using the Info Panel with Objects

The Info panel also gives you information about the document, text, and placed images.

To see the document information:

◆ Deselect any objects on the page. The Info panel displays the following information 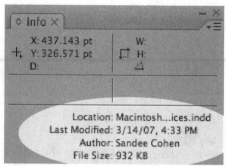:

  • **Location** of the file on the computer.
  • **Last Modification** date and time.
  • **Author** as entered in the File Info (**File > File Info**) dialog box.
  • **File size.**

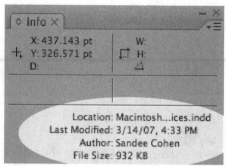

82 *With no objects selected, the Info panel displays* **document information**.

To see the text information:

◆ Place your insertion point inside a text frame.

  or

  Highlight the text in the frame. The Info panel displays the following 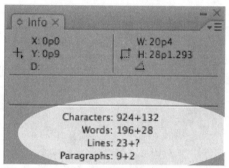:

  • **Characters** in the frame or selection.
  • **Words** in the frame or selection.
  • **Lines** in the frame or selection.
  • **Paragraphs** in the frame or selection.

TIP If there is any overset text, it is displayed as a number with a plus sign.

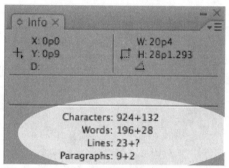

83 *With text selected, the Info panel displays* **text information**.

To see the placed object information:

◆ Select a frame that contains a placed image, or the placed image itself. The Info panel displays the following 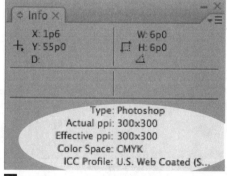:

  • **Type** of placed image.
  • **Actual ppi (points per inch)** resolution of the image.
  • **Effective ppi** resolution of the image if you have scaled the image in InDesign.
  • **Color Space** of the image.
  • **ICC Profile** (if applicable) may also be shown.

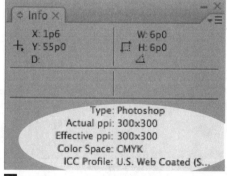

84 *With a placed image selected, the Info panel displays* **placed image information**.

85 *The **Padlock cursor** indicates that the Lock Position command has been applied.*

How Safe Are Locked Objects?

I sincerely hope that you lock your front door more securely than the Lock Position command locks objects, although what's bad for your home can be good for your layouts.

The Lock Position command only locks the position of the object. The object can still be selected using either the selection tools or the Select All command.

If there is text within the selected object, the text can be selected and otherwise modified.

If there is a placed image within the selected object, the image can be replaced by choosing a new object with the Place command.

If you need more security for your objects — for instance, to avoid inadvertently changing the color of an object — then you should lock the object's layer.

Locking Objects

You can also lock objects so they cannot be moved or modified. This prevents people from inadvertently destroying your layout.

TIP Locking objects is not the same as locking the layers of a document. *(See Chapter 11, "Layers," for more information on working with layers.)*

To lock the position of an object:

1. Select the objects you want to lock.

2. Choose **Object > Lock Position.** A small padlock appears if you try to move or modify the object **85**.

TIP Locked objects can be selected, copied, and pasted, and their colors and contents can be modified.

To unlock objects:

1. Select the objects you want to unlock.

2. Choose **Object > Unlock Position.**

Selecting Frames

Use this chart as a guide to let you know what type of object you have selected and which parts of the object can be selected using the Selection tool or the Direct Selection tool.

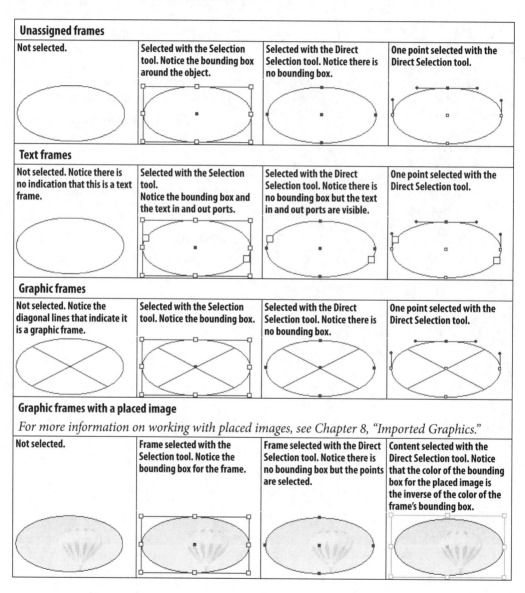

Unassigned frames

| Not selected. | Selected with the Selection tool. Notice the bounding box around the object. | Selected with the Direct Selection tool. Notice there is no bounding box. | One point selected with the Direct Selection tool. |

Text frames

| Not selected. Notice there is no indication that this is a text frame. | Selected with the Selection tool. Notice the bounding box and the text in and out ports. | Selected with the Direct Selection tool. Notice there is no bounding box but the text in and out ports are visible. | One point selected with the Direct Selection tool. |

Graphic frames

| Not selected. Notice the diagonal lines that indicate it is a graphic frame. | Selected with the Selection tool. Notice the bounding box. | Selected with the Direct Selection tool. Notice there is no bounding box. | One point selected with the Direct Selection tool. |

Graphic frames with a placed image

For more information on working with placed images, see Chapter 8, "Imported Graphics."

| Not selected. | Frame selected with the Selection tool. Notice the bounding box for the frame. | Frame selected with the Direct Selection tool. Notice there is no bounding box but the points are selected. | Content selected with the Direct Selection tool. Notice that the color of the bounding box for the placed image is the inverse of the color of the frame's bounding box. |

Selecting Frames

WORKING IN COLOR 5

When I first started in advertising, only the senior creative teams could work in color. The junior teams were assigned only black-and-white ads. Later on they might be able to work on a two-color job, but the four-color work was handled by senior art directors.

Fortunately, you're not limited by such constraints. InDesign gives you, right from the first day you use it, all the color controls you could ever wish for. However, with that power comes some responsibility.

When you define colors and use them on your pages, you are wearing two hats. Your first hat is that of a designer who looks at the aesthetics of the page and then applies colors. This is where you have fun with your creativity.

Your second hat is that of production manager. Wearing that hat you need to understand some of the principles of color and printing color documents. You also need to make sure your colors are defined so they print correctly.

The Basics of Color

Here's a quick primer to help you understand what happens when you define and apply colors in your InDesign layout, as well as other programs.

Type of color	How it is used	How it is created	Comments
CMYK	CMYK stands for the cyan, magenta, yellow, and black inks that are combined to create other colors. Also called process color, this is the primary type of color used in color printing. Most magazines and brochures are printed using the four process color inks.	Use the Color panel set to CMYK or the New Color Swatch dialog box set to CMYK or the Color Picker in the CMYK mode.	Color images are saved in the CMYK mode before they are imported into InDesign.
RGB	RGB stands for the red, green, and blue lights that are used in computer monitors to display colors. Because RGB colors are based on light waves, not inks, there will always be a slight difference between colors defined as RGB and those defined as CMYK. RGB colors can be used to define colors for documents that will be displayed onscreen. But you should not use them for print work.	Use the Color panel set to RGB or the New Color Swatch dialog box set to RGB or the Color Picker in the RGB mode.	Most scanners save images as RGB files. You must use a program such as Adobe Photoshop to convert those images to CMYK.

Type of color	How it is used	How it is created	Comments
LAB	The LAB is another light-based color model that uses luminance (L) combined with the green to red (A) plus yellow to blue (B). As with RGB, you should not define print colors using this system.	Use the Color panel set to LAB or the New Color Swatch dialog box set to LAB or the Color Picker in the LAB mode.	
Spot colors	Spot colors are specialty colors that are printed without using the four process color inks. For instance, a metallic gold in a brochure is printed using metallic gold ink, not a combination of CMYK colors. Spot colors can be mixed to display colors that could not be created using simple CMYK colors.	Use the New Color Swatch dialog box set to Spot.	Spot colors can be defined by the user or you can use the commercial spot color libraries produced by companies such as Pantone and Dicolor and Toyo. Other names for spot colors are specialty, second color, fifth or sixth color, or flat colors.
Tints	Tints are colors that have been screened so that only a percentage of their color appears on the page.	Tints can be created from named colors using the New Tint dialog box.	
Mixed inks	Mixed inks are combinations of at least one spot color and another spot or process color.	Mixed inks can be created using the Swatches panel menu. One spot color must also have been previously defined.	Mixed Ink Groups are combinations of different percentages for Mixed ink colors.

The Basics of Color

Using the Color Panel

There are three different models for defining colors: CMYK, RGB, and LAB. Each model is used for different purposes. You choose the color mode and mix colors in the Color panel. *(See Chapter 6, "Styling Objects," for how to apply colors to objects and text.)*

1 The **Color panel** *with the options turned off shows only the spectrum or ramp for choosing colors.*

To choose the options in the Color panel:

1. If the Color panel is not visible, choose **Window > Color** to open the panel **1**.

   or

   If the Color panel is behind other panels, click the Color panel tab.

2. If the color sliders are not visible, click the panel tab or choose Show Options from the Color panel menu **2**.

TIP Hold the Shift key as you drag one slider to have the others move along with it.

2 The **Color panel menu** *lets you choose among the three color models.*

The CMYK color model is used primarily for print work. CMYK colors are mixed using percentages of the four inks used in process printing: cyan, magenta, yellow, and black.

To define CMYK colors:

1. Choose CMYK from the Color panel menu. This opens the panel in the CMYK mode **3**.

2. Choose one of the following methods to define the amount of cyan, magenta, yellow, or black ink in the color:

   • Type a value from 0 to 100% in each of the four color fields.

   • Drag the sliders for each of the four color fields.

   • Click a color in the CMYK spectrum area.

TIP Click the solid white or black rectangles to the right end of the spectrum to quickly get 100 percent black or white.

3 The **Color panel with the CMYK** *(cyan, magenta, yellow, and black) color controls.*

The Black Color Panel

If your Color panel displays a single slider for Black, it is because the Black color in the Swatches panel is your default color. Simply change it to CMYK to get the full set of CMYK color sliders.

Understanding CMYK Color

Each of the colors in CMYK corresponds to one of the inks used in typical four-color printing. Cyan is a shade of blue. Magenta is a shade of red. Yellow is … well, yellow. And black is black — I want my baby back.

If you are creating print documents, you will want to define your colors using CMYK colors. Not only is the CMYK system overwhelmingly used for print work, it is the system you are most familiar with, whether you're aware of it or not. Yellow and cyan make green; magenta and yellow make orange, and so on.

In theory, you shouldn't need more than three colors for printing. If you mix cyan, magenta, and yellow together, you should get a solid black color. In reality, however, those inks are not pure enough to create solid black; instead they create a dark brown.

That's why process printing uses four colors. In addition to cyan, magenta, and yellow, a fourth key color — black, indicated by the letter K — is added to create the really black areas. That's where the term CMYK comes from.

4 *The **Color panel set for mixing RGB** (red, green, blue) color controls for onscreen display such as Web sites.*

The RGB color model is used primarily for onscreen work such as presentations and Web sites. The RGB colors — red, green, and blue — are mixed using representations of the three colors of light. This is what you see on television screens and computer monitors. RGB colors have a wider range of colors than CMYK colors.

To mix RGB colors:

1. Choose RGB from the Color panel menu. This opens the panel in the RGB mode **4**.

2. Choose one of the following methods to define the amount of red, green, or blue in the color:

   - Type the value from 0 to 255 in each of the three color fields.

   - Drag the sliders for each of the three color fields.

   - Click a color in the RGB spectrum area.

Mixing Colors in RGB

Maybe some Web designers and video engineers can think in RGB, but I confess, I can't. With the RGB sliders, red plus green creates yellow; green plus blue creates a shade of cyan, and all three colors together create white. To create black, you set all three colors to zero. It's the exact opposite of CMYK where the four colors combine to create black.

Using the Color Panel

The LAB color model defines colors according to a *luminance* (lightness) component, and two color components, A and B. The A component defines green to red values. The B component defines blue to yellow values. LAB colors are device-independent so that colors don't change from one source to another.

TIP The proper name for LAB is L*A*B and is pronounced by spelling out the name (*el-ay-bee*), not by saying the word "LAB."

To mix LAB colors:

1. Choose LAB from the Color panel menu. This opens the panel in the LAB mode **5**.

2. Choose one of the following methods to define the three components of the color:

   • Type the value from 0 to 100 in the L field or type the value from -128 to 127 in the A or B field.

   • Drag the sliders for each of the fields.

   • Click a color in the LAB spectrum area.

The out-of-gamut symbol appears if you choose an RGB or LAB color that cannot be printed using process inks **6**.

To convert out-of-gamut colors:

◆ Click the small square next to the out-of-gamut symbol. This converts the color to the closest process-color equivalent.

You can use the Color panel to apply colors to selected objects.

TIP This technique, while convenient to use, creates unnamed colors or colors that are not listed in the Swatches panel. *(See the sidebar "Avoiding Unnamed Colors" for why creating unnamed colors can be a problem.)*

5 *The* **LAB Color panel** *mixes colors that look consistent no matter whether you print them or display them onscreen.*

Out-of-gamut symbol

Color conversion square

6 *The* **out-of-gamut symbol** *for RGB or LAB colors indicates that the color shown on screen will not print as seen using process color inks.*

Using the Color Panel

7 *With an object selected,* **click the color ramp in the Color panel** *to apply a color to an object.*

8 Drag a color from the Color panel *to apply a color to an object.*

To apply colors to a fill or stroke:

◆ With an object or text selected, use the Color panel to define a fill color. This applies the unnamed color to the fill of the object or text.

or

With an object or text selected, use the Color panel to define a stroke color. This applies the unnamed color to the stroke of the object or text.

TIP You can choose colors by clicking the ramp section of the Color panel **7**.

TIP You can also drag a color directly from the Color panel onto objects **8**. This also creates unnamed colors.

TIP A square dot appears next to the cursor when you drag a swatch color onto objects. This indicates you are dragging a fill color onto the object.

You can add colors from the Color panel to the Swatches panel so you can easily reuse them.

To transfer colors from the Color panel:

1. Define the color in the Color panel.

2. Choose Add to Swatches from the Color panel menu. The color appears as a new color swatch in the Swatches panel.

Using the Color Panel

Defining and Storing Swatches

Although it is very quick to create a color using the Color panel, you will find it more efficient to create color *swatches*. A swatch is a color that has been defined and is stored in the Swatches panel.

TIP Unnamed colors are not available for all places where you use colors. For instance, only named color swatches can be used as part of text styles.

To work with the Swatches panel:

1. If the Swatches panel is not visible, choose **Window > Swatches** to open the panel .

   or

   If the Swatches panel is behind other panels, click the Swatches panel tab.

2. To see the different types of swatches, click the icons at the bottom of the panel as follows:

   • **Show All Swatches** displays both the color and the gradient swatches.

   • **Show Color Swatches** displays only the color swatches.

   • **Show Gradient Swatches** displays only the gradient swatches.

3. To change the display of the swatches in the panel, choose the following from the Swatches panel menu:

   • **Name** displays a list of the swatch names in a large typeface.

   • **Small Name** uses a more compact typeface to display the swatch names.

   • **Small Swatch** displays only the square of the swatch color or gradient.

   • **Large Swatch** displays a larger square of the swatch color or gradient.

C=100 M=50 Y=0 K=0
C=33 M=66 Y=64 K=2
C=2 M=3 Y=98 K=0

All Swatches   **Gradients**   **Delete Swatch**

Colors   **New Swatch**

9   *The* **controls for the Swatches panel.**

The Color "Paper"

The swatch labeled [Paper] in the Swatches panel allows you to change the background color of the pages in your document. This can be helpful if your document will be printed on colored paper, specialty paper, or even newsprint that is not completely white. You can modify the paper color to help judge how your images will look when printed.

Defining and Storing Swatches

10 *You can* **drag colors from the Color panel** *into the Swatches panel.*

The Registration Color

"Registration" is a color that is set to print on all plates of a document. For instance, if your document will be printed using process colors, you might want to create a note or mark that should be seen on all four plates. Rather than make the note in a combination of cyan, magenta, yellow, and black, you can apply the color Registration to the text for the note. This prints the note as a combination of all four inks.

Although you can apply colors to objects and text directly from the Color panel, this is not considered a good production workflow. Instead, use the Swatches panel to add the color currently defined in the Color panel.

TIP If you apply colors from the Color panel, they are called unnamed colors. Unnamed colors can cause production problems later on and should be avoided.

To add a color to the Swatches panel:

1. Use the Color panel to define a color.

2. Click the New Swatch icon at the bottom of the panel. The new color, named with the color values, is automatically added to the Swatches panel.

TIP You can also add colors to the Swatches panel using the Color Picker.

InDesign also lets you drag colors from the Color panel into the Swatches panel.

To drag colors into the Swatches panel:

1. Create the color in the Color panel.

2. Drag the color from the Color panel fill or stroke box to the bottom of or between two colors in the Swatches panel.

3. Release the mouse when a black line appears in the Swatches panel **10**. The new color is added and automatically takes its name from the color values.

TIP The cursor displays a plus sign as you drag the color into the Color panel. On the Mac the cursor is the image of a fist. On Windows the cursor is an arrow.

You can define and add new colors to your document using only the Swatches panel.

To define a new color swatch:

1. Choose New Color Swatch from the Swatches panel menu. This opens the New Color Swatch dialog box .

   or

   Opt/Alt-click the New Swatch icon at the bottom of the Swatches panel.

2. To name the color swatch yourself, deselect the checkbox for Name with Color Value and then type a name in the Swatch Name field.

   or

   Leave the setting checked to name the color swatch using the values that define the color. This option is not available for spot colors.

3. Choose Process or Spot from the Color Type pop-up list .

4. Choose Lab, cmyk, or rgb from the Color Mode menu 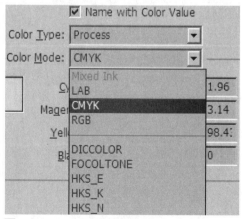.

   or

   Choose one of the Swatch Libraries at the bottom of the Color Mode menu 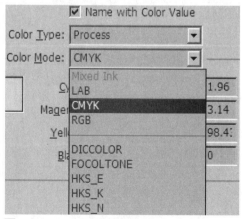.

5. If you have chosen Lab, cmyk, or rgb, use the sliders to change the values from the ones originally defined.

6. Click ok. This adds the swatch and closes the dialog box.

   or

   Click Add to add the swatch without closing the dialog box. This allows you to define additional colors.

11 *Use the* **New Color Swatch dialog box** *to define colors to be added to the Swatches panel.*

12 *Use the* **Color Type menu** *to choose either process or spot colors.*

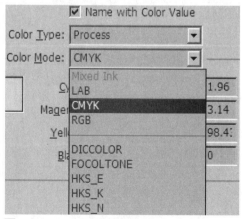

13 *The* **Color Mode menu** *in the New Swatch dialog box.*

Protected

CMYK

Spot

LAB

RGB

Mixed Ink

Process

14 *The* **icons in the Swatches panel** *identify the different types of colors and color modes.*

15 *Once you define a swatch, you modify it in the* **Swatch Options dialog box**.

The colors that appear in the Swatches panel are displayed with icons that give you information about the type of color, the color mode, and other attributes **14**. Of course, once you have defined a color swatch, you can modify its color definition. This changes the appearance of all text and objects that use that color, even if they are not selected.

TIP The color Black is protected and cannot be modified. If you need a variation of Black, create a new color swatch.

To modify a color swatch:

1. Select the swatch and choose Swatch Options from the Swatches panel menu. This opens the Swatch Options dialog box **15**. These are the same controls as in the New Color Swatch dialog box.

   or

   Double-click the swatch in the panel.

2. Make changes to the color.

TIP Click the Preview checkbox to see how the changes affect the colors applied to objects in the document.

3. Click OK to apply the changes.

TIP The Swatch Options dialog box does not have an Add button. This is because you use this dialog box only to modify existing colors — not to add new ones.

Defining and Storing Swatches

Process or Spot?

Process colors are those printed using small dots of the four process inks: cyan, magenta, yellow, and black. Spot colors are printed using special inks. For example, if you look at the process-color green printed in a magazine, that color is actually a combination of cyan and yellow printed together in a series of dots. However, a spot-color green is printed by using actual green ink.

One benefit of spot colors is that you can exactly match a special color or use specialty colors such as fluorescents or metallics that could never be created using process inks. You can also use a spot color together with black as a two-color job. This is cheaper than printing four-color process colors. The benefit of process colors is that you use just four inks to create thousands of different color combinations.

Once you create color swatches, you can apply them via the Fill and Stroke controls in the Tools panel or Color panel.

To apply a swatch color:

1. Create the object or text that you want to color.

2. Select either the Fill or Stroke icons in the Color panel or Tools panel. *(See Chapter 6, "Styling Objects," for more information on the Fill or Stroke icons.)*

3. In the Swatches panel, click the color you want. This applies the swatch to the object.

To delete swatches:

1. Select the color you want to delete.

TIP To select a series of adjacent swatches, select the first swatch and then hold the Shift key and select the last swatch in the series. This highlights the first and last swatch and all the swatches in between.

TIP Hold the Command/Ctrl key to select nonadjacent swatches.

2. Click the Delete Swatch icon or choose Delete Swatch from the Swatches menu.

3. If the swatch is used within the document, the Delete Swatch dialog box appears, asking how you want to replace the deleted swatch :

   • To swap the color with one from the Swatches panel, choose Defined Swatch and then pick a swatch from the pop-up list.

   • To leave the color as an unnamed color applied to the object, choose Unnamed Swatch.

TIP The default swatches None, Paper, Black, and Registration cannot be deleted.

16 *Click the* **Delete Swatch icon** *to delete the selected swatches.*

17 *The* **Delete Swatch dialog box** *controls what happens to colors when they are deleted from a document.*

Defining and Storing Swatches

The following menu commands are shown in the panel:

New Color Swatch...
New Tint Swatch...
New Gradient Swatch...
New Mixed Ink Swatch...
New Mixed Ink Group...
Duplicate Swatch
Delete Swatch...

Swatch Options...

Load Swatches...
Save Swatches...

Select All Unused
Add Unnamed Colors

✓ Name
Small Name
Small Swatch
Large Swatch

Merge Swatches

Ink Manager...

Hide Options

18 *The* **Swatches panel menu** *contains the commands for working with color swatches.*

If you have many colors in your document that you are not using, you may want to delete them to avoid confusion when the file is sent to a print shop.

To delete all unused swatches:

1. Choose Select All Unused in the Swatches panel menu **18**.

2. Click the Delete Swatch icon or use the Delete Swatch command in the Swatches panel menu.

You can also select several swatches and merge them into one color.

TIP The Merge Swatches command makes it easy to globally replace all instances of one defined color with another.

To merge swatches:

1. Click to select the first color. This is the final color that you want the other colors to change to.

2. Hold the Cmd/Ctrl key and click to select another swatch. This is the color that you want to delete.

   or

   Hold the Shift key and click to select a range of swatches. These are the swatches you want to delete.

3. Choose Merge Swatches from the Swatches panel menu **18**. This deletes all the swatches except the swatch that was first selected. That swatch is applied to all text and objects that used the deleted swatches.

Defining and Storing Swatches

The position that swatches occupy in the panel comes from the order in which they were created. You can easily change the order of the swatches.

To move swatches to new positions:

1. Select a swatch in the panel.
2. Drag the swatch to a new position. A black line indicates where the swatch will be located .
3. Release the mouse button.

You may find it easier to duplicate a swatch and modify it than to start from scratch.

To duplicate a swatch:

◆ Select the swatch and choose Duplicate Swatch from the Swatches panel menu.

or

Select the swatch and click the New Swatch icon.

or

Drag the swatch onto the New Swatch icon.

You can save a selection of swatches for use in other InDesign documents, or in Adobe Illustrator or Adobe Photoshop documents.

To save selected swatches:

1. Select the swatches in the Swatches panel that you want to save.
2. Choose Save Swatches For Exchange from the Swatches panel menu.
3. Use the operating system dialog box to save the swatches as an Adobe Swatch Exchange (.ase) file.

19 **Drag a swatch** *to move it from one position to another.*

The Cost of Unused Colors

Why is it important to delete unused colors?

One reason is if you are going to send your documents to a service bureau or print shop for final output. It can be confusing to the people who are going to open your file if they see many colors in a document that's supposed to be printed in black and white.

At the very least, they're going to wonder if they've received the right instructions. At the worst, they'll delay printing the file until they talk to someone to make sure.

Also, it may seem like a little thing, but every color adds to the size of the file. Even in these days of huge hard drives, it's always better to keep your files as lean as possible.

Defining and Storing Swatches

Avoiding Unnamed Colors

Why do I warn you against creating unnamed colors? Why may your service bureau warn you not to create unnamed colors?

Your job will most certainly print, even with unnamed colors. The problem comes when someone checks to make sure all your colors are defined correctly.

Because the unnamed colors don't appear in the Swatches panel, there is no way for someone to easily find or make a universal change to the colors in your document. So the checker will have to search, page by page, to see if there are any unnamed colors.

So although there is nothing actually wrong with unnamed colors, it is better to always use the Swatches panel to apply colors. That way you'll have more control over the colors in your document.

You can import the swatches from one InDesign document into another. You can also import the swatches from an Adobe Swatch Exchange file.

To import swatches from other documents:

1. Choose Load Swatches from the Swatches panel menu. The operating system dialog box appears.

2. Navigate to find the document or Adobe Swatch Exchange file you want to import swatches from.

3. Click Open. The swatches are imported into the current document.

Unnamed colors are colors that are applied to objects directly from the Color panel or the Color Picker instead of through the Swatches panel. It is a good idea not to have unnamed colors floating around your document. Fortunately, you can easily convert unnamed colors into named colors.

To name unnamed colors:

◆ Choose Add Unnamed Colors from the Swatches panel menu. All unnamed colors are added to the panel named with their percentage values.

You can create colors that are available as the default colors for all new documents.

To create default colors:

1. Close all documents but leave InDesign running.

2. Use any of the methods in this section, "Defining and Storing Swatches," to define and store a color in the Swatches panel. The color will appear in the Swatches panel of all new InDesign documents.

Defining and Storing Swatches

Using Swatch Libraries

Rather than defining your own color mixtures, you can use the swatch libraries for professional color systems from companies such as Pantone or Trumatch. These color libraries usually have printed samples that you can refer to in order to see how the color will appear when printed.

To add colors from swatch libraries:

1. Open the New Swatch dialog box or the Swatch Options dialog box.

2. Choose one of the swatch libraries listed in the Color Mode list **20**. This displays the colors in the library **21**.

3. Scroll through the library to select the color you want to add to your document.

   or

   Instead of scrolling through a long list, type the name or number associated with the color in the Swatch Library field.

20 *The* **swatch libraries** *in the Color Mode list.*

21 *An example of the window that displays* **a swatch library,** *such as the Pantone Solid Coated colors.*

You can use the swatch libraries to open color panels from other InDesign documents and Adobe Illustrator documents.

To import swatches from other documents:

1. Choose Other Library from the Color Mode list **20**.

2. Navigate to select the InDesign or Illustrator document. The colors appear in the window.

The Swatch Libraries

InDesign ships with a collection of third-party swatch libraries that contain the color definitions used by professional color systems. Here is a description of each of the types of libraries.

ANPA Color is commonly used for newspaper production. The colors can be found in the ANPA Color Newspaper Color Ink Book.

DIC Color Guide contains spot colors used mainly in Japan. These colors can be matched using the color guides from Dainippon Ink and Chemicals, Inc.

Focoltone holds the process colors that can be matched using materials that are available from Focoltone International, Ltd. These colors are very popular in both France and the United Kingdom.

HKS is a system of process and spot colors used in Europe.

Pantone is the major color-matching system company used in North America. All Pantone colors can be matched to materials available from Pantone, Inc.

System (Macintosh) includes the colors of the Macintosh operating system.

System (Windows) includes the colors of the Windows operating system.

Toyo consists of spot colors used primarily in Japan. Color matching materials are available from the Toyo Ink Manufacturing Co., Ltd.

Trumatch provides a library of process colors. These colors have been specially designed for digital prepress as well as desktop color printers and copier machines. Color matching materials are available from Trumatch, Inc.

Web consists of the 216 colors that are shared by both the Macintosh and Windows system colors. These are sometimes called the Web-safe colors.

Using Swatch Libraries

Creating Mixed Inks

Mixed inks is the term InDesign uses for a color that combines a spot color with other spot colors or process colors. (QuarkXPress calls this type of color a *multi-ink*.) Mixed inks give you more flexibility in creating colors, especially for two-color jobs.

To create a single Mixed Ink swatch:

1. Choose New Mixed Ink Swatch from the Swatches panel menu. This opens the New Mixed Ink Swatch dialog box **22**.

TIP The command to create mixed inks is not available unless you have first defined a spot color in the Swatches panel.

2. Enter a name for the mixed ink swatch.

3. Click the ink controls to select the colors in the mixed ink swatch. You must choose two inks, and one of them must be a spot color ink **23**.

4. Use the sliders or fields to set the amount of each ink in the swatch.

5. Click the OK button to create the mixed ink swatch.

   or

   Click the Add button to create the mixed ink swatch and then use the dialog box to define a new mixed ink swatch.

Ink names

Preview Ink option   Sliders   Fields

22 The **New Mixed Ink Swatch dialog box** *allows you to combine a spot color with other colors.*

Nonactive ink   Active ink

23 *Use the* **ink controls** *to define the colors in the mixed ink swatch.*

Using Mixed Ink Swatches

Mixed ink swatches have a variety of uses. Perhaps the most common use is to define a mixed ink as a single spot color plus a percentage of process black. This allows you to create a slightly darker version of a spot color. I find this extremely helpful when working on two-color jobs where I need to darken my spot color.

You can also use mixed ink swatches to combine two spot colors. For instance, you can combine a spot yellow with a spot blue to create a green mixed ink swatch. However, be careful when you try to mix spot colors. The color in the preview box is only a very rough representation of the actual color on press.

Finally, you can use mixed inks to combine varnishes with process colors. This is a sophisticated technique and you should consult with your print shop.

24 *The* **New Mixed Ink Group dialog box** *allows you to automatically create a series of mixed inks.*

25 *Use the Inks controls to set the mixed ink colors, the initial amounts, the repetitions, and the increments by which they change.*

You might want to create a collection of mixed inks that combine colors in an increasing series of mixtures. InDesign calls this a Mixed Ink Group and makes it easy to automatically create the mixtures of colors.

TIP A Mixed Ink Group makes it easy to create a variety of mixed inks that can be quickly applied as you work.

To create a Mixed Ink Group:

1. Choose New Mixed Ink Group from the Swatches panel menu. The New Mixed Ink Group dialog box appears **24**.

2. Enter a name for the group in the Name field.

3. Click the Inks controls to select the colors in the mixed ink swatch. You must choose at least two inks and one of them must be a spot color ink.

4. Use the Initial field to define the amount of color that the first instance of an ink has **25**.

5. Use the Repeat field to set how many new mixed inks will be created with the color.

TIP Set the Repeat to zero to keep that color constant throughout the mixed ink group.

6. Use the Increment field to set the color increases for each new mixed ink.

7. Click the Preview Swatches button to see the result of the settings in the Swatches panel **24**.

8. Click OK to create the Mixed Ink Group. The group appears in the Swatches panel.

Creating Mixed Inks

Once you have created a mixed ink group, you can make changes to the entire group or the individual swatches in the group.

To modify all the swatches in a mixed ink group:

1. Select the mixed ink group in the Swatches panel and choose Swatch Options from the Swatches panel menu.

   or

   Double click the name of the mixed ink group in the Swatches panel. The Mixed Ink Group Options dialog box appears **26**.

2. Use the Name field to change the name of the group.

3. Use the ink controls to delete inks from the mixed ink group.

   TIP While you can delete inks from the group, you cannot add inks. So a two-ink group can't be changed to a three-ink group.

4. Use the Inks list to swap one ink for another **27**. The list shows both the process and spot colors in the document.

5. If desired, check Convert Mixed Ink Swatches to Process. This changes all the colors in the mixed ink swatches to their process color equivalents.

   TIP The option to convert the colors to process is permanent and cannot be changed except as part of InDesign's undo chain.

6. Click OK. The changes are applied to the inks used in the mixed ink swatches that you originally created.

   TIP Watch out! Once you have deleted inks from the mixed ink group, you can't go back and add them to the mixed ink group. You'll have to regenerate the entire mixed ink group.

26 *Use the* **Mixed Ink Group Options dialog box** *to make changes to the inks used in a mixed ink group.*

27 *Use the* **Inks list** *to change the colors used in a mixed ink group.*

Creating Mixed Inks

Creating Tints

Tints are screened, or lighter, versions of colors. Spot color tints create screens of the base color. Process color tints reduce the amounts of the process inks that define the color.

To create a tint swatch:

1. Select the *base color,* that is, the swatch color that you want to tint.

2. Use the Tint field in the Swatches panel to create a screen of the swatch color **28**.

3. Click the New Swatch icon to store the tint percentage as a swatch in the Swatches panel.

TIP The tint swatch appears in the Swatches panel with the same name as the base color but with the tint percentage listed **29**.

TIP The tint field percentage continues to tint other swatches in the panel until you reset the field to 100%.

As you select a color swatch as a base color, the Color panel displays a slider and a ramp of the color.

To tint a swatch using the Color panel:

1. Select the swatch color that you want to tint.

2. In the Color panel, use the slider or click in the ramp to create a percentage of the base color **30**.

3. Click the New Swatch icon to create a tint swatch of the percentage you defined.

28 Use the **Tint field** to create a screened version of a swatch color.

29 A **tint swatch** is listed with the same name as the base color and the tint percentage.

30 The Color panel displays **a slider and tint ramp** when a base color is chosen.

You can also create a tint swatch using the Swatches panel menu.

To store a tint swatch of a color:

1. In the Swatches panel, select the base color, that is, the color you want to tint.

2. Choose New Tint Swatch from the Swatches panel menu. The New Tint Swatch dialog box appears .

3. Adjust the tint slider to a percentage.

4. Click OK. The tint swatch appears in the Swatches panel with the same name as the base color but with the tint percentage listed.

   or

   Click Add to add the tint to the Swatches panel and then create additional tints.

Once you store a tint swatch, you can modify the tint percentage. This updates all the objects that use that tint swatch.

To modify tint swatches:

1. Double click the name of the tint swatch in the Swatches panel. This opens the Swatch Options dialog box for tints .

TIP This dialog box is slightly different from the ordinary Swatch Options dialog box, which does not have a tint slider.

2. To change the tint value, adjust the Tint slider at the bottom of the dialog box.

TIP You can also modify the sliders for the base color when you open the Swatch Options dialog box to modify a tint.

3. Click OK to apply the changes.

TIP Anytime you modify the swatch used as a base color, all tints of that color update automatically.

31 *The* **New Tint Swatch dialog box** *lets you set the percentage of a tint.*

32 *The* **Swatch Options for a tint swatch** *let you change the tint percentage or modify the base color of the tint.*

33 *The* **Fill and Stroke icons** *in the Tools panel or Color panel let you open the Color Picker.*

34 *The* **Color Picker in the RGB mode** *lets you define and store RGB colors.*

35 *The* **Color Picker in the LAB mode** *lets you define and store LAB colors.*

36 *The* **Color Picker in the CMYK mode** *lets you define and store CMYK colors.*

Using the Color Picker

If you have used Photoshop, you are probably familiar with Photoshop's Color Picker, which is accessed through the foreground or background color icons in the Tools panel. InDesign also has a Color Picker, which is opened through the Tools panel.

To define a color using the Color Picker:

1. Double-click either the Fill icon or the Stroke icon in the Tools panel **33**. This opens the Color Picker.

2. Use the RGB, LAB, or CMYK fields (**34**, **35**, and **36**)to define the color.

3. Click OK to apply the color to the current fill or stroke.

TIP When you click the RGB or LAB controls, the Color Space area at the left of the dialog displays one of those color controls. When you click the CMYK controls, however, the Color Space area does not display the CMYK color controls.

To define a color swatch using the Color Picker:

1. Double-click either the Fill icon or the Stroke icon in the Tools panel to open the Color Picker.

2. Use the RGB, LAB, or CMYK fields to define the color.

3. Click the Add [RGB, LAB, or CMYK] Swatch button to add the color to the Swatches panel.

4. Click OK to close the Color Picker.

Using the Color Picker

Creating Gradient Swatches

Gradients are blends that change from one color into another. InDesign creates gradients as swatches that can then be applied to objects. *(See Chapter 6, "Styling Objects," for information on applying gradients.)*

To define a gradient:

1. Choose New Gradient Swatch from the Swatches panel menu. The New Gradient Swatch dialog box appears **37**.

2. Enter a name for the gradient in the Swatch Name field.

3. Choose Linear or Radial in the Type field **38**.

4. Click a color stop on the gradient ramp to define a color in the gradient **39**.

5. Choose the type of color for the selected stop from the Stop Color list **40**:

   • Swatches shows you the list of colors in the Swatches panel.

   • LAB, CMYK, or RGB displays the sliders that let you define the color using the LAB, CMYK, or RGB values.

6. Click the other gradient stop to define a color for it.

7. Adjust the midpoint control to change the position where the two colors blend equally.

8. Click OK to add the gradient to the Swatches panel **41**.

   or

   Click the Add button to add the current gradient to the Swatches panel and continue defining additional gradients.

TIP If you don't see the gradient listed in the Swatches panel, click either the Show All Swatches or Show Gradient Swatches icon at the bottom of the Swatches panel.

37 *Use the* **New Gradient Swatch dialog box** *to define a gradient of blended colors.*

38 *A linear gradient changes colors along a line. A radial gradient changes colors in a circular pattern.*

39 *Use the color stops and midpoint controls along the gradient ramp to modify a gradient.*

40 *Use the* **Stop Color menu** *to choose the format for the colors used for the color stops.*

41 *Gradients are stored in the* **Swatches panel.**

42 *Click under the gradient ramp to add a color stop to the gradient.*

43 *Drag a color stop off the gradient ramp to delete that color from the gradient.*

All gradients must have at least two colors. However, you can easily add more colors to a gradient by using the color stops.

To add gradient color stops:

1. Open the New Gradient Swatch or the Gradient Options dialog box.

2. Click the area below the gradient ramp. This adds a color stop to the ramp area **42**.

3. Make whatever changes you want to the color stop.

4. If necessary, move the color stop to a new position.

5. Click OK to apply the changes to the gradient swatch.

To delete a gradient color stop:

◆ Drag the color stop away from the ramp area and release the mouse **43**. The gradient reblends according to the colors that remain.

To modify a gradient swatch:

1. Select the gradient swatch and choose Swatch Options from the Swatches panel menu. This opens the Gradient Options dialog box.

   or

   Double-click the gradient in the panel.

TIP Use the Preview checkbox to see how the changes affect the gradients in the document.

2. Adjust the midpoint, color stops, or gradient type.

3. Click OK to apply the changes.

Creating Gradient Swatches

Just as you can create colors on the fly, you can also create gradients without using the Swatches panel. These gradients are created only within the Gradient panel and are not stored in the Swatches panel.

To work with the Gradient panel:

1. Choose **Window > Gradient** to open the Gradient panel .

2. Choose Show Options from the Gradient panel menu to see all the controls.

44 *Use the* **Gradient panel** *to create on-the-fly gradients.*

To create gradients from the Gradient panel:

1. Use the Type pop-up list to choose between Linear and Radial.

2. Select a color stop and adjust the sliders in the Color panel to define the color at that position.

   or

   Hold the Opt/Alt key and click the name of a swatch in the Swatches panel.

3. Select another color stop and use the sliders in the Color panel to define the color at that position.

4. Set the angle of the gradient in the Angle field.

5. Click the Reverse icon to reverse the positions of the color stops.

Once you have a defined a gradient in the Gradient panel, you can store it as a swatch.

To store an unnamed gradient:

1. Create the gradient in the Gradient panel.

2. Click the New Swatch icon in the Swatches panel.

   or

   Drag the preview of the gradient from the Gradient panel into the Swatches panel.

3. Double-click the name of the gradient in the Swatches panel to rename it.

Process and Spot Colors in Gradients

A gradient that's defined using process colors is separated onto CMYK plates.

A gradient that contains two tints of the same spot color will be separated onto the single spot color plate. If you want the gradient to fade to white, create a gradient between the spot color and a 0% tint of the spot color.

You can create a gradient between two spot colors. However, to avoid moiré patterns in the gradient, you must assign different screen angles to those spot colors in the Inks dialog box.

For instance, if you had a gradient of spot red to spot yellow, you would want to make sure each color had a screen angle that was 45 degrees different from the other. Ask your print shop for details on setting the screen angles for spot colors.

A gradient that contains both spot and process colors will be separated onto both the spot and process color plates.

---

*The **Eyedropper tool** lets you sample colors from placed images.*

 *Click with the **Eyedropper tool** over an area of an image that you want to sample.*

Using the Eyedropper

The Eyedropper tool lets you sample colors from graphics that are placed in your document. *(See Chapter 8, "Imported Graphics," for more information on placing graphics.)*

To sample and store colors from placed graphics:

1. Click the Eyedropper tool in the Tools panel **45**.

2. Move the Eyedropper cursor over the color of a placed graphic **46**.

3. Click to sample the color.

TIP If you have already used the Eyedropper to sample a color, hold the Opt/Alt key to sample a new color.

4. Click the New Swatch icon in the Swatches panel. The sampled color is stored as a color swatch.

TIP The Eyedropper samples the color in the same color mode as the placed graphic. So RGB images yield RGB colors, and CMYK images yield CMYK colors.

TIP The Eyedropper can also sample and apply fills, strokes, and transparency attributes of objects and text formatting. *(See Chapter 6, "Styling Objects," and Chapter 14, "Automating Your Work.")*

Using the Eyedropper

Overprinting Colors

Overprinting is a technique that allows you to set the color of one object to mix with any colors underneath. For instance, without overprinting, a yellow object placed over a blue background knocks out the blue and prints as yellow. But with overprinting turned on, the yellow object mixes with the blue background to create green.

To set a fill or stroke to overprint:

1. Select the object.
2. If the Attributes panel is not visible, choose **Window > Attributes** to open the panel .

   or

   If the Attributes panel is behind other panels, click the Attributes panel tab.
3. Check Overprint Fill to set the object's fill color to overprint.
4. Check Overprint Stroke to set the object's stroke color to overprint.
5. Check Overprint Gap to set the color of the gap applied to stroke effects to overprint.

TIP Check Nonprinting in the Attributes panel to set an object not to print. This is helpful if you want to add comments for production use that aren't meant to be seen in the finished piece.

In some desktop publishing programs, the only way to see the effects of setting an object to overprint is to wait until the object is separated and printed. InDesign lets you see a simulation of overprinting onscreen.

To turn on the overprint preview:

◆ Choose **View > Overprint Preview**. InDesign shows the effects of those colors set to overprint ▮48▮.

47 *Use the* **Attributes panel** *to set the colors of an object to overprint.*

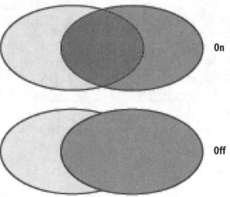

48 *Turn on the* **Overprint Preview command** *to see the effects of overprinting onscreen.*

Overprinting Colors

FILLS, STROKES, AND EFFECTS | 6

Here's where you get a chance to express your creativity. Styling refers to applying fills, strokes, gradients, and effects to frames, lines, and text. If you're bored with plain black text on a white background, InDesign lets you change the text and background colors to almost anything you can imagine.

Most other graphics programs let you style objects and text with fills, strokes, and gradients. InDesign certainly does that also.

However, InDesign has broken new ground in offering sophisticated effects such as transparency, drop shadows, and glows. These are the effects that art directors and designers could only dream about creating with other page-layout programs.

With InDesign, they can make those dreams a reality.

Applying Fills

Fills are the effects applied to objects, which can be the interior of frames or text within a frame. So you can apply one color fill to the text inside a frame and another color fill to the frame itself. A fill can be a solid color or a gradient.

To apply a fill to an object:

1. Select an object.

2. Make sure the Container icon is chosen in the Tools panel or the Swatches or Color panel **1**. This indicates that the object will be modified.

3. Click the Fill icon in the Tools panel or in the Swatches or Color panel **2**.

4. Choose a color or gradient in the Color, Gradient, or Swatches panel.

You don't have to select an object to apply a fill. You can just drag a swatch onto any object to apply a color or a gradient.

To drag fill effects onto objects:

1. Drag a gradient or color swatch from the Tools panel or the Color, Gradient, or Swatches panel onto the object **3**.

2. Release the mouse button when the swatch is inside the object. A square dot appears to indicate you are inside the object.

TIP If you release the mouse button when the swatch is on the edge of the object, you will apply the effect to the object's stroke.

1 *The **Container icons** (circled) indicate an effect will be applied to an object, not text.*

2 *The **Fill icons** (circled) indicate an effect will be applied inside an object.*

3 *You can drag a swatch inside an object to apply a fill.*

The **Wonderful** Wizard of Oz

4 *Choose a swatch to apply the color or gradient to selected text.*

5 *The **Text icons** (circled) set an effect to be applied to all the text within a frame.*

6 *The **T inside the Fill icon** (circled) indicates that text is going to be styled.*

7 The **Gradient icon in the Tools panel** *indicates that a color or gradient will be applied.*

8 The **gradient in the Fill box** *indicates that the gradient will be applied as a fill.*

You can also apply fill colors to selected text in a text frame.

To apply a fill to selected text:

1. Use the Text tool to highlight the text.
2. Click the Fill icon in the Tools panel or the Swatches or Color panel.
3. Choose a swatch in the Color, Gradient, or Swatches panel **4**.

TIP When text is highlighted, the color of the text is inverted. Deselect to see the actual text color.

You can also apply a fill to all the text in a frame with just the frame selected.

To apply a fill to all the text in a frame:

1. Select the text frame that contains the text to which you want to apply the fill.
2. Click the Fill icon in the Tools panel or the Swatches or Color panel.
3. Click the Text icon in the Tools panel or the Swatches or Color panel **5**.

TIP The *T* inside the Fill icon indicates the text will be affected, not the frame **6**.

4. Choose a swatch in the Color, Gradient, or Swatches panel.

You can also apply a gradient to text or objects.

To apply a gradient fill:

1. Click the Fill icon in the Tools panel or the Swatches or Color panel with the container or text icons selected.
2. Click the Gradient icon in the Tools panel **7**.

   or

   Click a gradient in the Swatches or Gradient panel. The gradient is displayed in the Fill box **8**.

Applying Fills

Once you have applied a gradient to an object or text, you can modify how it is applied using the Gradient tool.

To adjust a gradient fill:

1. Select the object that contains the gradient you want to modify.

2. Choose the Gradient tool in the Tools panel .

3. Drag the Gradient tool along the angle that the linear gradient should follow **10**.

   or

   Drag the Gradient tool to define the start and end points of a radial gradient **11**.

TIP The start of the drag positions the first color. The end of the drag positions the final color.

The **Gradient tool in the Tools panel** *lets you modify the appearance of gradients.*

10 *Drag the Gradient tool to set the start and end points and the angle of a linear gradient.*

11 *Drag with the Gradient tool to set the start and end points of a radial gradient.*

Applying Fills

White fill

None fill

12 *The difference between a text frame with a white fill and a none fill.*

You can also apply a fill of None to an object. This makes the background of the object transparent **12**.

To apply a fill of None:

1. Select the object.
2. Click the None icon in the Tools panel or the Swatches or Color panel **13**.

TIP If the object is not in front of others, you may not see a difference between a white and a none fill. Check the icon to be sure **14**.

13 *The None icons (circled) apply no fill to an object.*

Another way to style objects is to create a compound path. A compound path allows one path to punch a hole in another. This makes the inside path transparent while the outside path is solid **15**.

To create a compound path:

1. Select two paths that overlap.
2. Choose **Object > Paths > Make Compound Path.**

TIP If the second object is not completely contained inside the first, the hole appears only where the objects overlap.

TIP Compound paths must contain the same fill and stroke effects.

14 *The None symbol in the Fill icon (circled) indicates there is no fill applied to the object.*

You can release a compound path back to separate objects to restore the inside path to a solid color.

To release a compound path:

1. Select the compound path.
2. Choose **Object > Paths > Release Compound Paths.**

Before

After

15 *An example of how a compound path creates a hole in an object.*

Applying Fills

Applying Stroke Effects

Strokes are the effects applied to the edge of objects and text, or along lines.

TIP In QuarkXPress, stroke effects are called frames or line effects.

To apply a stroke to an object:

1. Select the object.

2. Make sure the Container icon is chosen in the Tools panel or the Swatches or Color panel ⚫. This indicates that the object will be modified.

3. Click the Stroke icon in the Tools panel or the Swatches or Color panel .

4. Choose a swatch in the Color, Gradient, or Swatches panel.

You can also apply a stroke color by dragging a swatch onto the edge of any object on the page.

To drag stroke effects onto objects:

1. Drag a gradient or color swatch from the Tools panel or the Color, Gradient, or Swatches panel onto the edge of the object.

2. Release the mouse button when you see a small line appear next to the mouse cursor ⚫. This applies the color or gradient to the stroke.

TIP If you release the mouse button when the swatch is inside the object, you apply the effect to the object's fill.

InDesign makes it easy to swap the fill and stroke colors applied to an object.

To swap the fill and stroke settings:

◆ Click the double-headed arrow in the Tools panel ⚫. This switches the colors of the fill and stroke applied to the object.

Tools panel   **Color panel**   **Swatches panel**

16 *The Stroke icons (circled) set an effect to be applied to the outside of an object or text.*

17 *Drag a swatch onto the edge to apply a stroke effect to an object.*

18 *Click the Swap Fill and Stroke icon in the Tools panel to switch the settings.*

Dorothy

19 *A stroke effect applied to text.*

Tools panel **Color panel** **Swatches panel**

20 *The outlined T in the Stroke icon (circled) indicates that a stroke has been applied to text.*

21 *The effect of a linear gradient applied as a stroke with three different types of fills.*

Permission to Stroke Text

If you have worked with other desktop publishing programs, you may have found that strokes on text deform the shape of the characters. This happens because the stroke is applied on both the outside and the inside of the text. As a result, most teachers like me warned our students never to add a stroke to text—not in headlines and never in body copy.

InDesign puts its strokes only on the outside of text. This means that it does not distort the characters. So you have complete permission to stroke headline text in InDesign. (Body text is too small to stroke.)

You can also add a color or gradient stroke to the outside edges of text with a color or gradient **19**.

To apply a stroke to selected text:

1. Use the Text tool to highlight the text.
2. Click the Stroke icon in the Tools panel or Color panel **20**.
3. Choose a swatch in the Color, Gradient, or Swatches panel.

To apply a stroke to all the text in a frame:

1. Select the text frame that contains the text to which you want to apply the stroke.
2. Click the Text button in the Tools panel or Color panel.
3. Click the Stroke icon in the Tools panel or Color panel.
4. Choose a swatch in the Color, Gradient, or Swatches panel.

You can also apply a gradient as a stroke to text or objects.

To apply a gradient stroke:

1. Click the Stroke icon in the Tools panel or the Swatches or Color panel.
2. Click the Gradient icon in the Tools panel or the Swatches or Gradient panel.
3. Use the Gradient tool to modify the angle or length of the gradient applied to a stroke.

TIP A linear gradient applied as a stroke creates a beveled effect. This may be combined with a solid or gradient fill for a three-dimensional effect **21**.

Color is only one aspect of a stroke effect. The Stroke panel controls the rest of the stroke attributes.

To work with the Stroke panel:

◆ If the Stroke panel is not visible, choose **Windo w > Stroke** to view it .

or

If the Stroke panel is behind other panels, click the Stroke panel tab.

One of the most important attributes of a stroke is its thickness. This is controlled by changing the stroke weight 23.

To set the stroke weight (thickness):

1. Select the object.

2. Use the Weight field controls to set the thickness of the stroke 24.

TIP The stroke can be positioned on the outside, in the center, or inside the path using the Align Stroke controls.

22 *The Stroke panel with all its options displayed.*

23 *Different stroke weights.*

24 *The Weight controls let you change the stroke thickness.*

25 *The Cap icons control the end points of strokes.*

26 *The three Cap settings applied to strokes.*

27 *The Join buttons control how the corners of strokes are displayed.*

28 *The three Join settings applied to strokes.*

29 *The Miter Limit field controls how long a miter point may extend.*

A stroke's style is also controlled by the end caps and joins, which form points and corners.

To set the caps and joins:

1. Select an object that has a stroke applied to it.

2. In the Stroke panel, use the Cap icons **25** to change the way the ends of open paths are treated **26**:

   - **Butt** ends the stroke in a square. This is the default setting for a plain stroke.
   - **Round** ends the stroke in a semi-circle.
   - **Projecting** ends the stroke in a square that extends out from the end point.

TIP The Cap settings have no effect on closed paths such as rectangles, ellipses, and polygons.

3. Use the Join buttons **27** to change the way two segments of a path meet at corners **28**:

   - **Miter** joins the segments at an angle.
   - **Round** joins the segments with a curve.
   - **Bevel** joins the segments with a line between the segments.

Sometimes a mitered join becomes too long and pointed. Fortunately, you can stop the point from becoming too long by setting the miter limit.

To set the miter limit:

1. Select an object with a mitered join.

2. In the Stroke panel, increase the amount in the Miter Limit field to control the size of the angle between the segments **29**.

TIP If the size of the angle exceeds the miter limit, a bevel is substituted **28**. It does not mean a shorter point is substituted.

Applying Stroke Effects

In traditional drawing programs, a stroke is distributed evenly on the outside and inside of its path. InDesign lets you choose the alignment of the stroke on the path **30**.

TIP This is different from the position of a stroke applied to text.

To set the alignment of a stroke:

1. Apply a stroke to an object.

2. Choose one of the three alignment options for the stroke as follows **31**:

   • **Center** aligns the stroke so that half the stroke weight is inside the path and half is outside the path.

   • **Inside** aligns the stroke so that the entire thickness of the stroke weight is inside the path.

   • **Outside** aligns the stroke so that the entire thickness of the stroke weight is outside the path.

30 *Set the Align Stroke controls to set the position of the stroke along the path.*

31 *Examples of how the Align Stroke controls change the position of the stroke on the path.*

Uses for the Stroke Alignment

Most people will find they don't ever need to change the alignment options for a stroke. They use the traditional Center alignment all the time. However, for many others, the ability to specify where the stroke aligns on the path is a real benefit.

Say you have a placed image inside a frame. After you import the graphic, you may want to add a stroke to its frame, but you don't want the stroke to cover any part of the placed image.

If you applied a stroke with the traditional Center alignment, you would then have to enlarge the size of the frame by half the size of the stroke. By setting the stroke alignment to Outside, you ensure that the stroke does not cover any part of the image.

Or say you want to apply a stroke to an object without increasing its size. With the Center alignment, every time you change the stroke weight, the size of the object would increase or decrease. By setting the stroke alignment to Inside, the stroke only appears inside the object and doesn't add to the size of the object.

Applying Stroke Effects

32 *The 18 default strokes in the Stroke Type menu in the Stroke panel.*

33 *Use the Gap Color menu in the Stroke panel to set the color of the clear areas of a stroke.*

34 *Use the Gap Tint controls to set a tint for the gap color.*

The default setting for strokes is a solid line. However, you can choose one of the specialty strokes such as stripes, dashes, hashes, dots, or diamonds. You can even pick a stroke that curves up and down along the path.

To apply stroke styles to strokes:

1. Apply a stroke to an object.

2. Choose one of the styles from the Stroke Type menu **32**.

The color of a stroke comes from choosing the Stroke icon and then picking a color. This method only colors the solid portion of a stroke. For strokes such as stripes and dashes, you can also color the gap, or the clear area between the solid colors of the stroke.

TIP This is the same technique used to set the gap color for the underline and strikethrough effects.

To set a stroke gap color:

1. Choose one of the specialty strokes that have both solid and clear areas.

2. Use the Gap Color menu to choose the color for the clear areas of the stroke **33**.

TIP This list contains the same colors and gradients as the Swatches panel.

3. If necessary, use the Gap Tint controls to set a screen for the gap color **34**.

Applying Stroke Effects

The stroke list contains a dashed stroke that you can customize to set the size of the dashes and the gaps between them.

To create custom dashed strokes:

1. Apply a stroke to an object.

2. Choose Dashed from the Stroke Type pop-up menu. The dashed settings appear at the bottom of the Stroke panel .

TIP The dashed settings only appear when you select the stroke style named Dashed and not the ones labeled Dashed (3 and 2) or Dashed (4 and 4).

3. Enter an amount in the first dash field for the length of all of the dashes in the line.

4. Enter an amount in the first gap field for the size of the space between all of the dashes.

5. To create a series of dashes and gaps with irregular lengths, enter other values in the rest of the dash and gap fields.

6. If necessary, use the Corners list to adjust the dashes and gaps :

   - **None** leaves the dashes and gaps as they are. This can cause unequal dashes at the corners.

   - **Adjust dashes** changes the stroke so that the corner dashes are equal.

   - **Adjust gaps** changes the stroke so that the gap lengths are equal.

   - **Adjust dashes and gaps** changes the stroke to make the best fit so that both the corner dashes and gaps are equal.

   - **Dash (3 and 2)** creates a dash that is 3 times the stroke weight with a gap that is 2 times the stroke weight .

   - **Dash (4 and 4)** creates dashes and gaps that are 4 times the stroke weight .

35 *The Dashed settings at the bottom of the Stroke panel. These only appear when the Dashed stroke type is chosen.*

36 *Use the Corners menu to adjust how dashes and gaps are distributed on a stroke.*

37 *Examples of how the Corners settings affect the appearance of a dashed stroke.*

38 *The effects of the two preset dash styles on 3-point strokes.*

Applying Stroke Effects

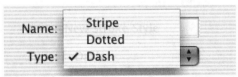

39 *The Stroke Styles dialog box lets you create, edit, and manage custom stroke styles.*

40 *The New Stroke Style dialog box is where you define the pattern for a custom stroke.*

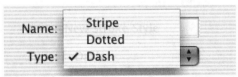

41 *Use the Type menu to choose the type of custom stroke style.*

Creating Custom Stroke Styles

Stroke styles allow you to create custom stripes, dashes, and dots that you can add to your Strokes panel for reuse.

To create custom styles for strokes:

1. Choose Stroke Styles from the Stroke panel menu. The Stroke Styles dialog box appears **39**.

   TIP This dialog box contains the seven default stripe styles. You can't edit these default stripes, but you can use them as the basis for new stripe styles.

2. Click the New button to open the New Stroke Style dialog box **40**.

   or

   Choose one of the default stripes and then click the New button. This opens the New Stroke Style dialog box with the stripe style already set as the starting pattern.

3. Use the Name field to enter a name for the custom stroke style.

4. Choose the type of stroke style from the Type menu as follows **41**:

   • **Stripe** allows you to create multiple lines that run parallel to each other along the stroked path.

   • **Dotted** creates a series of dots repeated along the path.

   • **Dash** creates a single line that is broken into a series of individual elements.

5. The dialog box changes its controls according to the stroke style chosen in the Type menu.

6. When you have finished setting the stroke style, click OK to create the style.

   or

   Click the Add button to create the style and then define additional styles.

To create a custom stripe stroke style:

1. Choose Stripe from the Type menu of the New Stroke Style dialog box. The stripe controls appear .

2. Click inside the Stripe area to add a stripe to the stroke.

TIP New stripes appear in the Stripe area with no width and need to be adjusted in order to appear as part of the finished stroke.

3. Drag the Start control triangle on the percentage ruler or enter an amount in the Start field to set the initial position for the stripe on the stroke .

TIP A setting of 0% positions the stripe to start at the very top of the stroke width.

4. Drag the Width control triangle on the percentage ruler or enter an amount in the Width field to set the width of the stripe 43.

TIP The width of the stripe is a percentage of the final stroke weight of the stroke. For example, a stripe width of 50% applied to a 4-point stroke creates a 2-point stripe.

5. Drag the stripe itself up or down in the Stripe area to position it without changing its width.

6. If you need to delete a stripe, drag it up or down so that it is off the Stripe area.

7. Use the Preview control to increase or decrease the size of the preview for the stroke style .

TIP A larger preview helps you see small elements added to the custom stroke style. However, it does not change the appearance of the stroke used in the document.

The New Stroke Style dialog box set for the Stripe controls.

The stripe controls in the New Stroke Style dialog box.

Use the Preview display and Preview Weight to see what the stripe style will look like.

Stripe area

Start controller

Width controller

Creating Custom Stroke Styles

45 *The New Stroke Style dialog box set for the Dash controls.*

46 *The Dash controls in the New Stroke Style dialog box.*

47 *Use the Corners list to choose how dashes are distributed along a stroke.*

To create a custom dashed stroke style:

1. Choose Dash from the Type menu of the New Stroke Style dialog box. The dash controls appear **45**.

2. Click inside the Dash area to add a dash to the stroke **46**.

TIP New dashes appear in the Dash area with no length and need to be adjusted in order to appear as part of the finished stroke.

3. Drag the Start control triangle on the percentage ruler or enter an amount in the Start field to set the initial position for the dash **46**.

TIP Unlike the Stripe controls, the length of a dash is set as an absolute amount, not a percentage of the stroke width.

4. Drag the dash itself to move it without changing its width.

5. Use the Pattern Length field to increase the length of the space that the dashes repeat within **46**.

6. If you need to delete a dash, drag it up or down so that it is off the Dash area.

7. Use the Corners list to choose how the dashes should be arranged around corners **47**.

8. Choose a Cap style to set how the dashes appear on the stroke.

9. Use the Preview control to increase or decrease the size of the preview for the stroke style.

Creating Custom Stroke Styles

To create a custom dotted stroke style:

1. Choose Dotted from the Type menu of the New Stroke Style dialog box. The dotted controls appear **48**.

2. Click inside the Dotted area to add a dot to the stroke **49**.

3. Drag the Center control triangle on the ruler or enter an amount in the Center field to set the initial position for the dot **49**.

4. Use the Pattern Length field to increase the length of the space that the dots repeat within **49**.

5. If you need to delete a dot, drag it up or down so that it is off the Dotted area.

6. Use the Corners list to choose how the dots should be arranged around corners **50**.

TIP Unlike the choices for dashes, the Corners list for dots only allows you to adjust gaps, as the dots themselves cannot change their length.

7. Use the Preview control to increase or decrease the size of the preview for the stroke style **51**.

To edit a stroke style:

1. Select the custom stroke style in the Stroke Styles dialog box and choose Edit. The Edit Stroke Style dialog box appears.

TIP The Edit Stroke Style dialog box is the same as the New Stroke Style dialog box, except that there is a Preview checkbox to help you see what your changes do to the stroke **52**. Also, the Edit Stroke Style dialog box does not have an Add button.

2. Click OK to apply the changes.

48 *The New Stroke Style dialog box set for the Dotted controls.*

49 *The Dotted controls in the New Stroke Style dialog box.*

50 *Use the Corners menu to control how dotted styles are applied to corners.*

(sidebar) **Creating Custom Stroke Styles**

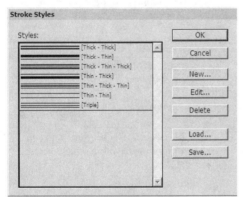

51 *Use the Preview display and Preview Weight to see what a dotted style will look like.*

52 *Click the Preview checkbox to see how the stroke edits appear when applied to objects.*

53 *The Stroke Styles dialog box lets you create, edit, and manage custom stroke styles.*

Once you have defined a stroke style, it appears in the Type menu of the Stroke panel for that document. You may want to transfer strokes from one document to another. You do so using the Stroke Styles dialog box **53**.

To save strokes for use in another document:

1. Choose Stroke Styles from the Stroke panel menu.

2. Select the custom strokes that you want to transfer to another document.

TIP Hold the Shift key to select a range of strokes.

TIP Hold the Cmd/Ctrl key and click to select noncontiguous strokes.

3. Click the Save button. A dialog box appears where you can save the strokes as an .inst file, which contains the custom stroke definitions.

To transfer strokes from another document:

1. Choose Stroke Styles from the Stroke panel menu.

2. Click Load from the Stroke Styles dialog box.

3. Navigate to find the .inst file that contains the custom stroke definitions.

4. Click the Open button to add the strokes to the document.

TIP You can also add custom strokes by copying and pasting objects from one document to another.

To delete a stroke from document:

1. Choose Stroke Styles from the Stroke panel menu.

2. Select the stroke or strokes you want to delete.

3. Click the Delete button.

TIP You can't delete the seven default strokes.

Creating Custom Stroke Styles

Arrows and Corner Options

You can add arrowheads and other shapes to the open-ended objects that have strokes applied to them .

To add arrowheads and end shapes:

1. Select an object with open ends.

2. Add a graphic to the beginning of the object by choosing a shape from the Start menu in the Stroke panel .

3. Add a graphic to the end of the object by choosing a shape from the End menu.

InDesign can modify the shape of objects by adding special corner options. You can apply these effects to any object that has corner points — even open-ended objects.

TIP You can change a star's points to curves by applying a rounded corner effect. Or you can convert an L-shaped line into a soft curve.

To apply corner options:

1. Select an object with corner points.

2. Choose **Object > Corner Options.** The Corner Options dialog box appears .

3. Choose one of the options from the Effect menu.

4. Set the size of the effect.

TIP Check Preview so you can see how the settings look.

5. Click OK to apply the settings .

TIP You can change corner options later by selecting the object and reopening the dialog box. However, the individual points within the effect cannot be manipulated.

54 *The 12 different types of arrowhead styles for paths.*

55 *Choose an arrowhead style from the Start or End menu in the Stroke panel.*

56 *The Corner options dialog box lets you apply different corners to objects.*

57 *An example of applying the special corner options to rectangles.*

58 The **Effects panel**.

59 The **Transparency controls** in the *Effects dialog box*.

60 The **Opacity slider in the Effects panel** *lowers the visibility of objects*.

61 *An example of how a white text frame with the fill set to 50% opacity creates a ghost area in the image.*

Opacity and Blend Mode Effects

What I call *transparency* (the ability to see through objects, images, or text), InDesign calls *opacity*.

To apply opacity effect to an object:

1. Choose **Window** > **Effects** to open the Effects panel **58**.

   or

   Click the Opacity slider in the Control panel.

   or

   Choose **Objects** > **Effects** > **Transparency** to open the Effects dialog box set to the Transparency option **59**.

   or

   Choose Transparency from the Effects panel menu.

2. Drag the Opacity slider or enter an amount in the Opacity field **60**. The lower the opacity percentage, the more you can see through the object.

TIP Once you have activated the Opacity field or slider, you can use the up and down arrow keys on the keyboard to increase or decrease the amount of opacity.

TIP Place a text frame filled with the color Paper at a reduced opacity over an image to "ghost" that area in the image **61**.

Blend mode effects allows the colors and shades in one object to interact with the objects beneath .

To add a blend mode effect:

1. Select the object.
2. Choose a blend mode from the list in the Effects panel or from the Transparency controls in the Effects dialog box.

   - **Normal** applies no change to the objects.
   - **Multiply** multiplies the bottom color with the top color.
   - **Screen** is the inverse of Multiply.
   - **Overlay** preserves the highlights and shadows of the base color while mixing in the top color.
   - **Soft Light** is similar to shining a diffused spotlight on the artwork.
   - **Hard Light** is similar to shining a harsh spotlight on the artwork.
   - **Color Dodge** lightens the bottom color to reflect the top color.
   - **Color Burn** darkens the bottom color to reflect the top color.
   - **Darken** displays either the bottom or top color — whichever is darker.
   - **Lighten** selects the bottom or top color — whichever is lighter.
   - **Difference** subtracts one color from another depending on brightness.
   - **Exclusion** is similar to Difference but is lower in contrast.
   - **Hue** replaces the hue of the bottom object with the hue of the top one.
   - **Saturation** replaces the saturation of the bottom object with the top.
   - **Color** colorizes the bottom object with the top color.
   - **Luminosity** changes the bottom object's luminance with the top.

Normal

Multiply

Screen

Overlay

Soft Light

Hard Light

Color Dodge

Color Burn

Darken

Lighten

Difference

Exclusion

Hue

Saturation

Color

Luminosity

62 *An example of how the 16 blend modes interact when placed over an image.*

Opacity and Blend Mode Effects

Knockout
Group off

Knockout
Group on

63 *With the Knockout Group turned on, blended objects do not interact with each other.*

64 *The Knockout Group checkbox in the Effects panel.*

As you apply a blend mode or an opacity setting, you may need to control how the transparency is applied. One such control is called a *knockout group*. Objects in a knockout group display their blend modes or opacity settings on other objects, but not with each other **63**.

To create a knockout group:

1. Apply a blend mode or opacity setting to an object.

2. Repeat for any additional objects.

TIP Each object can have its own blend mode or opacity setting, or they all can have the same settings.

3. Use the Selection tool to select the objects. These are the objects you *don't* want to have interact with each other.

4. Choose **Object > Group**.

5. With the group selected, click the Knockout Group checkbox in the Effects panel **64** or the Transparency controls in the Effects dialog box.

Opacity and Blend Mode Effects

The Isolate Blending command creates the opposite effect of a Knockout group. With this command, the objects in the group display their blend modes with each other, but not with objects outside the group .

To isolate the blending in objects:

1. Apply a blend mode to as many objects as you want.

2. Use the Selection tool to select the objects that have the blend mode.

3. Choose **Object > Group**.

4. Keep the group selected, click the Isolate Blending checkbox in the Effects panel or the Transparency options in the Effects dialog box.

You can also specify where the opacity or blend mode is applied.

To specify to which attributes the effect is applied:

◆ Use the Settings for menu in the Effects dialog box to choose one of the following:

- **Object** sets the effect to the entire object.

- **Fill** sets the effect to just the fill.

- **Stroke** sets the effect to just the stroke.

- **Text** sets the effect to just the text.

or

Click to target the object attribute in the Effects panel 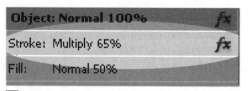.

TIP Use this technique when working with the other effects such as shadows, glows, bevel and emboss effects, satin, and feathers covered in the next sections.

Isolate Blending off

Isolate Blending on

65 *With the Isolate Blending command turned on, blended objects only interact with each other, not the objects below.*

66 *The* **Isolate Blending checkbox** *in the Effects panel.*

67 *Use the* **Settings for list** *to choose to which parts of the object the opacity or blend mode is applied.*

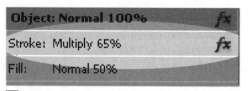
68 *Select the* **object attribute in the Effects panel** *to apply the opacity of blend mode to just one part of the object.*

Opacity and Blend Mode Effects

69 *The* **Effects dialog box** *lets you choose effects as well as change their appearance.*

70 *The* **fx** *icon in the* **Effects panel** *lets you apply special effects.*

71 *The* **Delete Effect icon** *in the Effects panel removes effects from selections.*

72 *The* **Clear All Transparency icon** *in the Effects panel removes all effects and makes the object opaque.*

Working with Effects

In addition to opacity and blend modes, you can also apply special effects such as shadows, glows, and feathers to objects. All these effects are controlled from the Effects dialog box **69**.

To open the Effects dialog box:

◆ Click the fx icon in the Effects panel or the Control panel to choose an effect from the menu **70**.

or

Choose **Object** > **Effects** and then one of the effects in the submenu.

or

Choose one of the effects in the Effects panel menu.

To remove effects:

◆ Uncheck the effect in the Effects dialog box.

or

Select the effect in the Effects panel and then click the Delete Effect icon in the Effects panel **71**.

or

Click the Clear All Transparency icon in the Effects panel to remove all effects as well as any opacity and blend mode settings **72**.

or

Choose Clear Effects from the Effect panel menu or **Object** > **Effects** submenu.

or

Choose Clear All Transparency from the Effects panel menu or **Object** > **Effects** submenu. This removes all effects as well as any opacity and blend mode settings.

Working with Effects

Shadow Effects

One of the most popular effects is a drop shadow set behind objects, text, or images .

To add a drop shadow:

1. Select the object.

2. Open the Effects dialog box **74** as described previously.

3. Click the Drop Shadow checkbox.

4. Set the controls as follows:

   - The **Blending area** controls the color and opacity of the shadow as well as how the shadow interacts with other objects.

   - The **Position area** controls the placement of the shadow in relationship to the object.

   - The **Options area** controls the size and other attributes of the shadow.

5. Click OK to apply the shadow.

An inner shadow creates the appearance that the object is cut out of the page it is on **75**.

To add an inner shadow:

1. Select the object.

2. Open the Effects dialog box **76** as described previously.

3. Click the Inner Shadow checkbox.

4. Set the controls as follows:

   - The **Blending area** controls the color and opacity of the shadow as well as how the shadow interacts with other objects.

   - The **Position area** controls the placement of the shadow in relationship to the object.

   - The **Options area** controls the size and other attributes of the shadow.

5. Click OK to apply the shadow.

73 *A **drop shadow** applied to text.*

74 *The **Drop Shadow controls** in the Effects dialog box.*

75 *An **inner shadow** applied to text.*

76 *The **Inner Shadow controls** in the Effects dialog box.*

An **outer glow** *applied to text.*

The **Outer Glow controls** *in the Effects dialog box.*

An **inner glow** *applied to text.*

The **Inner Shadow controls** *in the Effects dialog box.*

Glow Effects

You can also add an outer glow around objects or an inner glow inside an object ⁊⁊ – ⁊⁊.

To add an outer glow:

1. Select the object.
2. Open the Effects dialog box ⁊⁊ as described previously.
3. Click the Outer Glow checkbox.
4. Set the controls as follows:
   - The **Blending area** controls the color and opacity of the glow as well as how the glow interacts with other objects.
   - The **Options area** controls the size and other attributes of the glow.
5. Click OK to apply the glow.

To add an inner glow:

1. Select the object.
2. Open the Effects dialog box ⁊⁊ as described previously.
3. Click the Inner Glow checkbox.
4. Set the controls as follows:
   - The **Blending area** controls the color and opacity of the shadow as well as how the glow interacts with the inside of the object.
   - The **Options area** controls the size and other attributes of the glow.
5. Click OK to apply the glow.

Glow Effects

Bevel and Emboss Effects

A great way to add dimension to objects is with the bevel and emboss effects **81**.

TIP Bevels and emboss effects are simply variations in the style of one effect.

To add a bevel or emboss:

1. Select the object.
2. Open the Effects dialog box **82** as described previously.
3. Click the Bevel and Emboss checkbox.
4. Set the controls as follows:
   - The **Structure area** controls the style of the bevel or emboss as well as the size and other attributes.
   - The **Shading area** controls what colors are used for the highlights and shadows of the effect as well as the direction of the light that creates the effects.
5. Click OK to apply the bevel or emboss.

Satin Effect

The satin effect gives the appearance of a fabric texture applied to the object **83**.

To add a satin effect:

1. Select the object.
2. Open the Effects dialog box **84** as described previously.
3. Click the Satin checkbox.
4. Set the controls as follows:
   - The **Structure area** controls how the satin texture is applied as well as the size, angle, and other attributes.
   - Choose **Invert** to reverse the appearance of the satin effect with the object's color.
5. Click OK to apply the satin effect.

EFFECTIVE EFFECTS

81 A **bevel effect** *applied to text.*

82 *The* **Bevel and Emboss controls** *in the Effects dialog box.*

EFFECTIVE EFFECTS

83 A **satin effect** *applied to text.*

84 *The* **Satin controls** *in the Effects dialog box.*

EFFECTIVE EFFECTS

85 *A* **basic feather** *applied to text.*

```
Basic Feather
  Options
    Feather Width  0p9
    Choke:  0%
    Corners:  Diffused
    Noise:  0%
```

86 *The* **Basic Feather controls** *in the Effects dialog box.*

EFFECTIVE EFFECTS

87 *A* **directional feather** *applied to text.*

```
Directional Feather
  Feather widths
    Top:  0p0          Left:  0p0
    Bottom:  0p0       Right:  0p0
  Options
    Noise:  0%         Choke:  0%
    Shape:  Leading Edges    Angle:  0°
```

88 *The* **Directional Feather controls** *in the Effects dialog box.*

Feather Effects

Feather refers to softening the edge of an object so that it fades to transparent. InDesign gives you three different types of feather effects. The Basic Feather creates a soft edge around the outside of objects **85**.

To add a basic feather effect:

1. Select the object.
2. Open the Effects dialog box **86** as described previously.
3. Click the Basic Feather checkbox.
4. Use the Options area to control the size and other attributes of the feather.
5. Click OK to apply the feather.

A Directional Feather allows you to specify different amounts of softening for the top, bottom, left, and right sides of the object **87**.

To add a directional feather:

1. Select the object.
2. Open the Effects dialog box **88** as described previously.
3. Click the Directional Feather checkbox.
4. Set the controls as follows:
   - The **Feather widths area** controls the size of the feather for the four sides of the object.
   - The **Options area** controls the size and other attributes of the feather.
5. Click OK to apply the feather.

Feather Effects

The Gradient Feather effect allows you to create a color that fades in and out of opacity. So instead of a gradient that changes color, a gradient feather changes opacity for each of the gradient stops (transition points) .

TIP The Gradient Feather effect only changes the opacity of the gradient. If you need to change the color of the gradient, you need to create a separate color gradient.

To add a gradient feather:

1. Select the object.
2. Open the Effects dialog box as described previously.
3. Click the Gradient Feather checkbox.
4. Set the controls as follows **90**:
   - The **Gradient Stops area** allows you to set the opacity and location for each of the gradient transition points.
   - The **Options area** controls the type of gradient (linear or radial) and the angle of the gradient.
5. Click OK to apply the feather.

Setting the Global Light

The Global Light setting allows you to set an angle and position of the electronic "light" that creates shadows and other dimensional effects. You can use the Global Light controls to coordinate the appearance of the effects.

To set the Global Light:

1. Choose Global Light from the Effects panel menu or the **Object > Effects** submenu.
2. Use the Global Light dialog box to set the angle and altitude of the global light **91**.

89 *A* **gradient feather** *applied to text.*

90 *The* **Gradient Feather controls** *in the Effects dialog box.*

91 *The* **Global Light dialog box.**

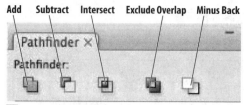

Add   Subtract   Intersect   Exclude Overlap   Minus Back

92 *Click the* **Pathfinder** *icons in the Pathfinder panel.*

Command	Objects before	Objects after
Add		
Subtract		
Intersect		
Exclude Overlap		
Minus Back		

93 *Examples of how the* **Pathfinder** **commands** *change selected objects.*

Before   After

94 *An example of how the* **Exclude Overlap** **command** *creates separate objects when the Compound Path is released.*

Using the Pathfinder Commands

I can't draw. So rather than struggle to create certain shapes, I use the Pathfinder commands to use multiple objects to create different shapes.

To use the Pathfinder commands:

1. Select the objects that you want to have interact with each other. You must select at least two objects.

2. Click one of the Pathfinder icons at the top of the Pathfinder panel **92** (**Window** > **Object & Layout** > **Pathfinder**).

    or

    Choose one of the following from the **Object** > **Pathfinder** menu:

    - **Add** combines the outer edges of the objects in a single shape **93**.

    - **Subtract** uses the frontmost objects as cookie cutters that change the shape of the backmost object **93**.

    - **Intersect** creates a new shape based on the area intersected by the objects **93**.

    - **Exclude Overlap** creates a hole where the objects overlap **93**.

    - **Minus Back** uses the backmost objects as cookie cutters that change the shape of the frontmost object **93**.

Depending on the command and the position of the objects, you may create a compound path. If you want to separate the objects, you need to release the compound path:

To separate the results of the Pathfinder commands:

1. Select the objects created by the Pathfinder command.

2. Choose **Object** > **Paths** > **Release Compound Paths**.

3. Deselect the objects and then move each one to new positions **94**.

the Convert Shape commands to
cts from one shape to another.

...... shape of objects:

1. Select the object that you want to convert.

2. Click one of the Convert Shape icons in the Pathfinder panel **95** and **96**.

   or

   Choose one of the following from the **Object > Convert Shape** menu:

   - **Rectangle** converts to a rectangle.
   - **Rounded Rectangle** converts to a rectangle with rounded corners.
   - **Beveled Rectangle** converts to a rectangle with flat, angled corners.
   - **Inverse Rounded Rectangle** converts to a rectangle with inverted rounded corners.
   - **Ellipse** converts the object to an ellipse.
   - **Triangle** converts to a triangle.
   - **Polygon** converts to a polygon using the current settings for the Polygon tool.
   - **Line** converts the object to a line. The length is the diagonal of the bounding box of the object.
   - **Orthogonal Line** converts the object to a line. The length is the width or height of the bounding box, whichever is greater.

TIP The size of the corner options comes from the current corner radius setting in the Corner options.

95 *The **Convert Shape** icons in the Pathfinder panel allow you to change the shape of objects.*

Icon	Function
▭	Rectangle
▢	Rounded Rectangle
⬡	Beveled Rectangle
✛	Inverse Rounded Rectangle
○	Ellipse
△	Triangle
⬡	Polygon
╱	Line
✛	Orthogonal Line
◔	Open Path
◕	Close Path
⟲	Reverse Path

96 *The **Convert Shape** icons and their functions.*

Draw a rectangle and duplicate it in place

Apply the corner option to one of the rectangles

Change the size of the rectangle to expose the rounded corners

Change the size of the rounded rectangle to expose the corners

Apply the Add Pathfinder command

97 *The steps used to create a rectangle with two rounded corners.*

Three of the icons in the Convert Shape area are actually path modification commands.

To modify paths:

1. Select the object that you want to modify.

2. Click one of the Convert Shape icons in the Pathfinder panel **95** and **96**.

   or

   Choose one of the following from the **Object > Paths** menu:

   - **Open Path** opens a closed path at a point.

   - **Close Path** creates a segment between the end points of a path.

   - **Reverse Path** changes the direction of a path.

TIP Apply the Close Path command to expand the electronic corner options into actual points on the path. This is similar to applying Illustrator's Object > Expand command.

Creating Special Shapes

The Pathfinder and Convert Shape commands can be used to create special shapes. Here are a few ideas for working with those commands.

You can use the Pathfinder commands to merge two different shapes into one. For instance, many people want to create a rectangle with only two rounded corners. That shape is easily created by applying the Pathfinder > Add command to merge an ordinary rectangle with a rounded-corner rectangle **97**.

Using the Pathfinder Commands

Using the Eyedropper

Imagine you've finished styling an object with exactly the right combination of fill, stroke, and effects. And now you'd like to apply those same settings to a different object. That's where the Eyedropper tool comes to the rescue.

TIP As handy as the Eyedropper tool is, it doesn't come close to the power of object styles *(covered in Chapter 15, "Style")*.

To set the eyedropper options:

1. Double-click the Eyedropper tool in the Tools panel **98** This opens the Eyedropper Options dialog box **99**.

2. Click the triangles to open each of the attribute categories.

TIP The object settings categories are Fill, Stroke, and Transparency.

3. Use the checkboxes to choose which attributes you want the Eyedropper tool to sample.

4. Click OK to set the options.

Once you set the eyedropper options, you can sample and apply object attributes.

To sample and apply object attributes:

1. Choose the Eyedropper tool.

2. Click with the white eyedropper cursor inside the object that you want to sample **100**. The cursor changes from white to black.

TIP If an object has a stroke, but no fill, click the object's outline to sample its stroke.

3. Click the black eyedropper cursor inside the object that you want to change **101**. This applies the first object's attributes to the second.

4. Click the eyedropper inside any other objects that you want to change.

98 *The* **Eyedropper tool** *in the Tools panel lets you sample object attributes.*

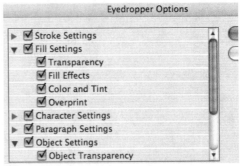

99 *Use the* **Eyedropper Options dialog box** *to set which attributes the Eyedropper will sample and apply.*

100 *The* **white eyedropper** *lets you sample the object attributes.*

101 *The* **black eyedropper** *applies object attributes from one object to another.*

102 *The* **white precision eyedropper** *allows you to sample a specific color.*

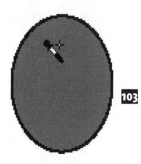

103 *The* **black precision eyedropper** *lets you apply a specific color to either the fill or a stroke.*

As you work with the Eyedropper tool, you may change your mind and want to unload one set of attributes to sample new ones.

To sample new attributes:

1. Hold the Opt/Alt key. The eyedropper cursor changes to the white sample mode.

2. Click the cursor inside a new object that you want to sample.

3. Release the Opt/Alt key to apply the new attributes to objects.

You may not want to sample all the attributes in an object — just the fill or stroke. That's when you can use the Eyedropper tool in its precision mode. The precision mode allows you to sample and apply just the color to either a fill or a stroke.

To use the precision eyedropper:

1. Choose the Eyedropper tool. Hold the Shift key. A plus sign appears next to the white eyedropper cursor **102**. This indicates that the Eyedropper tool is in the precision mode.

2. Click the precision white eyedropper cursor on the fill or stroke color you wish to sample. The cursor turns into the precision black eyedropper **103**.

3. Click the precision eyedropper on either a fill or a stroke of the object that you want to change. Only the fill or stroke is changed.

Using the Eyedropper

Setting Object Defaults

You can make any of the object settings the default for any new objects you create. You can set the object defaults for the current document or globally for all new documents.

104 *Click the* **Default Fill and Stroke icon** *in the Tools panel to set the fill to none and stroke to black.*

To set current document defaults:

1. With a document open, deselect any objects.

2. Make whatever changes you want in the Stroke panel or other panels. This sets the defaults for the open document.

3. Set whatever amounts you want for the Effects or Corner options dialog boxes.

To set global defaults:

◆ With no document open, make whatever changes you want in the Stroke or other panels. This sets the global defaults for all new documents.

InDesign also has its own default fill and stroke setting of a black stroke and no fill. These are separate from the defaults you set yourself. This can be easily applied to objects.

To apply the InDesign fill and stroke defaults:

◆ Click the Default Fill and Stroke icon in the Tools panel 104.

Setting Object Defaults

POINTS AND PATHS 7

I remember the first time I tried to use the Pen tool in a computer graphics program. I clicked the tool and dragged across the screen in the way I thought would create a simple curve. Instead, I got a wild series of lines that shot out in different directions. When I tried to change the shape of the curves, things got even worse. I was so startled I immediately closed up the program and didn't use the Pen tool for a long, long time.

However, I really wanted to use the Pen tool, as I knew it was the best way to create curved shapes. So I forced myself to try the tool again. It took a lot of trial and error but eventually I was able to understand the Pen and Bezier controls. Later on, working with tools such as the Pencil and Eraser made it even easier to work with Bezier curves.

Once I got it, I realized the principles are simple. Even better, if you have used the Pen tool in Adobe Illustrator or Adobe Photoshop, you will find InDesign's Pen tool almost the same.

I wish someone had written out easy-to-understand, step-by-step instructions on how to use the Pen tool. So think of this chapter as the instructions for the Pen tool that I wish I had had back then.

Pen Points

One of the most important tools in any graphics program is the Pen tool. Fortunately, InDesign has a Pen tool that lets you create much more sophisticated shapes in your layout than can be created with the basic shape tools. *(See Chapter 4, "Working with Objects," for more information on working with the basic shapes.)*

TIP If you are familiar with the Pen tool in Adobe Illustrator or Macromedia FreeHand, you will find it very easy to master the Pen in InDesign.

If you've never used a Pen tool in any graphics program, you will understand more if you first become familiar with the elements of paths.

Elements of Paths

Paths are defined by points and line segments. When you draw with the Pen tool you create the following:

- **Anchor points,** which define a path at points where the path changes . These can be plain corner points, smooth curve points, and corner curve points, as explained on the following pages.

- **Segments,** which are the paths that connect anchor points .

- **Control handles** that extend out from anchor points; their length and direction control the shape of the segment's curves .

Control handle
Deselected anchor point
Path segment
Selected anchor point

1 *The elements of a path.*

The Father of Bezier Curves

Some people call the curves created by the Pen tool *Bezier curves.* This is in honor of Pierre Bézier (*Bay-zee-ay*), the French mathematician.

Monsieur Bézier created the system of mathematics that is used to define the relationship of the control handles to the shape of the curve.

Adobe Systems, Inc., adopted this mathematical system when it created the PostScript language that is used as the basis of graphics programs. InDesign, along with many other programs, uses Bezier curves as the mathematics behind each curve.

Drawing in a Page Layout Program?

I limit using InDesign's Pen tool to simple things. If I need some sort of curved or wavy line, I use InDesign's Pen tool. For instance, all the curved arrows in this book were created with the Pen tool. However, if I want a perfect spiral, I use Illustrator's Spiral tool. *(See Chapter 8, "Imported Graphics," for how to bring Illustrator paths into InDesign.)*

If I need to jazz up some text, I stay within InDesign. But if I need a complete map of New York State with highways, rivers, and scenic attractions, I work in Illustrator.

Pen Points

Click the **Pen tool in the Tools panel** *to create lines.*

The **start icon** *for the Pen tool.*

Click with the Pen tool to create **a corner point,** *shown as a small square.*

Straight lines extend between the plain corner points.

The small circle next to the Pen cursor indicates that you will close the path.

Drawing Lines

Different types of anchor points create different line shapes. Straight lines are formed by creating *plain corner points*.

To create straight lines:

1. Click the Pen tool in the Tools panel **2**.

2. Position the cursor where the path should start. A small X appears next to the Pen, which indicates that you are starting the path **3**.

3. Click. A plain corner point appears as a colored square. The Pen cursor is displayed without any symbol next to it **4**.

4. Position the cursor for the next point and click. This creates another plain corner point with a straight line that connects the first point to the second.

TIP Hold the Shift key to constrain the straight lines to 45-degree angles.

5. Continue clicking until you have created all the straight-line sides of the object **5**.

TIP If you have not closed the path (see the next exercise), hold the Cmd/Ctrl key and click with the Selection tool. This deselects the path and allows you to start a new one.

To close a path with a straight line:

1. Move the Pen over the first point. A small circle appears next to the Pen **6**. This indicates that you can close the path.

2. Click. This closes the path with a plain corner point and allows you to start a new path.

Drawing Lines

Drawing Curves

Smooth curve points create curves like the track a roller coaster follows. There are no abrupt changes from one curve to another.

To create smooth curves:

1. Drag the Pen tool where you want to start the curve. Handles extend out from the point.

TIP The length and angle of the handle control the curve's height and direction.

2. Release the mouse button.

TIP You do not see a curve until you create the next point of the path.

3. Move the cursor to where you want the next part of the curve. Drag to create the curved segment between the two smooth curve points **7**.

4. Continue to create curved segments by repeating steps 2 and 3 **8**.

To close a path with a smooth curve:

1. Move the Pen over the first point. A small circle appears, indicating that you can close the path.

2. Drag backwards to close the path **9**.

A *corner curve point* creates curves with an abrupt change in direction. The path of a bouncing ball illustrates a corner curve.

To create a corner curve:

1. With the Pen tool active, drag to create an anchor point with control handles.

2. Without releasing the mouse button, hold the Opt/Alt key and then drag to pivot the second handle **10**.

3. Release the mouse button when the second handle is the correct length and direction.

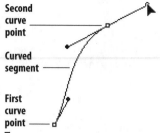

7 *Drag with the Pen tool to create* **smooth curves.**

8 *A path with a series of curved segments.*

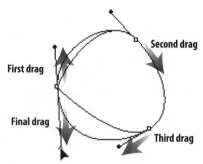

9 *Dragging backwards closes a path with a smooth curve.*

10 *Hold the Opt/Alt key to pivot the handles, which creates a* **corner curve.**

Move the cursor back over a point and click to **retract a handle along a curve.**

Drag with the Pen tool over an existing anchor point to **extend a handle out from the point.**

General Pen Rules

As you work with the Pen tool, there are some rules you should follow:

- Use the fewest number of points to define a path. Too many points add to the size of the file and make it difficult to edit the path later.

- Try to limit the length of the control handles to one-third the length of the curve. This is sometimes called the *One-Third Rule*. The One-Third Rule makes it easier to edit and control the shape of curves.

Changing Curves and Corner Points

If you retract the handle that extends out from a curve point, the next segment becomes a straight line.

To retract a handle:

1. Drag to create a smooth curve point.

2. Move the Pen cursor back over the anchor point. A small angle symbol appears next to the cursor.

3. Click. The handle retracts back into the anchor point. The point is now a corner point with only one handle **11**.

4. Continue the path with either a straight line or a curved line.

TIP Click to make the next path segment straight. Drag to make the next path segment curved.

If you create a corner point with no control handles, you can extend a single handle out from that anchor point.

To extend a handle from a point:

1. Click to create a corner point with no handles.

2. Move the Pen cursor back over the anchor point you just created. A small angle symbol appears next to the cursor.

3. Drag to pull a single handle out from the anchor point **12**.

4. Continue the path with a curved line.

Changing Curves and Corner Points

Modifying Paths

Once you create a path, you can still change its shape and the position of the points. You can also split a path into two separate segments or join two segments together. When you move points, you use the Direct Selection tool.

The **Direct Selection tool** *in the Tools panel; use it to move points.*

To move individual points:

1. Click the Direct Selection tool in the Tools panel **13**.

2. Position the tool over the point you want to move.

3. Drag the point to the new position.

To select and move multiple points:

1. Click the Direct Selection tool in the Tools panel.

2. Drag to create a rectangular marquee around the points you want to select **14**. The selected points appear solid. The unselected points appear hollow.

   or

   Hold the Shift key as you click to select the points.

TIP You can select points in one path or multiple paths.

3. Drag the points to the new position.

The Direct Selection tool also lets you change the length and direction of the control handles.

To move control handles:

1. Click the Direct Selection tool in the Tools panel.

2. Click a point on the path. This displays the control handles for that point.

3. Position the Direct Selection tool over the end point of the handle.

4. Drag the handle to the new position **15**.

Drag a marquee to select multiple points. *The center point does not turn black.*

The Direct Selection tool changes the length and position of a control handle.

16 *The* **Scissors tool** *in the Tools panel allows you to snip paths in two.*

 17 *The Scissors tool splits a path into two points, one on top of the other.*

 18 *The* **Close Path command** *joins the two end points of a path.*

19 *The results of applying the* **Reverse Path command** *to a path with an arrowhead.*

You may want to separate one path into two parts — for instance, to separate two halves of a circle. The Scissors tool makes it easy to split or break a path into segments.

To split paths:

1. Select the path.
2. Click the Scissors tool in the Tools panel **16**.
3. Position the cursor where you want to split the path.
4. Click to split the path at that point.

TIP The Scissors tool creates two points, one on top of the other. Use the Direct Selection tool to move one point away from the other **17**.

TIP Paths that contain text cannot be split into two distinct segments.

To open paths using a command:

1. Select the path.
2. Choose **Object > Path > Open Path**. This opens the path by creating two points, one on top of the other.

To close paths using a command:

1. Select the path.
2. Choose **Object > Path > Close Path**. This closes the path by creating a line segment between the end points of the path **18**.

The path direction comes from the order in which you draw the path. You can change the path direction.

To change the path direction:

1. Use the Direct Selection tool to select the path.
2. Choose **Object > Path > Reverse Path**. This switches the start and end points of the path **19**.

Modifying Paths

Modifying Points

So what happens if you create the wrong point with the Pen tool? Are you stuck? Does it mean you have to redraw the entire path? Thankfully, no—there are many ways to change the paths made with the Pen tool, as well as paths made with other tools. *(See Chapter 4, "Working with Objects," for more information on working with the basic shapes.)*

A simple way to change a path is to add a point. This helps you turn one shape into another.

To add points to a path:

1. Select the path.
2. Choose the Add Anchor Point tool in the Tools panel .
3. Click the path where you want to add the point.

TIP The Pen tool automatically changes to the Add Anchor Point tool when positioned over a selected path segment .

You can delete points from a path without causing a break in the path.

To delete points from a path:

1. Select the path.
2. Choose the Delete Anchor Point tool in the Tools panel **22**.
3. Click to delete the point of the path.

TIP The Pen tool changes to the Delete Anchor Point tool when positioned over a point on a selected path **23**.

20 *The* **Add Anchor Point tool** *in the Tools panel.*

21 *The Add Anchor Point tool displays a plus sign over a path segment.*

22 *The Delete Anchor Point tool in the Tools panel.*

23 *The Delete Anchor Point tool displays a minus sign over a point.*

24 *When you select and delete a segment, you keep the points on either side of the segment.*

25 *When you select and delete a point, you delete both segments that were attached to the point.*

26 *The Convert Direction Point tool in the Tools panel.*

27 *Drag with the Convert Direction Point tool to change a corner point into a smooth curve point.*

28 *Click with the Convert Direction Point tool to change a smooth curve point into a corner point.*

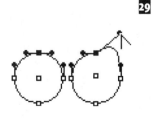

29 *Drag a handle with the Convert Direction Point tool to change a smooth curve point into a corner curve point.*

You may also want to create an open path by deleting a segment or the point between two segments.

To delete a segment in a path:

1. Use the Direct Selection tool to select the segment that you want to delete.

2. Press the Delete key or choose **Edit > Clear**. This deletes the segment and opens the path **24**.

TIP If you select a point with the Direct Selection tool, the two segments on either side of the point can be deleted **25**.

You can also change the control handles around an anchor point. This changes the shape of the segments controlled by that anchor point.

To modify an anchor point:

1. Select the path.

2. Choose the Convert Direction Point tool in the Tools panel **26**.

3. Use the tool as follows to change the anchor points:

   - Press and drag a corner point to create a smooth curve point with two handles **27**.

   - Click a smooth curve point to create a corner point with no handles **28**.

   - Drag one of the handles of a smooth curve point to create a corner curve point **29**.

Modifying Points

Using the Pencil Tool

Unlike the Pen tool, which uses mathematical principles to draw paths, InDesign's Pencil tool works more like a traditional Pencil. However, the Pen tool is a little more precise than the Pencil.

TIP If you are familiar with the Pencil tool in Adobe Illustrator, you will find you already know how to work with InDesign's Pencil tool.

To draw with the Pencil tool:

1. Click the Pencil tool in the Tools panel . A small cross next to the Pencil cursor indicates that you are about to start the path .

2. Press and drag with the Pencil .

3. To close the path, hold the Opt/Alt key. A small circle next to the cursor indicates that the path will be closed **33**.

4. Release the mouse to create the path.

The Pencil tool can also be used to edit existing paths and reshape paths.

To edit paths with the Pencil tool:

1. Select the path that you want to reshape.

TIP The Pencil tool can edit paths created by tools such as the Pen or the frame tools.

2. Move the Pencil tool near the selected path. The cross next to the cursor disappears. This indicates that you are about to edit the path.

3. Drag along the path. When you release the mouse button, the path is reshaped **34**.

TIP If you don't get the results you expect, drag the Pencil tool in the opposite direction.

30 *The Pencil tool in the Tools panel.*

31 *The cross next to the Pencil cursor indicates that you are about to start a new path.*

32 *Press and drag to create a path with the Pencil tool.*

33 *The circle next to the Pencil cursor indicates that the Opt/Alt key will close the path.*

34 *Drag the Pencil tool next to a selected path to reshape the path.*

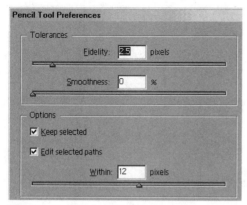

35 *The* **Pencil Tool Preferences dialog box** *allows you to control the appearance of the path.*

Fidelity 2.5 pixels **Fidelity 11 pixels** **Fidelity 11 pixels**
Smoothness 0% **Smoothness 0%** **Smoothness 70%**

36 *The* **Pencil tool Fidelity and Smoothness settings** *change the appearance of the path.*

You can change how the Pencil tool responds to the movements of the mouse as you drag. The preferences also control how the Pencil tool edits paths.

To set the preferences for the Pencil tool:

1. Double-click the Pencil tool in the Tools panel. This opens the Pencil Tool Preferences dialog box **35**.

2. Set the amount of Fidelity using the slider or field. The lower the amount of Fidelity, the more the path will follow the motions of the mouse **36**.

3. Set the amount of Smoothness using the slider or field. The higher the setting for Smoothness, the more the path will follow curved shapes **36**.

4. Check Keep Selected to keep the path selected after you have drawn it. This makes it easier to reshape the path.

5. Check Edit Selected Paths to turn on the reshape option.

6. If the Edit Selected Paths option is turned on, use the slider or field to set how close the Pencil tool must come, in pixels, to the path you want to reshape.

Using the Pencil Tool

Using the Smooth Tool

Once you have created a path, you may want to delete extra points so that the path is smoother.

TIP If you are familiar with Illustrator's Smooth tool, you will find it easy to use the Smooth tool in InDesign.

To smooth paths with the Smooth tool:

1. Select the path that you want to smooth.

2. Click the Smooth tool in the Tools panel .

3. Press and drag the Smooth tool along the path.

4. Release the mouse. The path is redrawn with fewer points .

You can change how the Smooth tool responds to the movements of the mouse as you drag.

To set the preferences for the Smooth tool:

1. Double-click the Smooth tool in the Tools panel to open the Smooth Tool Preferences dialog box .

2. Use the slider or field to set the Fidelity amount. The lower the amount, the more the new path will follow the original path.

3. Use the slider or field to set the Smoothness amount. The higher the setting, the more curved the path.

4. Check Keep Selected to keep the path selected after you have smoothed it. This makes it easier to increase the smoothness of the path.

37 *The* **Smooth tool** *in the Tools panel.*

Original path · After using the Smooth tool

38 *Drag the Smooth tool along a path to* **remove points and eliminate small bumps and curves**.

39 *The* **Smooth Tool Preferences** *allow you to control how much the Smooth tool affects the appearance of paths.*

Using the Smooth Tool

40 *The* **Erase tool** *in the Tools panel.*

Original path

After using the Erase tool

41 *The Erase tool deletes points as you drag it along a path.*

Deleting or Removing Points: Which tools or commands do what?

You may find yourself confused by all the different tools and commands for deleting or removing points and segments.

When does the action cause a break in a path? When does an action remove points without opening the path?

See the table on the next page for a review of how points are removed from paths, and the result.

Using the Erase Tool

You may want to delete parts of paths. Rather than selecting and deleting individual points, you can use the Erase tool to drag to delete parts of a path.

TIP If you are familiar with the Erase tool in Adobe Illustrator, you will find it easy to use the Erase tool in InDesign.

To delete paths with the Erase tool:

1. Select the path that you want to delete parts of.

2. Choose the Erase tool in the Tools panel **40**.

3. Press and drag the Erase tool along the path.

4. Release the mouse to display the new path **41**.

TIP The Erase tool will always open a closed path.

TIP If you drag the Erase tool over the middle of an open path, you create two separate open paths. Both open paths will be selected.

Adding or Deleting Points on Paths

The following table compares the different tools and commands as to their effect when adding or deleting points on a path.

Tool or Command	Action	Result
Add Anchor Point tool	Click a segment on the path	Always adds a point to the path.
Delete Anchor Point tool	Click an existing point on the path	Deletes the point. Path reshapes without any break.
Erase tool	Drag along a path	Creates a break in the path
Scissors tool	Click a point or a segment	Creates two end points at that position. Points can then be separated to create a break in the path.
Open Path command	Applied to a path	Creates two end points at the origin of the path. Points are indicated by selection. Points can then be separated to create a break in the path.
Close Path command	Applied to a path	Creates a segment that joins two end points of a path.
Delete command	Applied to points or segments selected with the Direct Selection tool	If applied to a selection in the middle of a path, the command breaks the path into two segments. If applied to a selection at the end of a path, the command shortens the path.

IMPORTED GRAPHICS 8

One reason desktop publishing became so popular is how easy it made combining graphics such as photographs and illustrations with type for layouts.

In the years before designers began using personal computers, specialized workers, toiling under the exotic name of *strippers*, manually trimmed away the blank areas around graphics so that text could be placed around the image. (The name stripper is derived from combining strips of film together.)

Even more complicated was placing text over an illustration. The image and text had to be combined by photography and then stripped into the layout.

Certainly you expect InDesign to import images in the formats that are used by other page-layout programs. But since this is *Adobe* InDesign, you also get some special benefits when working with other Adobe products.

Here's where you learn how to add imported artwork to your page layouts. It only takes a few clicks of a mouse to combine type and artwork together. It's enough to make old-time strippers hang up their tassels!

Placing Artwork

Most artwork that's used in InDesign comes from other sources such as scanners or digital cameras. Artwork can also be created using programs such as Adobe Photoshop, Adobe Illustrator, Adobe FreeHand, or Adobe Acrobat. You can even place the contents of one InDesign file as a graphic into another. This is extremely helpful for working with ads, coupons, or other inserts.

The easiest way to place artwork is to automatically create the frame that contains it when you import the artwork.

To place artwork without drawing a frame:

1. Choose **File > Place.** This opens the Place dialog box .

2. Navigate to find the file you want to import.

3. Check Show Import Options to open the Import Options dialog box before you place the file.

4. Click Open to load the graphic into an image cursor .

TIP Hold the Shift key as you click Open to open the Import Options dialog box, even if the option is not checked.

5. Click the cursor to place the graphic in a rectangular frame the same size as the artwork.

    or

    Drag the image cursor to define the size of the rectangular frame.

    or

    Position the cursor over an empty frame and click. Curves appear around the cursor indicating you are about to place the image within the frame .

TIP Hold the Opt/Alt key to place the image into a frame that already contains an image.

1 *Use the* **Place dialog box** *to open a file you wish to place. Check Show Import Options to make refinements to the imported file.*

2 *The* **loaded image cursor** *appears when you prepare to place artwork.*

3 *The* **curved loaded image cursor** *appears when you position the loaded cursor over an existing frame.*

File Formats

A wide variety of graphic formats can be added to InDesign documents. These formats are recommended for professional printing:

- **Adobe Illustrator** (AI)
- **Adobe Photoshop** (PSD)
- **Adobe InDesign** (ID)
- **Encapsulated PostScript** (EPS)
- **Desktop Color Separation** (DCS)
- **Joint Photographic Experts Group** (JPEG)
- **Portable Document Format** (PDF)
- **Portable Network Graphics** (PNG)
- **PostScript** (PS)
- **Scitex Continuous Tone** (SCT)
- **Tagged Image File Format** (TIFF)

Although the following formats can be inserted into InDesign documents, they are not recommended for use in commercially printed documents. These formats are acceptable for low-resolution, onscreen PDF review, or non-PostScript printers:

- **Enhanced Metafiles** (EMF)
- **Macintosh Picture** (PICT)
- **Graphics Interchange Format** (GIF)
- **PC Paintbrush** (PCX)
- **Windows Bitmap** (BMP)
- **Windows Metafile** (WMF)

You can also place artwork directly into a selected frame. This is handy if you have set up empty frames as placeholders for graphics.

To place artwork into an existing frame:

1. Use one of the tools to create a rectangular, elliptical, or polygonal frame.

TIP You can use either the frame tools that create graphic frames or the tools that create unassigned frames.

2. Use either the Selection or Direct Selection tool to select the frame.

3. Choose **File** > **Place** and navigate to find the image you wish to place in the frame.

4. Click Open in the Place dialog box. The file automatically is inserted within the frame.

TIP You can also use the Pen tool to create frame shapes.

To replace the artwork in an existing frame:

1. Use either Selection tool to select the frame that contains the artwork you want to replace.

2. Choose **File** > **Place** and navigate to find the image you wish to place.

3. Click Replace Selected Item in the Place dialog box ▮.

4. Click Open in the Place dialog box. The new image automatically replaces the contents of the frame.

To move or copy artwork between frames:

1. Use the Direct Selection tool to select the artwork you want to replace.

2. Choose **Edit** > **Cut** or **Edit** > **Copy**. This places the artwork on the clipboard.

3. Select the frame that you want to move the artwork into.

4. Choose **Edit** > **Paste Into**. The contents of the clipboard are pasted into the frame.

Placing Artwork

You can also select multiple items in the Place dialog box and then add all the items to your document. This way you don't have to keep going back to the Place dialog box.

To place multiple items at once:

1. Choose **File** > **Place** to open the Place dialog box.

2. Use the Cmd/Ctrl key to select the items you want to place.

   or

   Use the Shift key to select a range of items.

3. Click the Open button. The cursor displays a preview of the placed file. A number next to the preview indicates there are multiple files ▣.

4. Click or drag to place each item. The number reduces as you place each item.

TIP Use the up/down or left/right arrow keys to cycle through the placed items.

TIP Use the ESC key to delete an item from the loaded cursor.

TIP Use the Opt/Alt key to swap the item in a frame with the item in the loaded cursor.

TIP You don't have to stay within the same type of item. You can load the cursor with Photoshop, PDF, or other types of files. You can even mix text files with image files!

(7)

▣ *The* **numbered loaded cursor** *indicates you have more than one placed item.*

What can you do with a loaded cursor?

Be careful when you've got a loaded cursor in your hand. Never point it at anyone unless you intend to use it.

Once you have the loaded cursor, what can you do without losing the placed items? Surprisingly, there's a lot you can do.

You can go to any menu, open panels, or even go to another document. Your cursor remains loaded when you come back to your document.

However, you will lose the items in a loaded cursor if you choose any tool in the Tools panel or press a key that chooses a tool.

Placing ID files into another ID file

There's something very existential about it, but you can place an InDesign file as a graphic into another InDesign file.

The placed file behaves exactly like a placed PDF document. When you modify the placed graphic, it updates in the InDesign layout. You can turn the layers on or off as you can with PDF documents.

Placing Artwork

5 **Drag an image from Adobe Bridge** *to place it onto an InDesign page.*

6 **The multiple image preview** *appears when you drag multiple items from Bridge into InDesign.*

Using Bridge to Place Artwork

Adobe Bridge not only lets you organize and view artwork, it also lets you drag graphics directly onto InDesign pages.

To place artwork from Bridge:

1. Position the Bridge and InDesign windows so that both are visible.

2. Select one or more files in the Bridge window.

3. Drag the file or files from Bridge onto the InDesign page **5**. The preview displays a single image if you have selected one file. The preview displays a multiple image if you have selected more than one item **6**.

4. Release the mouse button to place the item.

5. If you have dragged multiple files, click or drag to place the additional images.

TIP When Bridge is in the Compact Mode, you can choose Compact Window Always on Top from the Bridge panel menu to keep the Bridge window visible over the InDesign document window.

Using Bridge to Place Artwork

Specialty Frames

Frames don't have to be single items drawn from scratch. You can join frames into one compound shape or you can convert text into frames that can hold images. You can also bring paths from other programs into InDesign to act as frames.

You can make multiple frames act as a single item by converting them to a compound shape. Frames combined into a compound shape display a single image across all the items in the compound.

To create a compound shape:

1. Select the frames you want to combine into a compound shape.

TIP If the frames overlap, InDesign displays a transparent hole where they overlap.

2. Choose **Object > Paths >Make Compound Path**. If the frame is a graphic frame, the diagonal lines cross through all the frames in the compound **7** and **8**.

To add an image to a compound shape:

1. Use either Selection tool to select the compound shape.

2. Use any of the techniques described on the previous pages to place the image in the selected frame. The image tiles across the spaces between the elements of the compound shape **9**.

To split a compound shape:

1. Select the compound shape.

2. Choose **Object > Paths > Release Compound Path**. The image is shown only through the first frame; the rest of the compound frames are available to hold other images.

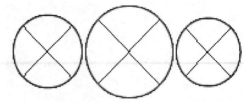

7 *Individual frames that act independently display diagonal lines within each object.*

8 *A* **compound shape displays the diagonal lines** *across the entire set of frames.*

9 *A* **placed image is seen across all the items** *in a compound shape.*

Frame

 Paths

10 *The* **Create Outlines command** *converts text into paths that can then be modified.*

11 *Text converted to paths can also hold imported graphics.*

You can also create unique frame shapes by converting text to frames so graphics assume the shapes of letters.

TIP If you can't draw for beans, you can convert the characters in dingbat or symbol fonts into graphic shapes such as hearts, arrows, snowflakes, and so on.

To convert text to frames:

1. Use the Selection tool to select the frame that contains the text.

   or

   Highlight the selected text within the frame.

2. Choose **Type > Create Outlines.** Each character of text is converted to paths that can be modified **10**.

TIP You can also place images into the converted text paths as you can with compound shapes **11**.

TIP The converted paths are created as compound paths. If you want to place different images or colors in each of the frames, release the compound shape first.

TIP If you select only a portion of the text within the frame, the highlighted text is converted to inline graphics within the frame.

Specialty Frames

If you work with a vector-drawing program such as Adobe Illustrator or FreeHand, you can also convert the paths in those programs to InDesign frames.

TIP In addition to Illustrator and FreeHand, this technique can be used with any other program that copies paths using the AICB (Adobe Illustrator Clipboard). Check your vector-drawing program manual for more information.

Specialty Frames

To import paths as frames:

1. Position the windows of the vector-drawing program and InDesign so they are both visible onscreen.

2. Select the paths in the vector-drawing program with the appropriate tool in that application.

3. Drag the paths from the vector-drawing program onto the window of the InDesign document.

4. When a black line appears around the perimeter of the InDesign window, release the mouse button. The paths are converted to InDesign unassigned frames 12.

TIP If you don't have the screen space to see both windows at once, you can also use the clipboard to copy the paths from the vector program and paste them into InDesign.

TIP Once the vector path has been converted to an InDesign frame, it can be used to hold an image or text 13.

12 *Artwork can be dragged from a vector program and converted into InDesign frames.*

13 *Graphics converted to frames can hold images or text.*

Dragging from Illustrator

If you want to import paths from Adobe Illustrator, you need to make sure that Illustrator's preferences are set correctly.

Choose File Handling And Clipboard in Illustrator's Preferences dialog box. Under the Clipboard section, check the AICB (no transparency setting) option. Then click the Preserve Paths button.

If this is not done, the Illustrator paths will not be converted to frames.

---

14 *The* **Image Import Options dialog box for** TIFF **and** JPEG **images.**

Best File Format from Adobe Illustrator?

If you work in Adobe Illustrator, you will notice that there are several file formats you can choose from when you save your work: native Illustrator, EPS, or Adobe PDF. Which one works best with InDesign?

All three file formats can be placed into InDesign documents. However, native Illustrator files have the best preview.

You may have old Illustrator documents that were saved as EPS files. There's no need to resave them. You can place them into InDesign too.

However, you may see a white background behind artwork that has been saved on a Macintosh as an EPS. If that is a problem, use the Rasterize the PostScript option during import to eliminate the white background.

Setting the Image Import Options

When you import a graphic, you can use the Image Import Options dialog box to control how that image is placed.

TIP The following chart shows which types of import options are applied to pixel images.

Import Options for Placed Images	
TIFF	Image Import Options with controls for Image and Color
JPEG	Image Import Options with controls for Image and Color
PSD	Image Import Options with controls for Image, Color, and Layers
EPS	EPS Import Options
Illustrator	PDF Import Options with controls for Layers
PDF	PDF Import Options with controls for Layers
InDesign	PDF Import Options with controls for Layers

To set the options for TIFF **and** JPEG **images:**

1. In the Place dialog box, check Import Options.

2. Choose a TIFF or JPEG image and click Open. This opens the Image Import Options dialog box for TIFF or JPEG images **14**.

3. Select the Image tab. If the image has a clipping path, you can choose Apply Photoshop Clipping path.

4. Select the Color tab. Use the controls to set the Color Management settings.

5. Click OK to place the image.

Setting the Image Import Options

To set the options for PSD images:

1. In the Place dialog box, check Show Import Options.

2. Choose a Photoshop image and click Open. This opens the Image Import Options dialog box for Photoshop files .

3. Choose Show Preview to see a preview of the file.

4. Select Image Settings. If the image has a clipping path, you can choose Apply Photoshop Clipping path.

5. Select the Color tab. Use the controls to set the Color Management settings.

6. Select Layers. If the images has layers or layer comps, you can choose which layers are visible in the InDesign layout.

7. Click OK to place the image.

To set the import options for EPS images:

1. In the Place dialog box, check Show Import Options.

2. Choose an EPS file. This opens the EPS Import Options dialog box .

3. Don't check Read Embedded OPI Image Links unless your service bureau has instructed you to have InDesign perform the image swapping.

4. If the image has a clipping path, you can choose Apply Photoshop Clipping Path.

5. Set the options in the Proxy Generation to control the preview of the image:

   • **Use TIFF or PICT Preview** uses the preview that was created with the file.

   • **Rasterize the PostScript** displays the actual PostScript data as a preview. This lets you see custom PostScript code such as is found in FreeHand.

6. Click OK to place the image.

15 The **Image Import Options** for Photoshop files.

16 The EPS **Import Options** dialog box *lets you control imported EPS files.*

Working with Photoshop Layer Comps

A layer comp is a snapshot of a state of the Layers panel. Layer comps record the visibility, position and appearance of the layers in a Photoshop file.

You create layer comps in Photoshop. The names of the layer comps are then available within InDesign.

Using layer comps makes it possible to have several variations of the same file within InDesign.

17 *The* **Place PDF dialog box** *lets you preview and control the options for PDF files.*

18 *The* **page selectors** *let you preview the pages of a multipage PDF.*

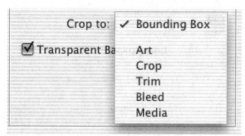

19 *The* **Crop To Menu** *in the Place PDF dialog box controls the size of the placed artwork.*

Transparency off   Transparency on

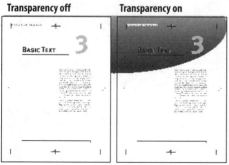

20 *The effect of the* **Transparent Background** *on a placed PDF image.*

InDesign also lets you place PDF files as graphics.

To set the options for PDF files:

1. In the Place dialog box, check Show Import Options.

2. Choose a PDF file. This opens the Place PDF dialog box **17**.

3. Choose Show Preview to see a preview of each page of the PDF.

4. Use the page selectors to select the page you want to place **18**. If you select multiple pages, use the following exercise to place the multiple pages.

5. Click the General tab to see those options.

6. Use the Crop To list to determine how the PDF should be cropped within the frame **19**. Choose the crop options:

   • **Bounding Box** crops to the active page elements, which includes printer marks.

   • **Art** crops to the area defined as placeable art.

   • **Crop** crops to only the printable area, not to the printer marks.

   • **Trim** crops to the area that is the final trim size.

   • **Bleed** crops to the area that is the total size of the image if a bleed area has been specified.

   • **Media** crops to the page size of the original document.

7. Choose Transparent Background to show only the elements of the page, without the opaque background **20**.

TIP If you choose Transparent Background, you can make it opaque by adding a fill color to the frame that contains the PDF.

8. Click the Layers tab to set the layers for the PDF.

9. Click OK to place the image.

PDF documents can contain more than one page. If you want, you can place those multiple pages all at once, without having to go back to the Place PDF dialog box.

To place multiple pages from a PDF:

1. In the Place PDF dialog box, choose one of the following:

   - **Previewed Page** selects whatever page is selected in the Preview area.

   - **All** selects all the pages in the document.

   - **Range** allows you to specify individual pages or a range of pages. Use commas to separate individual pages; use a hyphen to specify a range of pages.

2. Click OK to load the cursor.

TIP The cursor for a PDF displays a plus (+) sign when it is loaded with multiple pages .

3. Click as many times as necessary to load all the pages. When the plus sign disappears from the cursor, you have reached the last page to be placed.

21 *The* **plus sign (+) in the PDF cursor** *indicates that you can place multiple pages from the PDF.*

Placing Multiple PDF Pages from Bridge

Part of my job is not only to tell you what you *can* do in InDesign, but also to tell you what you *can't* do. Sadly, this sidebar is to tell you what you can't do when placing a PDF file from Adobe Bridge into InDesign.

When you select a PDF in Bridge, the Preview pane adds page controls that allow you to view the various pages in the PDF.

I would have sworn that the Adobe engineers would have designed the program so that whatever page was displayed in the Bridge Preview would automatically be the page placed when you dragged from Bridge onto an InDesign page.

Nope, it doesn't work that way. Even if you set the PDF import option to place a specific page, dragging from Bridge places only the first page of the PDF.

As much as I am a big fan of using Bridge in my workflow, this is an example of where Bridge is not as useful as working with the ordinary Place dialog box.

*Sidebar heading (rotated left margin):* Setting the Image Import Options

Frame and image   Image only   Frame only

22 *The* **display of the bounding boxes and points** *indicates what items are selected.*

23 *If you move an object quickly, you see only a bounding box as the item is being moved.*

24 *If you press and pause before you move, you see a preview of the image being moved.*

Working with Images Inside Frames

After you place an image, you may want to move or modify it. Which tool you use and where you click affects what will be selected.

To select and move both the frame and the image:

1. Use the Selection tool and click the frame holding the image. A bounding box appears that indicates that the frame and its content are selected **22**.

2. Press and drag the selection to move both the frame and the image.

TIP If you move quickly, you will see only a bounding box of the moved items **23**. If you press and pause for a moment, you will see a preview of the items being moved **24**.

To select the image within the frame:

1. Use the Direct Selection tool and click inside the frame where the image is visible. A bounding box for the image appears **22**.

TIP If the image is larger than the frame, this bounding box will appear outside the boundaries of the frame.

2. Press and drag the image to move it without disturbing the frame.

TIP As you press, the areas of the image that are outside the frame are displayed lighter than the area within the frame **24**.

To select and move just the frame:

1. Use the Direct Selection tool and click the edge of the frame. The points on the frame appear **22**.

2. Hold the Opt/Alt key and click the frame again to select all the points.

3. Release the Opt/Alt key and drag the frame to move it to reveal a new part of the image.

When you apply transformations to frames that contain placed images, you have a choice as to which objects — the frame, the image, or both — are transformed. Here are some helpful guides.

TIP If you pause before you drag with any of the transform tools, you will see a preview of the image as you transform it.

To transform both the frame and the placed image:

1. Use the Selection tool to select both the frame and the placed image.
2. Use any of the Transform panel fields or transform tools .

To modify the frame only:

1. Use the Direct Selection tool to select the frame that contains the image.
2. Use any of the Transform panel fields or transform tools to modify only the selected frame **26**.

To modify the placed graphic only:

1. Use the Direct Selection tool to select the artwork within the frame.
2. Use any of the Transform panel fields or transform tools to modify only the selected image **27**.

25 *To transform both the frame and its image use* the Selection tool to select the items.

26 *To transform just the frame that contains an image, use* the Direct Selection tool to select just the frame *and then transform the item.*

27 *To transform just the image within a frame, use the* Direct Selection tool to select just the image within a frame.

Using the Position Tool

The Position tool works like a combination of the Selection and Direct Selection tools. Originally created for PageMaker users who missed that feature when they switched to InDesign, the Position tool may be the solution for confused designers who don't know which tool to use for what purpose.

To use the Position tool:

1. Click the Position tool in the Tools panel **28**.

2. Use the Position tool with a graphic frame as follows:

   - Move the cursor over the edge of a frame to select the frame. A square next to the cursor indicates that the frame will be selected **29**.

   - Move the cursor over one of the bounding boxes of the frame. The double-headed arrow indicates that both the frame and the graphic can be resized **30**.

   - Move the cursor over the center point of the frame. The curved arrow indicates that you can move the frame and its contents **31**.

   - Move the cursor over the placed graphic within the frame. The Hand cursor indicates that the graphic may be repositioned inside the frame **32**.

   - Click the Hand cursor inside the frame. The bounding box for the placed graphic indicates that the graphic may be resized.

   - Move the cursor over the bounding box for the graphic. The double-headed arrow indicates that the graphic can be resized **33**.

TIP The Position tool does not allow you to reshape frames.

The **Position tool in the Tools panel** *works as a combination of the Selection and Direct Selection tools.*

29 *Place the* **Position tool over the edge of a frame** *to select the frame.*

30 *Place the* **Position tool over the bounding box** *to resize a frame and graphic.*

31 *Place the* **Position tool over the center point** *to move a frame.*

32 *Place the* **Position tool over the image** *to move the graphic inside a frame.*

33 *Place the* **Position tool over the bounding box** *for a graphic to resize the graphic.*

Fitting Graphics in Frames

Placed images don't always fit perfectly into preexisting frames. InDesign gives you several commands that let you quickly position and resize artwork in frames.

To resize the graphic to the frame size:

1. Use either selection tool to select the frame or the graphic inside the frame.

2. Choose **Object > Fitting > Fit Content to Frame.** This changes the size of the graphic to fit completely within the area of the frame .

TIP This command does not preserve the proportions of the artwork; the artwork may become distorted.

To proportionally resize to the frame size:

1. Use either selection tool to select the frame or the graphic inside the frame.

2. Choose **Object > Fitting > Fit Content Proportionally.** This changes the size of the graphic to fit completely, and without distortion, within the frame .

TIP Use the Fit Frame to Content command to resize the frame to the size of the graphic.

The Fit Content Proportionally command usually leaves some empty space between the graphic and the frame. What if you want to resize the image so that it fills the entire frame? That's where the Fill Frame Proportionally command comes to the rescue.

To resize the graphic to fill the frame:

1. Use either selection tool to select the frame or the graphic inside the frame.

2. Choose **Object > Fitting > Fill Frame Proportionally.** This changes the size of the graphic to fit completely, and without distortion, within the frame .

Before   **After**

34 *The effect of the* **Fit Content to Frame** *command.*

Before   **After**

35 *The effect of the* **Fit Content Proportionally** *command.*

| | **Fit Content Proportionally** | **Fill Frame Proportionally** |

Before

36 *The* **Fit Content Proportionally** *command may leave a gap between the frame and the image. The* **Fill Frame Proportionally** *command always fills the frame.*

"Why Does the Frame Say 100% Even Though I Resized the Image?"

Here's something that confuses my students. They import an image into a frame, and then choose Fit Content Proportionally to shrink the image.

When they look at the Control panel the frame size is listed at 100%. That seems impossible; how can the image which has just been shrunk down still be listed as 100%? The answer is that the *frame* may be listed as 100%, but if you select the *image* with the Direct Selection tool, you'll see the percentage that the image was scaled.

Before   **After**

37 *The effect of the* **Fit Frame to Content** *command.*

Before   **After**

38 *The effect of the* **Center Content** *command.*

Fit Content Proportionally
Fit Content to Frame   Fill Frame Proportionally
Fit Frame to Content   Center Content

39 *Use the* **Fit icons in the Control panel** *to modify placed images and frames.*

To resize the frame to the graphic size:

1. Use either selection tool to select the frame or the graphic inside the frame.

2. Choose **Object > Fitting > Fit Frame to Content.** This changes the size of the frame so that the artwork fits completely within the area of the frame **37**.

You can also resize a frame to the graphic size by clicking the frame handles.

To resize the frame by clicking the frame handles:

1. Use the Selection tool to select the frame.

2. Click the frame handles as follows:
   • Double-click a corner handle to resize both horizontally and vertically.
   • Double-click the left or right handles to resize either horizontally
   • Double-click the top or bottom handles to resize vertically.

TIP These techniques work on both images and text.

TIP These techniques work when the frame is either larger or smaller than the content.

Sometimes you just want to put a graphic in the center of a frame. This is especially helpful if an image has been transformed so it is no longer visible within the frame.

To center the graphic within the frame:

1. Use either selection tool to select the frame or the graphic inside the frame.

2. Choose **Object > Fitting > Center Content.** This centers the graphic within the frame without changing the size of either the graphic or the frame **38**.

TIP The Fitting commands are also available on the Control panel **39**.

Fitting Graphics in Frames

Many designers work with frames already in the layout to which they add images. What they want is their image to automatically be placed at the correct size — filling the frame, or scaled proportionally. InDesign lets you apply that setting to empty frames.

To apply the fitting commands to empty frames:

1. Select the frame.

2. Choose **Object > Fitting > Frame Fitting Options** to open the Frame Fitting Options dialog box .

3. Use the Crop Amount to specify how much area of the image should be outside the frame.

4. Set the Alignment Reference Point to choose how the image should be positioned when cropped or scaled.

5. Use the Fitting list to set how the image will be scaled when placed into an empty frame **41**.

   or

   Choose None to leave the image unscaled when placed.

40 *Use the* **Frame Fitting Options** *dialog box* *to set how images appear when placed into a frame.*

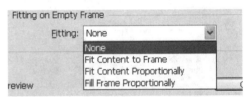

41 *The* **Fitting controls list** *lets you choose the Fitting options for how an image is scaled when placed in an empty frame.*

Fitting Graphics in Frames

Content offset on   **Absolute offset**

42 *Content offset positions the graphic relative to the frame. Absolute offset positions the graphic relative to the page.*

43 *The* **plus signs (+) next to the X and Y coordinates** *indicate that the position of the object is relative to the frame.*

In addition to the commands that position graphics, you can also position images numerically within frames using the X and Y coordinates in the Transform panel.

To numerically position graphics within frames:

1. Check Show Content Offset in the Transform panel menu.

2. Use the Direct Selection tool to select the graphic inside the frame.

3. Enter the X and Y coordinates in the Transform panel. The image moves to a new position relative to the frame **42**. This is called the *content offset*.

TIP Small plus signs (+) next to the X and Y coordinates in the Transform panel indicate that Show Content Offset is turned on **43**.

To numerically position graphics on the page:

1. Uncheck Show Content Offset from the Transform panel menu.

2. Use the Direct Selection tool to select the graphic inside the frame.

3. Set the X and Y coordinates in the Transform panel. The image moves to a new position relative to the page rulers. This is called the *absolute offset*.

Of course you can use any of the transformation commands to scale, rotate, and shear objects within the frame. This allows you to scale images numerically within a frame.

To transform images within a frame:

1. Use the Direct Selection tool to select the graphic inside the frame.

2. Use any of the Transform tools or the Transform panel.

Fitting Graphics in Frames

Nesting Graphic Elements

Once you have an image in a frame, you can then paste it into another frame. This technique is called *nesting elements* and it allows you much more flexibility in assembling various images than other programs.

TIP For instance, you can use nested elements to put a placed image inside a circular frame, and then put that circular frame inside a rectangular frame. The top rectangular frame crops the circular frame while the circular frame crops the placed image.

44 *Before nesting, the circular frame with the placed image is a separate object.*

To create a nested frame:

1. Use the Selection tool to select the element to be nested inside the frame **44**.

TIP A nested element can be a graphic or text frame.

2. Cut or copy the element to the clipboard.

3. Select the frame that is to hold the nested element.

4. Choose **Edit** > **Paste Into**. This pastes the element inside the frame **45**.

45 *After nesting, the circular frame is the content inside the rectangular frame.*

TIP The Selection tool moves all the elements in the nest.

TIP Frames can hold multiple levels of nested frames. So you can have a frame within a frame within a frame, and so on.

TIP Use the Fit Content commands to automatically position the nested frame inside the parent frame.

Nesting Graphic Elements

46 *The first click with the Selection tool selects the frame that holds the nested image.*

Select container   Select content

47 *You can also use the* **Select command icons** *in the Control panel.*

Once you have nested elements, you can select those elements using the Select commands. These commands make it very easy to select pasted-in elements and graphics.

To use the Select commands for nested elements:

1. Use the regular Selection tool to select the object. This selects the main container that holds the nested elements **46**.

2. Choose **Object > Select > Content**. This selects the item that was pasted into the main container. In the case of a nested element, this is the frame that holds the placed graphic.

TIP Use the Selection tool to move this object by dragging its center point.

3. You can choose **Object > Select > Content** again to select the placed graphic.

TIP If you have selected objects within the nested elements, you can choose **Object > Select > Container** to select upward through the nested elements.

TIP The Select commands are also available as icons on the Control panel **47**.

Nesting Graphic Elements

Styling Placed Images

Once you have placed a graphic within a frame, you can employ many techniques to style the frame or the image. For instance, you can change the color of the frame or the color of the image.

To color the frame fill or stroke:

1. Use the Selection tool to select the frame.
2. Click the Fill icon in the Tools panel or Color or Swatches panel.

   or

   Click the Stroke icon in the Tools panel or Color or Swatches panel.
3. Choose a color in the Swatches panel. If the Fill icon is chosen, you'll see the fill color wherever the image doesn't fill the frame **48**.

If you import a grayscale image, you can add color to it, so you change the black values in the image.

To color a grayscale image:

1. Use the Direct Selection tool to select the grayscale image.
2. Choose the Fill icon in the Color panel or Tools panel.

TIP The default fill color for grayscale images is black.

3. Change the tint value to lighten the image.

   or

   Choose a color in the Color or Swatches panel. The grayscale values change to a tint of the color chosen **49**.
4. Use the steps in the previous exercise to change the fill color of the frame. This colorizes the white areas of the image.

48 *When a frame is selected, choosing a fill color changes the background color of the frame.*

Original

Image color tinted

Image color tinted and frame darkened

49 *You can change the appearance of a grayscale image by changing the image color or the fill color of the frame.*

Colorizing Grayscale Images

Your service bureau may tell you not to colorize grayscale images. Or you may get a warning from a preflight program that checks your document before printing.

In theory there is nothing wrong with colorizing grayscale images, but individual production workflows may not be able to handle the images.

If you do get a warning, check with your print shop or service bureau to see whether or not it can handle them.

50 *The* **Links panel** *displays the names of the placed images in the document.*

Pasteboard

Comp

Missing link

Modified link

51 *The* **icons and page numbers next to a listing in the Links panel** *tell you the status of a placed image.*

Linking Graphics

When you place an image, you don't actually place the image into the document. You place a screen preview of the image that links to the original graphic. In order to print the file, InDesign needs to follow that *link* to the original graphic.

TIP It is possible to link text files as well as graphics, but those are primarily used together with InCopy.

To examine the links in a document:

1. Choose **Window > Links.** This opens the Links panel **50**. The Links panel shows all the linked images in the document with their page numbers. Special icons indicate the status of the image **51**.

   - **Missing Link** indicates that InDesign can't find the original graphic.

   - **Modified Link** indicates that the graphic has changed and has a different modification date from when it was originally placed.

2. Use the Links panel menu to sort the list of graphics as follows:

   - **Sort By Name** arranges the graphics in alphabetical order.

   - **Sort By Status** arranges the missing or modified graphics together.

   - **Sort By Page** arranges the graphics according to the page they are on.

   - **Sort By Type** arranges similar kinds of graphics together.

TIP You can also sort the images by choosing the context-sensitive menu over the name of the link in the panel.

Linking Graphics

The Missing or Modified Links notice appears when you open a file whose link is missing or has been changed .

To relink graphics when you open a document:

1. Click the Fix Links Automatically button in the Missing or Modified Links notice. All modified graphics are automatically updated.

2. If there are missing links, the operating system navigation dialog box opens. Use it to find each missing graphic.

You can use the Links panel to relink missing graphics to the screen preview.

To relink a missing graphic:

1. Select the missing link in the Links panel.

   TIP You can also select multiple links. Shift-click to select a range of links. Cmd/Ctrl-click to select noncontiguous links.

2. Click the Relink button. This opens the navigation dialog box, which you can use to find the missing file.

   or

   Choose Relink from the Links panel menu.

3. Navigate to find the missing file.

4. Check the Relink All Instances option to relink all instances of a missing graphic .

5. Check the Show Import Options to open the Import Options dialog box before you relink the graphic.

6. Click Open to relink the graphic.

*The **Missing or Modified Links notice** appears when you open a file that has a missing link to a text or graphics file.*

*Check the **Relink All Instances option** to update all instances of a missing image.*

Linking Graphics

54 *The* icon commands in the Links panel *allow you to access frequently used commands.*

Go to Link   Edit Original
Relink   Update Link

Links for Text Files

InDesign also has a preference that automatically creates a link for placed text files. With the preference turned on, if you modify the original text file that was placed in the InDesign document, you see a notice when you open the file that links are missing or modified.

It might seem like a good idea to use the Update Link command to update the text within the InDesign document. If you do, you will lose any formatting or changes you have applied within InDesign.

In most cases it is not necessary to keep the link for text files. You are probably better off embedding the text file within the document.

If you are working with InCopy or some other sort of workgroup software, you may not be able to embed text files within the document. In that case, check with your workgroup supervisor for the proper procedures.

If a graphic has been modified, you can use the controls at the bottom of the Links panel to update the link.

To update modified links:

1. Select the modified link in the Links panel.
2. Click the Update Link button **54**.

   or

   Choose Update Link from the Links panel menu.

TIP Shift-click to select a range of links. Cmd/Ctrl-click to select noncontiguous links.

The Links panel also lets you move quickly to a specific graphic.

To jump to a linked graphic in the document:

1. Select the link in the Links panel.
2. Click the Go to Link button **54**.

   or

   Choose Go to Link from the Links panel menu.

The Links panel can also be used to open and edit a graphic.

To edit a linked graphic:

1. Select the graphic you want to edit.
2. Choose Edit Original from the Links panel menu.

   or

   Click the Edit Original icon in the Links panel **54**. The graphic opens in the program that created it.

TIP You can also edit the graphic in its original program by holding the Opt/Alt key and double-clicking the graphic on the page.

Linking Graphics

You may want to find a placed image in the Macintosh Finder, Windows Explorer, or Bridge window.

To find the linked file:

1. Select the graphic in the Links panel.

2. Choose one of the following in the Links panel menu or the context-sensitive menu for the linked image:

   • **Reveal in Finder** (Mac) or **Reveal in Explorer** (Win) to select the file in the operating system directory.

   • **Reveal in Bridge** to select the file in the Bridge window.

The Link Information dialog box gives you information about an imported graphic.

To see the link information:

1. Select the graphic in the Links panel.

2. Choose Link Information from the Links panel menu. This opens the Link Information dialog box 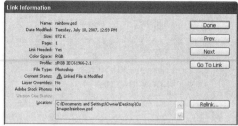.

3. Use the Go To Link button to move to and select the graphic within the InDesign layout.

4. If necessary, use the Relink button to find missing graphics.

5. Use the Next or Previous buttons to move to other graphics in the Links panel.

6. (Mac Only) Click the Spotlight button to see information used by the Macintosh Spotlight find command 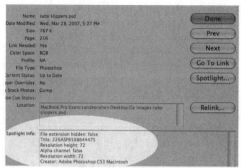.

7. Click the Done button when finished.

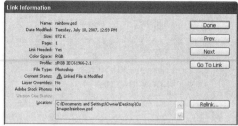

55 *The* **Link Information dialog box** *gives you information about a placed graphic.*

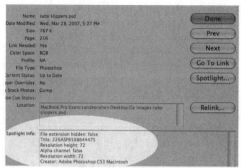

56 *The* **Macintosh Spotlight Info** *gives additional information about linked graphics.*

Linking Graphics

57 *The* **Embed icon in the Links panel** *indicates that all the information necessary to print the graphic is stored in the InDesign file.*

58 *The* **Unembed alert box** *lets you choose to link back to the original file or create a new file.*

When to Embed Graphics

You may be tempted to embed many, if not all, of your graphics within the InDesign document. After all, it makes it much easier to send a file to the service bureau if you don't have to remember to send the graphic files along with it.

Embedding graphics increases the size of the InDesign file. Just a few large graphics can make the InDesign file balloon in size. This means the file will take a long time to open or save.

You shouldn't have problems, though, if you embed small graphics, such as logos. Just remember that each time you embed a small graphic, it adds to the file size. Page after page of small graphics adds up.

My own feeling is to avoid embedding graphics. That way I don't have to worry about the file size. But I do have to remember to send the necessary files along to the printer.

Embedding Graphics

Usually, only the preview of a graphic is contained within an InDesign file. You can, however, embed a graphic within the InDesign file. This means that all the information necessary to print the file is contained within the InDesign document.

TIP Embedded graphics will increase the size of the InDesign file.

To embed placed images or text:

1. Select the placed image.

   or

   Select the frame that contains the imported text.

2. Choose Embed File from the Links panel menu. If you have selected a graphic, the Embed icon appears next to the file name in the Links panel **57**.

   or

   If you have selected text, the file name disappears from the Links panel.

TIP Embedded text files do not add to the size of the InDesign file.

TIP Once you embed a graphic, InDesign no longer needs to find the original file on your hard disk.

To unembed images:

1. Select the embedded image.

2. Choose Unembed File from the Links panel menu. The Unembed alert box appears **58**.

3. Click Yes to link the embedded graphic back to the original file that was placed into InDesign.

   or

   Click No. A dialog box appears asking you to choose the destination for a new file.

Setting Layer Visibility

When you import Photoshop, Illustrator, InDesign, and PDF files, you have the chance to set the visibility of the layers in those files. This makes it possible to import one file, but then use it with various combinations of the layers turned on or off.

To set the layer options as you import files:

1. Choose Show Import Options when you place a layered Photoshop, Illustrator, InDesign, or PDF file.

2. Click the Layers option in the Show Import Options dialog box 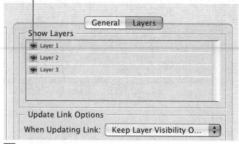.

3. Click the visibility icon for each layer to show or hide that layer.

4. If you have chosen a Photoshop file with layer comps, use the Layer Comp list to choose the layer comp that you want to apply to the image 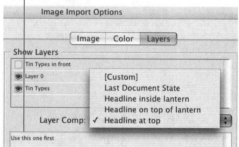.

TIP The layer comp description appears in the field under the Layer Comp list.

5. Select one of the following from the When Updating Link list:

   • **Use Photoshop's/PDF's Layer Visibility** resets any overrides you have made in InDesign to the settings of the original.

   • **Keep Layer Visibility Overrides** maintains any layer settings you have made in InDesign.

TIP A symbol appears in the Links panel if you have set the layers differently from the saved state of the file .

Once you have imported a layered file, you can change the visibility of the layers.

To edit the layer options of a placed file:

1. Select the placed image.

2. Choose **Object > Object Layer Options**.

3. Make whatever changes you want.

Show/Hide Layer Icons

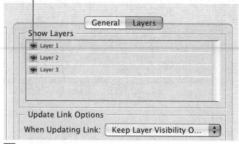

59 *The* **Layer controls** *of the* Place PDF dialog box.

Layer Comp description

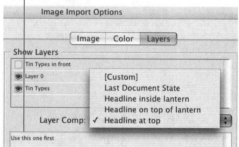

60 *The* **Layer Comp list of the Image Import Options** *for a Photoshop file.*

61 *The* **Eyeball icon in the Links panel** *indicates that the visibility of the layers is different from the saved state of the file.*

62 Photoshop's **Paths panel** *shows the paths saved with the file. Clipping paths are shown in outlined type.*

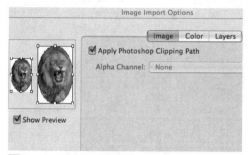

63 *InDesign's* **Image Import Options dialog box** *lets you choose to apply a clipping path to a file.*

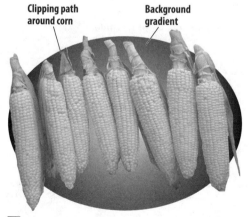

64 *An example of how a clipping path creates a transparent area around an image.*

Using Clipping Paths

Raster images saved as TIFF or EPS files are always rectangular. If you want to see only part of the image you import, you can create a *clipping path* that surrounds the part of the image that you want to see. The rest of the image becomes transparent. One way to create a clipping path is to use Adobe Photoshop to create paths for the file.

To import a file with a clipping path:

1. In Photoshop, use the Path tools to create a path around the image **62**.

TIP Although you will not see the clipping effect in Photoshop itself, the areas of the image inside the path will be visible in InDesign. The areas outside the path will be invisible.

2. Use Photoshop's Paths panel menu to designate the path as a clipping path.

3. Save the file as a TIFF, EPS, or Photoshop file.

TIP You can have many paths saved as part of a Photoshop file, but only one path can be designated as a clipping path.

4. In InDesign, choose **File > Place** and choose the file you have created.

5. In InDesign's Import Options dialog box, check Apply Photoshop Clipping Path **63**. The image is automatically clipped so that only the areas inside the path are visible in the layout **64**.

Once you have a clipping path applied to a graphic, you can change the shape of the path to hide or show more of the image.

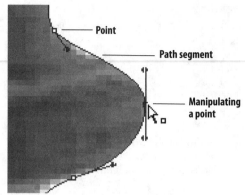

To modify the shape of a clipping path:

1. Use the Direct Selection tool to select the placed image. If the image has a clipping path, the path appears as a series of points and path segments **65**.

2. Use any of the path techniques to change the shape of the clipping path.

You can also turn a clipping path into a frame. This lets you apply a stroke to the path.

65 *Use the* **Direct Selection tool** *to manipulate the shape of a* **clipping path** *around an image.*

To convert a clipping path into a frame:

1. Use either selection tool to select the image with the clipping path.

2. Choose **Object > Clipping Path > Convert Clipping Path to Frame.** The clipping path is converted into an ordinary frame.

You don't have to designate a clipping path in Photoshop. InDesign lets you select any path saved with the image file as a clipping path.

To choose a path as an InDesign clipping path:

1. Select the placed image that includes a path.

2. Choose **Object > Clipping Path > Options.** The Clipping Path dialog box appears **66**.

3. Use the Type menu in the Clipping Path dialog box to select the Photoshop Path option **67**.

4. Use the Path menu to select which path should be used as a clipping path **68**.

5. Click the Preview button to see the effects of choosing a path.

6. Click OK to apply the path.

66 *The* **Clipping Path dialog box** *lets you create or modify a clipping path for a graphic.*

67 *Use the* **Clipping Path Type list** *to choose which type of clipping path to apply.*

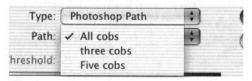

68 *Use* **the Path list** *to choose a specific path attached to a graphic.*

Using Clipping Paths

69 *The* **Clipping Path dialog box** *gives you controls for creating a clipping path based on the appearance of the image.*

What happens, though, if an image doesn't contain a clipping path? Fortunately, InDesign can create a clipping path from the edges — or the differences between the dark and light colors — of the image.

To create a clipping path from an image:

1. In the Clipping Path dialog box, choose Detect Edges from the Type menu **69**.

2. Adjust the Threshold slider to define the color that is used as the area outside the clipping path; **0** is pure white.

3. Adjust the Tolerance slider to allow a slight variation in the Threshold color. A high number for the tolerance often smooths out small bumps in the path.

You can also use an alpha channel saved with the file as a clipping path.

TIP Alpha channels are grayscale images that are saved along with the color or black channels of an image.

To choose an alpha channel as a clipping path:

1. Use the Type menu in the Clipping Path dialog box to select Alpha Channel.

2. Use the Alpha menu to select which channel should be used as a clipping path.

3. Because alpha channels can contain shades of gray, adjust the Threshold slider to define the color that is used as the area outside the clipping path; **0** is pure white.

4. Adjust the Tolerance slider to allow a slight variation in the Threshold color. A high number for the tolerance often smooths out small bumps in the path.

Using Clipping Paths

All clipping paths can be further modified by using the controls at the bottom of the Clipping Path dialog box.

To modify the effects of a clipping path:

1. Type a positive value in the Inset Frame field to shrink the entire path into the image.

   or

   Type a negative value to expand the path outside the image.

2. If necessary, check Invert to switch, which areas the path makes visible and which areas it leaves invisible.

3. Check Include Inside Edges to add areas to the clipping path that are enclosed by the foreground image .

4. Check Use High Resolution Image to create the path from the high-resolution version of the file rather than the preview. This is a slower but more accurate way of calculating the path.

5. Check Restrict to Frame to prevent the clipping path frame from displaying any part of the image that is outside the frame that holds the image.

To delete the clipping path around an image:

1. Select the placed image.

2. Choose **Object > Clipping Path > Options.** The Clipping Path dialog box appears.

3. Choose None from the Type pop-up list.

70 *The **Include Inside Edges in a clipping path** option creates transparent areas within the image such as the area inside the basket handles.*

The End of the Clipping Path?

Clipping paths are not suitable for all images. A clipping path acts like a knife that cuts out the background of an image. This is good if you need a really sharp edge on an image. However, soft, curly hair may need variations in transparency that a clipping path can't provide.

Fortunately, InDesign lets you use the transparency in Photoshop files to make parts of an image transparent.

71 A **transparent Photoshop file** *lets you see through the glass to the text behind the image.*

Importing Transparent Images

InDesign offers you a special advantage when you place native Photoshop (PSD) or Illustrator (AI) files. If there is any transparency in the placed image, InDesign displays the image with the same transparency as in the original file.

To use the transparency in a Photoshop file:

1. In Photoshop, use any of the Tools to silhouette or fade the edges of the image. The Photoshop transparency grid indicates which parts of the image are transparent.

2. Save the file as a Photoshop (PSD) file.

3. Choose **File > Place** to import the file into the InDesign document.

TIP The Image Import Options dialog box automatically sets the Alpha Channel import option to Transparency. You do not have to set the transparency option for native Photoshop files.

4. Click to place the file. The areas that were transparent in Photoshop will be transparent in InDesign **71**.

TIP You can combine the use of a Photoshop path together with transparency to create a silhouette with a see-through transparency.

To use the transparency in an Illustrator file:

1. In Illustrator, use any of the commands to apply transparency to the artwork.

2. Save the file as an Illustrator (AI) file.

3. Make sure that the PDF Compatibility option is checked in the Save dialog box.

4. Import the file into the InDesign document. The areas that were transparent in Illustrator will be transparent in InDesign.

In addition to importing Photoshop files with transparent layers, InDesign can also apply an alpha channel saved with flattened files. This allows you to display transparency in file formats that do not support layers or a transparency grid.

To apply an alpha channel to an image:

1. Add an alpha channel to the image in Photoshop. The alpha channel should be created as follows:

   - Black designates those areas that are not transparent.

   - White designates those areas that are completely transparent.

   - Shades of gray are used for those areas that are partially transparent.

2. Save the file as a TIFF, GIF, JPEG, or BMP file.

3. Choose **File** > **Place** to import the file into the InDesign document.

4. Use the Show Import Options checkbox to open the Image Import Options dialog box.

5. Choose the name of the alpha channel from the Alpha Channel menu and click OK to place the file 72.

6. If necessary, click to place the file on the page. The alpha channel is applied to the image to create opaque, transparent, and semi-transparent areas.

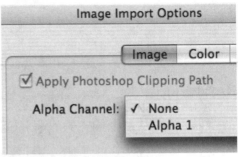

72 *Use the* **Alpha Channel menu in the Image Import Options** *to apply the channel to an image.*

73 The **Display Performance Preferences**
dialog box *controls how images and*
transparency effects are displayed.

74 The **Default View Settings list** *lets*
you choose which display performance
setup is applied to images.

75 *Check* **Preserve Object-level**
Display Settings *to let each*
object's settings override the overall
document display setting.

Viewing Images

When you have a large document with a lot
of images in it, you might find that the redraw
time is delayed as you move around. However, you can set preferences for how your
images are displayed by lowering some of the
image detail for increased speed as you move
through pages. These display settings can be
applied to the entire document or to individually selected objects.

TIP The display settings for images don't affect
how the document will print.

To set the default appearance of previews:

1. Choose **Edit > Preferences > Display**
   Performance (Win).

   or

   Choose **InDesign > Preferences > Display**
   Performance (Mac). This opens the
   Display Performance Preferences dialog
   box **73**.

2. Choose one of the three options from the
   Default View Settings menu **74**.

   • **Fast** is used when you want fast screen
     redraw and the best performance.

   • **Typical** is used when you want a better
     representation of the images.

   • **High Quality** is used when you want to
     see as much detail as possible onscreen.
     This option may cause InDesign to
     work slower than it will with the other
     choices.

TIP Each of the menu choices corresponds
to one choice in the Adjust View Settings
list.

3. Check Preserve Object-level Display
   Settings to use the display settings that
   have been applied to individual images **75**.

As you work, you can switch between the menu commands without having to open the Display Performance Preferences dialog box.

To switch the default view setting:

1. With no object selected, Right-click (Win) or Control-click (Mac). This opens a context-sensitive menu 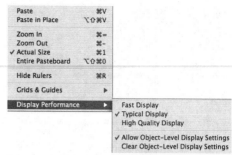.

2. Choose one of the view settings from the Display Performance submenu.

3. Choose Allow Object-Level Display Settings to override any individual image previews. This does not delete those individual settings, it only overrides them.

4. Choose Clear Object-Level Display Settings to delete any individual image previews.

TIP You can also use the View menu to choose the view settings or to override any individual image previews.

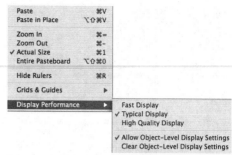

76 *The* **Display Performance context-sensitive menu** *lets you switch from one display performance setup to another.*

You can also set each individual image to its own display setting. This lets you set one large image to faster screen redraw while showing more detail in other objects.

To set individual image previews:

1. Select the image.

2. Right-click (Win) or Control-click (Mac). This opens the context-sensitive menu for the display of that object .

3. Choose one of the options from the Display Performance submenu of the context-sensitive menu.

TIP The Use View Setting command sets the object back to the current View Setting in the Display Performance Preferences.

TIP You can also use the **Object > Display Performance** submenu to choose the view settings for a selected object.

77 *The* **Display Performance context-sensitive menu** *for an object.*

78 The **Adjust View Settings menu** *gives you three display settings to apply to a document or individual images.*

79 The **Raster Images and Vector Graphics sliders** *let you control how those formats are displayed.*

80 *An example of the* **Gray Out view setting.**

Proxy display   **High Resolution display**

81 *The difference between the Proxy setting and the High Resolution setting.*

The labels Fast, Typical, and High Quality are merely guides. You can customize the specific displays for raster images, vector art, and transparency effects in the Adjust View Settings area of the Display Performance Preferences.

To set the raster and vector displays:

1. Choose **Edit** > **Preferences** > **Display Performance** (Win).

   or

   Choose **InDesign** > **Preferences** > **Display Performance** (Mac).

2. Choose one of the options in the Adjust View Settings menu **78**.

3. Drag the slider for the Raster Images or Vector Graphics as follows **79**:

   - **Gray Out** (far left) displays a gray background instead of the image **80**. This is the fastest performance.

   - **Proxy** (middle) displays a 72-ppi screen preview of the image **80**. This setting provides the best performance that still shows what the image looks like.

   - **High Resolution** (far right) displays the maximum resolution for the image **81**.

4. Repeat the process for each of the other menu settings.

TIP Raster Images and Vector Graphics settings don't have to be set for the same resolution. This allows you to have a faster redraw for large raster files, and more details in the lines of vector graphics.

Viewing Images

You can also adjust the display for the transparency effects as well as the drop shadows and feather effects.

To set the transparency effects displays:

1. Choose one of the listings in the Adjust View Settings menu.

2. Drag the Transparency slider to each notch setting as follows 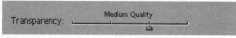 (The labels appear as you drag the slider.)

   - **Off** (far left) displays no transparency effects. This is the fastest performance.

   - **Low Quality** (second from left) displays basic opacity and blend modes. Drop shadows and feathers are displayed in low resolution only. Some blend modes may change in the final output.

   - **Medium Quality** (second from right) displays drop shadows and feathers in low resolution.

   - **High Quality** (far right) displays high resolution drop shadows and feathers. Blend modes appear in their correct CMYK color display.

3. Repeat the process for each of the other Adjust View menu items.

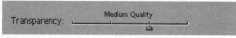

82 *The* **Transparency slider** *lets you control the display of drop shadows, feathers, and transparency effects. The setting labels appear as you move the slider.*

Viewing Images

TEXT EFFECTS

Go back and look at the newspaper magazine advertisements created in the 1800s. (Yes, that was *way before* I worked in advertising.) In those ads, the text marches along in a straight line without swerving toward or moving around the images.

Back then, it was extremely difficult to wrap text around an image. Each line of text had to be cut and pasted around the edges of an image.

The paste-up artists never dreamed of setting text along a path so that it follows the shape of a rollercoaster — that would have been far too much work!

Adding short horizontal rules to divide paragraphs was another tedious task. In fact, if you look closely at some old advertisements, you can see that the rule isn't perfectly centered in the column.

Fortunately, electronic page-layout programs such as InDesign make it easy to do all these special text effects with incredible precision.

...te effects to apply to text is
...ow around images and other
...s. This is called *text wrap* in InDesign,
a text runaround in some other programs.
(InDesign doesn't give you the runaround.)

To apply a text wrap:

1. Select the object that you want the text
   to wrap around. This can be an imported
   graphic, a text frame, or an unassigned
   frame.

2. Choose **Window > Text Wrap**. This opens
   the Text Wrap panel .

3. Choose one of the following options for
   how the text should flow around the
   object . *(Options shown in the chart on
   the following page.)*

   - **No wrap** lets the text flow across the
     object.

   - **Bounding Box** flows the text around
     the bounding box for the object.

   - **Object Shape** flows the text around the
     shape of the frame or the shape of the
     placed graphic.

   - **Jump Object** flows the text to the next
     available space under the object.

   - **Jump to Next Column** flows the text to
     the next column or text frame.

4. Check Invert to force the text to flow
   inside the object .

5. Enter an amount in the offset fields to
   control the distance between the text and
   the object .

TIP Click the Make All Settings the Same icon
(chain) so that all the offsets are equal.

TIP The number of available offset fields
depends on the type of text wrap you
choose.

1 The **Text Wrap panel** *controls the settings
for how text flows around an object.*

2 The **five different text wrap
buttons** *let you choose how the
text wraps around objects.*

3 When the **Invert command** *is turned
on, the text wrap causes the text to
flow inside, not outside, an object.*

4 Use the **text wrap Offset controls** *to set
the distance between text and a graphic.*

Wrapping Text

Wrap Chosen	Offset Available	Results
No Wrap	No offset options available.	There were only four witches in all the Land of Oz, and two of them, those who live in the North and the South, are witches. I know this is for I am one of them myself, and cannot be mistaken.
Bounding Box	Top, bottom, left, and right offset options available.	There were only four witches in all the Land of Oz, and two of them, those who live in the North and the South, are good witch- es. I know this is true, for I am one of them myself, and cannot be mistaken.
Object Shape	Top offset option is the only one available. The amount is used as the space around the entire graphic.	There were only four witches in all the Land of Oz, and two of them, those who live in the North and the South, are good witches. I know this is true, for I am one of them myself, and can- not be mistaken.
Jump Object	Top, bottom, left, and right offset options available. How-ever, only the top and bottom offsets affect the text.	There were only four witches in all the Land of Oz, and two of them, those who live in the
Jump to Next Column	Top, bottom, left, and right offset options available. How-ever, only the top offset affects the text.	There were only four witches

Wrapping Text

TIP Unless you change the preference setting, lines that wrap below the text wrap object skip to the next available leading increment below the object.

When you choose Object Shape for the text wrap, InDesign lets you set how the text wraps as well as the contour options for that shape.

To set the text wrap contour options:

1. Use the Direct Selection tool to select the image.

2. Click the Object Shape text wrap button in the Text Wrap panel.

3. Choose Show Options from the Text Wrap panel menu to display the Contour Options at the bottom of the Text Wrap panel.

4. Use the Contour Options Type menu to choose the type of element that should be used to create the text wrap 5:

   - **Bounding Box** uses the rectangle that contains the image.

   - **Detect Edges** uses the differences between the pixels of the image and its background.

   - **Alpha Channel** lets you choose an embedded alpha channel.

   - **Photoshop Path** lets you choose an embedded path.

   - **Graphic Frame** uses the shape of the frame that contains the image.

   - **Same As Clipping** uses whatever shape has been designated as the clipping path for the image.

5. If you choose Alpha Channel or Photoshop Path, use the second pop-up menu to choose a specific channel or path.

6. Check Include Inside Edges to make the text wrap inside any holes in the image, path, or alpha channel 6.

5 *The* **Contour Options Type menu** *lets you choose what type of element controls the shape of the text wrap.*

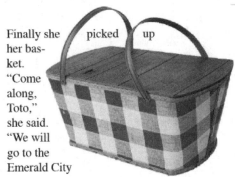

Finally she picked up her basket. "Come along, Toto," she said. "We will go to the Emerald City

6 *Use the* **Include Inside Edges** *option to have text wrap within the edges of the image, such as within the handles of the basket.*

Wrapping Text

7 *The* **Wrap To menu** *lets you choose the orientation for text wraps around objects.*

IN THE BOOKS, THE ORIGINS OF THE
CHARACTER ARE RATHER GRUESOME.
ORIGINALLY AN ORDINARY MAN BY
THE NAME OF NICK CHOPPER, THE TIN
WOODMAN USED TO MAKE HIS LIVING
CHOPPING DOWN TREES IN THE FOR-
ESTS OF OZ. THE WICKED WITCH
OF THE EAST ENCHANTED HIS AXE
TO PREVENT HIM FROM MARRY-
ING THE GIRL THAT HE LOVED.

8 *The Wrap To option set to wrap the text on both sides of the object.*

IN THE BOOKS, THE ORIGINS OF THE CHARAC-
TER ARE RATHER GRUESOME. ORIGINALLY AN
ORDINARY MAN BY THE
NAME OF NICK CHOP-
PER, THE TIN WOOD-
MAN USED TO MAKE
HIS LIVING CHOPPING
DOWN TREES IN
THE FORESTS
OF OZ. THE

9 *The Wrap To option set to wrap the text on whichever side has the largest area.*

Just as you can set the alignment for a paragraph, you can also set how text wraps to the object.

To set the wrap to options for a text wrap:

1. Use the Direct Selection tool to select the image.

2. Click the Object Shape text wrap button in the Text Wrap panel.

3. Choose Show Options from the Text Wrap panel menu to display the Wrap Options in the Text Wrap panel.

4. Use the Wrap To menu to choose the orientation for the text wrap **7**:

   - **Right Side** wraps only around the right side of the object.

   - **Left Side** wraps only around the left side of the object.

   - **Both Left & Right Sides** wraps to both sides of the object **8**.

   - **Side Towards Spine** wraps to either the left or right side of the object depending which side of a facing page document the object is on.

   - **Side Away From Spine** does the opposite of the above.

   - **Largest Area** wraps only on the side that has the most area. This may cause the text to flip from left to right **9**.

A text wrap doesn't have to be around visible objects. You can use an object with no fill or stroke as the shape to wrap text around . This creates a special effect for text around an image.

To wrap text around an invisible object:

1. Draw an object with no fill or stroke.

2. Set the Text Wrap to Object Shape.

Once you set a text wrap, you can still manipulate it so that the text reads more legibly or fits more attractively into the contour of the object. This is called a *custom text wrap.*

To create a custom text wrap:

1. Use either selection tool to select the object that has the text wrap applied to it.

TIP Apply the Object Shape text set for Graphics Frame to create a simple text wrap without a lot of points.

2. Use the Direct Selection tool to move the points on the text wrap path .

TIP You can preview how the text reflows around the text wrap. Press and hold for a moment before you move the point of the text wrap. You can then see the text reflow as you move the point.

3. Click the Pen tool between points on the text wrap path to add a new point to the path .

4. Click the Pen tool on a point on the text wrap path to delete the point from the path .

TIP Hold the Cmd/Ctrl key to access the Direct Selection tool while using the Pen tool.

10 *An example of how an invisible object can be used to create a text wrap.*

11 *Use the Direct Selection tool to change the shape of a text wrap path.*

12 *The plus sign next to the Pen tool indicates that you can add a point to the text wrap path.*

13 *Position the Pen tool over a point and click to delete points from a text wrap path.*

Wrapping Text

Text frame that ignores the text wrap   **Text frame that follows the text wrap**

There was no garret at all, and no cellar --- except a small hole dug in the ground, called a cyclone cellar, where the family could go in case one

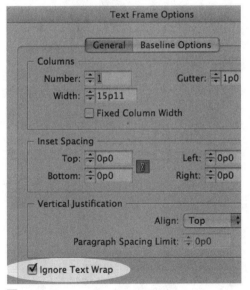

14 *An example of how* **Ignore Text Wrap** *keeps the map title from being affected by the text wrap applied to the outline of the state.*

15 *The* **Ignore Text Wrap checkbox** *in the Text Frame Options dialog box prevents text from being affected by any text wrap settings.*

You may find that you don't want some text to be affected by a text wrap. For instance, you might want to have the body text in one frame run around an image but have the text label in another frame appear over the image **14**. That's when you need to direct the text frame to ignore a nearby text wrap.

To ignore the text wrap:

1. Select the text frame that contains the text that you don't want affected by the text wrap command.

2. Choose **Object > Text Frame Options.** This opens the Text Frame Options dialog box **15**.

3. Check Ignore Text Wrap. The text in that frame is unaffected by any objects that have a text wrap applied.

TIP Text wrap is applied even if the object that has the wrap is on a hidden layer. Use the Layer Options dialog box to change this so that hidden layers do not exert a text wrap.

Master pages *(covered in Chapter 10, "Pages and Books")* allow you to place an object on many pages at once. You can set the text wrap for an object so that it is only applied on the master page, not any document pages.

To set the text wrap for an object on a master page:

1. Place the object on a master page.

2. Choose Apply to Master Page Only from the Text Wrap panel menu. (This command is only available for objects on a master page.)

Wrapping Text

Text on a Path

When you create an object such as a text frame, the outside shape of the frame is considered the object's path. Not only can InDesign fit text inside a text frame, it also lets you position text so that it runs along the outside of the frame.

To run text on the outside of a path:

1. Choose the Path Type tool in the Tools panel .

2. Move the tool so that it is near the path. A small plus sign appears next to the tool cursor **17**.

3. Click with the Path Type tool. A blinking insertion point appears on the path.

4. Type the text. Use any of the text controls to select or modify the text.

TIP Use the Direct Selection tool to select the path and change its fill or stroke to None to make the path invisible.

Once you apply text to a path, you can drag to position the text.

To position text on a path:

◆ Drag the indicator at the start or end of the text on a path to change the start or end point of the text **18**.

   or

   Drag the small indicator within the text to change the center point of the text **19**.

TIP You can also drag the center point indicator to the other side of the path.

TIP You can use the Paragraph panel to change the alignment of the text between the start and end indicators.

16 *The* **Path Type tool** *in the Tools panel is used to add text to a path.*

17 *The plus sign next to the Path Type cursor indicates you can click to add text to a path.*

18 *Drag the indicator line to move the text along a path.*

19 *The* **center point indicator** *allows you to move text or flip it from one side of the path to another.*

The **Path Type Options dialog box** *allows you to control how text is applied to a path.*

The **Effect menu** *controls the appearance of the text on the path.*

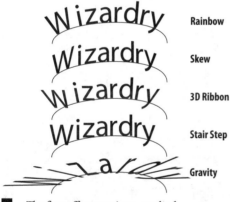

Rainbow

Skew

3D Ribbon

Stair Step

Gravity

The **five effect settings** *applied to text on a path.*

To apply effects to text on a path:

1. Choose **Type** > **Type on a Path** > **Options**. This opens the Path Type Options dialog box .

2. Use the Effect menu to control how the text is positioned in relationship to the path .

   - **Rainbow** positions the text in an arc along any curves in the path.

   - **Skew** distorts the text vertically as it is positioned along curves in the path.

   - **3D Ribbon** distorts the text horizontally as it is positioned along curves in the path.

   - **Stair Step** aligns the individual baselines of each letter so that the text stays vertical as it is positioned along curves in the path.

   - **Gravity** uses the shape of the path to distort the text as it is positioned along curves in the path.

3. Click the Flip checkbox to position the text on the other side of the path.

4. If the spacing of the text is uneven, use the spacing control to tighten the character spacing around sharp turns and acute angles on the path.

TIP Higher values remove more space from between the characters.

Text on a Path

You can also control where the letters are positioned vertically on the path.

To set the vertical alignment of text on a path:

1. Use the Align menu to control how the text is positioned in relationship to the path .

   - **Ascender** positions the text so that the tops of the tallest letters touch the path.

   - **Descender** positions the text so that the bottoms of the lowest letters touch the path.

   - **Center** positions the text so that the middle of the text touches the path.

   - **Baseline** positions the text so that the baseline of the text touches the path.

2. Use the To Path menu to position the vertical alignment in one of the following positions:

   - **Top** positions the text relative to the top of the path's stroke weight.

   - **Center** positions the text in the middle of the path's stroke weight.

   - **Bottom** positions the text relative to the bottom of the stroke weight.

TIP If you do not see any changes between the To Path settings, try increasing the thickness of the stroke weight.

TIP You can also use the Baseline Shift controls to move the text up or down relative to the path.

The **Align menu** controls how the text is positioned in relationship to the path.

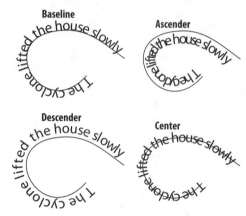

The **Align choices** applied to text on a path.

The **To Path menu** positions the vertical alignment of the text on the path.

The effect of the To Path settings on the **position of text on a stroked path.**

Text on a Path

27 *The* **Paragraph Rules dialog box** *controls the settings for paragraph lines.*

28 *Choose* **Rule Above or Rule Below** *to position the line above or below a paragraph.*

Why Use Paragraph Rules?

If you want a line (technically called a *rule*) to appear above or below a paragraph, you might draw a line using the Pen or the Line tool. Unfortunately, if the text reflows, that line does not travel with the text. You could also paste the line into the text as an inline graphic, but you would not have much control over that line.

The proper way to create lines above or below paragraphs is to use the Paragraph Rules commands. Because the rules are applied as part of the paragraph settings, they automatically move if the paragraph moves. In addition, they can be precisely positioned in relationship to the paragraph.

Working with Paragraph Rules

The correct way to create a line above or below a paragraph is with paragraph rules. These are lines that travel with the paragraph and that can be applied as part of style sheets.

To apply paragraph rules:

1. Select the paragraph to which you want to apply the rule and choose Paragraph Rules from the Paragraph panel menu. This opens the Paragraph Rules dialog box **27**.

2. Choose Rule Above or Rule Below to specify whether the rule appears before or after the selected paragraph **28**.

3. Check Rule On to activate the rule.

TIP If you want rules both above and below the paragraph, repeat steps 2 and 3.

Working with Paragraph Rules

Once you have turned on the rule, you can style its appearance. This is somewhat similar to styling the stroke for an object.

To style the appearance of a rule:

1. Set an amount for the weight (or thickness) of the rule .

2. Use the Type list to set a stroke style .

3. Use the Color list to apply one of the pre-defined swatch colors or gradients .

TIP The Text Color setting sets the rule to the same color as the text.

4. If desired, check Overprint Stroke to set the ink to overprint.

5. Use the Tint controls to create a shade of the color .

6. If you have chosen a rule style that has a gap, use the Gap Color list to apply a color or gradient swatch to the gap 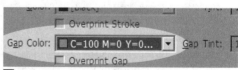.

7. If you have chosen a gap color, use the Gap Tint controls to create a shade of the gap color .

8. If desired, check Overprint Gap Color to set the gap ink to overprint.

If a paragraph rule falls at the top of a paragraph, you may want to control whether the rule is displayed inside or outside the frame.

To control the position of the rule within a frame:

1. Select the paragraph with the rule.

2. Open the Paragraph Rules dialog box.

3. Check Keep in Frame.

29 Use the **Weight control** to define the thickness of the paragraph rule.

30 Use the **Type list** to choose the stroke style for the paragraph rule.

31 Use the **Color list** to choose the main color for the paragraph rule.

32 Use the **Tint control** to set the screen for the color of the paragraph rule.

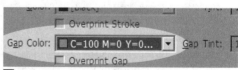

33 Use the **Gap Color list** to set the secondary color of the paragraph rule.

34 Use the **Gap Tint control** to set the screen for the gap color of the paragraph rule.

35 *The Width list lets you choose the length of paragraph rules.*

"From the Land of Oz," said Dorothy gravely. "And here is Toto, too. And oh, Aunt Em! I'm so glad to be at home again! **Column**

"From the Land of Oz," said Dorothy gravely. "And here is Toto, too. And oh, Aunt Em! I'm so glad to be at home again! **Text**

36 *Column width fits the rule to the width of the column. Text width fits the rule to the neighboring text.*

37 *The Left Indent and Right Indent fields let you modify the length of a rule.*

"From the Land of Oz," said Dorothy gravely. "And here is Toto, too. And oh, Aunt Em! I'm so glad to be at home again! **No indent**

"From the Land of Oz," said Dorothy gravely. "And here is Toto, too. And oh, Aunt Em! I'm so glad to be at home again! **Left and right indents**

38 *How changing the Left and Right Indent settings changes the look of rules.*

"From the Land of Oz," said Dorothy gravely. "And here is Toto, too. And oh, Aunt Em! I'm so glad to be at home again! **No offset**

"From the Land of Oz," said Dorothy gravely. "And here is Toto, too. And oh, Aunt Em! I'm so glad to be at home again! **0p8 offset**

39 *Change the Offset amount to move a rule up or down relative to the text.*

The length of a rule (called its width) can be set to cover the width of the column or the width of the text. The rule can also be set to be indented from the column or text margins.

To control the width of a rule:

1. Choose from the Width list in the Paragraph Rules dialog box as follows **35**:

   - **Column** creates a rule that is the same width as the column that holds the text **36**.

   - **Text** creates a rule that is the same width as the closest line of text **36**.

   TIP If you set a rule below a paragraph that ends in a short line, the rule will be the same length as the last line.

2. Set the Left Indent to the amount that the rule should be indented from the left side of the column or text **37**.

3. Set the Right Indent to the amount that the rule should be indented from the right side of the column or text **37**.

   TIP Use positive numbers to move the rule in from the margin **38**. Use negative numbers to move the rule outside the margin. The rule can extend outside the text frame.

By default the paragraph rule is positioned on the baseline of the text. You can control the position above or below the baseline **39**. This is called the *offset* of the rule.

To control the offset of a rule:

◆ In the Paragraph Rules dialog box, enter a value in the Offset field.

   - For a Rule Above, positive numbers raise the rule above the baseline.

   - For a Rule Below, positive numbers lower the rule below the baseline.

   TIP Negative numbers move rules in the opposite direction.

Working with Paragraph Rules

You can create many special effects with paragraph rules. One of the most common is to superimpose text inside paragraph rules to create the effect of reversed text. Most reversed text is white type inside a black background. However, any light color can be used inside any dark background .

TIP Don't forget that you can also use the underline or strikethough styles to create reversed text.

To reverse text using rules:

1. Apply a light color to a line of type.

2. Open the Paragraph Rules dialog box.

3. Create a Rule Below.

4. Set the weight of the rule to a point size large enough to enclose the text. For instance, if the text is 12 points, the rule should be at least 12 points.

TIP If you have more than one line of text, you need to calculate the size of the leading times the number of lines.

5. Set a negative number for the offset value.

TIP The offset amount should be slightly less than the weight of the rule. For instance a rule of 14 points might take an offset of minus 11 points.

6. Check Preview so you can see the effect of the weight and offset settings you choose.

7. Adjust the weight and offset, if necessary.

8. Click OK to apply the rule **41**.

The Guardian of the Gate

It was some time before the Cowardly Lion awakened, for he had lain among the poppies a long while.

40 *A paragraph rule can create the effect of reversed text.*

41 *A dialog box showing the sample settings for a paragraph rule that create the effect of reversed text.*

True Story

When I first started learning page layout software, I used the art director's computer at the advertising agency where I worked. I stayed after hours to explore the programs and create my own documents.

When I saw the command "Rules" in the menu, I figured that was where they kept the laws governing the program. Since I didn't want to mess up the art director's machine, I never chose the command.

It was several years later (and several horrible jobs without any paragraph rules) that I discovered what the "Rules" were.

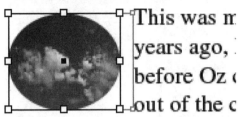

who walked in the forest

This was m

years ago,

before Oz o

out of the c

to rule over this land.

"There lived here then,

42 *An* **inline object** *flows along with the text.*

Inline and Anchored Objects

Another type of nested element is called an *inline object*. An inline object is a frame that is pasted as a character into the actual text.

TIP An inline object can also be used to add images to a table.

To create an inline object:

1. Select the element that you want positioned.

2. Cut or copy the element to the clipboard.

3. Click to place an insertion point where you want the inline object to be positioned.

4. Choose **Edit > Paste**. The element is pasted into the text and flows along with any changes to the text **42**.

TIP Use the Direct Selection tool to move the graphic within its inline frame.

TIP Use the Selection tool to select and move inline objects up or down inside the text.

TIP Use any of the Text Wrap commands to force text around the inline object.

You can also place an image directly into the text as an inline object.

To import an image directly as an inline object:

1. Place your insertion point where you would like the graphic to appear.

2. Choose **File > Place** and select the image you want to import. The image appears inside an inline frame.

Uses for Inline Objects

The biggest problem with inline objects is that most people forget they are available.

Have you ever wanted to use a little picture instead of a plain bullet? Inline graphics make it easy to add the picture so it flows along with the text.

You can also use an inline object to keep a picture of an author along with her biography.

Inline objects don't have to be graphic elements. You can insert an inline text frame to create two columns of text within a single column story.

Finally, you can paste a horizontal line as an inline graphic to make the fill-in-the-blank lines in a coupon.

Inline and Anchored Objects

In addition to inline objects, InDesign also allows you to insert anchored objects into text flow. Anchored objects require a little more preparation but are much more powerful than inline objects.

To create an anchored object:

1. Place the insertion point in the text where you want to anchor the object.

TIP This does not have to be the exact position where you want the anchored object to appear.

2. Choose **Object > Anchored Object > Insert**. The Anchored Object dialog box appears **43**.

3. Set each of the options for the Anchored Object as described in the following exercises.

4. Click OK to insert the anchored object into the story. An anchored object hidden character symbol appears in the text.

To set the Object Options for an anchored object:

1. Use the Content list to choose the type of object to be anchored. These are the same as the **Object > Content** options **44**.

2. Use the Object Style list to choose a graphic style for the object. *(See Chapter 15, "Text and Object Styles," for more information on graphic styles.)*

3. If you select Text as the content, use the Paragraph Style list to choose the style for the text.

4. Use the Height and Width controls to set the size of the anchored object.

TIP Anchored objects are always defined as rectangles by default. You can use any of the drawing tools or the Convert Shape commands to change the rectangle to other shapes.

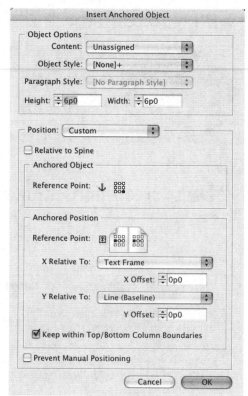

43 *The* **Insert Anchored Object** dialog box *lets you control the options for an anchored object.*

44 *The* **Content list** *lets you choose the type of anchored object.*

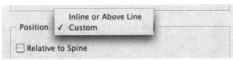

45 *The* **Position list** *lets you choose the location for anchored objects.*

46 *The Position options for* **Inline or Above Line** *anchored objects.*

I divide anchored objects into two different types based on their position on the page.

To set the Position for the anchored object:

◆ Use the Position list to choose the type of positioning for the anchored object **45**:

 - **Inline or Above Line** positions the anchored object within the text frame.

 - **Custom** allows you to position the anchored object outside the text frame.

Once you have chosen the positioning for the anchored object, you can set the options for the location of the anchored object **46**.

To set the options for inline objects:

1. Click the Inline radio button to specify that option for the object. This removes all the options except the Y Offset.

2. Use the Y Offset controls to move the object above or below the baseline of the text.

TIP Positive numbers move the object above the baseline. Negative numbers move the object below the baseline.

Inline and Anchored Objects

To set the options for Above Line objects:

1. Click the Above Line radio button to position the object above the line that contains the anchor insertion point .

2. Use the Alignment list to position the object in the text frame as follows 48:

   - **Right** aligns the object on the right.

   - **Left** aligns the object on the left.

   - **Center** aligns the object in the center.

   - **Text Alignment** uses whatever alignment was set for the paragraph that contains the anchored object.

3. If you have a facing-page document, you have two additional options. These options flip the anchored object if it is a left- or right-hand page.

   - **Towards Spine** positions the object so that it is closest to the spine.

   - **Away From Spine** positions the object so that it is furthest away from the spine.

4. Use the Space Before or Space After control to add space above or below the object.

5. Check the Prevent Manual Positioning option to stop the object from being moved with any of the selection tools.

Anchored object indicator in the text

47 *An* **Above Line** *anchored object inside a text frame.*

48 *The* **Alignment list** *for Above Line anchored objects.*

Inline and Anchored Objects

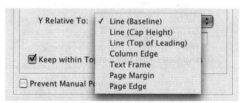

49 *The* **Custom Anchored Objects dialog box.**

50 *The* **X Relative To list** *for custom anchored objects.*

51 *The* **Y Relative To list** *for custom anchored objects.*

52 *The* **indicator for custom anchored objects.**

The other type of anchored object is the custom object. This option offers the most choices for positioning the anchored object.

TIP I find the Custom Anchored Objects dialog box baffling **49**. The only way I can apply the settings is to first insert the anchored object and then close the dialog box. Next, with the anchored object still selected, I choose **Object > Anchored Object > Options**. This opens the Options dialog box that has a Preview that lets me see what the settings are doing.

To set the options for custom objects:

1. Use the Anchored Object Reference Point proxy box to choose which point on the anchored object should be used as the orientation of the anchored object.

2. If the document has facing pages, you can choose Relative to Spine to allow the settings to flip depending on whether they are left- or right-hand pages.

3. Click the Anchored Position Reference Point to choose the position on the page where the object should align.

4. Use the X Relative To list to set the point from which the horizontal axis should start **50**.

5. Use the Y Relative To list to set the point from which the vertical axis should start **51**.

6. Use the X Offset and Y Offset controls to move the anchored object from the X and Y reference points.

7. Select Keep Within Top/Bottom Column Boundaries to insure that the anchored object does not move above or below the frame that contains the text.

8. Select Prevent Manual Positioning to prevent the object from being moved.

TIP Custom anchored objects are indicated on the page by a little anchor *(cute!)* **52**.

Inline and Anchored Objects

As I said on the previous page, it's a lot easier to set the options for a custom anchored object if you edit the settings for an existing anchored object.

To edit the settings for an anchored object:

1. Use the Selection tool to select the anchored object.

2. Choose **Object > Anchored Object > Options**. This opens the Anchored Object Options dialog box, which gives you a Preview option in addition to all the settings to control the anchored object.

So what if you want to convert the anchored object into a regular object but position it in the same spot as when it was anchored? I thought I could cut and paste the object to get it out of the text flow. Nope; instead you need to release the anchored object.

To release an anchored object:

1. Use the Selection tool to select the anchored object.

2. Choose **Object > Anchored Object > Release**. This converts the anchored object into an ordinary object.

Inline and Anchored Objects

Tips for Using Anchored Objects

Although the settings for custom anchored objects may take a while to master, you should not give up learning to use them. There are quite a few ways to use custom anchored objects.

It is important to remember that custom anchored objects can be positioned well outside the frame of text that contains the anchor position. This lets you use the custom anchored object for marginalia, notes, or images. Many textbooks, for example, require notes for teacher editions. Custom anchored objects make it easy to insert those notes.

Anchored objects have to start off as rectangles, but once you insert the object, you can apply any of the Convert Shape commands to change their shape. My favorite is to use the Orthogonal Line command to change the anchored object into a stroked line that I can extend down the side of the text frame. This makes it easy to highlight important paragraphs.

Also, you may feel limited that you can insert only one anchored object in certain positions in the text flow. For example, the illustrations in this book consist of both a graphic frame and a text frame. Fortunately, both of those elements can be made into a single anchored object by grouping them and then pasting them into position.

PAGES AND BOOKS 10

Most people who lay out documents work on projects that have more than one page — booklets, brochures, newsletters, menus, annual reports, magazines, books, and so on. Even a lowly business card has two pages if you design a front and back.

When you work with multipage documents, you need to add pages, flow text, apply page numbers, and force text to move to certain pages.

If you are working on very complex documents, you need to make sure all the pages have the same structure.

If you are working on a book, you will want to join individual chapters together. You may also want to automate the process of creating a table of contents or an index.

Here's where you'll learn how to automate and organize working with multipage layouts. In addition, you'll learn how to use InDesign's Book features to synchronize multiple documents in a large project. You'll also discover special features for creating a table of contents from text.

Changing the Pages Panel

You may want to change the display of the Pages panel.

To open the Pages panel:

◆ If the Pages panel is not visible, choose **Window > Pages** to open the panel .

To control the display of the Pages panel:

1. Choose Panel options from the Pages panel menu. This opens the Panel Options dialog box **2**.

2. Use the Pages Icon Size menu to choose the size of the document pages icons.

3. Uncheck Show Vertically to display the pages horizontally in the panel **3**.

4. Uncheck Show Thumbnails to hide the thumbnail preview of the pages in the Pages panel.

TIP Turning the Show Vertically option off makes it easier to fit more pages in a smaller panel area.

5. Use the Masters Icon Size menu to change the size of the master page icons. These choices are the same as the Pages Icon Size menu.

6. Choose Pages on Top to position the document pages at the top of the panel.

7. Choose Masters on Top to position the master pages at the top of the panel.

8. Use the Resize list to control what happens when you resize the panel:

   • **Proportional** maintains the same relative area as you change the size of the panel.

   • **Pages Fixed** adds new space only to the masters area.

   • **Masters Fixed** adds new space only to the pages area.

Changing the Pages Panel

1 The **Pages panel** *is the command center for multipage documents.*

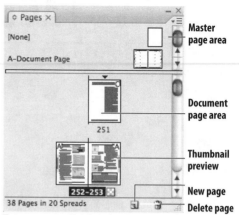

2 The **Panel Options dialog box** *lets you control the appearance of the Pages panel.*

3 *The Pages panel with Show Vertically turned off (left) and turned on (right).*

4 *The* **checkerboard grid** *next to a page indicates that an effect such as a transparency or a drop shadow has been applied to that page.*

5 *Drag a master page from the master page area of the Pages panel to the document area to add pages to a document.*

Adding Blank Pages

Although you probably specified a certain number of pages before you started your document, you might need to add more pages after you've started working on it. You can add pages as you work or you can add a particular number of pages at a precise location.

TIP A checkerboard grid next to the number of the page in the Pages panel indicates that an effect that requires flattening such as a transparency, drop shadow, feather, or Photoshop transparency has been applied on that page **4**. *(See Chapter 19, "Output" for more information on flattening.)*

If you need to add just a few pages, you can add them one by one, manually.

To manually add pages:

1. Click the New Page icon in the Pages panel to add a single page.

   or

   Drag a master page or a nonmaster page from the master page area to the document area of the panel **5**.

2. Repeat as many times as necessary until you have added all the pages you need.

Glossary of Page Terms

As you work with pages and the Pages panel, it helps if you understand the following:

Document pages: The main pages of your document. These are the pages that contain your project. Items that are on the document pages are *document page items.*

Master pages: The pages that contain elements that are repeated on all the document pages. Items that are on the master pages are called *master page items.*

Local Overrides: Normally you cannot select or modify master page items. However, if you apply a local override to the master page items on a specific document page, they can be modified on the document page.

Adding Blank Pages

If you need to add many pages, rather than dragging pages over and over in the Pages panel, you can add them using the Insert command. This also lets you specify where to add the pages.

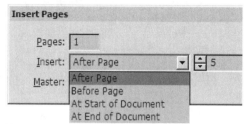

To add pages using the Insert command:

1. Choose Insert Pages from the Pages panel menu. The Insert Pages dialog box appears 6.

2. Type the number of pages you want to insert in the Pages field.

3. Choose where to add the pages within the document from the Insert menu as follows 7:

   • **After Page** lets you insert new pages after a specific page.

   • **Before Page** lets you insert new pages before a specific page.

   • **At Start of Document** inserts new pages at the beginning of the document.

   • **At End of Document** inserts new pages at the end of the document.

4. Use the Master menu to choose the master page that the new pages should be based on.

   or

   Choose None from the Master menu to have an empty page that does not act as a master applied to the new pages.

5. Click OK. The new pages appear in the Pages panel.

6 *The* **Insert Pages dialog box** *lets you add many pages at once to a document.*

7 *The* **Insert menu** *gives you specific choices as to where to insert pages.*

Adding Blank Pages

8 *The colored highlight on the targeted pages (pages 4-5) shows they are not the active pages (pages 2-3).*

9 *The highlight on both the page number and the page for the active pages (pages 2-3) shows they are both targeted and active.*

Navigating and Moving Pages

As you work with pages in the Pages panel, you should understand the difference between targeting a page and working on a page. The active page is the page you are currently working on. The targeted page is the page chosen in the Pages panel.

To target a page:

◆ Click the page in the Pages panel. A highlight appears on the page **8**.

TIP When a page is targeted, it means you can apply a command in the Pages panel even without working on the page.

To work on a page:

◆ Double-click the page number or name of the master page spread in the Pages panel. A highlight appears on the number or name of the page **9**.

TIP When you work on the page, that page or spread is centered within the document window.

InDesign has several different ways to move from page to page.

To move to a specific page using the Pages panel:

◆ Double-click the page in the Pages panel that you want to move to. The page is centered within the document window.

or

Double-click the name of the spread to fit both pages in the document window.

TIP You can also scroll or use the Hand tool to move through the document.

Navigating and Moving Pages

You can also use the navigation controls at the bottom of the document window.

To navigate using the window page menu:

◆ Click a page number in the window page menu to navigate through the document 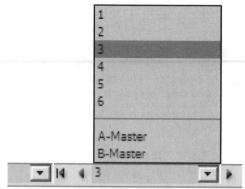.

or

Enter a number in the Page field to move to a specific page.

To use the navigation controls:

◆ Click each of the navigation arrows to move through the document 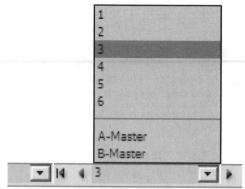.

You can also navigate using the commands in the Layout menu in the menu bar at the top of the application.

TIP The Layout menu commands can be applied using keyboard shortcuts. This lets you move through the document without using the mouse.

To navigate using the Layout menu:

◆ Choose one of the following:
   - **Layout > First Page** moves to the first page of the document.
   - **Layout > Previous Page** moves to the previous page.
   - **Layout > Next Page** moves to the next page.
   - **Layout > Last Page** moves to the last page of the document.
   - **Layout > Next Spread** moves to display the next spread of pages.
   - **Layout > Previous Spread** moves to display the previous spread of pages.
   - **Layout > Go Back** moves to the page that was previously active.
   - **Layout > Go Forward** moves to the page that was active before the Go Back command was applied.

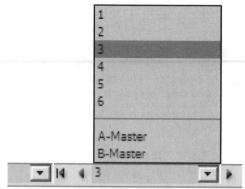

10 *The* **pop-up page list** *at the bottom of the document lets you navigate through the document.*

First page   Previous page   Next page   Last page

11 *Use the* **navigation controls** *at the bottom of the document window to move through the document.*

Navigating and Moving Pages

Maximum Number of Pages?

The maximum number of pages in an InDesign document is 9,999. While most documents fall well below that number, many people do need to create books and catalogs that contain 10,000 or more pages.

If you need to create those types of super-long documents, you should break your projects into separate documents. Then, use the Book feature (covered later in this chapter) to maintain proper pagination as well as synchronize master pages and styles.

You can also use the Pages panel to duplicate and delete pages from the document.

To duplicate pages:

1. Select the page or spreads you want to duplicate.
2. Drag the pages onto the New Page icon.

   or

   Choose Duplicate Spread from the Pages panel menu.

To delete pages:

1. Use the Pages panel to select the pages.

TIP Hold the Shift key to select contiguous pages. Hold the Cmd/Ctrl key to select noncontiguous pages.

2. Choose Delete Pages from the Pages panel menu.

   or

   Click the Delete Page icon at the bottom of the Pages panel ▯.

TIP The command may change to Delete Spreads if you have a spread or spreads selected.

3. When the confirmation dialog box appears, click OK to confirm your choice.

TIP Hold the Opt/Alt key to bypass the confirmation dialog box.

Navigating and Moving Pages

You can use the Pages panel to change how pages are arranged in the document.

To rearrange pages in a document:

◆ Drag a page next to or between the pages of a spread as follows :

- With Allow Document Pages to Shuffle turned on, the new page forces other pages to a new spread .

- With Allow Selected Spread to Shuffle turned off, the new page is added to the existing spread without moving the other pages .

TIP The arrow cursor indicates which side of a spine the new page is inserted on .

TIP You can drag pages between documents. When you do a dialog box appears asking where you would like the pages to appear.

To move pages in a document:

1. Choose Move Pages from the Pages panel menu. This opens the Move Pages dialog box .

2. Use the Move Pages field to list the pages you want to move.

TIP Use hyphens to designate contiguous pages. Use commas to separate noncontiguous pages.

3. Use the Destination list to choose where you want the pages to move.

4. If you have chosen After Page or Before Page, enter the page number in the field.

5. Use the Move To list to choose the document location. This can be the current document or any open documents.

6. If you choose an external open document, you can check Delete Pages after Moving to delete the pages from the original file.

7. Click OK to move the pages.

Arrow points in direction page will be added

 Pages can be moved by dragging their icons in the Pages panel.

Before page drag **After page drag**

 When Allow Document Pages to Shuffle is turned on, a page moved between two other pages forces one of the pages to the next spread.

Before page drag **After page drag**

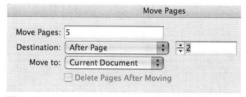 *When **Allow Document Pages to Shuffle** is turned off, a page moved between other pages is added between the two pages in the spread.*

Move Pages: 5
Destination: After Page ⇕ 2
Move to: Current Document ⇕
☐ Delete Pages After Moving

The Move Pages dialog box.

Navigating and Moving Pages

16 *An example of how three pages can be put together to form an island spread.*

17 *The thick vertical line indicates that the new page will be added as an island spread.*

18 *An example of an island spread in the Pages panel.*

19 *You can dismantle an island spread by changing the number of pages in the spread.*

20 *The brackets around the numbers indicate that Allow Selected Spread to Shuffle has been turned off for the pages.*

Creating and Separating Spreads

Most documents are either single-page or facing-page documents. However, you can create spreads with more than one or two pages. These are *island spreads*, like the fold-outs found in special issues of magazines **16**.

To create an island spread:

1. Deselect Allow Document Pages to Shuffle in the Pages panel menu.

TIP This command is turned off so that the pages that are already in the spread do not move to new positions.

2. Drag a page from the pages area, or a master page, next to the spread.

3. Release the mouse when the vertical line appears next to the spread **17**. This adds the page to the island spread **18**.

To dismantle an island spread:

1. Drag each page outside the spread.

    or

    Choose Allow Document Pages to Shuffle from the Pages panel menu. A dialog box asks if you want to maintain the current number of pages in the spread **19**.

2. Click the No button. This dismantles the island spread into the default number of pages per spread in the document.

You can also control whether or not the pages in a spread are kept together or allowed to separate.

To keep the pages in a spread together:

1. Select the spread you want to protect.

2. Deselect Allow Selected Spread to Shuffle from the Pages panel menu. Brackets appear around the page numbers **20**. This prevents the spread from separating if you add pages.

Importing Text

If you have a short amount of text, you can easily type it directly in InDesign's text frames. However, if you are working with long amounts of text, most likely you will want to import the text from a word processing program. You will also want to place the text so that it flows from page to page.

To import text:

1. Choose File > Place. The options for placing text are at the bottom of the Place dialog box 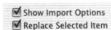.

2. Navigate to find the file you want to import.

3. Click Show Import Options to open the specific import options for that type of text file.

4. Click Replace Selected Item to replace the contents of a selected text frame with the new text.

5. Click Open to load the text into a text cursor *(also called a loaded cursor)* 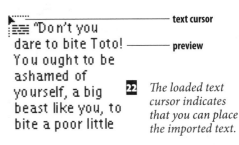.

TIP The text cursor also contains a preview area to show the type of object being placed. For the rest of this book, however, I will show only the text cursor itself to make it easier to see its behavior.

TIP If you hold the Shift key as you click Choose, you open the Import Options dialog box even if the option is not checked.

TIP If the text file uses fonts not installed on your computer, an alert box informs you that the fonts are missing.

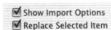

21 *The Import options in the Place dialog box.*

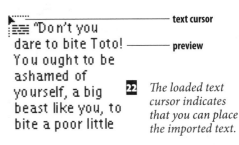

22 *The loaded text cursor indicates that you can place the imported text.*

Importing Text Files

InDesign lets you import text files saved from Microsoft Word 98 or higher. You simply save the Word DOC file and import that into InDesign.

If you have an earlier version of Word, you should save the text as a RTF (Rich Text Format) document. RTF files retain most of their original formatting and can be imported by InDesign.

InDesign can also import ASCII text. ASCII stands for American Standard Code for Information Interchange. This is a standard character-coding scheme used by most computers to display letters, digits, and special characters. It is the most primitive computer text format. For example, when text is saved in the ASCII format, any italic or bold formatting is lost.

Although ASCII text is stripped down, it is useful for importing text from databases or Internet sites. However, you do have to reformat text imported in the ASCII format.

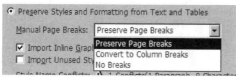

23 *The Microsoft Word Import Options dialog box is used to import Word files.*

24 *The Manual Page Breaks list controls how Word page breaks are converted.*

The options for importing text change depending on which type of text file you choose to import.

To open the import options for Microsoft Word files:

◆ Choose Import Options to open the Microsoft Word Import Options dialog box **23**.

To set the Word import options:

1. Use the Include area to include Word's Table of Contents Text, Index Text, Footnotes, or Endnotes.

2. Choose whether dumb quotes and apostrophes (such as ' and ") should be converted into proper typographer quotes (such as ' and ' or " and ").

To control the formatting in the Word import options:

1. Select Remove Styles and Formatting from Text and Tables to remove the formatting that was applied in Word.

2. If you choose to remove styles and formatting, you can select Preserve Local Overrides to keep attributes such as italic and bold.

3. Use the Manual Page Breaks list to control how Word page break commands are handled **24**.

4. Select Import Inline Graphics to include images inserted into the Word text.

5. Select Import Unused Styles to add all styles from the Word document even if some have not been applied to text.

6. Select Track Changes to see the edits applied to the text when using InCopy.

7. Select Convert Bullets & Numbers to Text to convert Word's electronic bullets and numbers into actual characters.

Importing Text

If your Word document contains a table, you can control how those tables are imported.

To control the formatting in the Word import options:

♦ Use the Convert Table To list to choose one of the following 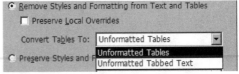:

- **Unformatted Tables** creates a table with InDesign's default settings.

- **Unformatted Tabbed Text** converts tables into tab-delimited text.

TIP The import options for RTF files contain the same options as the Microsoft Word Import Choices.

When you import a Microsoft Excel file, you can set the import options for the file. *(See Chapter 13, "Tabs and Tables," for more information on working with the tables imported from Excel files.)*

To set the options for Microsoft Excel files:

♦ Choose Import Options to open the Microsoft Excel Import Options .

To choose which data to import from Excel files:

1. Use the Sheet list to control which parts of the spreadsheet you want to import.

2. Use the View list to control which view information to import.

3. Use the Cell Range list to control which cells to import.

4. Check Import Hidden Cells not Saved in View to import that data.

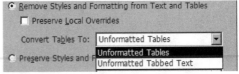

25 *The* **Convert Tables To list** *controls how Word tables are converted.*

26 *The* **Microsoft Excel Import Options dialog box** *is used to import Excel tables.*

Importing Text

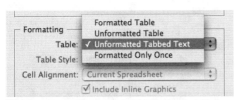

27 *The* **Formatting Table list** *controls how tables are imported.*

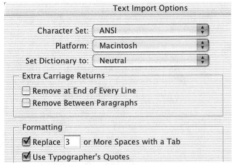

28 *The* **Text Import Options dialog box** *is used to import raw ASCII text files.*

To choose how the Excel data is formatted:

1. Use the Formatting Table list to choose how the table should be formatted **27**.

2. Use the Formatting Table Style list to apply one of InDesign's table styles.

3. Use the Cell Alignment list to choose the paragraph alignment for the information in the table.

4. Check Include Inline Graphics to include placed images along with the text.

You can also control how plain text files, such as ASCII files, are imported into an InDesign document.

To set the options for ASCII files:

1. Choose Import Options to open the Text Import Options dialog box **28**.

2. Choose the character set, platform, and dictionary to ensure that special characters are imported correctly.

3. Choose how to handle extra carriage (paragraph) returns at the ends of lines and paragraphs.

4. Choose how to delete extra spaces inserted into the text.

Importing Text

Flowing Text

Once you have imported the text into the loaded text cursor, you can choose how the text flows into the document.

To import text into a new frame:

◆ Drag the loaded text cursor to create a text frame that contains the text . The straight lines indicate the text will be placed into a new frame.

   or

   Click the loaded text cursor on the page. InDesign creates a text frame the width of the margins of the page.

TIP To unload the text cursor, choose any tool in the Tools panel.

You can place text automatically into text frames that are master page items. This makes it easy to flow text from page to page.

To create master text frames:

◆ Choose Master Text Frame when you first create the document . This creates a text frame that fits within the margins of the master page.

To import text into an existing or master frame:

1. Move the loaded text cursor inside the frame. Curved lines appear [31].

TIP Do not select the text frame.

2. Click the loaded text cursor inside the frame. The text flows into the frame.

To import text within the margins:

1. Move the loaded text cursor near the top-left corner of the margins.

2. Click the loaded text cursor. The text flows into the frame.

TIP Look for the cursor arrow to turn white. This indicates you will pour the text exactly within the margin.

[29] *The* **straight lines around the loaded text cursor** *indicate that the text will be placed into a new text frame.*

[30] *Apply the* **Master Text Frame** *option when you create a new document.*

[31] *The* **curved lines around the loaded text cursor** *indicate that the text will be placed into an existing frame.*

Do you need master frames?

Coming from QuarkXPress as my first page layout program, I used master frames in InDesign. I felt there was no other way to flow text through many pages.

But as I've worked with InDesign over the past six years, I've come to the conclusion that I don't need master frames to flow text from one page to another.

All you have to do is flow the text within the margins and the text will make as many pages as you want.

Flowing Text

32 *Move the loaded cursor inside an existing or master frame to flow text onto a page.*

33 *If there is more text than can fit on the page, an overflow (plus sign) symbol appears at the bottom of the frame.*

34 *Click the overflow symbol to manually load the overflow text into the cursor.*

35 *Click the link cursor to flow the text to the next page.*

36 *The text flows onto the next page.*

If you want, you can import many pages of text so they're linked from one page to another. There are several techniques for flowing the text. The manual method lets you choose exactly where the text should appear. For instance, you can use this method to place text onto noncontiguous pages.

To manually flow text:

1. Import the text so that you have a loaded cursor.

2. Move the cursor inside the area where the master text frame is located.

   or

   Move the cursor inside the top-left corner of the margins.

TIP The cursor displays curved lines when it is within the area of the master text frame **32**.

3. Click inside the area where the master text frame is located. The text fills the frame. If there is more text, an overflow symbol appears at the bottom of the frame **33**.

4. Click the overflow symbol to load the overflow text into the cursor **34**.

5. Move to another page. The cursor changes to a link symbol **35**. Click to flow the text onto that page **36**.

6. If there is additional overflow text, repeat steps 3, 4, and 5 until all the text has been manually flowed onto the pages.

Flowing Text

Flowing text manually is tedious and cumbersome. Rather than manually load the overflow text onto the cursor, you can use the semi-autoflow command to easily load the cursor with the overflow text.

 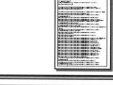

*The **semi-autoflow cursors** let you flow text page by page.*

To semi-autoflow text:

1. Import the text so that you have a loaded cursor.

2. Hold the Opt/Alt key to display the semi-autoflow cursor .

TIP The cursor displays curved lines if you place it inside an existing frame or within a master frame.

3. Click the cursor within a frame or the margins.

   or

   Drag to create a text frame. The semi-autoflow cursor automatically loads any overflow text into a new cursor, which can be placed into a new frame .

After clicking with the semi-autoflow cursor the text is automatically loaded into a new cursor.

4. Hold the Opt/Alt key and click or drag to create another text box linked to the first.

5. Repeat step 4 as many times as necessary to place all the text in the story .

Each click with the semi-autoflow cursor loads the text onto new pages.

What Can You Do With a Loaded Cursor?

Once you load a cursor with text, it may seem like all you can do is click to place the text. However, there are some things you can do without losing the text loaded into the cursor. You can:

- Use any of the menu or Pages panel commands to add pages to the document.
- Use the keyboard shortcuts to zoom in or out.
- Use the scroll bars to move through the page or the document.
- Move the onscreen elements, such as the panels, to new positions.

But remember, never point a loaded cursor at anyone. It always seems funny till someone loses an icon!

Flowing Text (sidebar tab)

40 *Use the* **autoflow cursors** *to create all the pages necessary to hold the imported text.*

41 *After clicking with the autoflow cursor new pages are created to hold the text.*

42 *Use the* **fixed-page autoflow cursors** *to flow text only onto the existing pages.*

43 *The* **fixed-page autoflow cursor** *indicates the text will flow only onto existing pages in the document.*

If you have many pages of text, you can automatically flow the text and create new pages at the same time using the autoflow feature.

To autoflow pages with text:

1. Import the text so that you have a loaded cursor.

2. Hold the Shift key. This cursor changes to the autoflow text cursor **40**.

3. Move the cursor over the area inside an existing frame or the master frame of the page.

   or

   Click the cursor at the top-left corner of the margins.

4. Click the mouse button. This flows the text onto that page and creates as many additional pages as are necessary to hold all the text **41**.

TIP Do not select the master text frame before you flow the text or you will lose the ability to autoflow the text.

What if you want to automatically flow text onto the existing pages of a document without adding any new pages?

To flow text onto a fixed number of pages:

1. Import the text so that you have a loaded cursor.

2. Hold the Shift+Opt/Alt keys. The cursor changes to the fixed-page autoflow cursor **42**.

3. Click anywhere inside a master text frame or the margins of the page **43**. This flows the text automatically onto as many pages as are in the document. If there is more text, an overflow symbol appears on the last page.

Flowing Text

You can fill a frame with dummy text instead of importing real text.

To fill a frame with placeholder text:

1. Click inside a frame.

2. Choose Type > Fill with Placeholder Text. The dummy text fills the frame 44.

TIP You can use your own text for the placeholder by saving a file named placeholder.txt in the InDesign application folder.

Creating Text Breaks

InDesign has special characters that force the text to break to a new position.

To insert break characters:

1. Place the insertion point where you want to jump to the next location.

2. Choose Type > Insert Break Character.

   or

   Control-click (Mac) or right-click (Win) to choose Insert Break Character from the contextual menu.

3. Choose one of the following:

Lonre I dionsectet, velit will num ot prat send verosto eu facin a ullan eix lyx ero prize enis awt. Duisismod to lesequamet the eum delisim first nisl exeriureet person acoing ercilla who alissed tant.

Loir sends anid te mincillan me hendre an eugiat email praestio ewa with amet ip the estrud dit irn page hendignis number enim delenim ver goit velisi bla feugue delesequipit ulluptat of alis nostrud this doluptat. Unt prat secret luptat allit message

44 *A sample of the* placeholder text *that is used to fill text frames.*

Insert Break Character Shortcuts

Use the following shortcuts to insert break characters:

Enter (on the number pad) inserts a column break.

Shift-Enter inserts a frame break.

Cmd-Enter (Mac) or **Ctrl-Enter** (Win) inserts a page break.

Break character	Description	Symbol
Column break	Jumps text to the next column. If there is no column in the frame, the column break forces the text to the next page.	⌄
Frame break	Jumps text to the next frame.	⌄⌄
Page break	Jumps text to the next page.	●⌄
Odd page break	Jumps text to the next odd page.	▪⌄
Even page break	Jumps text to the next even page.	▪▪⌄

TIP To see a representation of the break characters, choose Type > Show Hidden Characters.

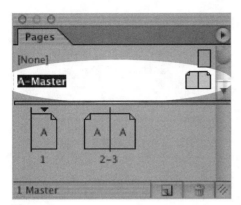

45 *Double-click a master page in the Pages panel to view that* **master page in the document window.**

Uses for Master Pages

Master pages allow you to automate page layout changes. For instance, if you have a hundred-page book, you wouldn't want to have to draw a text frame on every page and type the name of the chapter or book title.

Master pages allow you to place an object or frame on the master page and have it appear on all the document pages.

If you place an object on the master page, it will always be positioned in exactly the same spot on every page that has that master applied.

You can also use master pages to store design alternatives such as different column layouts or margin settings.

Think of master pages as the style sheets for pages.

Working with Master Pages

Every new document includes a master page. When you add objects to the master page, they appear on all the document pages based on that master page.

To add objects to a master page:

1. In the Pages panel, double-click the name of the master page **45**. This opens the master page in the document window.

2. Add text boxes, graphics, or any other elements you want on the master page.

TIP If the document has been set for facing pages, there are two sides to the master page, left-hand and right-hand. The left-hand master page governs the left-hand document pages. Similarly, the right-hand master page governs the right-hand document pages.

3. Double-click the name of the document page to make it the active page. Any items placed on the master page now appear on the document page.

You can also add master pages from one document into another.

To import masters from one document into another:

1. Choose Load Master Pages from the Pages panel menu.

2. Use the dialog box to select the document that contains the masters you want to import.

3. If the masters contain the same name, you will be asked how to resolve the conflict.

4. An alert will tell you if the masters are not the same page size.

You can have many master pages in a document. This allows you to have different layouts for different parts of your document.

To create new master pages:

1. Choose New Master from the Pages panel menu. This opens the New Master dialog box .

2. Choose a letter for the prefix for the master page.

TIP The prefix is the letter that appears inside the pages that have that master page applied to them.

3. Enter a name for the master page.

4. Use the pop-up menu to set which master page, if any, the new master page should be based on.

TIP Basing one master page on another allows you to make changes on one master page that are applied to the other.

5. Enter the number of pages for the master. This allows you to create spreads that serve as master pages.

TIP To create a new master page without opening the New Master dialog box, hold the Cmd/Ctrl key and click the New Page icon at the bottom of the Pages panel.

As you work, you might want to convert a document page into a master page. InDesign makes it easy to turn a document page into a master page.

To convert a document page to a master page:

1. Select the page or pages.

2. Drag the page or pages from the document area to the master page area .

    or

    Choose Save as Master from the Pages panel menu.

46 *The New Master dialog box allows you to set the attributes for the master page.*

47 *Drag a document page into the master page area to convert the document page to a master.*

Strategies for Basing Master Pages on Each Other

I have three master page spreads for this book. One master — the main master — holds only the guides and page numbers for the book. The master for ordinary pages is based on that main master. The master for the chapter opener is also based on that main master.

That way, if I need to move the page numbers I only need to change the page number on the main master. The other masters update automatically.

48 *The* **Apply Master dialog box** *allows you to change the master that governs pages.*

49 **The rectangle around the single page** *indicates that the master will be applied to that page only.*

50 **The rectangle around the spread** *indicates that the master will be applied to the spread.*

Master based on other masters

Spread based on B-Master

Spread based on [None] page

51 *The* **letters inside the page icons** *indicate what masters are applied to pages or other masters.*

New pages are based on the master page applied to the last existing page of the document. You can easily change the master page that governs pages.

To apply a new master to a page:

1. Select the page or pages.

2. Choose Apply Master to Pages from the Pages panel. This opens the Apply Master dialog box **48**.

3. Use the Apply Master menu to apply a master to the pages.

4. Use the To Pages field to change the selected pages.

TIP Selecting None creates pages that have no master page applied.

To apply masters with the Pages panel:

◆ Drag the master page onto the document pages as follows:

• To apply to a single page, drag the master page icon onto the page. A rectangle appears around the page **49**.

• To apply to a spread, drag the master page icon onto the spread. A rectangle appears around the spread **50**.

You can also base one master page on another using the Pages panel.

To base masters on existing masters:

1. Create a new master or spread.

2. Drag one master page onto another.

• To base the spread on the master, drag the master onto the spread.

• To base one page on the master, drag the master onto a single page.

3. Release the mouse button. The prefix of the master appears inside the second master page **51**. The prefix indicates that the master page governs the other master page.

Ordinarily you modify the elements of a master page only on the master page itself. The elements on the document pages are protected from being selected or modified. However, you can release that protection and modify the master elements by creating local overrides.

To modify master elements on document pages:

1. Hold Cmd/Ctrl-Shift and click the element you want to modify. This releases the protection and selects the element.

2. Make any local override changes to the element.

You might want to modify all the master elements on a page. Rather than release each item one by one, InDesign lets you do it with a single command.

To release all master elements on a page:

♦ Choose Override All Master Page Items from the Pages panel menu. This releases the objects so they can be modified on the document page.

You may want to set master page items, such as page numbers and headers, to never be modified on the document page.

To set a master page item to not be overridden:

1. Select the item on the master page.

2. Deselect Allow Master Item Overrides on Selection from the Pages panel menu.

You can also set a master page item to apply its text wrap to other master page items, and not any document page items.

To control the text wrap of a master page item:

1. Select the item on the master page.

2. Apply a text wrap setting.

3. Use the Text Wrap panel menu to select or deselect Apply to Master Page Only.

Overriding Master Page Elements

If you modify a master page element on a document page, the local override loses its link to the master page element. However, the element may have partial links to the master page element.

Let's say you add a stroke to an object on the document page. From that point on, the stroke of the element is removed from the control of the element on the master page.

But other attributes of the element maintain their link to the master page item. For instance, the position of the element maintains a link to the master page item. So if you move the element on the master page, the item on the document page also moves.

Similarly, the fill color of the elements on the document pages changes if you change the master page element. Only the formatting for the stroke is separated from the master page element.

How Many Master Pages?

While it may seem like a lot of work to set up master pages, the more masters you have the easier it is to lay out complicated documents.

A weekly magazine can easily have 50 or more master pages — some for special editorial spreads and others for different types of advertising spaces.

Some publishers insist that every page must be based on a master and do not allow any modifications of the master page elements. Others let the designers override the master pages.

You decide which way best suits your work habits and the project.

Stacking Order of Master Page Items

The items on the master page are always behind any new items you may put on a page. But when you release the master page items from the master page, they always spring to the front of the document page.

If you want, you can use the Object > Arrange menu to change the stacking order of the items. However, if you release many items on many pages, it may seem cumbersome to move them backwards.

Instead, create two layers in your document (*see Chapter 11, "Layers"*). Put all the master page elements on the bottom layer, and your regular document objects on the top layer. That way when you release the master page items, they will not move in front of your regular page items.

Once you have created a local override on a master page element, it may still have links to the original master page item. You can completely sever all ties between the master page item and the item on the document page.

To separate an item from the master item:

1. Select the object that has been released.

2. Choose Detach Selection From Master in the Pages panel menu.

Of course you can also separate all the objects on a page from their links to the master page items.

To separate all the master items on a page:

1. Use the command Override All Master Page Items to first release all the master page items from the master page.

2. Choose Detach All Objects From Master in the Pages panel menu. This severs any remaining link between the item and the master page.

You can also hide master page items on document pages so they do not print.

To change the display of master page items:

♦ Choose Hide Master Items from the Pages panel menu.

   or

   Choose Show Master Items from the Pages panel menu.

InDesign also lets you quickly clear all local overrides and reapply the master page items to the document page.

To remove local overrides and reapply the master:

♦ Choose Remove All Local Overrides in the Pages panel menu. All local override elements will be deleted and the master page items will be reapplied.

Working with Master Pages

Adjusting Layouts

You certainly are not expected to set layouts perfectly the first time, or every time. Fortunately, InDesign has a powerful layout adjustment feature that moves and resizes objects as you change the page size or margins.

Once layout adjustment is turned on, any changes to the layout will alter the position of the elements on both the master pages and the document pages.

To set the layout adjustment options:

1. Choose **Layout > Layout Adjustment**. This opens the Layout Adjustment dialog box 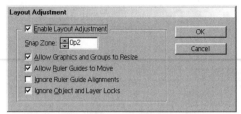.

2. Check Enable Layout Adjustment so that elements change position when page size, orientation, margins, or columns are changed **53**.

3. Set a value for the Snap Zone to specify how close an object must be before it will align and move to a margin or column guide, or page edge.

4. Check Allow Graphics and Groups to Resize so that elements change size as well as move during the adjustment.

5. Check Allow Ruler Guides to Move to have ruler guides move as part of the layout adjustment.

6. Check Ignore Ruler Guide Alignments to keep objects from moving along with ruler guides.

7. Check Ignore Object and Layer Locks to move objects that are locked or on locked layers.

8. Click OK to set the options. The document will change according to the new settings when the document setup or margins are changed.

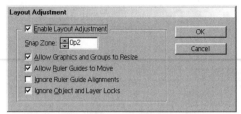

52 *The* **Layout Adjustment dialog box** *controls which elements change if you change document attributes such as the page size or margins.*

53 *When Enable Layout Adjustment is turned on, the items on the page adjust their size and position when the margins and page size are changed.*

54 *The* **current page number** *appears as a letter on master pages but as a number on document pages.*

55 *The* **New Section** *dialog box lets you change the formatting and numbering of pages.*

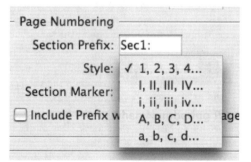

56 *The* **Style** *menu allows you to choose different formats for page numbering of a section.*

Page Numbers and Text Variables

The most common element that is added to a master page is the page-number character.

To add automatic page numbering:

1. Draw a text frame on the master page where you want the page number to appear.

2. Choose **Type > Insert Special Character > Markers > Current Page Number**. This inserts a special character in the text frame **54**.

TIP The current page number character is the prefix for the master page.

3. If the master page is a facing-page master, repeat steps 1 and 2 for the other page in the master.

You may want to change the format of page numbers or the number they start from. You do that by creating a new *section*.

To create a document section:

1. Move to the page where you want the section to start.

2. Choose **Layout > Numbering & Section Options**. The New Section dialog box appears **55**.

3. Check Start Section to open the options.

4. Choose the Page Numbering options:
   - **Automatic Page Numbering** continues the count from the previous pages.
   - **Start Page Numbering At** lets you enter a specific number to start the section from.

5. Use the Style pop-up list to set the format for the automatic page numbering **56**.

TIP The choices for roman numerals or letters are commonly used for front and back matter in book publishing.

You can also create a section prefix that appears in front of the current page number.

To work with a section marker

1. Choose **Layout > Numbering & Section Options** to open the New Section dialog box.

2. Type the label (up to five characters) for the section in the Section Prefix field.

3. Choose Include Prefix when Numbering Pages to add the section prefix to the page number.

4. Enter a label for the Section Marker .

Once you have created an entry for the section marker, you need to insert a section marker character in the text frame to see the entry on document pages.

To add a section marker character:

1. Place the insertion point in a text frame where you want the section marker to appear.

TIP The text frame can be on a master page or a document page.

2. Choose **Type > Insert Special Character > Markers** and then choose Section Marker from the menu.

TIP If the text frame that contains the section marker character is on the master page, the word "Section" appears on the master page. If the text frame is on the document page, the label for the section marker appears .

Page Numbering Options

Section Prefix: Sec1:

Style: 1, 2, 3, …

Section Marker: Chapter

☐ Include Prefix when Numbering Pages

57 *The entry in the* **Section Marker field** *allows you to create custom labels for pages.*

Section

Chapter

58 *The* **section marker** *appears as the word "Section" on master pages but as the label on document pages.*

Absolute or Section Numbering?

What if you create a document that has its first section start on page i and then starts a new section that starts on page 1? This could create some confusion if you try to print page "one." Which one of the "ones" would you print?

Fortunately, InDesign has a preference setting that allows you to change the section numbering to absolute numbering. This makes it easier to avoid confusion if a document has multiple sections that start with the same number.

However, you can also specify page numbers by using the plus (+) sign in the print dialog box. For instance +1 means the first page in the document even if that first page is numbered i or 1 or any other number.

Page Numbers and Text Variables

Document Chapter Numbering

Style: [1, 2, 3, 4... ▼]

● Chapter Number: [10]

○ Continue from Previous Document in the Bo

○ Same as Previous Document in the Book

59 *The* **Document Chapter Numbering** *allows you to set the chapter number for a document.*

Document Chapter Numbering

Style: ✓ 1, 2, 3, 4...
    I, II, III, IV...
● Chapter Number: i, ii, iii, iv...
○ Continue from Pre A, B, C, D... n the Bo
    a, b, c, d...
○ Same as Previous 01,02,03... ook

60 *Use the* **Document Style list** *to set the elements that are used for chapter numbers.*

Chapter
10#

61 *A* **text variable** *is displayed with a rectangle around the information.*

Books have more than just page numbers. They also have chapter numbers can specify the chapter number for yo document. Then you can insert the chapter number as a text variable in a frame.

To specify a chapter number:

1. Choose **Layout > Numbering & Section Options** to open the New Section dialog box.

2. Enter a number in the Chapter Number field **59**.

TIP The number can also be created automatically as part of a Book document, which is covered later in this chapter.

3. Use the Document Chapter Numbering Style list to choose the style of the characters used for the chapter numbers **60**.

TIP These are similar to the styles for page numbers with the exception of the 01, 02, 03, 04 style, which is used in many textbooks.

Chapter numbers are inserted as special characters that can appear anywhere.

To add a chapter number:

1. Place the insertion point in a text frame.

2. Choose **Type > Text Variables > Insert Variable** and then choose Chapter Number from the list of preset text variables. The text variable for Chapter Number appears with a line around the display **61**.

TIP Other text variables include creation date, file name, last page number, modification date, output date, and running headers.

Page Numbers and Text Variables

You can also insert special characters that create jump lines that show the page where the text flow continues to or from.

To create a continued to/from page number:

1. Place the insertion point in a text frame that touches the frame that holds the story.

2. Choose Type > Insert Special Character and then choose one of the following:

   - Next Page Number inserts the number of the page that the text jumps to or continues on .

   - Previous Page Number inserts the number of the page that the text continued from 63.

TIP The continued to/from character needs a separate text frame so that if the text reflows, the continued to/from character doesn't move along with the text.

TIP The continued to/from characters only insert the page number that the story is linked to. You have to type the words "Continued on" or "Continued from" yourself.

Duis etummolore facilla faci bla
sequissequis nulputpat. Duisim in
adigna conulla feuguer accumsan
commodolore magna faciliquisi t

Continued on page 3 — Overlap

 The Next Page Number character shows the page number that the story is continued on. The overlapping area is where the page number frame touches the story frame.

Continued from page 2 — Overlap

irit lutpatie vent nim irilit vullandree
feugait lobor sum ipis aliquisl dolor
eugait lut delessi tat, si.

63 *The Previous Page Number character shows the page number that the story comes from. The overlapping area is where the page number frame touches the story frame.*

64 *A saved book document appears with its own document icon.*

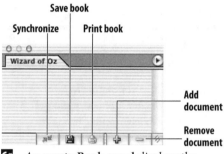

Save book

Synchronize   Print book

Add document

Remove document

65 *An* **empty Book panel** *displays the name of the book on its panel tab.*

Making Books

Most people who create long documents break them up so that each chapter is contained in its own document. They need a way to coordinate the page numbers, colors, and styles. An InDesign *book* is an electronic file that keeps track of all those documents.

To create an electronic book file:

1. Choose **File > New > Book**.

2. Use the dialog box to name the book document and save it in a location 64. The Book panel appears 65.

TIP The tab for the Book panel contains the name of the book.

Once you have created the book file, you can then add documents that make up the book.

TIP You don't have to create the book file first. For instance, I created these chapters before I added them to a book document.

To add documents to a book:

1. Click the Add Document button at the bottom of the Book panel.

   or

   Choose Add Document from the Book panel menu.

2. Use the dialog box to find the document you want to add to the book. The name of the chapter appears in the Book panel.

3. Repeat steps 1 and 2 to add other documents to the book.

To remove documents from a book:

1. Select the documents you want to remove.

2. Click the Remove Document button at the bottom of the Book panel.

   or

   Choose Remove Document from the Book panel menu.

Making Books

You can use the Book panel and Book panel menu to open, rearrange, and control the documents that make up the book.

To open documents in a book:

◆ Double-click the name of a document in the Book panel. The open book symbol next to the name indicates that the document is open .

66 *The* **open book icon** *indicates that a document of the book is open.*

The order that documents are listed in the Book panel determines the page numbers of the book.

To change the order of the documents in a book:

◆ Drag the name of a document in the Book panel to a new position in the panel .

67 **Drag a listing in the Book panel** *to change the order in which the documents appear in the book.*

One of the benefits of creating a book document is that you can have one file (called the *style source*) control the style sheets, swatches, and master pages for the other documents in the book. If you make changes to the style source, all the other files in the book synchronize to that file.

Style source icon

68 *The* **style source file** *is used to synchronize the style sheets and colors for other documents in a book.*

To set the style source for a book document:

◆ Click the Style Source box next to the name of the file that you want to control the rest of the documents in the book **68**.

To synchronize files to the style source:

◆ Click the Synchronize button in the Book panel.

or

Choose Synchronize Book in the Book panel menu.

TIP The menu command says Synchronize Selected Documents if only some of the files in the book are selected.

69 *Use the **Synchronize Options** dialog box to set which attributes of the style source file will be applied to the files in the book.*

70 *The **Alert** icon in the Book panel indicates that the file has been modified.*

71 *The **Missing** icon in the Book panel indicates that the file has been moved after it was imported into the book.*

To set the synchronizing options:

1. Choose Synchronize Options from the Book panel menu. The Synchronize Options dialog box opens **69**.

2. Choose the options that you want to apply from the style source document.

If the book is closed when you modify the files in the book, you need to update them when you do reopen the book document.

TIP This step is not necessary if you modify book files while the book document is open.

To update files in a book:

1. Choose **File > Open** and then navigate to the book document you want to work on.

2. Use the Book panel to open, then modify any files in the book document. An Alert icon appears next to the modified files **70**.

   or

   Use the Open command in the File menu to open, then modify any files in the book document.

3. If necessary, synchronize the files to the style source document.

You can also replace missing files in a book or swap one file for another.

TIP A Missing icon indicates that the file has been moved after being added to the book **71**.

To replace a file in a book:

1. Select the file in the Book panel that you want to replace.

2. Choose Replace Document from the Book panel menu.

3. Navigate to find the file you want to replace or relink.

4. If necessary, synchronize the files.

Making Books

Files in a book automatically run in consecutive numbers. As you add or delete pages in one document, the page numbers in the rest of the book adjust. You can control how the page numbers are adjusted.

To set how page numbers are adjusted:

1. Choose Book Page Numbering Options from the Book panel menu to open the dialog box .

2. Choose the Page Order options as follows:

   - **Continue from previous document** starts new pages sequentially from the end of the previous listing.

   - **Continue on next odd page** always starts new pages on an odd number.

   - **Continue on next even page** always starts new pages on an even number.

3. If using the odd or even options results in a skipped page, check Insert Blank Page.

4. Deselect Automatically Update Page & Section Numbering to stop InDesign from automatically numbering the files in a book.

To set the numbers for each document in a book:

1. Choose Document Numbering Options from the Book panel menu to open the dialog box 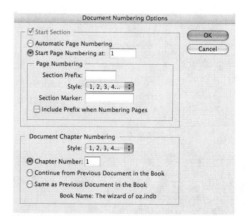.

2. Choose Automatic Page Numbering to number pages as they appear in the Book panel.

   or

   Choose Start Page Numbering At to set a specific page number to start that document on .

3. Set the rest of the options as described on page 273.

72 *Use the* **Book Page Numbering Options** *dialog box to set how pages will be numbered in a book.*

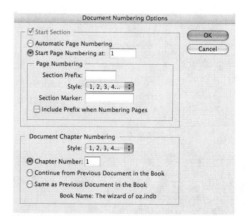

73 *Use the* **Document Numbering Options** *dialog box to set how an individual document is numbered in a book.*

74 *The* **Page Numbering options** *for a document in a book.*

Making Books

Document Chapter Numbering

Style: 1, 2, 3, 4...

● Chapter Number: 1

○ Continue from Previous Document in the Book

○ Same as Previous Document in the Book

Book Name: The wizard of oz.indb

75 *The* **Document Chapter Numbering options** *for a document in a book.*

Preflight Book...
Package Book For Print...
Export Book to Digital Editions...
Export Book to PDF...
Print Book...

Preflight Selected Documents...
Package Selected Documents For Print...
Export Book to Digital Editions...
Export Selected Documents to PDF...
Print Selected Documents...

76 *With no files selected, the* **Book panel menu controls all the files in a book** *(top). However, when you select individual files in the Book, the Book panel menu commands are applied only to those selected files (bottom).*

To set the chapter numbers for document in a book:

1. Choose Document Numbering Options from the Book panel menu to open the dialog box **75**.

2. Choose one of the following to set the number for the chapter:

   • Automatic Page Numbering to number pages as they appear in the Book panel.

   • Choose Start Page Numbering At to set a specific page number.

3. Set the Style options for the chapter number as described on page 273.

To update the numbering in a book:

◆ Choose one of the following from the Book panel menu's Update Numbering submenu:

   • Update Page & Section Numbers

   • Update Chapter & Paragraph Numbers

   • Update All Numbers

You can also apply output commands to the files in a book. *(See Chapter 19, "Output," for more information on printing files.)*

To set the Output options for a Book:

◆ Choose one of the following output commands from the Book panel menu:

   • **Print Book** prints the entire book.

   • **Preflight Book** preflights all the documents in the book.

   • **Package** collects the files for output.

   • **Export Book to PDF** creates a PDF of the documents in the book.

TIP Select just some of the files in the Book to print, preflight, package, or make a PDF of just those files **76**.

Making Books

Creating a Table of Contents

InDesign creates a table of contents (TOC) by looking at the styles applied to paragraphs and then listing the text and page numbers for those paragraphs. The TOC for this book lists the chapters and the section heads .

To prepare a document for a table of contents:

1. Add the page or pages that will hold the TOC.

TIP Most tables of contents are part of the front matter of a book and are numbered separately without affecting the regular page numbering.

TIP If the document is part of a book, make sure the book's pagination is current.

2. Apply paragraph styles to the paragraphs that you want to appear in the TOC.

To define the styles for TOC entries:

1. Choose **Layout > Table of Contents** to open the Table of Contents dialog box .

2. Set the Title and Listing controls as described in the exercises that start on the next page.

3. Click Save Style. This opens the Save Style dialog box 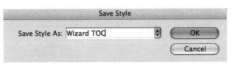.

4. Name the style and click Save.

To generate the TOC:

1. Choose **Layout > Table of Contents** to open the Table of Contents dialog box.

2. Set each of the controls as described in the following exercises.

3. Click OK. This closes the dialog box and creates a loaded text cursor that contains the TOC.

4. Click or drag the loaded cursor to apply the TOC text where you want it to appear in the document.

77 *The* **paragraph styles applied to chapter titles and section heads in this book** *can be used to create a table of contents.*

78 *The* **Table of Contents dialog box** *lets you select and format listings for a table of contents.*

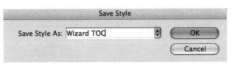

79 *The* **Save Style dialog box** *lets you save the settings from the Table of Contents dialog box.*

80 *Use the* **Title field in the Table of Contents dialog box** *to enter the text you want to appear before the listings.*

81 *Move styles from the Other Styles list to the* **Include Paragraph Styles list** *to choose which paragraphs are added to the table of contents.*

82 *Move styles from the Other Styles list to the* **Include Paragraph Styles list** *to choose which paragraphs are added to the table of contents.*

Benefits of an Automatic TOC

If all this seems like too much work just to create a short table of contents, you may be tempted to create one by hand — manually entering the items in the TOC.

For instance, I could easily create the TOC for this book by hand.

But there is a big benefit in creating an automatic TOC. When you export PDF files with an automatically created TOC, they will have hyperlinks from the TOC to the document pages.

This means someone reading the PDF document can just click on the page number listed in the TOC to go to that specific page. Without the electronic TOC, you'd have to manually add all those links in Acrobat.

The title is the label that is applied before each entry in the table of contents. You can set the type for the title as well as the paragraph style that formats the title.

To enter the title of the table of contents:

1. Type the text for the title in the Title field **80**.

2. Use the Style menu to the right of the Title field to choose which paragraph style is applied to format the title.

You create the entries for a table of contents by selecting the paragraph styles that are applied to those sections of your documents.

To choose the listings for the table of contents:

1. Select a paragraph style listed in the Other Styles area of the Table of Contents dialog box **81**.

2. Click the Add button. This moves the style to the Include Paragraph Styles list.

3. Repeat steps 1 and 2 for any additional styles.

If your TOC uses a style with auto numbers, you can set how the TOC styles those entries.

To set the options for numbered paragraphs:

1. Select a paragraph style listed in the Other Styles area of the Table of Contents dialog box **82**.

2. Choose one of the options from the Numbered Paragraphs list as follows:

   - **Include Full Paragraph** includes the text and the numbers.

   - **Include Numbers Only** includes just the numbers for the paragraph.

   - **Exclude Numbers** includes the text but not the numbers.

Most likely you will want to format the entries in a table of contents with a different style than the one used within the document.

To format the entries in the table of contents:

1. Select the entry listing in the Include Paragraph Styles area.

2. Choose a paragraph style sheet from the Entry Style menu under the Style: [Name] in the Table of Contents dialog box 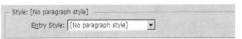.

3. Repeat steps 1 and 2 for any additional styles.

The Table of Contents dialog box has additional controls for more advanced options such as formatting the page numbers for each entry.

To open the additional table of contents controls:

- Click the More Options button in the Table of Contents dialog box **84**. This opens the advanced options at the bottom of the dialog box **85**.

TIP If the button says Fewer Options, then the dialog box already shows the advanced options.

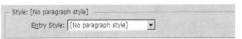

83 *Use the **Entry Style menu** to choose a style sheet that you have created to format the listing as it should appear in the table of contents.*

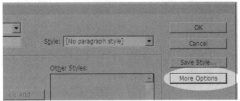

84 *Click the **More Options button** to expand the controls in the Table of Contents dialog box.*

85 *The **Table of Contents dialog box** with all the options available.*

Creating a Table of Contents

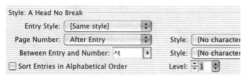

86 *The* **Style options area** *gives you controls to format how the entries are formatted and arranged in the* TOC.

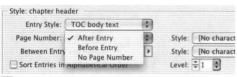

87 *The* **Page Number menu** *controls where the page number will appear in the* TOC *listings.*

Other Uses for a Table of Contents

You're not limited to using the Table of Contents commands just for listings of chapters and section heads.

If you have a sales catalog you can use the commands to create a list of all the items, which can be used as a price list. I could generate a separate file for this book that lists all the titles for sidebars such as this one. In a book of illustrations, you can use it to create a list of names of all the artists for each illustration.

The only thing you need to remember is to assign a style sheet to each item that you want to appear in the table of contents.

With the advanced options open, you have additional controls for the style for each entry in the TOC **86**. This gives you greater control over where the page numbers appear and how they are formatted.

To set the advanced Style options for each entry:

1. Choose one of the styles in the Include Paragraph Styles list. The style name appears in the Style options area.

2. If you have not already applied a listing from the Entry Style menu, do so as explained on the previous page.

3. Use the Page Number menu to choose a position for the entry's page number **87**.

4. If desired, choose a character style for the page number from the Style list to the right of the Page Number menu.

TIP The character style lets you apply formatting to the page number for each entry.

You can also control how the entry name and the page number are separated.

To control the separator character:

1. Select one of the character options from the Between Entry and Number menu **85**. The character symbol appears in the field.

2. If you want, type additional text before or after the character symbol. This lets you add a label before the page number.

3. If desired, apply a style from the Style menu for the Between Entry and Number character **85**.

Creating a Table of Contents

A table of contents doesn't have to be organized in the order that the items appear.

To alphabetize the table of contents:

◆ Check Sort Entries in Alphabetical order from the advanced options area **85**.

To indent the entries in a table of contents:

◆ Use the Level controls to indent each table of contents entry **85**.

TIP Each entry in the Include Paragraph Styles list is automatically indented. This is for display purposes in that dialog box and does not affect the final TOC.

There are additional options you can set for a table of contents **88**.

To set the table of contents options:

◆ Select each of the table of contents options at the bottom of the Table of Contents dialog box as follows:

- **Create PDF Bookmarks** adds bookmarks to the PDF that is created from the TOC. This is in addition to any hyperlinks within the TOC.

- **Replace Existing Table of Contents** lets you update or change the table of contents that has already been placed in the document.

- **Include Book Documents** lets you create a table of contents for all the documents in a book.

- **Run-in** creates a single paragraph table of contents with each entry divided by a semicolon (;) and a space.

- **Include Text on Hidden Layers** uses text that is on layers that are not visible.

- **Numbered Paragraphs** lets you format how paragraphs with auto numbering are formatted in the TOC.

88 *The* **Options for creating TOC documents.**

A TOC of Nonexisting Items

The following tip comes from *Real World InDesign CS3*, by Olav Martin Kvern and David Blatner. I strongly recommend this book for anyone who wants a deeper understanding of InDesign.

The items in a TOC don't have to be from items that are visible on each page. For instance, let's say you want a list of all photographers in your book and where their pictures appear. Simply put the names of the photographers next to their photos, but set the names to not print or on a layer set to not print.

Then, run the TOC for the items. You get a list of the photographers' names, even though those names don't actually appear on the printed pages.

Creating a Table of Contents

LAYERS 11

When I was in advertising, we used to lay clear acetate sheets over our mechanical board as a way to create variations for our layouts. One acetate layer might have copy and prices for a test market newspaper ad. Another piece of acetate might have prices for a special Sunday-circular ad. Yet another might have copy without prices for the national magazine ads. The artwork and other graphics stayed on the bottom layer and were visible through the acetate layers.

When the mechanical was sent to be printed, the print shop workers flipped the different acetate sheets on or off the board to create the different types of ads. Because a new mechanical didn't have to be created for each variation, it saved a lot of time and effort.

InDesign gives you the same sort of flexibility with electronic layers. You may have just two layers — one for text, the other for graphics. Or you may have a document with hundreds of different layers.

For instance, if you have English and French versions of a document, you can put the text for each language on its own layer. You can then display just one version at a time.

Creating and Deleting Layers

Every InDesign document opens with a default layer in the Layers panel. You don't have to do anything special to work with this default layer. It is instantly active, and everything you do is automatically on that layer.

1 *The* **Layers panel** *for all new documents contains one layer.*

To open the Layers panel:

◆ If the Layers panel is not visible, choose **Window** > **Layers** to open it **1**.

As you work, you may want additional layers in your document.

To create new layers:

1. Choose New Layer from the Layers panel menu **2**. This opens the New Layer dialog box.

   or

   Click the New Layer icon. This creates a new layer without opening the New Layer dialog box.

2. Set the layer options as described in the next section.

3. Click OK to create the layer.

TIP You can open the layer options at any time by double-clicking the name of the layer in the Layers panel or by choosing Layer Options from the Layers panel menu.

It may be easier to create different versions of a document by duplicating a layer, as well as the objects on that layer.

To duplicate a layer:

◆ Drag the layer onto the New Layer icon **3**. This creates a copy of the layer, as well as all objects on that layer.

2 *The* **Layers panel menu** *contains the commands for working with layers.*

3 *You can duplicate a layer by dragging it onto the* **New Layer** *icon.*

Before paste

After paste

4 *The* **Paste Remembers Layers command** *adds new layers when objects are pasted from one document to another.*

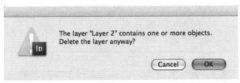

5 *An alert dialog box makes sure you don't inadvertently delete artwork when you delete a layer.*

You can also import the layers automatically when you paste items from one document to another. This behavior is controlled by the Paste Remembers Layers command.

To create new layers while pasting:

1. Choose Paste Remembers Layers from the Layers panel menu. If there is a check mark next to the command, then it is already turned on.

2. Drag and drop or copy and paste the items from one document into a second document. New layers are created in the second document as follows **4**:

   • The layers from the first document are added as new layers if they do not have the same name as the layers in the second document.

   • The layers from the first document are merged with the layers if they have the same name as layers in the second document.

TIP If Paste Remembers Layers is turned off, the items are pasted onto the active layer in the second document.

As you work, you may want to delete a layer. This also deletes all objects on the layer.

To delete a layer:

1. Select the layer you want to delete.

TIP Shift-click to select multiple layers.

2. Click the Delete Layer icon. If there are items on the layer an alert box appears **5**.

TIP Opt/Alt-click the Delete Layer icon to bypass the alert box.

You can quickly delete layers with no objects.

To delete all unused layers:

◆ Choose Delete Unused layers from the Layers panel menu.

Creating and Deleting Layers

Setting the Layer Options

The Layer Options dialog box contains some housekeeping options that make it easier to organize and work with layers .

To name a layer:

◆ Use the Name field to name the layer.

TIP If you have many layers, you should use descriptive names instead of the default names Layer 1, Layer 2, etc.

Each layer has a color associated with it. This is the color used to highlight object frames and paths.

To set the highlight color for a layer:

◆ Choose a color from one of the 37 colors in the Color list .

TIP Each new layer is automatically assigned the next color in the Color list. This means you can have 37 layers without ever repeating a color.

TIP Select Custom to choose your own color for a layer.

Layers help you organize your documents. For instance, if you lock a layer you lock all the objects, so they cannot be selected, moved, modified, or deleted.

To lock a layer:

◆ Choose Lock Layer from the Layer Options dialog box.

   or

   Click the Toggle Lock space in the Layers panel 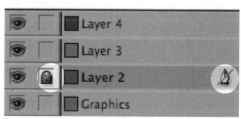. A padlock indicates that the layer is locked. A blank space indicates the layer is unlocked.

TIP Use the Lock Others command from the Layers panel menu or Opt/Alt-click the Toggle Lock space in one layer to lock all the other layers in the document .

6 *The* **Layer Options dialog box** *is the command center for all the attributes of a layer.*

7 *The* **Color list** *contains all the choices for highlighting objects.*

8 *Click the* **Toggle Lock space** *to lock the layer. The spotlighted icons indicate that the layer is locked.*

9 *Opt/Alt-click the* **Toggle Lock space** *to lock all the other layers in the document.*

10 Click the Toggle Visibility space *to hide or show the layer.*

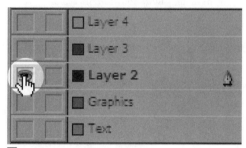

11 Opt/Alt-click the Toggle Visibility *space to hide all the other layers in the document.*

To prevent a layer from printing:

◆ Deselect Print Layer from the Layer Options dialog box.

TIP A layer set to not print is displayed in italic letters in the Layers panel

You can also use layers to hide and show the information on the layer. This can make it easy to focus on certain information.

TIP Hidden layers automatically do not print.

To hide a layer:

◆ Deselect Show Layer from the Layer Options dialog box.

or

Click the Toggle Visibility space in the Layers panel so that the space is blank **10**. When the space is blank, the layer is invisible.

TIP You cannot work on invisible layers.

TIP Use the Hide Others command from the Layers panel menu or Opt/Alt-click the Toggle Visibility space in one layer to hide all the other layers in the document **11**.

To show a layer:

◆ Select Show Layer from the Layer Options dialog box.

or

Click the Toggle Visibility space in the Layers panel. When the eyeball is visible, the layer is visible.

Setting the Layer Options

To control the visibility of guides on a layer:

1. Choose Show Guides in the Layer Options dialog box to display the guides for that layer.

2. Choose Lock Guides to protect the guides on the layer from being changed.

Although hidden layers don't print, they still can affect other objects on the page. The Layer Options dialog box contains the Suppress Text Wrap When Layer Is Hidden setting which controls what happens if you turn off the visibility for a layer that has a text wrap applied to images 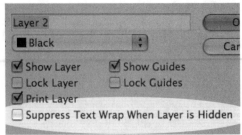.

To control the text wrap for hidden layers:

1. Apply a text wrap to an image that is on one layer.

2. Create text that is on another layer .

3. Set the Layer Options dialog box as follows:

   - Turn off Suppress Text Wrap When Layer Is Hidden to maintain the text wrap when the layer is not visible 14.

   - Turn on Suppress Text Wrap When Layer Is Hidden to discard the text wrap when the layer is not visible 15.

Setting the Layer Options

12 *The* **Suppress Text Wrap When Layer Is Hidden** *option controls what happens to the text wrap for hidden layers.*

When Dorothy stood in the doorway and looked around, she could see nothing but the great gray prairie on every side. Not a tree nor a house broke the broad sweep of flat country that reached to the edge of the sky in all directions. The sun had baked the plowed land into a gray mass, with little cracks running through it. Even the grass was not green, for the sun

13 *An image with a text wrap is placed on one layer affecting the text on another layer.*

When Dorothy stood in the doorway and looked around, she could see nothing but the great gray prairie on every side. Not a tree nor a house broke the broad sweep of flat country that reached to the edge of the sky in all directions. The sun had baked the plowed land into a gray mass, with little cracks running through it. Even the grass was not green, for the sun

14 *When the layer is hidden, the wrap continues to affect text when the* **Suppress Text Wrap option is turned off***.*

When Dorothy stood in the doorway and looked around, she could see nothing but the great gray prairie on every side. Not a tree nor a house broke the broad sweep of flat country that reached to the edge of the sky in all directions. The sun had baked the plowed land into a gray mass, with little cracks running through it. Even the grass was not green, for the sun had burned the tops

15 *When the layer is hidden, the wrap does not affect text when the* **Suppress Text Wrap option is turned on***.*

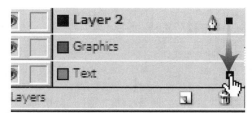

16 Drag the proxy square *to move an object from one layer to another.*

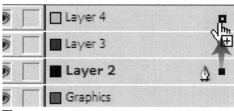

17 *Hold the Opt/Alt key as you drag the proxy square to copy an object from one layer to another.*

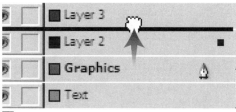

18 *Drag a layer up or down in the Layers panel to change the order of the layers.*

Working with Layers

Once you've created additional layers in your document, you can move objects onto the new layers.

To apply objects to layers:

◆ Click the layer in the Layers panel so that it's highlighted, and then create the object.

Rather than cutting or copying the object, selecting the new layer, and pasting it, you can use the Layers panel to move the object between layers.

To move objects from one layer to another:

1. Select the object. A square object proxy appears next to the name of the layer in the Layers panel.

2. Drag the object proxy from one layer to another **16**. This moves the object to a new layer.

TIP Hold the Opt/Alt key as you drag the proxy to create a copy of the object on the new layer **17**. The original object stays on its layer.

To reorder layers:

◆ Drag one layer above or below another to change the order in which objects appear in the document **18**.

You may want to combine the contents of one layer with another. This is called *merging* layers.

To merge layers:

1. Select the layers you want to merge.

2. Choose Merge Layers from the Layers panel menu. All the objects on the layers are combined onto one layer.

Working with Layers

So What About Photoshop, Illustrator, and Acrobat Layers?

"Hey, Sandee, didn't I see you speak at a conference and say that InDesign can show and hide the layers from Photoshop, Illustrator, and Acrobat files? How come you're not covering that topic in this chapter?"

You're right. InDesign does let you change the visibility of layers in those types of places graphics. But the layers in those graphics aren't controlled using the Layers panel. They're shown and hidden using the Image Import Options when you first place the graphic, or later, in the Object Layer Options. *(See Chapter 6, "Graphics," for how to control the layers in placed files.)*

Working with Layers

LIBRARIES AND SNIPPETS 12

Back when I worked in advertising, I noticed that the art directors would stick little bits and pieces of type and logos on their mechanical board, drafting table, lamp, and wall. This made it easy to grab an often-used logo or piece of art.

Similarly, when you work with electronic page layouts, you use certain elements over and over. For instance, if you're working on a magazine, you might want to have a series of different-sized frames to hold frequently used ads.

Rather than copying and pasting the frames from one part of the document to another, you can use InDesign's libraries or snippets to hold the elements you use repeatedly.

Then, when you need to use an item from the library or the saved snippet file, you can simply drag it onto the page.

Storing Items in a Library

A library allows you to store elements, such as text frames, images, or empty frames. When elements are in a library, they can be dragged easily into open documents. Libraries are especially useful when you need to use the same element in many different places.

TIP Libraries appear as panels that float above the open InDesign documents. Libraries are available to use with any InDesign document.

To create a library:

1. Choose **File > New > Library**. This opens the New Library dialog box.

2. Use this dialog box to name the library file and select its location.

TIP The name of the library file appears in the tab of the Library panel.

3. Click Save. The library appears as a floating panel **1**.

To add items to a library:

1. With a library open, select the item you want to insert in it.

2. Click the Add Item button at the bottom of the Library panel.

 or

 Drag the item into the library **2**. The item appears in the Library panel.

 or

 Choose Add Item from the Library panel menu **3**.

TIP Multiple objects are always entered as a single library item. If you want individual objects, you need to select and add them to the library one by one.

Item Information   Show Subset

Add Item

Delete Item

1 *A* **new Library panel** *does not contain any items.*

2 *You can* **add items to a library** *by dragging them from the page into the Library panel.*

3 *The* **Library panel menu** *contains the commands for working with a library.*

Strategies for Using Libraries

Libraries can be used in many different ways. I use a library to store items that I use often in a document.

For instance, I have one library labeled IDCS3VQS for this Visual QuickStart book. One of the elements is a graphic frame with a text frame underneath. I drag that out for the illustrations and captions.

Other elements are the empty circles, lines, and curved arrows I use to point to elements in the figures.

Another element is a gray text frame with a stroke around it. I drag it out when I write sidebars such as this.

You can also add all the items on the current page to a library.

To add a page to a library:

1. With a library open, move to the page you want to add to the library.

2. Choose Add Items on Page [number] from the Library panel submenu.

TIP The Add Items on Page [number] command automatically labels the entry as a single page in the library Item Information dialog box.

Instead of the Add Items on Page [number] command, you may want to add all the items on a page as individual library entries. Instead of dragging them one by one into the Library panel, you can add the items as separate elements.

To add all the items on a page separately:

1. With a library open, move to the page that contains all the items that you want to add to the library.

2. Choose Add Items on Page [number] as Separate Objects from the Library panel menu.

To delete items from a library:

1. Select the item in the library.

2. Click the Delete Item icon.

   or

   Choose Delete Item(s) from the Library panel menu.

3. A dialog box appears asking for confirmation that you want to delete the items. Click Yes.

TIP Hold the Opt/Alt key to bypass the dialog box when you delete a library item.

Storing Items in a Library

Applying Library Items to a Page

Libraries can be opened and the elements in the libraries dragged onto any InDesign documents.

4 *Items can be dragged from a library onto a document.*

To add library items to a document:

1. Select the item in the library.

TIP Shift-click to select multiple contiguous entries in the Library panel.

TIP Cmd/Ctrl-click to select multiple non-contiguous entries in the Library panel.

2. Drag the items from the library onto the page **4**.

   or

   Choose Place Item(s) from the Library panel menu.

TIP The Place Item(s) command adds the library item in the same position it was in when first defined.

You may want to modify an item in a library with a new object, text, or image. The Update Library Item command makes this easy to do.

To update an item in a library:

1. Select the item on the page that you want to use as the replacement in the library.

2. Select the item in the library that needs to be updated.

3. Choose Update Library Item from the Library panel menu. The library thumbnail updates to display the new item.

Libraries in the Bridge

Libraries appear in the Adobe Bridge as icons, not previewed documents.

Library icons can be opened through the Bridge as you would any InDesign file.

Although you can add descriptions to the items in a library, the library items in the Adobe Bridge cannot have keywords or other XMP metadata applied to them.

Applying Library Items to a Page (sidebar text)

Text icon — Chapter ope

Image icon — Dead witch

Page icon — Image and c

Structure icon — Long docum

EPS icon — oil can

Geometry icon — ruby shoes

InDesign icon — Scarecrow

PDF icon — Tornado Do

5 *The* **List View** *shows the name of the item and an icon that shows the type of item.*

Witch... | Boxes | Lantern

6 *The* **Thumbnail View** *shows the name of the item and a preview of the item.*

Item Information

Item Name: Witch
Object Type: Image
Creation Date: 8/8/03 1:10 PM
Description:

OK
Cancel

7 *The* **Item Information dialog box** *lets you change the information assigned to each item.*

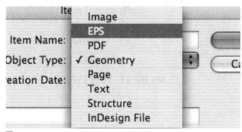

Item Name:
Object Type:
Creation Date:

Image
EPS
PDF
✓ Geometry
Page
Text
Structure
InDesign File

8 *Use the* **Object Type list** *to apply a label for the library element.*

Setting the Library Display

If you have many items in a library, you may want to change how the items are displayed.

To change the library display:

◆ Choose List View in the Library panel menu to see the item name and an icon that indicates the type of item **5**.

or

Choose Thumbnail View or Large Thumbnail View to see the name and a preview of the item **6**.

You can also add information such as file type and keywords that makes it easy to search for library entries.

To modify the library item information:

1. Select the item.

2. Click the Library Item Information icon.

or

Choose Item Information from the Library panel menu. This opens the Item Information dialog box **7**.

3. Enter the name in the Item Name field.

4. Use the Object Type list to choose one of following categories **8**:

   • **Text** contains text frames.

   • **Image** contains raster images.

   • **Page** is an entire page.

   • **Structure** contains XML elements.

   • **EPS** contains EPS files.

   • **PDF** contains PDF files.

   • **InDesign** contains InDesign files.

   • **Geometry** includes frames and rules that do not contain images or text.

TIP InDesign assigns a category when items are entered into a library. You can change that listing to any category you want.

5. Enter a description for the item.

Setting the Library Display

Searching and Sorting Libraries

If you have many items in a library, you may find it difficult to find specific library entries. InDesign has a powerful search feature that makes it easy to locate specific items in a library.

To search within a library:

1. Click the Show Library Subset icon.

   or

   Choose Show Subset from the Library panel menu. This opens the Subset dialog box .

2. Choose Search Entire Library to search all entries in the library 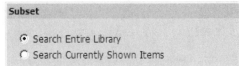.

   or

   Choose Search Currently Shown Items to search through only those items currently displayed in the library.

3. Use the Parameters menu and fields to set the search criteria .

4. Click More Choices to add up to five choices to the parameters list.

5. Choose Match All to choose only those items that match all the search parameters .

   or

   Choose Match Any One to find items that meet at least one of the search parameters.

6. Click OK to display the items that meet the search criteria.

TIP Use the Back or Forward button to move through the search settings in the Subset dialog box.

9 *The* **Subset dialog box** *lets you find specific library items.*

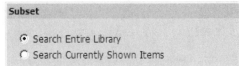

10 *The* **search criteria in the Subset dialog box** *let you specify where to search in the library.*

11 *The* **Parameters menu** *lets you choose which part of the item information is searched.*

12 *The* **match criteria** *in the Subset dialog box control how the search items are matched.*

Libraries or Snippets?

As you read about libraries and snippets you may wonder which one you should use. I agree that the two features are very similar. But I have noticed a few significant differences.

Libraries can hold hundreds, if not thousands of items, and can be sorted using sophisticated sorting commands.

Unlike library items, snippets can be dragged from the Bridge onto an InDesign document and can be set to appear on the page in exactly the same spot where they originated. Library items cannot be dragged onto the page in the same position. They must be added using the Place command.

Also, snippets have smaller file sizes than Libraries. Snippets should be used when you need to save just a few items from a page.

You can see a preview of the elements in snippets. Libraries only show the document icon.

Finally, snippets have a more fun name. I like reading the word *snippets*. I like writing the word *snippets*. I like saying the word *snippets*! Snippets make me happy.

Once you have sorted a library, you may need to show all the items at some other time.

To display all the library entries:

◆ Choose Show All from the Library panel submenu.

You can also control the order in which the library items are displayed. This makes it easier to find items in large libraries.

To sort library entries:

◆ Choose one of the Sort Items options from the Library panel menu:
  - **By Name** arranges the items in alphabetical order.
  - **By Newest** arranges the items in the order they were added, with the newest items first.
  - **By Oldest** arranges the items in the order they were added with the oldest items first.
  - **By Type** arranges the items in groups according to their categories.

Searching and Sorting Libraries

Creating and Using Snippets

Snippets are exactly what they sound like — little bits of a page that you snip off to use somewhere else.

To create snippets using the Export command:

1. Select the items on the page that you want to turn into a snippet.

2. Choose File > Export.

3. In the Export dialog box choose InDesign Snippet from the Format list .

TIP You cannot drag portions of text as a snippet, only the entire frame.

4. Name and save the file. The snippet icon appears in the directory.

13 *The* **Export dialog box** *lets you save items as InDesign snippets.*

To create snippets by dragging:

1. Select and drag the items that you want to turn into a snippet onto the desktop. The Snippet icon appears with a bizarre temporary name.

2. Change the name to something more understandable.

Once you have created snippets, you can drag them onto a page.

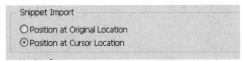

14 *The* **Snippet Import setting** *in the File Handling Preferences lets you control where snippets appear when dragged onto a page.*

To drag snippets onto a page:

1. Select the snippet on the desktop or in the file directory.

2. Drag the Snippet icon onto the InDesign document page.

TIP Use the Snippets Import setting in the **Preferences > File Handling** dialog to choose whether the snippet appears at its original coordinates or the cursor position **14**.

TIP Snippets also can be dragged from the Adobe Bridge onto a page.

Creating and Using Snippets

TABS AND TABLES 13

Before tabs and tables, there was chaos. Well, perhaps not chaos, but it was difficult to line up columns of text in an orderly fashion.

The word "tab" comes from the tabulator key on a typewriter. (Does anyone still use a typewriter?) The tabulator key moved the carriage a certain number of spaces.

The tabulator key was named because it allowed typists to create tabular data. Tabular data is information arranged in systematic rows and columns — otherwise known as a table.

However, mathematical information isn't the only thing arranged in tables. Resumes, menus, train schedules, calendars, and even classified ads are all arranged in some form of table.

Anytime you need to keep text or graphics aligned in either columns or rows, consider using the tabs and tables features in InDesign.

Not only can you align text using tabs, but you can create tab leaders that make it easy to read across the lines of text. You can also create tables with repeating headers and footers and add custom strokes and fills to the tables.

Inserting Tab Characters

There are two parts to working with tabs. The first part is to insert the *tab characters* that force the text to jump to a certain position.

To insert tab characters into text:

1. Position the insertion point where you want the tab character to be located.

2. Press the Tab key on the keyboard. This creates a tab character in the text 1.

TIP Choose **Type > Show Hidden Characters** to see the display of the tab character within the text.

TIP InDesign recognizes tab characters in imported text.

InDesign also has a special type of tab character called a right tab. This tab character automatically sets the text to the rightmost position in the frame 2.

To insert a right tab character:

1. Place the insertion point where you want the right tab character.

2. Press Shift-Tab.

   or

   Use the contextual menu to insert a right tab character from the Insert Special Character menu.

Franks»Writer

1 *A* **tab character** *is displayed as part of the hidden characters in text.*

Chapter·one   ⌡   5¶
Chapter·two   ⌡   45¶
Chapter·three ⌡   62#

2 *The* **right tab character** *automatically moves the text to the right side of the text frame.*

Inserting Tabs in Text

It's actually very simple to insert a tab character into text. Just tap the Tab key. However, there are some guides for working with tabs.

Insert only one tab character for each column. Even if the text doesn't line up correctly, don't add another tab character. Use the Tab panel and tab stops to line up the columns.

If you're over a certain age, you may have been taught to put a tab at the beginning of a paragraph to indent the first line. Don't do it! As mentioned in Chapter 3, "Basic Text," you can use the first line indent to format paragraphs.

Inserting Tab Characters (sidebar)

3 The **Tabs panel** *contains the controls for inserting tab stops and aligning the tabs.*

4 *Choose one of the four* **tab alignment icons** *to control how the text is aligned.*

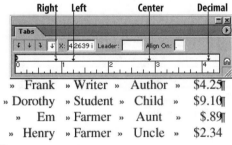

» Frank » Writer » Author » $4.25¶
» Dorothy » Student » Child » $9.10¶
»   Em » Farmer » Aunt » $.89¶
» Henry » Farmer » Uncle » $2.34

5 *Examples of how the four tab alignments control the text.*

Setting Tab Stops

The next — and most important — part to working with tabs is to set the *tab stops* or the formatting controls that set where the text should stop after it jumps to a new position. This is controlled using the Tabs panel.

To open the Tabs panel:

♦ Choose **Type** > **Tabs.** The Tabs panel appears above the text frame **3**.

TIP The Tabs panel can be kept onscreen like any other panel.

TIP If the Tabs panel is not positioned above the text, click the Magnet icon in the panel to automatically move the panel to the correct position.

To set tab stops:

1. Select the text.

2. Choose the type of tab alignment from the four tab icons in the ruler **4**. The four alignments work as follows **5**:

   • **Left** aligns the left side of the text at the tab stop.

   • **Center** centers the text on either side of the tab stop.

   • **Right** aligns the right side of the text at the tab stop.

   • **Decimal** aligns the text at the decimal point or period within the text.

3. Click the ruler area where you want the tab stop to be positioned.

   or

   Type a number in the Position field. A small tab arrow corresponding to the tab type appears that indicates the position of the tab stop.

TIP The default tab stops are invisible left-aligned tabs positioned every half inch. Adding tab stops to the ruler overrides all tab stops to the left of the new tab.

To change tab settings:

1. Select the text.

2. Open the Tabs panel.

3. To change the alignment of a tab stop, select the tab arrow and then click a new alignment icon.

   or

   Hold the Opt/Alt key and click the tab arrow in the ruler.

4. To change the position of a tab stop, drag the tab arrow to a new position.

TIP As you move a tab stop along the ruler, a line extends through the text, even if the Tabs panel is not aligned to the text frame 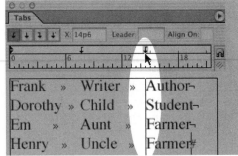. This helps you judge the position of the tab stop.

Many times you will want to have tab stops repeated at the same interval. InDesign makes it easy to set repeating tabs.

To set a repeating tab:

1. Position the first tab stop on the ruler.

2. With the tab stop still selected, choose Repeat Tab from the Tabs panel menu **7**. This adds new tab stops at the same interval along the ruler **8**.

TIP The tab stops created by the Repeat Tab command are not linked and move independently.

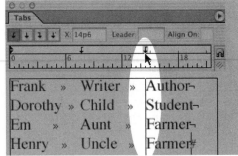

6 *As you move a tab stop,* **a line extends through the text** *to help you position the tab stop correctly.*

Clear All
Delete Tab
Repeat Tab
Reset Indents

7 *The* **Tabs panel menu** *gives you several important commands for working with tabs.*

8 *The* **Repeat Tab command** *allows you to easily add tab stops at the same interval along the ruler.*

Setting Tab Stops

9 *To remove a tab stop, drag it off the Tabs panel ruler.*

10 *You can enter a custom alignment character for the **Align On field**. Here the text aligns to the hyphen.*

Once you have added tab stops to the Tabs panel ruler, you can remove them easily.

To remove tab stops:

1. Select the tab stop on the Tabs panel ruler.

2. Drag the tab stop off the ruler. This deletes the tab stop **9**.

   or

   Choose Delete Tab from the Tab panel menu.

TIP If there are no tab stops to the left of the one you removed, this restores the invisible, default tab stops at the nearest half-inch position.

If you have many tab stops on the Tabs panel ruler, it may be easier to delete all the tab stops with a single command.

To clear all the tabs off the ruler:

♦ Choose Clear All from the Tabs panel ruler **7**. This restores the invisible default tab stops at every half-inch mark.

The Decimal tab aligns numerical data to a decimal point. However, you may need to align text to a different character. For instance, some European currency uses a comma instead of a decimal. InDesign lets you set a custom alignment character.

To set a custom alignment character:

1. Choose the Decimal Tab icon.

2. Add a tab stop to the ruler.

3. Replace the period in the Align On field with a different character. The text aligns around that character **10**.

Setting Tab Stops

Creating Tab Leaders

A *tab leader* allows you to automatically fill the space between the tabbed material with a repeating character. Tab leaders are often used in the tables of contents of books *(such as the one at the front of this book)*.

TIP Tab leaders are added when the reader needs to move horizontally across a wide column from one entry to another. The tab leader helps the reader's eye stay on the correct line of text.

To add tab leaders:

1. Select the tab stop arrow on the Tabs panel ruler.

2. Type up to eight characters in the Leader field of the Tabs panel.

TIP Add spaces between characters in the Leader field to give the leader a more pleasing look 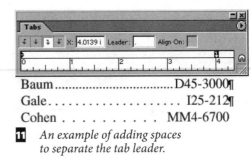.

TIP Press the Tab key on the keyboard to preview the characters in the Leader field.

TIP You can select the characters in a tab leader as you would ordinary text and change the point size, kerning, or other attributes.

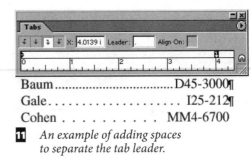

11 *An example of adding spaces to separate the tab leader.*

Choosing Between Tabs and Tables

For as long as I can remember, designers have wanted an easy way to create tables in page-layout documents. Now that InDesign lets you create tables, is there any reason to still use tabs?

Absolutely! I use tabs in this book to separate numbers from the text in the exercises. I also use tabs with leaders for the listings in the table of contents.

I use tables whenever I need side-by-side paragraphs such as in a résumé. I also use tables whenever I need to separate the information with horizontal and vertical lines.

Creating Tab Leaders

12 *Use the* **Insert Table dialog box** *to create an empty table in a text frame.*

Table and Cell Styles

As you read through the rest of this chapter, you may feel that it's too much work to create and format tables and the cells within tables. Relax, InDesign has powerful table and cell styles which make it easy to create very sophisticated-looking tables with just a few clicks.

However, rather than totally overwhelm you in this chapter, I'll cover the styles for tables and cells in Chapter 15, "Styles."

So, as you go through this chapter, consider this the part where you learn to bake bread from scratch. Later on I'll show you how to automate the whole process.

Creating and Using Tables

Tabs are limited to lining up only a single line of text. Tables can line up text so it extends down into several lines. Tables also let you add borders to the cell that contains the text or add fills of color behind the text.

To create a new table in a text frame:

1. Place an insertion point inside a text frame.

2. Choose **Table > Insert Table**. The Insert Table dialog box appears **12**.

3. Use the Body Rows control to set the number of rows in the table.

4. Use the Columns control to set the number of columns.

5. Use the Header Rows control to set the number of rows across the top of the table.

6. Use the Footer Rows control to set the number of rows across the bottom of the table.

TIP Headers and footers are special cells that are repeated when the table is divided between frames or pages.

7. If you have defined a table style, use the Table Style list to choose that style for the table.

8. Click OK. InDesign creates a table that fills the text frame as follows:

   • The width of the table is set to fill the width of the text frame.

   • The table columns are distributed evenly across the table.

Creating and Using Tables

Many times you will import text that you'd like to be converted into a table. Fortunately, this is rather easy to do.

To convert text into a table:

1. Select the text.

2. Choose **Table** > **Convert Text to Table**. The Convert Text to Table dialog box appears .

3. Use the Column Separator menu to choose which character should be used as the marker for each column in the table.

   or

   Type the character that you would like as the marker in the Column Separator field.

   TIP If you have imported tabbed delimited text, this is most likely a tab character although paragraph returns and spaces are sometimes used.

4. Use the Row Separator menu to choose which character should be used as the marker for each row in the table.

   or

   Type the character that you would like as the marker in the Row Separator field.

   TIP For most text, this is the paragraph symbol.

5. If you have chosen anything except a paragraph symbol for the Row Separator, use the Number of Columns field to choose how many columns there should be in the table.

6. If you have defined a table style, use the Table Style list to choose that style for the table.

7. Click OK to create the table **14**.

13 *The* **Convert Text to Table dialog box** *lets you choose how text is converted to a table.*

14 *The* **Convert Text to Table command** *transforms tabs and paragraphs into rows and columns.*

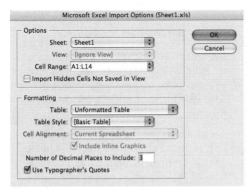

15 *The* **Microsoft Excel Import Options dialog box** *lets you choose which worksheet and cells are imported from an Excel document.*

16 *The* **Microsoft Word Import Options dialog box** *lets you choose how Word tables are imported into the InDesign document.*

What if you've already got a beautiful table, and some tabbed text, but they are separated from each other. InDesign lets you paste tabbed text into existing tables.

To paste text into a table:

1. Copy the tabbed text.

2. Highlight the cells in the table where you want the text to appear.

3. Choose paste. The text will populate the cells of the table and make additional table cells if necessary.

Most people use Microsoft Word and Excel to create text and spreadsheets. InDesign lets you import the tables created by both Word and Excel.

To import a table from Word or Excel:

1. Choose **File** > **Place** and navigate to the Word or Excel file.

2. If necessary, use the Microsoft Excel Import Options **15** or the Microsoft Word Import Options **16** to control how the file will be imported, as described on the next two pages. Click OK.

3. The imported document is inserted into the selected text frame.

   or

   Click or drag the loaded text cursor.

Creating and Using Tables

You can also customize which Excel data is imported.

To choose the cells that should be imported:

1. Use the Sheet menu to select a worksheet.

2. Use the View menu to choose a custom view.

3. Use the Cell Range field to select cells.

4. If desired, check the Import Hidden Cells Not Saved in View box.

To set the formatting for Excel cells:

1. Use the Table menu to change the formatting options as follows:

    • **Formatted Table** imports the cells with whatever formatting was applied in Excel.

    • **Unformatted Table** imports the cells with no formatting except a stroke around each InDesign cell.

    • **Unformatted Tabbed Text** converts the cells into text divided by tab characters.

2. If you have defined a table style, choose one from the Table Style list.

3. Use the Cell Alignment menu to choose:

    • **Current Spreadsheet** imports the text aligned with the alignment that was set in the spreadsheet.

    • **Left** sets the text aligned to the left side.

    • **Center** aligns the text to the center.

    • **Right** sets the text aligned to the right.

4. Use Number of Decimal Places to Include to set how many decimal places to include in the imported cells.

5. If desired, check Use Typographer's Quotes to convert straight "quotes" (like these) into open and closed "quotes" (like these).

Importing from Spreadsheets

Most likely, if you need to import data from Excel spreadsheets, the files have been created by accountants or others who know little about graphic design or page layout.

Try to talk to them before they send you the file for layout. Explain that they should not format their document using the controls in Microsoft Excel. Most of the time you will just have to strip out that formatting in order to make the file work in your layout.

You may also want to ask them for a test file so you can see how the information will be imported.

Creating and Using Tables

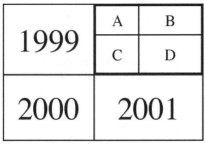

17 *An example of how a table can be inserted inside a cell of another table.*

18 *The* **Convert Table to Text command** *transforms table rows and columns into tabs and paragraph returns.*

You can also control how table information in Word documents is imported.

To set the formatting for Word tables:

1. Select Remove Text and Table Formatting in the Microsoft Word Import Options dialog box to change the original formatting applied in Word.

TIP Use this option to remove some of the hideous formatting that may have been applied to Word tables.

2. If you have set the option to remove the formatting, choose one of the following from the Convert Tables To menu:

   - **Unformatted Tables** imports the Word table with no formatting except a stroke around each cell.

   - **Unformatted Tabbed Text** converts the cells into text divided by tab characters.

To place a table in a table cell:

1. Click with the Text tool to place an insertion point inside a table cell.

2. Use the Insert Table command or a Place command to create a table within that cell **17**.

To convert a table to text:

1. Place an insertion point in any cell inside the table.

2. Choose **Table > Convert Table to Text**.

3. Use the Convert Table to Text dialog box to choose what elements should be used to designate the column and row separators **18**:

   - You can convert columns and rows to tabs, commas, or paragraph returns.

   - You can type your own character in the field to customize the conversion.

Creating and Using Tables

Navigating Through Tables

As you work with tables, you will want to add content to the cells, move from cell to cell, and select cells, rows, and columns.

To insert text into table cells:

1. Place an insertion point inside a table cell.

2. Type the text for the cell.

   or

   Choose **File > Place** to insert imported text in the cell.

To move from one cell to another:

◆ Press the Tab key to jump forward from one cell to another 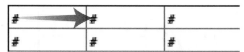.

   or

   Press Shift-Tab to move backward from one cell to another 20.

Since you navigate through a table using the Tab character, you need some special techniques to insert actual tab characters into a table.

To insert a tab character into a table:

◆ Press Opt/Alt-Tab to insert a tab character inside a cell 21.

   or

   Choose **Type > Insert Special Character > Tab Character**.

To jump to a specific row:

1. Choose **Table > Go to Row**. The Go to Row dialog box appears 22.

2. Use the menu to move to the body, header, or footer of the table.

3. Enter the number for the row you want to move to.

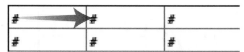

19 *Press the Tab key to* **jump forward from one cell to another** *in a table.*

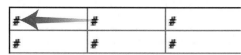

20 *Press Shift-Tab to* **jump backward from one cell to another** *in a table.*

21 *Press* **Opt/Alt-Tab** *to insert a* **tab character** *into a table.*

22 *The* **Go to Row dialog box** *lets you quickly jump from one row to another.*

Navigating Through Tables

Text only selected

23 *When the text in a cell is selected, only the text is highlighted. When the entire cell is selected, the entire cell area is highlighted.*

24 *Drag across and then down to select a specific group of cells in a table.*

25 *The* **down arrow cursor** *indicates you can click to select an entire column in a table.*

Selecting Tables

By clicking and dragging your cursor, you can select cells, columns, rows, or the entire table.

TIP When the entire cell, row, column, or combination of cells are selected, you can copy and paste cells from one part of a table to another.

To select text in a table cell:

1. Place an insertion point inside a table cell.

2. Drag across the cell until all the text in the cell is highlighted.

   or

   Choose **Edit** > **Select All** to select all the text within that cell.

TIP There is a difference in the appearance between just the text selected and the entire cell selected **23**.

To select text in multiple table cells:

1. Use the Text tool to drag across to select the cells in specific columns **24**.

2. If you want, continue to drag down to select the cells in additional rows.

To select a table column:

1. Place the Text tool cursor at the top of the table. A down arrow cursor appears.

2. Click the down arrow. The entire column is selected **25**.

3. Drag across with the down arrow cursor to select any additional columns.

   or

   Move the down arrow to another column and Shift-click to select multiple columns.

Selecting Tables

To select a table row:

1. Place the Text tool cursor at the left side of the table. A left arrow cursor appears.

2. Click the left arrow. The entire row is selected **26**.

3. Drag down with the left arrow cursor to select any additional rows.

   or

   Move the left arrow to another row and Shift-click to select multiple rows.

To select the entire table:

1. Place the Text tool cursor at the top corner of the table. A slanted arrow cursor appears.

2. Click the slanted arrow. The entire table is selected **27**.

To use the table selection commands:

1. Place the insertion point in a cell in the table.

2. Choose one of the following commands:

   • **Table > Select > Cell** selects the cell.

   • **Table > Select > Row** selects the row that contains the cell.

   • **Table > Select > Column** selects the column that contains the cell.

   • **Table > Select > Table** selects the entire table.

TIP The table selection commands are helpful for applying borders and fills to cells.

26 *The left arrow cursor indicates you can click to select an entire row in a table.*

27 *Position the cursor at the upper-left corner and click to* **select the entire table.**

28 *The* **Table Setup dialog box** *contains the basic options for a table's appearance.*

29 *The* **Table Dimensions area** *lets you set the number of rows, columns, header rows, and footer rows.*

Working with Rows and Columns

Once you've created a table, you may want to change the number of rows and columns in the table.

TIP In addition to the Table menu and dialog boxes, many adjustments to tables can be made using the Table panel or Control panel. *(See the section "Using the Table or Control Panels" at the end of this chapter for more information on modifying tables with those onscreen elements.)*

To change the number of rows and columns:

1. Select the entire table or any part of the table.

2. Choose **Table > Table Options > Table Setup** to open the Table Setup dialog box **28**.

3. Set the Body Rows controls in the Table Dimensions area to increase or decrease the number of rows in the main section of the table **29**.

4. Set the Header Rows controls to increase or decrease the number of rows in the header section of the table **29**.

5. Set the Columns controls to increase or decrease the number of columns in the table **29**.

6. Set the Footer Rows controls to increase or decrease the number of rows in the footer section of the table **29**.

TIP Use the Preview control at the bottom of the Table Setup dialog box to see the results of changing the controls.

TIP The commands in the Table Dimensions section always add rows and columns at the end of the table sections. The next exercise explains how to insert rows and columns into a specific location in the table.

You can also insert columns and rows into a specific location in a table.

To insert columns into a table:

1. Place an insertion point where you want to insert the columns.

2. Choose **Table > Insert > Column**. The Insert Columns(s) dialog box appears 30.

   or

   Choose **Insert > Column** from the Table panel menu.

3. Use the Number field to set the number of columns.

4. Choose either Left or Right to specify where the new columns should be inserted 31.

To insert rows into a table:

1. Place an insertion point where you want to insert the rows.

2. Choose **Table > Insert > Row**. The Insert Row(s) dialog box appears 32.

   or

   Choose **Insert > Row** from the Table panel menu.

3. Use the Number field to set the number of rows.

4. Choose either Above or Below to specify where the new rows should be inserted.

TIP The Insert Row(s) dialog box inserts rows into the header, footer, or main section of a table.

To insert rows as you type:

1. Place the insertion point in the final cell of the last row of the table main body, header, or footer.

2. Press the Tab key. A new row is automatically inserted.

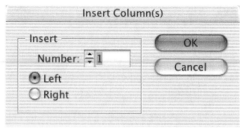

30 *Use the* **Insert Column(s) dialog box** *to add columns at a specific location within a table.*

Original table

	A	B	C	D
Y	84	94	34	55
Z	22	33	44	55
	AA	BB	CC	DD

Selected cell

After column is inserted   New column

	A	B		C	D
Y	84	94		34	55
Z	22	33		44	55
	AA	BB		CC	DD

31 *An example of* **how a column is added** *to the left of the selected cell.*

32 *Use the* **Insert Row(s) dialog box** *to add rows at a specific location within a table.*

Working with Rows and Columns

33 *Hold the Opt/Alt key as you drag across to* **add columns to a table**.

34 *Hold the Opt/Alt key as you drag down to* **add rows to a table**.

Selected cells   After deleting content

35 *An example of how you can* **delete the content of selected cells**.

To add columns as you drag the table edge:

1. Drag the last column of the table.

2. Press the Opt/Alt key as you drag. This expands the size of the table by adding columns **33**.

To add rows as you drag the table edge:

1. Drag the last row of the table.

2. Press the Opt/Alt key as you drag. This expands the size of the table by adding rows **34**.

To delete table columns:

1. Select the columns you want to delete.

2. Choose **Table > Delete> Column**.

To delete table rows:

1. Select the rows you want to delete.

2. Choose **Table > Delete> Row**.

To delete the entire table:

1. Select the table.

2. Choose **Table > Delete> Table**.

You may want to delete the content inside a cell without deleting the cell itself.

To delete the content in table cells:

1. Select the cells, columns, or rows.

2. Press the Delete/Backspace key or choose **Edit > Clear**.

TIP The content is deleted but the cells themselves remain in place **35**.

Working with Rows and Columns

You can't move cells from one place to another, but you can copy and paste cells and their content to new locations.

To copy and paste the content in table cells:

1. Select the cells, columns, or rows that you want to move to a new position.

2. Choose **Edit > Copy** or **Edit > Cut**. This puts the selected cells on the clipboard.

3. Select the new cells, columns, or rows.

TIP You should select at least the same number of cells, columns, or rows that were selected in step 1.

4. Choose Edit > Paste. The content on the clipboard is pasted into the selected cells **36**.

TIP If you selected more cells than were selected in step 1, the excess cells are not changed.

When you create a table, all the columns and rows are evenly spaced. However, you can modify the size of the rows and columns.

TIP A red dot inside a table cell indicates there is an overflow of text **37**. You can change the size of the cell to display the overflow text.

To change a single row height visually:

1. With the Text tool selected, place the cursor along the border of the row you want to adjust. The cursor changes to an up/down arrow **38**.

2. Drag to adjust the height of the row.

To change all the rows visually:

1. Place the cursor along the bottom border of the table. The cursor changes to an up/down arrow.

2. Hold the Shift key as you drag to adjust the height of all the rows in the table.

Working with Rows and Columns

Select and copy cells

W	55	65	
X	42	52	
Y	84	94	
Z	22	33	

Select and copy empty cells

W	55	65	
X	42	52	
Y	84	94	
Z	22	33	

Paste cells to new position

W	55	65	65
X	42	52	52
Y	84	94	94
Z	22	33	33

36 *The three-step process to* copy and move *cells from one position to another.*

July	August	Sep-
34	45	785
453	499	644

37 *A* red dot inside a table cell *indicates that there is an overflow of text inside the cell.*

April	May	June
12	67	54
6	7	2

38 *The* Up/Down arrow *indicates you can adjust the row height.*

39 *The* **Rows and Columns category** *of the Cell Options dialog box.*

40 *The* **Left/ Right arrow** *indicates you can adjust the column width.*

41 *The* **Column Width control** *of the Cell Options dialog box.*

To set the row height numerically:

1. Select the rows you want to adjust.

2. Choose **Table > Cell Options > Rows and Columns** to open the Cell Options dialog box to the Rows and Columns options **39**.

3. Set the Row Height menu as follows:
   - **At Least** sets a row height that can increase to hold text or an image.
   - **Exactly** sets a row height that does not get larger.

4. Enter an amount in the Row Height field.

5. Use the Maximum field to prevent the row from becoming too tall.

To change the column width visually:

1. With the Text tool selected, place the cursor along the border of the column you want to adjust. The cursor changes to a left/right arrow **40**.

2. Drag to adjust the width of the column.

To set the column width numerically:

1. Select the columns you want to adjust.

2. Enter an amount in the Column Width field **41**.

Working with Rows and Columns

You can adjust columns or rows so their spacing is evenly distributed.

To automatically distribute columns:

1. Set the rightmost column to the position it should be after the adjustment.
2. Select the columns you want to adjust.
3. Choose **Table > Distribute Columns Evenly**. The column widths adjust .

To automatically distribute rows:

1. Set the bottommost row to the position it should be after the adjustment.
2. Select the rows you want to adjust.
3. Choose **Table > Distribute Rows Evenly**. The row heights adjust so they are the same size .

You can control when and how the rows of a table break across text frames.

To set the keep options for rows:

1. Select the rows you want to control.
2. Choose **Table > Cell Options > Rows and Columns**.
3. Choose from the Start Row menu as follows :
   - **Anywhere** lets the row start anywhere in a text frame.
   - **In Next Text Column** forces the row to the next column in the frame or the next text frame.
   - **In Next Frame** forces the row to the next text frame.
   - **On Next Page** forces the row to the next page.
   - **On Next Odd Page** forces the row to the next odd-numbered page.
   - **On Next Even Page** forces the row to the next even-numbered page.
4. Check Keep with Next Row to make sure one row doesn't separate from another .

42 *The results of using the* **Distribute Columns Evenly command**.

43 *The results of using the* **Distribute Rows Evenly command**.

44 *The* **Start Row menu** *lets you choose where that row starts.*

45 *Check* **Keep with Next Row** *to force one row to always stay with the next one.*

Working with Rows and Columns

Here are the dates for the Spring classes.¶

April#	May#
12#	67#

No space around table

Here are the dates for the Summer classes.¶

June#	July#
12#	22#

Space added around table

46 **Add some space around a table** *to keep it from colliding with text.*

47 *The* **Table Spacing controls** *let you set the amount of space before and after a table.*

48 *The text threads show how tables can flow from one frame to another.*

Adjusting Tables Within a Text Frame

Tables are always contained within text frames. You can control how much space there is between the table and the text that precedes or follows it **46**.

To set the spacing around a table:

1. With the table selected, choose **Table** > **Table Options** > **Table Setup**. The Table Options dialog box appears.

2. Use the Table Spacing control for Space Before to set the amount of space between text and the top of the table **47**.

3. Use the Table Spacing control for Space After to set the amount of space between the bottom of the table and the text that follows it.

TIP A table is inserted into a text frame as an inline object in its own paragraph. This means that any space before or after the paragraph that holds the table is added to the space set by the Table Spacing controls.

If a table extends longer than a text frame, you get a text frame overflow. You can easily flow the rest of the table from frame to frame across pages.

To flow tables between frames:

1. Use the Selection tool to load the overflow cursor.

2. Click the overflow cursor inside the new frame to flow the rest of the table into the frame **48**.

Adjusting Tables Within a Text Frame

Working with Headers and Footers

Tables with lots of data often flow from one location to another. For easy navigation, you can repeat the first and last rows of the table each time it appears in a new place. When the first row of a table repeats, it is called a *header*. When the last row repeats, it is called a *footer*.

To add a header or footer to a table:

1. With the table selected, choose **Table > Table Options > Headers and Footers**. The Table Options dialog box opens to the Headers and Footers tab .

2. Use the Header Rows controls to set the number of repeating rows added to the top of the table .

3. Use the Footer Rows controls to set the number of repeating rows added to the bottom of the table.

TIP To turn off a header or footer, set the Header Rows or Footer Rows to zero.

TIP You can also set the number of header and footer rows in the Table Setup.

To set the repeat options for headers and footers:

1. Use the Repeat Header or Repeat Footer menu as follows 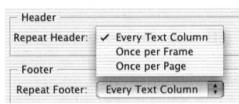:

   - **Every Text Column** repeats the header or footer whenever the table appears.

   - **Once per Frame** repeats the header or footer only once in the same frame. This is useful when a table flows from one column to another.

   - **Once per Page** repeats the header or footer only once in the same page. This is useful when a table flows into multiple frames on the same page.

2. Check Skip First (header) or Skip Last (footer) to display the header or footer only after the first instance of the table.

49 *The* **Headers and Footers area in Table Options** *lets you control the appearance of headers and footers in the table.*

50 *Use the* **Table Dimensions for Headers and Footers** *to control the number of header and footer rows.*

51 *Use the* **Repeat Header menu** *to set how frequently the header appears.*

Working with Headers and Footers

Body cells

Footer cells

 An example of what happens when a row is converted from body cells to header cells. Notice that the footer takes on the alternating fill.

As you work, you may want to convert body table cells into a header or footer.

To convert cells into a table header:

1. Select the rows that you want to convert. These rows must be the first rows of the table.

2. Choose **Table > Convert Rows > To Header**. The rows are converted from the body of the table to the table header 52.

TIP If there already is a header for the table, the cells are added to the bottom of the existing cells.

To convert cells into a table footer:

1. Select the rows that you want to convert. These rows must be the last rows of the table.

2. Choose **Table > Convert Rows > To Footer**. The rows are converted from the body of the table to the table footer.

TIP If there already is a footer for the table, the cells are added to the top of the existing cells.

Finally, you may want to convert the rows in a header or footer into the body of the table.

To convert header or footer cells into body cells:

1. Select the rows that you want to convert.

TIP The rows must be the bottom rows of the header or the top rows of the footer.

2. Choose **Table > Convert Rows > To Body**.

Working with Headers and Footers

Adding Images to Tables

Although table cells are created to hold text, you can easily add images as inline graphics to each cell.

To insert a graphic into a table cell:

1. Place an insertion point inside a table cell.

2. Choose **File** > **Place** to insert an image into the cell .

   or

   Paste a graphic copied to the clipboard into the cell.

TIP Graphics in cells are pasted as inline graphics.

If the graphic is larger than the size of the cell, some of the graphic may stick out beyond the cell. You use the Clipping setting to control whether placed graphics are seen outside a cell.

To control the display of a graphic inside a cell:

1. Place your insertion point inside the cell that contains the placed graphic.

2. Choose **Table** > **Cell Options** > **Text**. This opens the Cell Options dialog box .

3. Select Clip Contents to Cell to limit the display of the graphic to inside the cell 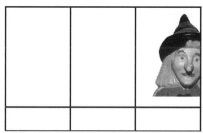.

   or

   Deselect Clip Contents to Cell to allow the graphic to be displayed outside the cell 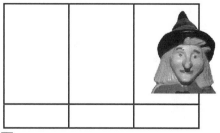.

TIP In addition to allowing a graphic to appear outside the cell boundaries, you can also drag a table so that the table itself extends outside the text frame.

An example of how a placed image can be inserted into a table cell.

*The **Clip Contents to Cell** option for inline graphics in a cell.*

*With the **clip options turned on**, an inline graphic is confined to the boundaries of the cell.*

*With the **clip options turned off**, an inline graphic extends outside the boundaries of the cell.*

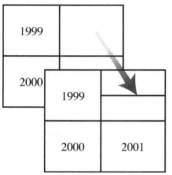

57 *The results of using the* **Merge Cells command.**

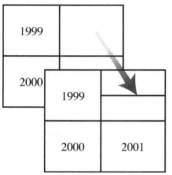

58 *The results of using the* **Split Cell Horizontally command.**

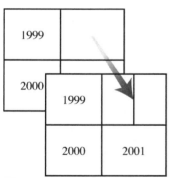

59 *The results of using the* **Split Cell Vertically command.**

Customizing Cells

In addition to setting the controls for the entire table, you can also make settings for individual cells. You can customize the arrangement of rows and columns by merging or splitting cells. You may want to merge cells to fit more text within a cell. You can also change the space of text within a cell.

To merge cells:

1. Select the cells you want to merge.

2. Choose **Table > Merge Cells**. The dividers between the cells are deleted **57**.

TIP If the merged cells contain text, the text will be divided into paragraphs.

To unmerge cells:

1. Select the cells you want to unmerge.

2. Choose **Table > Unmerge Cells**.

To split cells:

1. Select the cell you want to split.

2. Choose **Table > Split Cell Horizontally** or **Table > Split Cell Vertically 58** or **59**.

Customizing Cells

You can also control how text is positioned horizontally and vertically within each cell.

TIP These settings also control how inline graphics are positioned within frames.

To set the cell options for text:

1. Select the cells you want to adjust.

2. Choose **Table** > **Cell Options** > **Text**. This opens the Cell Options for text controls .

3. Use the Cell Insets fields to adjust the space between the text and the top, bottom, left, and right sides of the cells .

TIP Check the "link icon" to make all the cell insets the same amount.

4. Choose one of the four settings from the Text Rotation menu to rotate the text in 90° increments.

You can also set the vertical alignment for where the text is positioned in the cell.

To set the text vertical alignment:

1. Select the cells you want to adjust.

2. Choose **Table** > **Cell Options** > **Text**. This opens the Cell Options dialog box for text controls.

3. Use the Vertical Justification Align menu to choose one of the four alignment options as follows:

   • **Top** positions the text at the top edge of the cell.

   • **Center** positions the text in the middle of the cell.

   • **Bottom** positions the text at the bottom edge of the cell.

   • **Justify** distributes the lines of the text evenly so that it extends from the top to the bottom of the cell.

TIP The Justify setting overrides any leading applied to the text.

60 *The **Text area of the Cell Options** controls how text is positioned within each cell.*

61 *The **Cell Insets controls** let you specify how far text sits from the edge of a cell.*

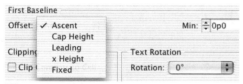

62 *When the* **Justify option is chosen in the Vertical Justification Align menu,** *the Paragraph Spacing Limit control is available.*

63 *The* **First Baseline controls** *let you set the position of the first baseline of text within a cell.*

If you choose Justify for the vertical alignment, you can then control the space between the lines or paragraphs.

To set the vertical justification spacing:

1. Select the cells you want to adjust.

2. Choose **Table > Cell Options > Text**. This opens the text controls for the cells.

3. Choose Justify from the Vertical Justification list.

4. Set an amount for the Paragraph Spacing Limit **62**.

TIP Increase the value for the paragraph spacing to avoid increasing the space between the lines within the paragraph.

Just as you can control where the first baseline of text appears in a text frame, you can also control the position of the text baseline within a cell.

To control the first baseline in a cell:

1. Select the cells you want to control.

2. Choose **Table > Cell Options > Text**. This opens the text controls for the cells.

3. In the First Baseline area, use the Offset menu to choose a setting **63**.

4. In the Min field, set the minimum amount of space for the first baseline.

Customizing Cells

Setting Borders, Strokes, and Fills

One of the benefits of using tables instead of tabs is how easy it is to add lines and colors to the table. (The line around a table is called the *border*. Lines around cells are called *strokes*. Colors inside the cells are called *fills* 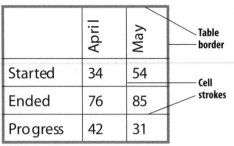.)

To add a border around the table:

1. Select at least one cell in the table.

2. Choose **Table** > **Table Options** > **Table Setup**. The Table Options dialog box opens with the Table Setup options selected .

3. In the Table Border category, use the Weight field to set the thickness of the border/line .

4. Use the Color menu to set the color of the border/line.

5. Use the Tint field to apply a screen to the color.

6. If desired, check overprint for the color.

7. Use the Type menu to set a stripe pattern for the border.

If you have applied a stroke to a cell that touches the table border, the Preserve Local Formatting checkbox controls how the table border changes the local settings to cells.

To preserve the formatting applied to cells:

1. Apple a stroke to the cells.

2. In the Table Options dialog box, select Preserve Local Formatting to maintain the appearance of the cell edges that touch the table border 🖸.

   or

   Deselect Preserve Local Formatting to allow the table border to override the stroke applied to the cell.

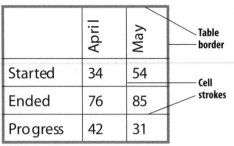

64 The **table border** *goes around the outside of a table.*

65 The **Table Setup dialog box** *lets you apply a border around the entire table.*

66 *You can format the line around a table with the* **Table Border controls.**

67 The **Preserve Local Formatting option** *maintains the appearance of cells that touch the table border.*

68 *The* **Strokes and Fills controls** *under Cell Options let you format cells in a table.*

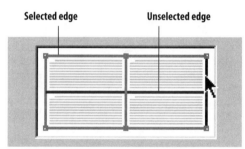

Selected edge   Unselected edge

69 *Click the* **proxy lines for the cell stroke** *to control which edges of the cell are stroked. The colored lines indicate the edge is selected.*

One cell   Two or more columns

Two or more rows Two or more columns and rows

70 *The* **cell preview area** *changes depending on how many cells, rows, or columns are selected.*

Tables are automatically created with strokes around the cells. You can remove those cell strokes, apply new ones, or customize them as you see fit.

To customize the strokes around individual cells:

1. Select the cells you want to modify.

2. Choose **Table > Cell Options > Strokes and Fills**. The Cell Options dialog box appears with the Strokes and Fills options selected **68**.

3. Click the proxy lines in the cell preview to select which edges of the selected cells should be formatted **69**. The top, bottom, left, and right edges of the preview area correspond to the position of the edges in the selected cells.

TIP *Important!* Select and deselect the proxy lines in the cell preview *before* you change any of the settings in the dialog box. This avoids applying partial settings to the cells.

TIP The cell preview area changes depending on the combination of cells, rows, or columns you have selected **70**.

4. Set the controls under Cell Stroke to format the appearance of the selected edges.

5. Click OK to apply the settings.

Setting Borders, Strokes, and Fills

If all your strokes are the same solid color, you don't have to worry about how the table is drawn. But as soon as you mix strokes or use nonsolid strokes, you need to set preferences for how the strokes appear when they cross each other.

To set the stacking order for the border and strokes:

1. Select at least one cell in the table.

2. Choose **Table > Table Options > Table Setup**. The Table Options dialog box appears.

3. Choose one of the following from the Draw menu :

   - **Best Joins** lets InDesign create the best possible appearance for how the strokes intersect.

   - **Row Strokes in Front** moves the strokes for the rows in front of the strokes for the columns.

   - **Column Strokes in Front** moves the strokes for the columns in front of the strokes for the rows.

   - **InDesign 2.0 Compatibility** uses a combination of the Best Joins for the table border and the rows in front of the strokes for the interior cells.

You can also fill the inside of a cell with a color or gradient.

To customize the fill inside individual cells:

1. Select the cells you want to modify.

2. Choose **Table > Cell Options > Strokes and Fills**. The Cell Options dialog box opens set to Strokes and Fills.

3. Set the controls under Cell Fill to format the color inside the selected cells .

TIP If you have already defined a gradient swatch, you can fill the selected cells with a gradient.

Best Joins

Row Strokes in Front

Column Strokes in Front

InDesign 2.0 Compatibility

71 *Examples of* **how the Draw menu settings are applied** *to tables.*

72 *The* **Cell Fill controls** *let you apply colors to individual cells in a table.*

73 *The* **Table Options for Row Strokes** *allow you to apply alternating patterns for the strokes applied to rows.*

74 *The* **Alternating Pattern menu** *for setting table rows.*

75 *The* **Alternating controls** *allow you to choose the appearance for the alternating row strokes.*

Alternating Strokes and Fills

Many people who work with tables find it helpful to set alternating strokes or fills for entire rows or columns in repeating patterns. This can help readers easily navigate down the column or across the row in lengthy tables.

TIP Even if you insert or delete rows or columns, the Alternating Pattern feature automatically reapplies the correct sequence of fills to your table.

To alternate repeating strokes for rows:

1. Select at least one cell in the table.

2. Choose **Table > Table Options > Alternating Row Strokes**. The Table Options dialog box opens set to the Row Strokes tab **73**.

3. Use the Alternating Pattern menu to choose how frequently the row strokes will alternate **74**.

4. Set the controls on the left side of the Alternating area to format the stroke appearance for the first set of rows **75**.

5. Set the controls on the right side of the Alternating area to format the appearance of the stroke for the next or second set of rows.

6. Use the Skip First and Skip Last fields to omit a certain number of rows at the start and end of the table from the alternating count.

TIP If you have applied custom strokes to individual cells and want to override the local formatting, uncheck the Preserve Local Formatting checkbox.

Alternating Strokes and Fills

To alternate repeating strokes for columns:

1. Select at least one cell in the table.

2. Choose **Table** > **Table Options** > **Alternating Column Strokes**. The Table Options dialog box opens set to Column Strokes .

3. Use the Alternating Pattern menu to choose how many column strokes will alternate .

4. Set the controls on the left side of the Alternating area to format the appearance of the stroke for the first set of columns 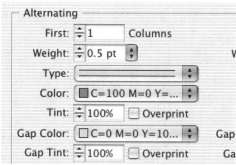.

5. Set the controls on the right side of the Alternating area to format the appearance for the second set of columns.

6. Use the Skip First and Skip Last fields to omit certain columns at the start and end of the table from the alternating count.

TIP If you have applied strokes to individual cells, the Preserve Local Formatting command controls whether the alternating strokes for columns override that local formatting.

76 *The* **Column Strokes controls** *under Table Options let you apply automatic alternating strokes to table columns.*

77 *The* **Alternating Pattern menu** *for table columns.*

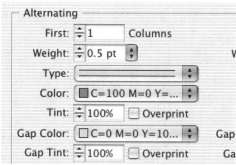

78 *The* **Alternating controls** *allow you to choose the appearance for the alternating column strokes.*

Alternating Strokes and Fills

79 *The* **Fills controls** *under Table Options let you apply automatic alternating fills to table rows or columns.*

80 *The* **Alternating Pattern menu** *for setting table fills.*

81 *The* **Alternating controls** *allow you to choose the appearance for the alternating fills.*

82 *An example of a table that uses the alternating fills for repeating rows.*

To alternate repeating fills:

1. Select at least one cell in the table.

2. Choose **Table > Table Options > Alternating Fills**. The Table Options dialog box appears set to Fills **79**.

   or

   Choose **Table Options > Alternating Fills** from the Table panel.

3. Use the Alternating Pattern menu to choose how many row or column fills will alternate **80**.

4. Set the controls on the left side of the Alternating area to format the appearance of the fill for the first set of columns or rows **81**.

5. Set the controls on the right side of the Alternating area to format the appearance of the second set of columns or rows.

6. Use the Skip First and Skip Last fields to omit certain rows or columns at the start and end of the table from the alternating count.

TIP If you have applied fills to individual cells, the Preserve Local Formatting command controls whether the alternating fills override that local formatting.

TIP My own personal favorite is to set repeating fills of light and dark rows **82**.

Alternating Strokes and Fills

Adding Diagonal Lines in Cells

Many people who design tables use diagonal lines to indicate empty data or corrected information. InDesign lets you apply diagonal lines inside cells.

To add diagonal lines in cells:

1. Select the cells you want to modify.

2. Choose **Table** > **Cell Options** > **Diagonal Lines**. The Cell Options dialog box opens with the Diagonal Lines options selected .

3. Click one of the direction controls to set the direction of the diagonal lines 84 and their styles 85.

4. Set the Line Stroke options to format the appearance of the line 86.

5. Choose one of the following from the Draw menu:
   - **Content in Front** positions the diagonal line behind any text in the cell.
   - **Diagonal in Front** positions the diagonal line in front of any text in the cell.

83 The **Diagonal Lines controls** *under Cell Options let you add diagonal lines to cells.*

84 The **direction controls** *for the diagonal lines in cells.*

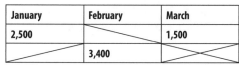

85 *Examples of how the diagonal lines can be used in cells.*

86 The **Line Stroke controls** *for diagonal lines let you style the appearance of the diagonal lines inside cells.*

87 *The* **Table panel** *provides an onscreen panel to modify many of the table controls.*

88 *When a table is selected, the* **Control** *panel displays the table controls.*

Using the Table or Control Panels

You can also work with the Table panel or the Control panel to modify the number of columns and rows, their width and height, and other settings in tables.

To work with the Table panel or Control panel:

1. Select the table or cells in the table.

2. Choose **Window > Type & Tables > Table**. This opens the Table panel **87**.

   or

   Choose **Window > Control**. This opens the Control panel **88**.

3. Use the controls, fields, and icons as shown in the following chart.

Table feature	Icon
Number of rows	⊟ ⇕ 4
Number of columns	▥ ⇕ 3
Row height menu	⊺ Exactly ▾
Row height	⇕ 1p4.32
Column width control	⊢ ⇕ 6p5.75
Text vertical justification	≡ = = ≡
Text rotation	T ⊣ 丄 ⊢
Top cell inset	⊟ ⇕ 0p4
Bottom cell inset	⊟ ⇕ 0p4
Left cell inset	⊹ ⇕ 0p4
Right cell inset	⊹ ⇕ 0p4

Table feature	Icon
There are also some table features that are only in the Control panel.	
Merge cells	
Unmerge cells	
Stroke weight	1 pt
Stroke type	
Cell preview	

TIP You can also use the commands in the Table panel menu or Control panel menu to modify the table.

AUTOMATING YOUR WORK 14

I have a general rule about working with a computer. Anytime I find myself doing the same thing more than ten times in a row, I stop. Most likely there is a command or tool that I can use to automate the process.

That's what this chapter is about — learning how to automate InDesign so the application does the dull, tedious chores for you. (Sadly, I can't apply this rule to other parts of my life, such as washing dishes, cleaning the litter box, or folding socks.)

There are many different automation features. You can use Find/Change, Spell Check, Footnotes, and Find Font to quickly change text formatting. Footnotes make it possible to simply choose the command and let InDesign do its stuff.

As amazing as these features are, they are not the ultimate in automation. Chapter 15 shows how text, tables, and object styles are even more powerful automation tools.

Of course, you're not required to learn any of these automation features. You are perfectly welcome to modify text by hand, one word at a time — especially if you don't care about doing anything else in your life.

Changing Case

InDesign gives you a command to quickly change text case.

To change text case:

1. Select the text you want to change.

2. Choose **Type** > **Change Case** and then choose one of the following: lowercase, Title Case, Sentence case, or UPPERCASE from the submenu.

Checking Spelling

One of the most popular features of page layout programs is the spelling checker, which searches for misspelled words.

To use the spell check command:

1. To check the spelling in a specific text frame or linked frames, click to place an insertion point anywhere within the text.

2. Choose **Edit** > **Spelling** > **Check Spelling**. The Check Spelling dialog box appears and displays the first word that needs attention .

3. Choose one of the Suggested Corrections for the word.

4. Click Change. The word is corrected and the next word is displayed.

   or

   Click Change All to change all instances of the word in the text.

5. Click Skip to continue the spelling check without changing that instance of the text.

   or

   Click Ignore All to continue the spelling check without changing any instance of that word in the text.

6. Click Done to stop the spelling check. The dialog box stays open if you want to run more spelling checks.

1 *The* **Check Spelling** *dialog box is the command center for a spelling check.*

Change To:

Whizard

Suggested Corrections:

Wizard
Wizards
Whizzed
Willard
Whisked
Wised
Wiser
Wiseacre

2 *InDesign gives you* **a list of suggested corrections** *for the unknown words found during a spelling check.*

The Limitations of the Spelling Check

Every once in a while, I read an article about how the use of spelling checkers in computers is contributing to the death of proper writing and language. It's true; too many people run a spelling check and don't bother to actually read the document. Consider the following text:

Their is knot any thing wrung with using a spelling cheque on a sent tents in a doc you mint. Ewe just haft to clique the write butt ends.

Obviously the paragraph is utter nonsense. Yet InDesign's spelling checker (as well as the spelling checker in most other programs) wouldn't flag a single word as being incorrect.

A spelling checker only flags words it doesn't recognize; but since everything in the paragraph is an actual word, InDesign doesn't see any problems. So, please, don't skip a session with a proofreader just because you've run a spelling check.

Once you have opened the Spelling check, you can set which text frames should be searched.

To set the search criteria:

1. In the Search list, choose where the spelling check should be performed:
   - **All Documents** checks all open files.
   - **Document** checks the entire active file.
   - **Story** checks all the linked frames of the selected text.
   - **To End of Story** checks from the insertion point.
   - **Selection** checks only the selected text.

2. Check the Case Sensitive option to require a match for upper- and lowercase characters.

Of course, the spelling checker wouldn't be very helpful if it couldn't make changes to suspect words.

To correct the error displayed:

1. Type a correction in the Change To box.

   or

   Select a word from the Suggested Corrections list **2**.

2. Click Change to change only that instance of the word in the text.

Checking Spelling

The Ignore commands only work during a particular session of InDesign. If you use specialized words frequently, you should add them to the dictionary that InDesign uses during a spell check.

To add words to the spelling check dictionary:

◆ Click Add when the word is displayed during the spelling check.

To edit the dictionary:

1. Choose **Edit** > **Spelling** > **Dictionary** to open the Dictionary dialog box **3**.

TIP You can also open the Dictionary by clicking the Dictionary button in the Check Spelling dialog box **1**.

2. Use the Target list to choose which dictionary you want to add the words to.

3. Choose the language from the Language list.

4. Choose Added Words, Removed Words, or Ignored Words from the Dictionary List.

5. Check the Case Sensitive option to ensure that the case of the word as entered in the dictionary is used during the spelling check.

6. Type the word you want to add in the Word field.

   or

   Select the word you want to remove.

7. Click the Add or Remove button.

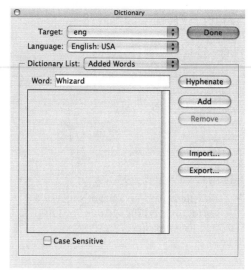

3 *The* **Dictionary dialog box** *allows you to add or delete words in the dictionary used during a spelling check.*

dorothy and
the the Munchkins.

4 *The **wavy underlines** indicate which words have been flagged by the dynamic spelling checker.*

dorothy and teh Munchkins   As typed

Dorothy and the Munchkins   After the autocorrection

5 *An example of how the **Autocorrect feature** corrects the capital letter and the misspelled word.*

You may want to send your dictionary list to others. To do this, you can export the list.

To export entries in the spelling check dictionary:

1. Click the Export button.

2. Name the file and save it.

To import entries into a spelling check dictionary:

1. Click the Import button.

2. Find the file you wish to import.

InDesign also flags suspect words in the layout or Story Editor the same way it would in the spelling checker.

To use the dynamic spelling:

◆ Choose **Edit > Spelling > Dynamic Spelling**. The dynamic spell checker displays unknown words and other spelling errors with wavy underlines **4**.

You can also set InDesign to automatically correct spelling errors as you type. This is called the Autocorrect feature.

To automatically correct spelling errors as you type:

◆ Choose **Edit > Spelling > Autocorrect**. A check appears in front of the command to indicate that Autocorrect is turned on.

TIP The Autocorrection feature only corrects words that are in the Autocorrect preferences or wrongly capitalized words **5**. It does not automatically correct unknown words or repeated words.

Checking Spelling

Using Find/Change

InDesign has a powerful Find/Change control panel that lets you find and replace text, font characters, or object attributes.

To choose the Find/Change mode:

1. Choose **Edit > Find/Change.** The Find/Change dialog box appears .

2. Click one of the following four Find/Change categories :

   - Text lets you search and replace strings of text as well as text formatting.
   - GREP lets you use codes that search for patterns within text.
   - Glyph lets you look for and replace specific glyphs using their Unicode or GID/CID values.
   - Object lets you search for and replace objects with certain formatting.

TIP Click the More Options button to see all the Find/Change controls.

The Find/Change dialog box lets you control which areas of the document are searched.

To set the search areas:

- Click one of the following icons to allow a search in the area .

  - **Locked layers** looks on layers that have been locked. This works only for the Find field.
  - **Locked stories** looks inside stories that have been checked out as part of the InCopy workflow. This works only for the Find field.
  - **Hidden layers** looks on layers that have been turned off in the Layers panel.
  - **Master pages** looks on master pages.
  - **Footnotes** looks inside InDesign's electronic footnotes.

6 *The* **Find/Change dialog box** *allows you to set the controls for searching for and replacing text.*

7 *The* **four categories for Find/Change** *are Text, GREP, Glyph, and Object.*

Locked layers Locked stories Hidden layers Master pages Footnotes

8 *Use* **the search areas** *to control which part of the document the Find/Change will look at.*

9 *The **Find/Change buttons** control the actions during a search.*

Undo after a Find/Change?

I get a lot of oohs and ahhhs when I show that even after a Find/Change that has made hundreds of changes across many pages of a document, I can still undo those changes in just one Edit > Undo command.

Just because InDesign has done a lot of work doesn't mean that you can't undo that work.

Of course, having said that, I'm sure that if I performed some incredibly complicated routine that worked across many documents with thousands and thousands of changes, I might exhaust the memory for the undo string.

But don't let that stop you from trying an undo. The worst you'll get is a slight "beep" from InDesign.

Although all four categories look for and replace different things, the control buttons work the same for all the searches **9**.

To use the Find/Change control buttons:

1. Click Find to start the search. Once something has been found, this button changes to Find Next.

2. Click Change to make the change without moving to the next instance.

   or

   Click Change/Find to make the change and move to the next instance.

   or

   Click Change All to change all the instances in the text.

3. Click Find Next to skip to the next occurrence without changing that instance of the found text.

4. Click Done if you wish to stop the search without going through the whole document.

Using Find/Change

Using the Text Find/Change

The Text category looks for text and changes it into new text or applies formatting. A simple Find/Change works with text only.

To set the Find/Change text strings:

1. To find and change within a specific text frame or linked frames, click to place an insertion point within the text.

2. In the Find What field, type or paste the text you want to search for.

3. In the Change To field, type or paste the text to be inserted.

4. In the Search pop-up list, choose where the search should be performed 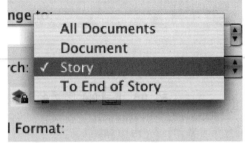:

   - **All Documents** checks all open documents.

   - **Document** checks the entire document.

   - **Story** checks all the linked frames of the selected text.

   - **To End of Story** checks from the insertion point.

   - **Selection** checks only the selected text.

5. Select Case Sensitive to limit the search to text with the same capitalization . For instance, a case-sensitive search for "InDesign" does not find "Indesign."

6. Select Whole Word to disregard the text if it is contained within another word . For instance, a whole-word search for "Design" omits the instance in "InDesign."

7. Click Find. InDesign looks through the text and selects each matching text string.

10 *The* **Search** *list lets you choose which documents or stories should be searched.*

Case sensitive   Whole word

11 *Use* **the case and whole word controls** *to modify the parameters of a text Find/Change.*

12 *The* **Find What** *list lets you enter the special characters to look for in a search.*

Using the Text Find/Change

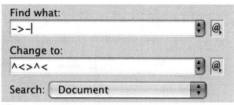

13 *An* **example of the metacharacter codes.** *Here the dashes around a > character are replaced using the codes for thin spaces.*

14 *The* **list of 15 previous search strings** *is saved for each session of InDesign.*

Delete formatting   Find formatting

15 *Click the* **formatting icons** *to add specific formatting to the Find/Change queries.*

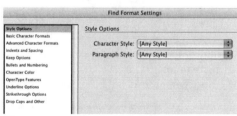

16 *The* **Find Format Settings** *for the Find or Change search criteria.*

Find Format Settings

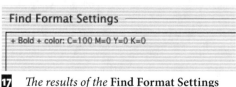

17 *The results of the* **Find Format Settings** *are displayed in the Find Format area.*

InDesign also lets you search for special characters such as spaces, hyphens, paragraph returns, tab characters, or inline graphic markers. These are called *metacharacters*.

To Find/Change metacharacters:

1. Choose the character you want to look for in the Find What menu **12**. The codes are entered in the Find What field **13**.

2. Choose the codes you want to substitute in the Change To menu.

TIP The metacharacter codes can also be entered using the keyboard.

3. Use the control buttons to run the Find/Change routine.

TIP InDesign also keeps a list of the past 15 strings for the Find What and the Change To fields **14**. You can also permanently save queries as described later in this chapter.

With the Find/Change dialog box expanded, you can set the formatting options for either the Find or Change field.

To set the Find/Change formatting options:

1. Click the Format button in the Find Format Settings area of the Find/Change dialog box. This opens the Find Format Settings dialog box **15**.

2. Choose those formatting categories on the left side of the Find Format Settings dialog box **16**.

3. Enter the criteria you want to search for in the fields for the chosen category.

4. Click OK. The search criteria are displayed in the Find Style Settings area **17**.

To delete the formatting options:

◆ Click the Delete icon to delete all the formatting in the Find Format Settings or Change Format Settings area.

Using the Text Find/Change

Using the GREP Find/Change

To perform GREP searches:

1. Click the GREP tab in the Find/Change dialog box .

2. Insert the GREP search codes in the Find what or Change to fields.

3. Set the rest of the dialog box controls the same way as for the Text Find/Change.

18 *The menu for the* **GREP** *codes.*

(sidebar:) Using the grep Find/Change

19 *The* **Glyph category** *of the Find/Change dialog box.*

20 *The* **Glyphs panel** *lets you visually choose the specialized glyphs to find and change.*

Using the Glyph Find/Change

As mentioned in Chapter 3, characters can have alternate glyphs used for fractions, ligatures, and other letter forms. The Glyph Find/Change area lets you search for these alternate glyphs using special codes as well as visual identification **19**.

TIP The Glyph Find/Change only searches and replaces one character at a time.

To perform glyph searches:

1. Click the Glyph tab in the Find/Change dialog box.

2. Use the Find Glyph and Change Glyph fields to choose one or more of the following:

   - Font Family chooses the typeface.
   - Font Style chooses the style.
   - ID lets you choose either the Unicode or the CID/GID numbering system. Then enter that number in the following field.
   - Glyph opens a version of the Glyphs panel, which lets you visually choose the letterform **20**.

3. Set the rest of the dialog box controls as described in the earlier section for Text Find/Change.

TIP The control buttons for the Glyph Find/Change are the same as the ones for the Text Find/Change with the exception of the additional Clear Glyphs button. This button clears all the information from the glyph fields to make it easier to perform new searches.

Using the Object Find/Change

The Object Find/Change lets you search for objects with certain attributes and change them to something else.

To perform object attribute searches:

1. Click the Object tab in the Find/Change dialog box .

2. Click the Find Formatting icons in the Find Object and Change Object fields. The Object Format Options dialog box opens 22.

3. Click each of the categories under the Basic Attributes to choose the object style or object attributes 22.

4. Use the Type list to choose Text Frames, Graphic Frames, or Unassigned Frames 23.

Saving Searches

You can save your searches so you don't have to type the codes and choose the attributes over and over.

To save searches:

1. Click the Save Query icon 24.

2. Name the search.

To apply saved searches:

◆ Choose the saved search from the Query pop-up list.

To delete saved searches:

1. Choose the search you want to delete from the Query list.

2. Click the Delete Query icon.

21 *The* **Object category** *of the Find/Change dialog box.*

22 *The* **Object Format Options dialog box** *lets you choose the attributes to search for or change.*

23 *Use the* **Type list** *to choose a specific type of object frame to search for.*

Save Query   Delete Query

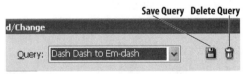

24 *Use the* **Query controls** *list to save, apply, and delete Find/Change searches.*

THE WONDERFUL WIZARD OF OZ

Chapter 1
The Cyclone

Dorothy lived in the midst of the great Kansas prairies, with *Uncle Henry*, who was a farmer, and *Aunt Em*, who was the farmer's wife. Their house was small, for the lumber to build it had to be carried by wagon many miles. There were four walls, a

	14.indd: THE WONDERFUL WIZARD...
Book Title	4.0
Chapter Number	
Chapter name	
Body copy first	

THE· WONDERFUL· WIZARD· OF· OZ¶
Chapter· 1¶
The· Cyclone¶
Dorothy· lived· in· the· midst· of· the· great· Kansas· prairies,· with· Uncle· Henry,· who· was· a· farmer,· and· Aunt· Em,· who· was· the· farmer's· wife.· Their· house· was· small,· for· the· lumber· to· build· it· had· to· be· carried· by· wagon· many· miles.· There· were· four· walls,· a· floor· and· a· roof,· which· made· one· room;·

25 *Text is displayed in the* **Story Editor** *without most of its special formatting. This makes it easier to make changes to the text.*

Styles	Vertical Depth Ruler	Text	Table	Inline graphic
Subhead	4.0	Wizard· of· Oz¶		
Subhead		⊞ ¶		
Subhead		⊡ ¶		
Body Text		It· succeeded· beautifull¦		

26 *The Story Editor displays the various elements within the story.*

or a dozen of the fierce Kalidahs.
Thus each of the little party was
satisfied except Dorothy, who longed
more than ever to get back to Kansas.
OV Overset
On the fourth day, to her great joy,
Oz sent for her, and when she entered
the Throne Room he greeted her

27 *The* **Overset Text indicator** *shows where the text extends outside the visible area of the text frame.*

Using the Story Editor

For people like me, one of the *good* things about electronic page layout is that I edit text as it appears on the page.

For others, one of the *bad* things about electronic page layout is that they edit text as it appears on the page. Those people like to edit text without seeing images, typefaces, sizes, and other design elements. For those people, InDesign has a Story Editor **25**.

To use the Story Editor:

1. Select the text frame that contains the text you want to edit, or place your insertion point inside the text.

2. Choose **Edit > Edit in Story Editor**. The Story Editor opens.

3. Use the right side of the Story Editor to make changes to the text. Any changes you make in the Story Editor appear on the document page.

4. Use the left side of the Story Editor to view the paragraph styles that may have been assigned to the text **26**.

5. If your text is overset inside the text frame, the overset text indicator displays where the overset appears **27**.

TIP The text within tables cannot be displayed in the Story Editor.

TIP The Story Editor appears as a separate window from your document page. You don't have to close the Story Editor to move back to the document. Just click the document page to work on it; then click to move back to the Story Editor.

TIP You can change the display of the Story Editor by changing the preference settings.

Using the Story Editor

Bullets and Numbering

InDesign can also automatically add bullets and numbers in front of paragraphs. This makes it easier to create and format those paragraph lists.

To apply bullets to paragraphs:

◆ Click the Bullets icon in the Control panel 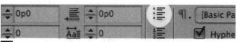.

   or

   Choose **Type > Bulleted & Numbered Lists > Apply Bullets**.

TIP This applies the last-used setting of the bullet options.

You will most likely want to format your own custom bullets.

To format the bullets in a paragraph:

1. Choose Bullets and Numbering from the Paragraph panel menu. The Bullets and Numbering dialog box appears .

2. Choose Bullets from the List Type menu. This displays the bullets options.

3. Choose a bullet from the Bullet Character glyph display.

TIP The letter **U** under the character indicates that the bullet can be styled with any font. Bullets without a **U** are confined to a single font.

4. Use the Text After field to type which characters you want to separate the bullet from the start of the text.

5. If desired, use the Character Style list to choose a character style to format the bullets. *(See Chapter 15, "Styles" for more information on character styles.)*

TIP The position settings described later in this section control how the bullets hang outside the text indent.

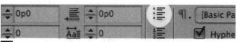

28 *The* **Bullets icon** *in the Control panel quickly applies bulleted lists.*

29 *The* **Bullets options** *of the* **Bullets and Numbering dialog box** *let you select and format bullets automatically.*

Bullets and Numbering

30 *The* **Add Bullets dialog box** *lets you add new bullet characters.*

31 *The* **Numbers icon** *in the Control panel quickly applies numbered lists.*

32 *The* **Numbers options** *of the* **Bullets and Numbering dialog box** *let you select and format numbers automatically.*

To add custom bullet characters:

1. Click the Add button in the Bullets and Numbering dialog box. The Add Bullets dialog box opens **30**.

2. Use the glyphs area to choose the character for the bullet.

3. If you want, choose the Font Family and Font Style for the bullet.

4. To set the bullet to a specific font, click Remember Font with Bullet.

5. Click Add or OK to add the character to the bullet list and choose new characters.

Bullets are just one type of character that can be added to paragraphs. You can also automatically create numbered lists with the Bullets and Numbering controls.

To apply numbers to paragraphs:

◆ Click the Numbers icon in the Control panel **31**.

   or

   Choose **Type > Bulleted & Numbered Lists > Apply Numbers.**

TIP This applies the last-used setting of the numbered options.

To format numbers in paragraphs:

1. In the Bullets and Numbering dialog box, choose Numbers from the List Type menu to display the numbers options **32**.

2. Use the Style list to choose Roman or Arabic numerals, or letters for the list.

3. Use the Separator control to choose a character that follows the number. You can also type your own character.

4. Use the Start At field to designate what number the list should start with.

5. Use the Font Family, Font Style, Size, and Color controls to style the number.

Bullets and Numbering

One of the benefits of the automatic bullets and numbers is that you don't have to worry about inserting tab characters or setting the left and first line indents. The Bullet or Number Position area lets you control those positions.

To set the position of bullets or numbers:

1. Open the Bullets and Numbering dialog box.

2. Use the Alignment list to choose Left, Center, or Right alignment .

TIP Use the Right alignment for numbers so that double-digit numbers align correctly.

3. Use the Left Indent field to set how the left margin of the text is indented.

4. Use the First Line Indent to set how the first line should be indented separately from the left indent.

5. Use the Tab Position field to set the position of the first character after the bullet or number.

There may come a time when you want the automatic bullets or numbers to become ordinary text and stop responding to the automatic controls.

To convert bullets or numbers to ordinary text:

1. Select the text.

2. Choose Type > Bulleted & Numbered Lists > Convert [Bullets or Numbering] To Text.

TIP Use this command if you are going to export the text or save the document to a previous version of InDesign.

33 *The* **Position controls** *of the* **Bullets and Numbering dialog box.**

Bullets and Numbers in This Book

You can see the results of using automatic bullets and numbered lists throughout this book.

All the numbered lists have been set with automatic numbering. This has made it possible for me to insert new items in a list without having to go back and renumber all the other steps.

It also has meant I can move list items around quickly and easily.

I also have used automatic bullets for all the bulleted lists in the book.

Bullets and Numbering

Reference **Footnote**

According to Littlefield, Baum wrote the book as a parable of the Populists, an allegory of their failed efforts to reform the nation in 1896.[1] Scholars soon began to find additional correspondences between Populism and The Wonderful Wizard of Oz. Richard Jensen, in a 1971 study of Midwestern politics and culture, devoted two pages to Baum's story.[2]

---

1 Littlefield, "Parable on Populism," 50, 58.
2 Richard Jensen, The Winning of the Midwest: Social and Political Conflict, 1888-1896 (Chicago, 1971), 282-83.

34 **Footnotes within text** *allow you to easily insert reference markers and the footnote text.*

35 *The* **Numbering controls** *of the Footnote Options dialog box.*

36 *The* **Style options** *for the footnote reference.*

Footnotes

Footnotes are the tiny reference markers inserted into text that correspond to comments usually inserted at the bottom of that column of text. InDesign makes it easy to insert, format, and update footnotes.

To insert a footnote into text:

1. Position the insertion point where you want the footnote reference to appear.

2. Choose **Type > Insert Footnote**. The reference appears in the text and the insertion point appears in the footnote position at the bottom of the text **34**.

3. Type or paste the text for the footnote.

You can also format the style for the reference and the footnote.

To format the style of the footnote:

1. Choose **Type > Document Footnote Options**.

2. Click the Numbering and Formatting tab to display those options **35**.

3. Use the Style list to choose Roman or Arabic numerals, symbols, letters, or asterisks for the reference **36**.

4. Use the Start At field to set what number the footnotes should start with.

5. If desired, click the options for Restart Numbering Every and then choose Page, Spread, or Section.

6. If desired, turn on the option for Show Prefix/Suffix in and then choose Footnote Reference, Footnote Text, or Both Reference and Text.

7. Use the Prefix field to choose a special character or to type in your own prefix for the reference.

8. Use the Suffix field to choose a special character or to type in your own suffix for the reference.

Footnotes

You can also control the appearance of the reference and the footnote text.

To format the reference:

1. Click the Numbering and Formatting tab to open the Formatting controls 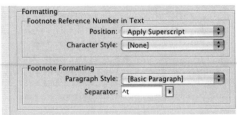.

2. Use the Position list to Apply Superscript, Apply Subscript, or Apply Normal position.

3. Use the Character Style list to apply a previously defined character style.

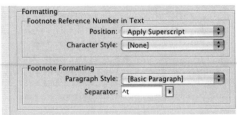

37 *The* **Formatting controls** *of the Footnote Options dialog box.*

To format the footnote:

1. Click the Numbering and Formatting tab to open the Formatting controls **37**.

2. Use Paragraph Style list to apply a previously defined paragraph style.

3. Use the Separator field to enter a tab or space between the footnote reference and the footnote text.

TIP You can enter your own character in this field, as well as have multiple characters in the field.

You can also control the appearance and position of the layout of the footnote.

To control the spacing options for the footnote:

1. Click the Layout tab of the Footnote Options dialog box to open the Layout controls **38**.

2. Use the Minimum Space Before First Footnote field to control how much space separates the bottom of the column and the first footnote.

3. Use the Space Between Footnotes field to control the distance between the last paragraph of one footnote and the first paragraph of the next.

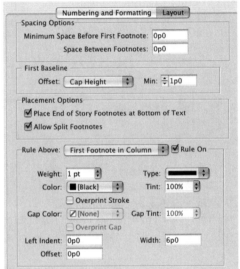

38 *The* **Layout controls** *of the Footnote Options dialog box.*

Footnotes

The **Layout controls** *of the Footnote Options dialog box.*

Importing Footnotes from Microsoft Word

When you import Word documents, the Word Import Options dialog box lets you import footnotes and endnotes.

The footnotes in Word documents are converted into electronic footnotes in InDesign documents.

Endnotes, however, are imported as ordinary text. This means that although you may see the reference in the text and the footnote at the end of the story, there is no electronic link between the reference and the footnote. Unlike electronic footnotes, if you delete the reference, you won't delete the endnote at the end of the text.

You can also control the position of the first baseline of the footnote.

To set the first baseline of the footnote:

1. Use the Offset list to choose the vertical alignment for the baseline.

2. Use the Min. field to increase or decrease this setting.

To set the placement options:

1. Check Place End of Story Footnotes at Bottom of Text to force a footnote that appears at the end of a story to the bottom of the text frame.

2. Check Allow Split Footnotes to permit long footnotes to flow from their original column to the next.

To set the controls for the footnote rule:

1. Choose if a separator rule is applied to one of the following:
   - **First Footnote in Column** applies the rule to the first footnote in the text column **39**.
   - **Continued Footnotes** applies the rule to footnotes that are continued from previous columns or pages **39**.

2. Check Rule On to apply the rule.

3. Use the rest of the controls to style the appearance of the rule.

Footnotes

Creating Tagged Text

If you import text from Microsoft Word, InDesign reads the paragraph and character styles applied in Word. But what happens if you want to import text from an application such as a database that doesn't have style sheets? Tags let you add the codes for styles **40** so that the correct formatting imports with the text **41**.

You can learn the correct tags for different formatting by exporting tags from InDesign.

To export tags from InDesign:

1. Select the text you want to export.

2. Choose **File > Export**.

3. Choose Adobe InDesign Tagged Text from the Save as File Type (Win) or Format (Mac) menu.

4. Click Save. The Export Options dialog box appears **42**.

5. Choose the type of tag:
   - **Verbose** shows the longer version of the tags.
   - **Abbreviated** shows the short version of the tags.

6. Choose the type of encoding **43**:
   - **ASCII**, for most English language files.
   - **ANSI**, for most international characters.
   - **Unicode**, a standard for most languages.
   - **Shift-JIS**, for Japanese characters.
   - **GB 18030**, for Chinese characters.
   - **Big 5**, for Taiwan and Hong Kong traditional Chinese characters.
   - **KSC5601**, for Korean characters.

```
<ASCII-MAC>
<dps:Normal=<Nextstyle:Normal><ct:>>
<ctable:=<Black:COLOR:CMYK:Process:0.0000
00,0.000000,0.000000,1.000000>>
<pstyle:Normal>The <ct:Bold>Scarecrow<ct:>
did not mind how long it took him to fill the
basket, for it enabled him to <ct:Italic>keep
away from the fire.<ct:> So he kept a good
distance away from the flames.
```

40 The **tagged text codes** *as they appear outside InDesign.*

The **Scarecrow** did not mind how long it took him to fill the basket, for it enabled him to *keep away from the fire.* So he kept a good distance away from the flames.

41 *The same text as it appears on the InDesign page.*

42 The **Export Options dialog box** *for setting the Tagged Text options.*

43 The **Encoding menu** *for how tagged text should be exported.*

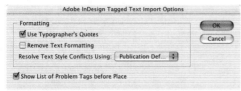

44 *The* **Adobe InDesign Tags Import Options dialog box** *controls how tagged text is imported.*

45 *The* **Revolve Text Style Conflicts Using menu** *lets you determine how two conflicting styles should be resolved.*

You can import tagged text as ordinary text. However, there are some special import options for tagged text.

To import tagged text:

1. Choose **File** > **Place**.

2. Navigate to find the text-only file with the tagged text codes.

3. If you want to control how the text is placed, click Show Import Options.

4. Click Open. The Adobe InDesign Tagged Text Import Options dialog box appears **44**.

The tagged-text import options control how any conflicts and missing tags are treated **45**.

To set tagged-text import options:

1. Check Use Typographer's Quotes to import text with the proper smart quotes.

2. Check Remove Text Formatting to import the text without any local formatting applied.

3. Use the Resolve Text Style Conflicts Using list to choose how to treat conflicts between the styles in the original document and those in the tagged text file. *(See Chapter 15, "Styles," for more information on working with styles.)*

   • **Publication Definition** uses the style as it is already defined in the document.

   • **Tagged File Definition** uses the style as defined in the tagged text. This adds a new style to the document with the word "copy" added to the style name.

4. Check Show List of Problem Tags before Place to display a list of incorrect or unrecognized tags.

Creating Tagged Text

Using Find Font

In addition to the Find/Change commands for text, InDesign lets you make global changes for font families. This helps if you open documents that contain missing fonts.

To make changes using Find Font:

1. Choose **Type** > **Find Font**. The Find Font dialog box appears .

2. Select the font that you want to change.

TIP The icons next to each font display the type of font and its status .

3. Use the Replace With controls to choose a replacement for the selected font.

4. Click Find First to find the first instance of the font. InDesign highlights the first place the font is used.

TIP When you find the first instance, the Find First button changes to Find Next.

5. Click one of the following options:
   - **Find Next** skips that instance.
   - **Change** replaces that instance.
   - **Change/Find** replaces that instance and finds the next instance.
   - **Change All** changes all the instances of the font.

6. Use the More Info button to find more information, such as if the fonts can be embedded in PDF documents 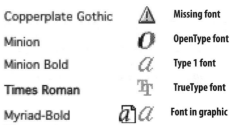.

7. Use Reveal in Finder (Mac) or Explorer (Windows) to locate where the font is on the computer.

To replace missing fonts:

1. Open the document. If fonts are missing, an alert box appears.

2. Click Find Font to open the Find Font dialog box.

3. Choose the missing font and follow the steps in the previous exercise.

46 *The* **Find Font dialog box** *lets you make global changes to the fonts in a document.*

47 *The* **Find Font icons** *tell you the status and type of fonts used in the document.*

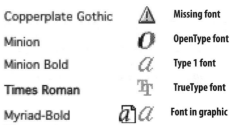

48 *The* **Info area** *of the Find Font dialog box gives you more information about the font.*

49 *The* **Keep Options dialog box** *controls how paragraphs break across columns or pages.*

50 *The* **Keep Lines Together** *controls of the Keep Options dialog box.*

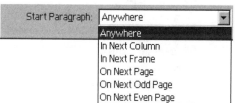

51 *The* **Start Paragraph list** *lets you choose where the next lines of the paragraph appear.*

Keeping Lines Together

Another automation technique is to sp how many lines of text must remain tog in a column or page. InDesign does this using the Keep Options controls.

To set the keep options for a paragraph:

1. Choose Keep Options from the Paragraph panel menu. This opens the Keep Options dialog box **49**.

2. Enter a number in the Keep With Next Lines field to force the last line in a paragraph to stay in the same column or page with the specified number of lines.

TIP This option ensures that subheads or titles remain in the same column as the body copy that follows.

3. Click Keep Lines Together and set one of these options **50**:

   - **All Lines in Paragraph** prevents the paragraph from ever breaking.

   - **At Start/End of Paragraph** lets you set the number of lines that must remain together for the start and the end of the paragraph.

4. Use the Start Paragraph menu to choose where the lines must jump to **51**.

   - **Anywhere** allows the text to jump anywhere.

   - **In Next Column** forces the text to the next column or page.

   - **In Next Frame** forces the text to the next frame or page.

   - **On Next Page** forces the text to the next page.

   - **On Next Odd Page** forces the text to the next odd-numbered page.

   - **On Next Even Page** forces the text to the next even-numbered page.

Keeping Lines Together

Using the Eyedropper on Text

The Eyedropper tool lets you quickly grab the formatting from one part of the text and apply it to another.

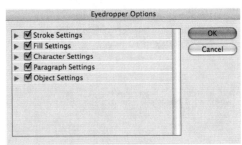

52 *The* **Eyedropper tool** *in the* **Tools panel** *lets you sample and apply text formatting.*

To set the eyedropper options for text:

1. Double-click the Eyedropper tool in the Tools panel **52**. This opens the Eyedropper Options dialog box.

2. Click the triangle control to open the Paragraph Settings from the list **53**.

3. Check which paragraph attributes you want the Eyedropper tool to sample.

4. Click the triangle control to open the Character Settings from the list **54**.

5. Check which character attributes you want the Eyedropper tool to sample.

Once you have set the eyedropper options, you can sample and apply paragraph or character attributes.

TIP Deselect the text frame as you use the Eyedropper tool to avoid styling the text frame itself.

53 *The* **Eyedropper Options** *dialog* **box** *contains the controls for text as well as object styling.*

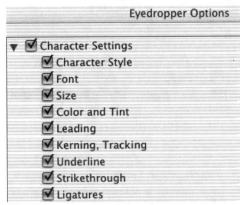

To sample and apply paragraph attributes:

1. Choose the Eyedropper tool.

2. Click the white eyedropper inside the paragraph that you want to sample **55**. The eyedropper changes from white to black.

3. Click the black eyedropper inside the paragraph that you want to change **56**. This changes the paragraph attributes.

TIP The black eyedropper does not apply character attributes when clicked unless a paragraph style was already applied to the sampled text.

4. Click the eyedropper inside any additional paragraphs that you want to change.

54 *Use the checkboxes to set the* **Paragraph Settings** *or the* **Character Settings**.

The·Wizard·of·
Oz.¶

By·L.·Frank·Baum¶

55 *Click the white eyedropper to sample the right alignment of the paragraph attributes.*

The·Wizard·of·
Oz.¶
By·L.·Frank·Baum¶

56 *Click the black eyedropper to apply the right alignment of the paragraph attributes.*

The·**Munchkins**·
and·the·Witch.¶

57 *Click the white eyedropper to sample local character attributes.*

The·**Munchkins**·
and·the·Witch.¶

58 *Drag the black eyedropper to apply character attributes to text.*

To sample and apply character attributes:

1. Choose the Eyedropper tool.

2. Click the white eyedropper inside the text that you want to sample **57**. The eyedropper changes from white to black.

3. Drag the black eyedropper across the exact text you want to change. This highlights the text **58**.

4. Release the mouse to apply the changes.

To sample new text attributes:

1. Hold the Opt/Alt key as you click the Eyedropper tool. The Eyedropper cursor changes to white.

2. Click the eyedropper inside the new text that you want to sample.

Using Scripts

Perhaps the most powerful way to automate working in InDesign is with AppleScripts on the Macintosh or VisualBasic scripts in Windows. You can also use JavaScripts, which work on both platforms. While you need to know code to *write* scripts, it's very easy to *run* scripts in InDesign. Writing code is much too difficult for me. Running scripts is totally easy. (Honestly, if I can do it, anyone can!)

To run scripts in InDesign:

1. Place the script file or the folder containing the script file inside the following directory path:

   InDesign Application Folder: Scripts: Scripts Panel.

2. Choose **Windows > Automation > Scripts** to open the Scripts panel 59.

3. If you have placed a folder inside the Scripts directory, click the triangle controller to open the scripts in the folder.

4. Double-click the script that appears in the panel. This prompts the start of the script.

TIP Certain scripts require an object or text to be selected. Follow any onscreen prompts that occur.

TIP You can also assign keyboard shortcuts to run scripts. Choose **Edit > Keyboard Shortcuts** to open the dialog box.

59 *Use the Scripts panel to run scripts from within InDesign.*

My Favorite Script

My favorite script was written for me by Peter Truskier of Premedia Systems (www.premediasystems.com). This script automates the process of creating the special spotlight used on certain screen shots in this book. *(See page 351, figure 27 for an example of the effect.)*

With Peter's marvelous script, I can do in just a single click that which used to take me almost a minute for each illustration. Ordinarily, it costs big bucks to hire people to write scripts for you, but if you go to the Adobe Studio Exchange, (www.adobestudioexchange.com) you will find other similarly wonderful scripts that are free to download.

STYLES 15

Awhile back I taught InDesign to a group of designers that included a young woman who was responsible for a yearly 100-page catalog of her company's products. When I got to the part of the class where I showed what text styles could do, she began to cry.

I'd never had a student break down and cry in a class, so I was very concerned. I didn't know what to do. "What's wrong?" I asked.

It took her a while to speak, but she eventually explained that it was "those styles." Turns out she had never been taught what styles did and she had been formatting the thousands of entries in the catalog by hand.

She now realized just how much time she could have saved by using text styles. Of course, this was before InDesign added object styles. And even more before table styles.

I dedicate this chapter to all of you who have been slaving away, working without text, object, and table styles. May the techniques you learn here bring smiles, not tears, to your faces.

Working with Paragraph Styles

InDesign has two types of text styles. *Paragraph styles* apply formatting for both character and paragraph attributes. *Character styles* apply formatting for only character attributes.

The Basic Paragraph style is the style that is always part of a document and is automatically applied to all new text 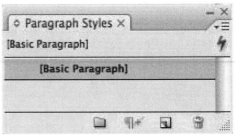. When you change the definition of the Basic Paragraph style, it automatically updates all text that has been styled with the Basic Paragraph style.

The **Basic Paragraph** *is the default style that appears in all new documents.*

To set the Basic Paragraph attributes by example:

1. Click inside a text frame and use the Control panel, Character panel, or Paragraph panel to change the text attributes.

2. A plus sign (+) appears next to the Basic Paragraph listing in the Paragraph Styles panel 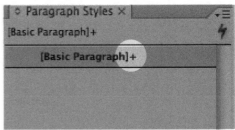. This indicates that local formatting has been applied to the Basic Paragraph.

3. Choose Redefine Style from the Paragraph Styles panel menu. This changes the definition of the Basic Paragraph to match the local formatting. The plus sign disappears.

The **plus sign (+) next to the style name** *indicates that local formatting has been applied to the text.*

To set the Basic Paragraph attributes by definition:

1. Double-click the Basic Paragraph listing in the Paragraph Styles panel. This opens the Paragraph Styles Options dialog box.

2. Make whatever changes to the style definition you like as explained on the following pages.

3. Click OK to make the changes.

TIP The Basic Paragraph style can be modified but not deleted.

New Style Group   New Style

Clear Overrides   Delete Style

3   *The* **Paragraph Styles panel** *lets you define and apply paragraph styles.*

4   *The* **New Paragraph Style dialog box** *set to the General options.*

You can use the Paragraph Styles panel to define new paragraph styles for a document.

To define a paragraph style manually:

1. Choose **Type** > **Paragraph Styles.** This opens the Paragraph Styles panel **3**.

2. Choose New Paragraph Style from the Paragraph Styles panel menu.

   or

   Opt/Alt-click the New Style icon in the Paragraph Styles panel. This opens the New Paragraph Style dialog box set to the General options **4**.

3. Use the Style Name field to name the style.

4. Set the Based On, Next Style, and Shortcuts options as described later in this chapter.

5. Click each category on the left side of the dialog box and set the criteria for each one **5**. *(These categories are the same as the character and paragraph formatting described in Chapter 3, "Basic Text.")*

6. Click OK to define the style. The name of the style appears in the Paragraph Styles panel.

General
Basic Character Formats
Advanced Character Formats
Indents and Spacing
Tabs
Paragraph Rules
Keep Options
Hyphenation
Justification
Drop Caps and Nested Styles
Bullets and Numbering
Character Color
OpenType Features
Underline Options
Strikethrough Options

5   *Click* **each category in the Paragraph Styles dialog box** *to set the format of the style.*

Working with Paragraph Styles

The easier way to define a style is to format the selection and define the style by example.

To define a paragraph style by example:

1. Select some text.

2. Use any of the commands to format the text.

3. Leave the insertion point in the formatted text.

4. Choose Type > Paragraph Styles.

5. With the insertion point blinking in the formatted text, click the New Style icon. This adds a new style to the Paragraph Styles panel.

TIP Check Apply Style to Selection to apply the newly-named style to the text originally selected.

TIP Double-click to rename the style created by the New Style icon.

The Next Style command for paragraph styles has two features. For typists who enter text directly into InDesign, it allows you to automatically switch to a new style as you type text. For instance, as I type this paragraph, I press the paragraph return after the period. This automatically switches to the next style, which is the exercise header.

To set the next paragraph style:

1. Select the General category in the New Paragraph Style dialog box.

2. Choose a style from the Next Style list in the New Paragraph Style dialog box 6. The chosen style is applied to the next paragraph when you press the Return key 7.

   or

   Choose Same Style from the Next Style list 6. This retains the original style until you manually change the style.

6 *The Next Style menu lets you choose [Same Style] or an already defined style.*

Checking Spelling

One of the most popular features of page layout programs is the Spelling Checker that checks a document for misspelled words.

Next style applied

Same style applied

To use the spell check command:

1. To check the spelling in a specific text frame or linked frames, click to place an insertion point within the text.

2. Choose Edit > Check Spelling. The Check Spelling dialog box appears 2.

3. In the Search list, choose where the spelling check should be performed 3:

7 *The Next Style command changes the paragraph style when the return key is pressed. The Same Style command keeps the style when the return is pressed.*

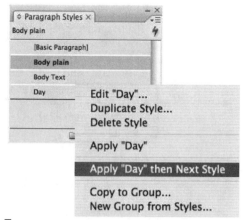

The Next Style feature does even more magic when you use it to apply the next style to selected text. This allows you to format many paragraphs in one simple click.

To apply the Next Style to multiple paragraphs:

1. Highlight the text that you want to style.

   or

   Select the text frame that contains the text that you want to style.

2. Position your cursor over the name of the paragraph style that you want to apply to the first paragraph.

3. Right-click (Windows) or Control-click (Mac) the name of the style. A contextual menu appears 8.

4. Choose Apply "name of style" then Next Style. This styles the text according to the Next Style controls 9.

TIP The command to apply the Next Style is only available if a Next Style has been defined for the paragraph style. If the style has Same Style for the Next Style, then the contextual menu will not display the Next Style option.

8 *The* **contextual menu over a style name** *allows you to apply a paragraph style and then the Next Style to the rest of the selected text.*

FRIDAY

The Princess Bride (1987) Directed by: Rob Reiner

SATURDAY

On the Waterfront (1954) Directed by: Elia Kazan

SUNDAY

The Wizard of Oz (1939) Directed by: Victor Fleming, Richard Thorpe

9 *An example of how the* **Next Style command** *applies for the style for the day. This changes to the movie listing and then back to the day, and so on.*

Working with Paragraph Styles

Working with Character Styles

Character styles allow you to set specific attributes that override the paragraph style character attributes. For instance, **this bold text** was set by applying a character style to the paragraph style.

To define a character style:

1. Choose **Type > Character Styles.** This opens the Character Styles panel 10.

2. Choose New Character Style from the Character Styles panel menu. This opens the New Character Style dialog box 11.

3. Name the style.

4. Set the Based On and Shortcut controls as described later in this chapter.

5. Click each category to set the character attributes 12.

6. Click OK to define the style. The name of the style appears in the Character Styles panel.

TIP Check Apply Style to Selection to apply the newly named style to the text originally selected.

You can also format the text and then define a character style by example.

To define a character style by example:

1. Select some sample text.

2. Format the text.

3. Leave the insertion point in the newly formatted text.

4. Choose **Type > Character Styles.**

5. Click the New Style icon. This adds a new style to the Character Styles panel.

New style group   **Delete style**

New style

10 *The* **Character Styles panel** *lets you define and apply character styles.*

11 *The* **New Character Style dialog box** *lets you specify settings for each of the categories for character styles.*

12 *Click each* **category in the Character Style dialog box** *to set the format of the style.*

Style Settings:

Body Text + next: [Same style] + size: 14 pt + color: C=0 M=100 Y=0 K=0

13 *When you base a new style on an existing style, you can see how they differ in the **Style Settings field** of the New Character Style dialog box.*

Basing Styles

The style for the numbers of the exercises in this book is based on the style of the subheads. If I change the style for the subheads, the number style and the numbers change automatically.

Similarly, the style for the exercises is based on the style for the body copy. So if my publisher asks me to make the copy a little smaller, I only have to change the point size for one style.

Limit how many levels you go when you base one style on another. Theoretically, you can base one style on another, which is based on another, which is based on another, and so on. However, this can be confusing if you go down too many levels.

I always use one style as the main one and base others on it. I think of the main style as the hub of a wheel, and the others are the spokes around it.

Working with Styles

The great thing about styles is that once you understand the basics of paragraph and character styles, you also know the basics for object and table styles. However, rather than wait till the end of this chapter to cover working with styles, I'm going to cover those techniques now. You can then use these techniques for the other types of styles.

Basing one style on another makes it easy to coordinate multiple text styles.

TIP You can only base like styles (paragraph on paragraph, character on character) on each other.

To base one style on another:

1. Start with at least one style.
2. Open the New Style dialog box to define a new style.
3. From the Based On pop-up menu, choose the style you want to use as the foundation of the new style.
4. Make changes to define the second style's attributes.

TIP The changes to the second style are displayed in the Style Settings area **13**.

TIP Any changes you make later to the original style also affect the second style.

If you have based one style on another, at some point you may want to remove any changes to the style so that it is like the first.

To reset to the base style:

◆ Click the Reset To Base button.

You can also set the text so that it no longer is governed by the style.

To break the link to a style:

◆ Choose Break Link to Style from the style panel menu.

Rather than create a new style from scratch, it may be easier to duplicate an existing style and then redefine it.

To duplicate a style:

1. Select the style.

2. Drag the style onto the New Style icon in the styles panel.

   or

   Choose Duplicate Style from the Styles panel menu.

To sort styles:

◆ Drag the style to the position where you want it to be.

   or

   Choose Sort by Name from the Styles panel menu.

You can also set keyboard shortcuts for styles. This makes it easy to apply styles as you type.

To set style keyboard shortcuts:

1. Open the New Style dialog box.

   or

   Double-click the name of the style to open the Style Options dialog box.

2. Click in the Shortcut field.

3. Press a keyboard modifier plus a number from the number pad. The keyboard modifiers can be a combination of one or more of the following keys:

   • Cmd (Mac) or Ctrl (Win) keys.

   • Shift key.

   • Opt (Mac) or Alt (Win) keys.

TIP In Windows, the Num Lock key must be turned on to set and apply keyboard shortcuts.

TIP The keyboard shortcut appears next to the style name in the Styles panel .

14 *The* **keyboard shortcut for a style** *is listed next to the name of the style.*

Style Guidelines

I like to arrange my styles by function in the styles panels. For instance, the styles that are applied only on master pages are grouped together; the styles for sidebars are grouped together. Rather than drag the styles all around, I use the Sort by Name command to do the work for me.

For instance, I have three different paragraph styles for the numbered lists in this book. Each style starts with the name *List* and is followed by a descriptive word such as *List Header, List Item, List Item Bulleted,* and so on. So when I sort the styles by name, the styles automatically group together. (I haven't used the style group folders as I have some troubles remembering the proper naming conventions for working with those style groups.)

If you use keyboard shortcuts, keep them in groups. For instance, the styles for the list items all use the keypad number 2 with variations of the keyboard modifiers. So *list item plain* is Shift-2, while *list item body* is Shift-Cmd/Ctrl-2.

Closed style group   Open style group

Styles not in group   Styles in group

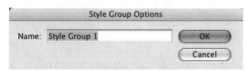

15 *The* **style groups** *as they appear in a styles panel.*

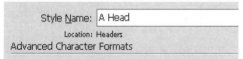

16 *The* **Style Group Options dialog box** *lets you name a style group.*

Style Name: A Head
Location: Headers
Advanced Character Formats

17 *A style in a style group has a name in the* **Location area** *of the Styles dialog box.*

Style Names in Style Groups

When you put styles in a style group, their name changes invisibly. For instance, I can have only one style named Tip at the top level of the styles panel.

But as soon as I put the Tip style into a style group, I can now have another style named Tip at the top level of the panel. I can also have other styles named Tip in other style groups.

Each of these Tip styles is independent of the other styles and they can each have different definitions.

Creating Style Groups

Just as you can create folders to organize files on your computer, so can you create folders (style groups) that allow you to organize your styles. Style groups are available for all types of styles.

To create a style group:

1. Click the New Style Group icon in the styles panel. A new style group folder appears **15**.

   or

   Choose New Style Group from the styles panel. The Style Group Options dialog box appears **16**.

   or

   Opt/Alt-Click the New Style Group icon in the styles panel. The Style Group Options dialog box appears.

2. You can double-click a style group folder to open the Style Group Options dialog box.

3. Choose a name for the Style Group and click OK.

TIP If a style is in a style group, the group appears next to the word Location in the Styles dialog box **17**.

To move styles into a style group:

1. Select the styles you wish to move.

2. Drag them into the style group folder.

TIP You can also select several styles and choose New Group from Styles in the styles panel menu to create a group and put the styles in the folder at once.

TIP Select the styles and choose Copy to Group from the style panel menu to make copies of those styles in a style group.

Creating Style Groups

Loading and Importing Styles

You can transfer or load styles from one document into another.

To transfer text styles into an InDesign document:

1. Choose one of the following from the Paragraph or Character Styles panel menus:

   - **Load Character Styles** transfers the character styles.
   - **Load Paragraph Styles** transfers the paragraph styles.
   - **Load All Text Styles** transfers both character and paragraph styles.

2. Navigate to find the document with the text styles you want to import.

3. Click Open. The text styles are added to the current document.

TIP Text style names are case-sensitive. Therefore, a paragraph style name of *Body Text* will be added as a separate style to a document that already has a paragraph style named *body text* **18**.

To transfer other styles into an InDesign document:

1. Choose Load [type of] Styles from the styles panel menu.

2. Navigate to find the document with the styles you want to import.

3. Click Open. The styles are added to the current document.

18 **Style names are case sensitive,** *so two styles can be listed by the same name but different character cases.*

How Many Styles?

I was taught to create a unique style for each type of element in my document. For instance, I might have a paragraph that I use in these sidebars that looks identical to the paragraph I use in the regular body text.

Some people might be tempted to define only one style and apply it to both paragraphs. That's not how I work. Instead, I have a unique paragraph style for each type of element.

There are two reasons for this. The first reason is that if I ever decide to change the appearance of one type of paragraph, I have that flexibility. The other reason comes from using styles as the tags that give my document structure.

With this type of structure applied to the text, I can export the text and reuse it in an XML workflow. While XML is way beyond the scope of this book, the concept of tagging each type of element with its own style is a good practice to learn.

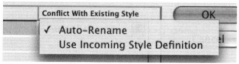

19 Load Styles dialog box *allows you to choose how style conflicts should be resolved.*

20 A check mark next to the style name *indicates the incoming style definition should be resolved.* No check mark *indicates the existing style definition should be used.*

21 *Use the* Conflict With Existing Style menu *to resolve a style conflict.*

When you load styles from one document to another, there may be times when the styles coming into the document have the same name, but different definitions. This is called a style conflict. When this happens you need to resolve the conflict between the styles.

To resolve style conflicts:

1. Choose one of the Load Styles commands. If there are conflicts, the Load Styles dialog box displays the incoming styles that have the same name as the existing styles **19**.

2. Check the styles that you want to load into the document, and resolve the conflict **20**.

   or

   Uncheck the styles that you don't want to load into the document.

TIP Use the Check All or the Uncheck All button to quickly make choices in a long list of styles.

3. For all the checked styles choose one of the following from the Conflict With Existing Style menu **21**:

   • **Auto-Rename** imports the style with a suffix to differentiate it from the existing style.

   • **Use Incoming Style Definition** changes the existing style to match the imported style definition.

Loading and Importing Styles

Importing Text Styles from Word

When you place text from word processing programs such as Microsoft Word into InDesign, the text styles from the imported text are added to the document.

To import styles in Microsoft Word text:

1. Choose **File > Place** and navigate to find the Word file you want to import.

2. Check Show Import Options and click Open. This opens the Microsoft Word Import Options dialog box .

3. Check Preserve Styles and Formatting from Text and Tables.

4. Check Import Styles Automatically.

   or

   Check Customize Style Import.

If you chose to import the styles automatically, you can choose how style conflicts are resolved.

To resolve style conflicts automatically:

1. To resolve paragraph style conflicts, choose one of the following from the Paragraph Style Conflicts menu 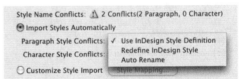.

   - Choose **Use InDesign Style Definition** to have the InDesign style override the incoming style.

   - Choose **Redefine InDesign Style** to have the incoming style override the InDesign style.

   - Choose **Auto Rename** to add the incoming style to the list of styles in the InDesign style panel.

2. To resolve character style conflicts choose from the Character Style Conflicts menu.

TIP A disk icon indicates the style definition came from the imported text 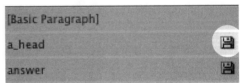.

TIP The disk icon disappears if you modify the imported style.

22 The **Microsoft Word Import Options** dialog box *allows you to control how styles are imported from Word files.*

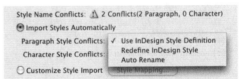

23 *Use the* **Paragraph Style Conflicts** *or* **Character Style Conflicts** menu *to resolve a style conflict.*

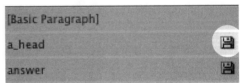

24 The **disk icon** *indicates that the style definition came from an imported text file.*

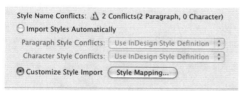

25 *Choose Customize Style Import to click the* **Style Mapping button**.

26 *The* **Style Mapping dialog box** *lets you choose how each Microsoft Word style should be applied.*

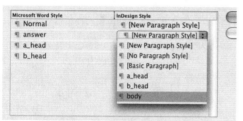

27 *The* **style choices list** *lets you map one style to another. Here the Word style* **answer** *has been mapped to the InDesign style* **body**.

What if you have a style name in Word that is totally different from the name of the style in the InDesign document? You need a way to tell InDesign which existing style to apply to the Word text. The custom style mapping controls let you change an incoming style to a specific existing style.

To map one style to another:

1. In the Microsoft Word Import Options dialog box, check Customize Style Import **25**. This makes the Style Mapping button available.

2. Click the Style Mapping button. This opens the Style Mapping dialog box **26**.

3. Under the InDesign Style column, choose one of the styles from the pop-up menu for each of the incoming Word styles **27**.

4. Click OK to close the Style Mapping dialog box.

TIP Only paragraph styles are shown in the pop-up menu for incoming Word paragraph styles. Similarly, only character styles are shown in the pop-up menu for incoming Word character styles.

5. Click OK to close the Style Mapping dialog box.

6. Click OK in the Microsoft Word Import Options dialog box to import the text.

Importing Text Styles from Word

Applying Styles and Style Overrides

Defining styles is just half of the process. You reap the benefits of your planning when you apply styles.

You can apply paragraph and character styles as you type new text, or you can add the styles to existing text **28**.

To apply paragraph styles:

1. Select the paragraphs.

TIP You do not need to select entire paragraphs. As long as a portion is selected, the paragraph style will be applied to the entire paragraph.

2. Click the name of the paragraph style.

   or

   Type the keyboard shortcut.

You can override the paragraph style by applying a character style or local formatting.

To apply local formatting:

1. Select the text.

2. Use the Control Panel or Character panel to format the text.

TIP A plus (+) sign next to the paragraph style name indicates that local formatting has been applied to the text **29**.

Rather than use local formatting, I prefer to use character styles on text. That way if I want to make changes later on, I can just redefine the character style.

To apply character styles:

1. Select the text.

TIP You must select all the text you want to format with a character style.

2. Click the name of the character style.

   or

   Type the keyboard shortcut.

Character styles

2. Navigate to find the document that contains the styles you want to import. — **Paragraph style**

3. Click **Open**. The styles are *automatically* added to the current document.

28 *An example of paragraph and character styles applied to text.*

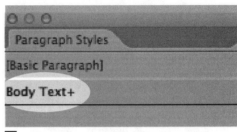

29 *The* **plus sign next to the paragraph style name** *indicates that local formatting has been applied to the text.*

Character Style Strategies

InDesign character styles only need to be defined with a single change from the paragraph attributes.

For instance, if you want to change text to italic, define a character attribute with just italic as the definition.

You can then apply the italic character attribute to many different paragraph styles, even if they are different typefaces or point sizes.

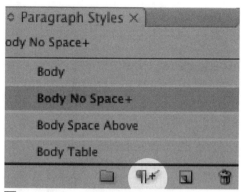

30 *The* **Clear Overrides button** *lets you remove local formatting applied to text.*

Clearing Style Overrides

When you apply local formatting or character styles, you have different ways to clear those style overrides.

You can use the Clear Overrides button to clear the overrides in a text selection.

To clear the local formatting in a text selection:

1. Select the text you want to clear.

2. Click the Clear Overrides button in the Paragraph Styles panel 30. This changes the local formatting in the selection to the underlying paragraph style.

You may find that you want to clear just the character attributes that were applied as local formatting, but you want to keep any paragraph attributes.

To clear only local character formatting in a text selection:

1. Select the text you want to clear.

2. Hold Cmd/Ctrl and click the Clear Overrides button. This changes the local character formatting in the selection to the underlying paragraph style.

A Summary for Clearing Overrides	
To do this:	**Do this:**
Clear all the local formatting in a selection	Select the text and click the Clear Overrides button
Clear just the local **character formatting** in a selection	Hold Cmd/Ctrl and click the Clear Overrides button
Clear just the local **paragraph formatting** in a selection	Hold Cmd/Ctrl-Shift and click the Clear Overrides button
Clear **all the local formatting** applied to a paragraph	Hold Opt/Alt and click the name of the paragraph style
Clear **all the local formatting and any character styles** applied to a paragraph	Hold Opt/Alt-Shift and click the name of the paragraph style

Clearing Style Overrides

The opposite to the previous exercise allows you to clear just the paragraph attributes that were applied as local formatting, but keep any character attributes.

To clear only local paragraph formatting in a text selection:

1. Select the text you want to clear.

2. Hold Cmd/Ctrl-Shift and click the Clear Overrides button. This changes the local paragraph formatting in the selection to the underlying paragraph style.

You can also remove all local formatting without making a specific text selection.

To override local formatting:

1. Place your insertion point in the paragraph you want to override.

2. Hold the Opt/Alt key as you click the name of the paragraph style **31**.

You may want to clear the character styles and local formatting applied to the text.

To override character styles and local formatting:

1. Place your insertion point in the paragraph you want to override.

2. Hold the Opt/Alt and Shift keys as you click the name of the paragraph style. This deletes both the character styles and the local formatting applied to the text **32**.

To break the link to a style:

1. Place your insertion point in the paragraph you want to override.

2. Choose Break Link to Style from the Paragraph Styles or Character Styles panel. This removes the style from the text, but does not change the formatting.

Original text with local formatting

Dorothy lived with **Uncle Henry,** and **Aunt Em.** Their house was small.

Opt/Alt-click removes local formatting

Dorothy lived with Uncle Henry, and Aunt Em. Their house was small.

31 Opt/Alt-click a paragraph style name *to remove any local formatting applied to text.*

Original text with character style applied

Their house was small. There were four *walls*, a *floor*, and a *roof.*

Opt/Alt-Shift-click removes character style

Their house was small. There were four walls, a floor, and a roof.

32 *Press* **Opt/Alt-Shift and click a paragraph style name** *to remove character styles and local formatting.*

Clearing Style Overrides

A Totally Style-Driven Workflow?

I use styles religiously. Everything in my book has a style applied to it. There is no text that has local formatting applied to it. So I never see a plus sign in my Paragraph Styles panel.

However, most of my students are not quite as strict as I am. They use paragraph and character styles for *almost* all their text. The one exception is the tracking they apply to text to avoid single words hanging around at the end of a paragraph.

This type of local formatting isn't really so bad — especially since you can easily override it.

Redefining and Deleting Styles

One of the advantages of using text or other styles is that when you redefine the style, it changes all the existing text or objects that have that style applied to it.

To redefine a style:

1. Double-click the style name in the panel. This opens the Style Options dialog box, where you can change the style attributes.
2. Click OK. The style is redefined, and text and objects that have the style applied are modified to reflect the new definition of the style.

To redefine a style by example:

1. Select the text or objects that have the style applied.
2. Use the commands to make any changes to the text or objects.

TIP A plus (+) sign appears next to the style name.

3. Choose Redefine Style from the Styles panel. The style is redefined based on the modified example.

TIP The plus (+) sign disappears.

You may have styles that you do not need in your InDesign document. You can shorten the styles list by deleting unused styles.

To delete unused styles:

1. Select the styles you want to delete.
2. Drag the styles onto the Delete Style icon.

   or

   Choose Delete Styles from the Style panel menu.

TIP Use Select All Unused to delete all the unused styles from a document.

Redefining and Deleting Styles

You can also delete styles that are being used in the document. In that case, you have a choice as to how to handle the text that has the style applied to it.

To delete paragraph styles that are in use:

1. Select the style you want to delete.
2. Delete the style as described in the previous exercise. An alert box appears .
3. Use the pop-up menu in the alert box to choose [No Paragraph Style], [Basic Paragraph], or one of the other paragraph styles.

To delete character styles that are in use:

1. Select the style you want to delete.
2. Delete the style as described in the previous exercise. An alert box appears .
3. Use the pop-up menu in the alert box to choose [None] or one of the other character styles.
4. Check Preserve Formatting to convert the character style into local formatting.

33 *The* **Delete Paragraph Style** **alert box** *lets you assign another paragraph style to deleted styles.*

34 *The* **Delete Character Style** **alert box** *lets you assign another character style to deleted styles.*

Redefining and Deleting Styles

35 *The* **Drop Caps and Nested Styles** *dialog box* *allows you to automate the style applied to drop caps.*

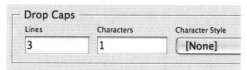

36 *Set the* **Lines and Characters fields** *to the number of lines for the drop cap and the number of characters to be formatted.*

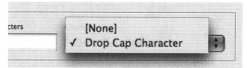

37 *Use the* **Character Style menu** *to assign a character style to format the drop cap character.*

Very soon the Rabbit noticed Alice, as she went hunting about, and called out to her in an angry tone, "Why, Mary Ann, what ARE you doing out here?"

Very soon the Rabbit noticed Alice, as she went hunting about, and called out to her in an angry tone, "Why, Mary Ann, what ARE you doing out here?"

38 *An example of how the* **Scale for Descenders command** *avoids problems when descenders are used in drop caps.*

39 *The* **Drop Caps and Nested Styles category** *for paragraph styles allows you to automate drop cap characters as you apply a paragraph style.*

Automatic Drop Cap Styling

Each chapter of this book has a drop cap that is not the same font as the rest of the text in the paragraph. This is an example of an automatic drop cap with a character style.

To apply automatic drop cap character styling:

1. Define a character style that contains the formatting for the drop cap character.

2. Select the paragraph that you want to style with the drop cap.

3. Choose Drop Caps and Nested Styles from the Paragraph panel menu. The Drop Caps and Nested Styles dialog box appears **35**.

4. Use the Lines field to set the number of lines that the drop cap character will descend into the text **36**.

5. Use the Characters field to set the number of characters for drop cap characters **36**.

6. Use the Character Style menu to choose the predefined character style **37**.

7. Click Align Left Edge to force the left edge of the character to align to the left indent of the text.

8. Click Scale for Descenders to scale and adjust the drop cap so that descenders don't collide with the lines below **38**.

9. Click OK.

TIP Choose the Drop Caps and Nested Styles category from the Paragraph Styles dialog box **39** to make the drop cap part of a paragraph style.

Using Nested Styles

Every once in a while I see a feature that is revolutionary in the field of desktop publishing. Nested styles are such a feature. Nested styles allow you to automate how character styles are applied to paragraphs.

Imagine you are formatting a phone directory. Each paragraph starts with a person's name followed by a colon. After that comes a phone number, and then a new line symbol forces the rest of the address to the end of the paragraph. These are repeating elements that you can reliably count on to use as markers for formatting using nested styles.

You want the person's name to be italic, the phone number to be bold, and the text after the new line symbol to be the regular paragraph style.

Before nested styles, you would have had to manually highlight each element in the paragraph and apply a character style. With nested styles all the formatting is applied in one fell swoop **40**!

TIP As you work with nested styles, remember that you need predictable elements that you can use as part of the automatic formatting. If you can't predict where the elements will be in the text, you probably can't use nested styles for that text.

To prepare to use nested styles:

◆ Define all the character styles that will be used to apply the formatting for nested styles.

TIP You can only use character styles as part of nested styles, not local formatting from the Character panel.

Dorothy·Gale:·**(620)·555-5432**↵
3·Farmhouse·Lane,·Very·Small·Town,·
KA,·12345¶
Scarecrow:·**(620)·555-5432**↵
Middle·of·Cornfield,·Very·Small·
Town,·KA,·12345¶
Woodman:·**(620)·555-5432**↵
Deep·in·Forest,·Very·Small·Town,·
KA,·12345¶

40 *An example of the kind of formatting that can be automated using nested styles. The predictable elements can be used to apply the automatic formatting.*

Searching for Repeating Elements

It may seem difficult to find repeating elements, but they are much easier to find than you might think.

Consider the steps in my exercises. The numbers are always separated from the rest of the body copy by a tab character. So I can easily set the tab as the repeating element for a nested style.

If you are formatting any text that comes from databases, it is extremely easy to have the people who create the database add tab characters to divide the different parts of the text. Then you can use the repeating tab characters to format with the nested styles.

---

41 *The Nested Styles area of the* **Drop Caps and Nested Styles** *dialog box allows you to apply multiple character styles to predictably occurring text elements.*

Style menu Duration menu Count field Repeating Element

42 *The* **New Nested Style** *button creates a new listing in the Nested Styles area.*

43 *Click the* **Character Style** *menu to choose the character style that should be applied as the formatting for the nested style.*

44 *Click the* **Duration** *menu to set the extent to which the formatting is applied.*

45 *Click the* **Repeating Element** *menu to choose the element that ends the nested style.*

Once you have defined the character styles, you can apply them using the Nested Styles command.

To apply the Nested Styles command to text:

1. Place your insertion point inside the paragraph that you want to format.

2. Choose Drop Caps and Nested Styles from the Paragraph panel menu. The Drop Caps and Nested Styles dialog box appears **41**.

3. Click the New Nested Style button. This adds a new listing under the Nested Styles area **42**.

4. Use the Character Style menu to choose which character style will be applied to the repetitive element **43**.

5. Use the Duration menu to choose the extent to which the character style is applied **44**:

   • **Through** applies the style so it includes the repeating character.

   • **Up to** applies the style so it ends before the repeating character.

6. Use the Count field to set how many repeating characters should occur before the character style ends.

7. Use the Repeating Element menu to set which element controls the nested style **45**.

8. Click OK to apply the nested style.

   or

   Click the New Nested Style button to add more nested styles for other parts of the text.

TIP Choose the Drop Caps and Nested Styles category from the Paragraph Styles dialog box **39** to make the nested style settings part of a paragraph style.

Using Nested Styles

To change the order of multiple nested styles:

1. Select the nested style you want to move.

2. Click the up or down arrow to move the nested style to a new position .

What if you know your repeating elements are going to repeat over and over? For instance, you want to change from bold to italic after every comma. Instead of setting a long string of nested styles, you can loop them.

To loop two or more nested styles:

1. Choose Repeat from the Character Style list ⁴⁷.

2. Set the number for how many styles should loop.

TIP If you type multiple characters, InDesign uses any of those characters as the repeating element.

If you don't have any repeating element in the text, you can insert the End Nested Style Here Character to control the appearance of a nested style.

To manually insert the End Nested Style Here Character:

1. Place your insertion point where you want the End Nested Style Here Character to appear.

2. Choose **Type > Insert Special Character > Other > End Nested Style Here**. This inserts the End Nested Style Here character into the text ⁴⁸.

TIP The End Nested Style Here character can be seen if you choose **Type > Show Hidden Characters**.

TIP The End Nested Style Here character can be inserted as part of Find/Change text or GREP searches.

46 *Use the* **up/down arrows** *to change the order of nested styles.*

[None]	up to	1	End Neste
Bold	through	1	End Neste
[Repeat]	last	2	Styles

47 *The* **Repeat command in the Character Style list** *is used to loop two or more nested styles.*

48 *The* **End Nested Style Here** **character** *can be inserted to end the effects of a nested style.*

Using the End Nested Style Here Character

When might you need to insert the End Nested Style Here character? Imagine that you want to style the last set of information in an address such as a zip code or postal code.

You can't rely on a certain number of commas appearing before the zip code appears, nor can you rely on the code to only have numbers if you have a mixture of U.S. and European addresses.

That's when you want to insert the End Nested Style Here character in front of the code.

If necessary, you can ask the editorial department that generates the text to insert a special character before the code. For instance, the zip code 10003 might appear as CODE10003. You can then use the Find/Change command to change the word CODE into the End Nested Style Here character.

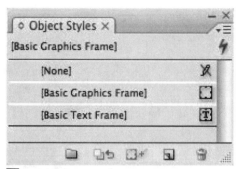

49 *The* **three built-in object style settings** *in the Object Styles panel.*

50 *The* **Object Style Options dialog box** *lets you modify the object style attributes.*

51 *Click the* **Style Settings controls** *to see the description of the settings for each category.*

Defining Object Styles

Just as character and paragraph styles make it easy to apply formatting to text, object styles make it easy to apply formatting to objects. InDesign comes with three built-in object style settings.

TIP If you understand the principles of text styles, it will be easy to work with object styles.

To apply the built-in object styles:

1. Select the object you want to style.

2. Choose **Window > Object Styles** to open the Object Styles panel **49**.

3. Click one of the following in the Object Styles panel:
   - [**Basic Graphics Frame**] applies the default object settings for graphic frames.
   - [**Basic Text Frame**] applies the default settings for text frames.
   - [**None**] removes all formatting from the object.

To modify the default styles:

1. Double-click the Basic Graphics Frame or Basic Text Frame style. This opens the Object Style Options dialog box.

TIP The [None] style can't be modified.

2. Click each of the categories on the left side of the dialog box. This displays the settings for each category **50**.

3. Make whatever changes you like to each of the category settings.

4. Use the Style Settings controls to see a description of the settings for each category **51**.

Defining Object Styles

You will most likely want to create your own object styles.

To create a new object style:

1. Choose New Style from the Object Styles panel menu.

   or

   Hold the Opt/Alt key and click the New Object Style icon in the Object Styles panel. The New Object Styles dialog box appears .

2. Use the Name field to name the style.

3. Use the checkboxes to control which categories are part of the style 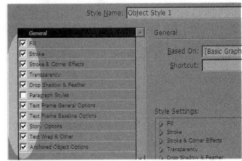. Unchecked categories are not part of the style 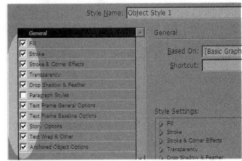.

4. Use the Based On field to base one style on another.

5. Click the Reset To Base button to remove all differences between one style based on another.

6. Click OK to create the style.

The easier way to define an object style is to format the object and define the style by example.

To define an object style by example:

1. Select a sample object.

2. Use the panels and commands to format the object.

3. Choose New Object Style from the Object Styles panel menu.

   or

   Hold the Opt/Alt key and click the New Style icon in the Object Styles panel. The New Object Styles dialog box appears.

4. Name the style.

5. Click OK to create the style.

TIP Object styles can be duplicated just like text styles.

*Use the **New Object Styles dialog box** to define the attributes of an object style.*

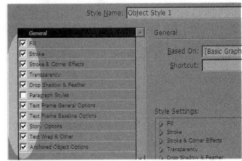

*Click the **category controls** to choose which attributes should be included in the object style.*

Default text frame **Default graphic frame**

54 *The* **two default icons for objects styles** *indicate which style is the default for new objects.*

Clear Overrides Not Defined in the Style icon **Clear Overrides icon**

55 *There are* **two ways to clear overrides** *applied to object styles.*

Working with Object Styles

For the most part, you work with object styles as you would text styles. However, there is a difference in how the default object style is applied. With text styles, whichever style is highlighted with no text selected will become the default style. But with object styles, you need to choose a default for either graphic frames or text frames.

To change the default object styles:

◆ Drag the default graphic frame icon to a new object style **54**.

or

Drag the default text frame icon to a new object style.

Like text styles, a plus (+) sign next to an object style name indicates that local formatting changes have been made to the object. However, you may also have made changes to the object in categories that were not selected in the object style. This local formatting is not indicated by a plus sign.

To clear local formatting not defined in the style:

1. Select the object that has the modifications to the object style.

2. Click the Clear Overrides Not Defined in the Style icon to clear the local formatting applied to the object **55**.

TIP The only way to know if that local formatting has been applied to the object is if the icon is visible in the Object Styles panel.

Working with Object Styles

Defining Table and Cell Styles

If you create just one or two tables in a document, you most likely won't have to worry about table and cell styles. But anyone who creates a lot of tables will enjoy how these features automate their work. As you work with table and cell styles, it is best to start by defining cell styles.

To define cell styles:

1. Choose New Cell Style from the Cell Styles panel menu. The New Cell Style dialog box appears .

2. Name the style and set the Style Info controls.

3. If you want, you can use the Paragraph Style list to choose a default paragraph style for table cells.

4. If desired, choose each of the Cell Styles categories to select the attributes of the style 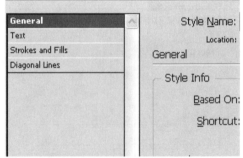.

TIP Unlike the relationship between paragraph and character styles, the formatting of cell styles is not duplicated by a table style. This means you must define a cell style if you want the cells in a table to be controlled by a style.

TIP The Style Settings area displays a description of the attributes for the cell style .

56 Use the **New Cell Style dialog box** *to define the attributes of cells.*

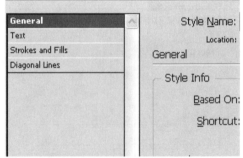

57 *The* **Cell Styles categories** *let you define the attributes of a cell style.*

58 *The* **Style Settings area** *shows you the attributes of a cell style.*

59 Use the **New Table Style dialog box** to define the attributes of tables.

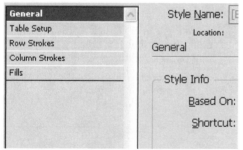

60 Use the **Cell Styles pop-up lists** to apply a cell style to the cells in the various positions of the table.

61 The **Table Styles categories** let you define the attributes of a table style.

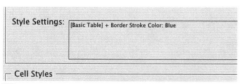

62 The **Style Settings area** shows you the defined attributes of a table style.

Once you have defined your cell styles, you can then "move up the ladder" to define table styles.

To define table styles:

1. Choose New Table Style from the Table Styles panel menu. The New Table Style dialog box appears **59**.

2. Use the Cell Styles pop-up lists to apply a cell style to the cells in each position of the table **60**. (That's why you needed to define the cell styles first.)

3. If desired, choose each of the Table Styles Categories to select the attributes of the style **61**.

TIP The Style Settings area displays a description of the attributes for the table style **62**.

TIP Unlike paragraph styles, table styles do not have to have all their attributes defined. This is why the Style Settings area displays only a description of the defined attributes for the table style.

Defining Table and Cell Styles

Using the Quick Apply Feature

Once you have defined your text and object styles, there is a very easy way to quickly apply them to text and objects. The Quick Apply feature works entirely from the keyboard — no mouse required!

To use Quick Apply to apply styles:

1. Select the text, table, or object that you want to apply the style to.

2. Press Cmd/Ctrl and then press Return/Enter to open the Quick Apply panel .

   or

   Click the Quick Apply icon on any of the style panels or the Control panel.

   TIP The panel can be moved to other positions on your screen.

3. Type a few of the letters that appear in the name of the style. As you type, the Quick Apply area shows just those styles that contain the letters.

   TIP The letters you type do not have to appear in sequence in the name of the style.

4. Keep typing until you have the style you want .

   or

   Use the up and down arrow keys to move to the style you want.

5. Press the Return/Enter key to select the style.

   TIP Quick Apply remembers the last selected style, so you can open Quick Apply and simply press Return/Enter to apply the same style to another selection.

   TIP Press Shift-Return/Enter to apply the Quick Apply item without closing the Quick Apply panel.

63 *The **Quick Apply icon** appears in all the style panels as well as the Control panel.*

64 *As you type in the **Quick Apply field**, the list shows just the styles that contain those letters.*

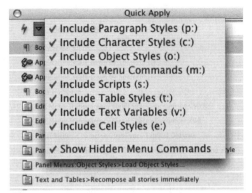

65 *Use the* **Quick Apply menu control** *to open the list of items that will be displayed as part of Quick Apply.*

You can even use Quick Apply to edit the styles dialog box for the selected Quick Apply style.

To edit a style through Quick Apply:

1. Open the Quick Apply panel.

2. Type or navigate to get to the style that you want to edit.

TIP This technique only works with styles, not the menu commands, scripts, or text variables.

3. Press Cmd-Return (Mac) or Control-Enter (Windows). This opens the dialog box for that style.

In addition to paragraph, character, object, table, and cell styles, Quick Apply can also apply menu commands, text variables, and scripts. However, you may not want to wade through hundreds of menus and scripts before getting to your own style. That's when you can customize the settings for Quick Apply.

To customize the results for Quick Apply:

1. Open the Quick Apply panel.

2. Press the menu control to open the list of items that Quick Apply will apply **65**.

3. Check those items you want to have displayed using Quick Apply. Unchecked items are not displayed using Quick Apply.

Using the Quick Apply Feature

You can also use the prefix letters for each of the styles, commands, or scripts that are part of a Quick Apply display.

To use the letter commands with Quick Apply:

1. Open Quick Apply.

2. Type one of the following prefixes before the name of the item you want to apply:

   - **p:** for paragraph styles
   - **c:** for character styles
   - **o:** for object styles
   - **m:** for menu commands
   - **s:** for scripts
   - **t:** for table styles
   - **v:** for text variables
   - **e:** for cell styles

3. Type the rest of the command or style name.

TIP Don't put a space after the colon when you type the rest of the name. For example, to apply a paragraph style called Callouts, you would type p:Callouts.

4. Press Return/Enter to apply the Quick Apply item.

Using the Quick Apply Feature

TYPOGRAPHY 16

The one thing that truly separates the amateurs from the experts in page layout is the control they take over their text. Amateurs are pleased if they can apply simple formatting such as fonts, sizes, alignment, tracking, and so on.

Experts, though, want more from a page-layout program. They want sophisticated control over kerning. This includes the ability to move one character in so that it tucks under the stroke of another.

They want to control how lines are justified within a text frame. This means that if one line looks too crowded and the next has big gaps between the words, the experts tell the program to reapportion the spaces.

The experts also want to work with the newest typefaces that give more choices for how letters look and act together.

These are advanced text effects. Once you apply these features, you move from being an ordinary designer to a typographer.

Optical Margin Alignment

One of the most sophisticated text effects in InDesign is the ability to apply hanging punctuation to justified text, in which a slight adjustment of the margin creates a more uniform appearance for the edge of the text. Hanging punctuation is applied by setting the *optical margin alignment*. This moves punctuation characters slightly outside the text margin ■. In addition, optical margin alignment moves the serifs of letters outside the margin ■.

Optical margin alignment is set using the Story panel.

To set optical margin adjustment:

1. Select the text.

2. Choose **Type>Story**. This opens the Story panel ■.

3. Check Optical Margin Alignment. The text reflows so that the punctuation and serifs lie outside the margin edges.

4. Enter a size for the amount of overhang.

TIP As a general rule, set the overhang the same size as the text.

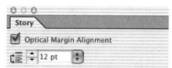

Off　　　　　　　On

■ *To create the effect of a straight edge,* **optical margin alignment** *moves punctuation outside the margin edges.*

■ *The* **Optical Margin Alignment** *setting also moves the serifs of letters slightly outside the margin.*

■ *The* **Story panel** *lets you set the Optical Margin Alignment to hang punctuation in the margin.*

The road was still paved with yellow brick, but these were much covered by dried branches and dead leaves from the trees, and the walking was not at all good.

Off

The road was still paved with yellow brick, but these were much covered by dried branches and dead leaves from the trees, and the walking was not at all good.

On

4 *Turn on* **Adobe Paragraph Composer** *to improve the spacing between words.*

When to Use Paragraph Composition?

Why would anyone want to turn off the miracle of paragraph composition? Well, there are times when the Paragraph Composer insists on breaking a paragraph where you don't want it to break. If that happens, you can turn off the Paragraph Composer.

You may also want to turn off the Paragraph Composer if you have converted a QuarkXPress document into InDesign and you want to keep the text from reflowing.

Also, some statistical data may be easier to work with if you turn off the Paragraph Composer.

Using Adobe Paragraph Composer

InDesign has two ways of composing (layi out) text. Single-line composition looks at the current line and evaluates the best place to break the line or apply hyphenation. Paragraph composition looks at all the text in a paragraph — forward and backward — when it evaluates the best place to break lines. When paragraph composition is turned on, the result is more even spacing for the text and fewer hyphens **4**.

To apply paragraph composition:

1. Select the text.
2. Choose **Type** > **Paragraph** to open the Paragraph panel.
3. Choose Adobe Paragraph Composer from the Paragraph panel menu. The text reflows.

TIP Adobe Paragraph Composer is a paragraph attribute and is applied to all the text in a paragraph.

TIP Adobe Paragraph Composer is turned on by default when you first open InDesign.

TIP Choose Adobe Single-line Composer to apply standard line-by-line composition.

Using Adobe Paragraph Composer

Applying Justification Controls

Justification determines how lines fit between margins. *(See the sidebar below for information on how justification affects text.)* InDesign provides three different ways to control justification: word spacing, letter spacing, and glyph spacing. *Word spacing* changes the space between words.

To set word spacing:

1. Select the text.

2. Choose **Type** > **Paragraph** to open the Paragraph panel.

3. Choose Justification from the Paragraph panel menu. This opens the Justification dialog box ⑤.

4. Set the Word Spacing options as follows ⑥:

   - **Minimum** controls the smallest amount of space you want between words. For instance, a value of 80% means that you are willing to allow the space to be 80% of the normal space.

   - **Desired** controls the preferred amount of space between words. A value of 100% indicates that you want the same amount that the designer of the typeface created.

   - **Maximum** controls the largest amount of space you want between words. A value of 120% means that you are willing to allow the space to be 120% of the normal space.

5. Click OK to apply the changes ⑦.

TIP The Minimum, Desired, and Maximum settings apply only to text that is set to one of the Justified settings. Other alignments, such as left-aligned text, use only the Desired setting.

⑤ The **Justification dialog box** *controls word and letter spacing.*

	Minimum	Desired	Maximum
Word Spacing:	80%	100%	133%
Letter Spacing:	0%	0%	0%
Glyph Scaling:	100%	100%	100%

⑥ The **spacing controls** *in the Justification dialog box.*

Welcome, my child, to the Land of Oz — Min: 80, Desired: 100, Max: 120

Welcome, my child, to the Land of Oz — Min: 80, Desired: 100, Max: 100

⑦ The effect of changing the **word spacing.** *Notice the change in the amount of space between the words.*

Understanding Justification

The lines in this paragraph are justified — that is, both ends of the line are aligned with the paragraph margins. Not all the words can fit evenly between the margins, so some lines have a bit more space between the words and others have less. The justification settings control how much space is added to make the lines fit between the margins.

Applying Justification Controls

Welcome, my child, to the
Land of Oz

Min: 0,
Desired: 0,
Max: 0

Welcome, my child, to the Land
of Oz

Min: -4,
Desired: 0,
Max: 4

8 *The effect of changing the* **letter spacing***.*
Notice how there is less space between
the characters within the words.

What Are the Best Justification Settings?

Perhaps the most debated issue in desktop publishing is what the best settings are for the Justification controls. The answer depends on a variety of factors. The typeface, width of the columns, even the type of text all need to be considered in setting the Justification controls.

For body text, such as the text here, I use word spacing of 70%, 100%, and 110%. (Here in New York City, most designers like to set copy tightly.) However, for headlines, I fit letters tighter, with word spacing of 60%, 90%, and 100%.

I keep all the letter spacing values at 0%. I set the glyph spacing values at 100%. I don't like to scrunch up the space between letters, and I definitely don't like to change the shape of the text, which happens with glyph scaling *(see the next page)*.

But that's just me. And that's why they call them preferences!

The space between letters is *letter spacing*, sometimes called character spacing. InDesign lets you change the letter spacing for text whether justified or not.

To set letter spacing:

1. Select the text.

2. Choose **Type** > **Paragraph** to open the Paragraph panel.

3. Choose Justification from the Paragraph panel menu.

4. Set the Letter Spacing options as follows:

   - **Desired** controls the preferred amount of space between letters. A value of 0% indicates that you do not want to add or subtract any space.

   - **Minimum** controls the smallest amount of space between letters. A value of –5% allows the space to be reduced by 5% of the normal space.

   - **Maximum** controls the largest amount of space between letters. A value of 5% allows the space to be increased by 5% of the normal space.

5. Click OK to apply the changes **8**.

TIP If a paragraph cannot be set according to the justification controls you choose, InDesign violates the settings by adding or subtracting spaces. Set the Composition preferences to have those violations highlighted.

Applying Justification Controls

Another way to control justification is to use *glyph scaling*. (*Glyph* is the proper term for all the letters, numbers, punctuation marks, and other parts of text.) Glyph scaling applies horizontal scaling to the letters themselves so that the text takes up more or less space within the line.

To set glyph scaling:

1. Select the text.

2. Choose **Type** > **Paragraph** to open the Paragraph panel.

3. Choose Justification from the Paragraph panel menu.

4. Set the Glyph Scaling options as follows:

   • **Desired** controls the preferred amount of scaling. A value of 100% indicates that you do not want to apply any scaling to the character shape.

   • **Minimum** controls the smallest amount of scaling that you are willing to apply to the text. A value of 98% means that you are willing to allow the characters to be reduced by 2% of their normal width.

   • **Maximum** controls the amount that you are willing to expand the space between words. A value of 105% means that you are willing to allow the characters to be increased by 5% of their normal width.

5. Click OK to apply the changes 9.

TIP Glyph scaling distorts the shape of letters. Most people say you can't see the slight distortion. However, typographic purists (such as this author) try to avoid distorting the letterforms whenever possible 10.

The road was still paved with yellow brick, but these were much covered by dried branches and dead leaves from the trees, and the walking was not at all good.

Min: 100
Desired: 100
Max: 100

The road was still paved with yellow brick, but these were much covered by dried branches and dead leaves from the trees, and the walking was not at all good.

Min: 80
Desired: 100
Max: 120

9 *The effects of changing the* **glyph** *scaling.*

10 *The black area shows the original shape of the character. The gray area shows the effects of 80% glyph scaling.*

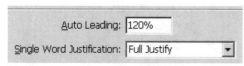

11 *The* **Auto Leading field** *controls how InDesign calculates the leading when set to Auto.*

12 *The* **Single Word Justification menu** *controls what happens when a single word occupies a line of justified text.*

Full Justify

Align Left

Align Center

Align Right

13 *The effects of the* **Single Word Justification** *settings.*

The Auto Leading field controls how much space is put between the lines whenever automatic leading is chosen.

To set the Auto Leading percentage:

1. Choose Justification from the Paragraph panel menu.

2. Enter an amount in the Auto Leading field **11**.

TIP The Auto Leading percentage is based on the point size of the text. So an Auto Leading of 120% applied to 12-point text creates a leading of 14.4 points ($12 \times 1.20 = 14.4$).

TIP Most professional designers use an absolute amount for leading by entering a specific number, rather than relying on the automatic leading.

Have you ever seen a paragraph of justified text where a single word stretched out along the entire line? InDesign lets you control what happens to a single word in a justified paragraph.

To set the single word justification:

1. Choose Justification from the Paragraph panel menu.

2. Choose a setting from the Single Word Justification menu **12**. Any text that is set to Justify in the Paragraph panel will be set according to the menu command **13**.

Applying Justification Controls

...ng Hyphenation

...ts you turn on hyphenation in the ...anel. Once hyphenation is turned on, you can then control how the hyphenation is applied.

To turn on hyphenation:

1. Select the text.

2. Check Hyphenate in the Paragraph panel .

To control the hyphenation:

1. Choose Hyphenation from the Paragraph panel menu. The Hyphenation Settings dialog box appears .

2. Click the Hyphenate checkbox to set the following controls 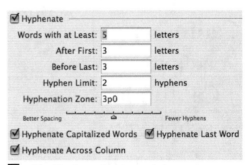:

   - **Words with at Least** controls the minimum number of letters a word must contain before it can be hyphenated.

   - **After First** sets the minimum number of letters before the hyphen.

   - **Before Last** sets the minimum number of letters after the hyphen.

   - **Hyphen Limit** sets how many consecutive lines can end with hyphens.

   - **Hyphenation Zone** controls the amount of whitespace at the end of a nonjustified line.

3. Check Hyphenate Capitalized Words to allow those words to be hyphenated.

4. Check Hyphenate Last Word to let the last word in a paragraph be hyphenated.

5. Check Hyphenate Across Column to let words that break across a column be hyphenated.

6. Adjust the hyphenation slider to control the total number of hyphens in the paragraph.

Controlling Hyphenation

14 *Click the* **Hyphenate checkbox** *to turn on automatic hyphenation for a paragraph.*

15 *The* **Hyphenation Settings dialog box** *lets you control how hyphenation is applied.*

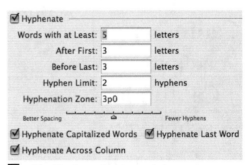

16 *The Hyphenation controls let you enter values for how words are hyphenated.*

Hyphenation Units are Nigels

The units in the hyphenation slider are called Nigels in honor of Nigel Tufnel (Christopher Guest), the "Spinal Tap" guitarist, whose amplifier went to 11.

Behold! I am the great and mighty, all-pow-erful Oz.

Behold! I am the great and mighty, all-powerful Oz.

17 *In the bottom example the word* powerful *was selected and the* **No Break** command *was applied to prevent the text from hyphenating.*

A·docиment·
can·not·be·

18 *A* **discretionary hyphen** *appears within the word but prints only when it appears at the end of a line.*

Setting Hyphenation Controls

My own preference is to set "Words with at Least" to six or more. This allows a word such as *person* to be hyphenated. I also prefer a minimum of three letters before the hyphen and three after. This avoids breaking words as *un-excited* or *relunctant-ly*.

Hyphenate Capitalized Words?

Some people automatically turn this off so that capitalized words do not hyphenate. I don't. The command doesn't distinguish between proper nouns and words that begin a sentence. So I would rather selectively control how proper nouns break by using the No Break command or by inserting a discretionary hyphen before the word.

Sometimes you may want to prevent words or phrases from being hyphenated or breaking across lines. For instance, you might not want the words *Mr. Cohen* to be separated at the end of a line. You might not want a compound word such as *self-effacing* to be broken with another hyphen **17**.

To apply the No Break command:

1. Select the text.

2. Choose **Type > Character** to open the Character panel.

3. Choose No Break from the Character panel menu.

You can also control hyphenation by inserting a *discretionary hyphen,* which forces the word to hyphenate at that point if it breaks at the end of a line.

To use a discretionary hyphen:

1. Place the insertion point where you want the hyphen to occur.

2. Press Command/Ctrl-Shift-(hyphen).

   or

   Control-click (Mac) or Right-click (Win) and choose **Insert Special Character > Hyphens and Dashes > Discretionary Hyphen** from the contextual menu.

TIP The discretionary hyphen prints only when it appears at the end of the line **18**.

TIP Insert a discretionary hyphen before a word to prevent that instance of the word from being hyphenated.

Controlling Hyphenation

a word is hyphenated.

the dictionary:

ing > Dictionary.

want to modify in the

rs :

icates the best possible hyphenation position.

- **Two tildes (~~)** indicates the next best possible position.

- **Three tildes (~~~)** indicates the least acceptable position.

- **A tilde before the word** prevents the word from being hyphenated.

3. Click Add to add the new hyphenation preferences to the dictionary.

Baseline Grid

InDesign has an electronic grid that you can force text to align to. This ensures that text lines up correctly in two separate frames .

To set the baseline grid:

1. Choose **Edit > Preferences > Grids (Win)** or **InDesign > Preferences > Grids (Mac)**. This opens the Grids dialog box .

2. Use the Color menu to set the grid color.

3. Use the Start field to control where the grid should start vertically in the document.

4. Use the Relative To menu to choose between the top of the page or the top margin .

5. Use the Increment Every field to control the space between the gridlines.

6. Set View Threshold for the magnification amount above which the grid is visible.

Dictionary List: Added Words

Word: in~~~di~~~vid~~u~~~al~ism

19 *The tilde characters control the preference for where hyphenation should occur.*

Align to Baseline Grid off

"From the Land of Oz." said Dorot grave

And oh, Aunt Em! I'm so

Align to Baseline Grid on

"From the Land of Oz." said Dorothy gravely.

And oh, Aunt Em! I'm so glad to be at home again!

20 *When **Align to Baseline Grid** is turned on, the text in two different frames lines up.*

Baseline Grid

Color:	■ Light Blue
Start:	3p0
Relative To:	Top of Page
Increment Every:	1p6
View Threshold:	75%

21 *The **Baseline Grid settings** in the Grids preferences.*

Relative To:	✓ Top of Page
ncrement Every:	Top Margin

22 *The **Relative To field** lets you choose where the baseline grid should start.*

Do not align to baseline grid

Align to
baseline grid

23 *The* **Align to Baseline Grid buttons** *in the Paragraph panel.*

Align to Baseline Grid off

Chapter·Two:·The·
Council·with·the·
Munchkins¶

She·was·awakened·by·a·shock,·so·sudden·and
severe·that·i
soft·bed·she

As·it·was,

Align to Baseline Grid on

Chapter·Two:·The·
Council·with·the·
Munchkins¶

She·was·awakened·by·a·shock,·so·sudden·and
severe·that·if·Dorothy·had·not·been·lying·on·the
soft·bed·she·might·have·been·hurt.¶

As·it·was,·the·jar·made·her·catch·her·breath

24 *When text is* **aligned to the baseline grid,** *the leading may increase. Also the space between paragraphs may adjust.*

Align all lines to grid

As it was, the jar made her catch her breath   This sou
and wonder what had happened; and Toto put   very mu
his cold little nose into her face and whined   like the
dismally. Dorothy sat up and noticed that the   opening
house was not moving; nor was it dark, for the   the movi
bright sunshine came in at the window, flood-
ing the little room.

Only align first line to grid

As it was, the jar made her catch her breath   This sounds
and wonder what had happened; and Toto put   very much
his cold little nose into her face and whined   like the
dismally. Dorothy sat up and noticed that the   opening for
house was not moving; nor was it dark, for the   the movie
bright sunshine came in at the window, flood-
ing the little room.

25 *Use the* **Only Align First Line to Grid command** *to align just the first line of a paragraph without affecting the leading.*

To align text to a baseline grid:

1. Select the text.

2. Click the Align to Baseline Grid icon in the Paragraph panel **23**. The text aligns to the grid.

TIP When you align to the baseline grid, the grid setting overrides the leading. Most designers set the baseline grid to the same amount as the leading for the text **24**.

TIP Aligning to the baseline grid may also change the space between paragraphs **24**.

In addition to setting the baseline grid, you can choose to set just the first line of a paragraph to the baseline grid.

To align just the first line to the baseline grid:

1. Select the text.

2. Click the Align to Baseline Grid icon in the Paragraph panel. All the lines in the paragraph will be aligned to the baseline grid.

3. Choose Only Align First Line to Grid in the Paragraph panel menu.

   or

   Choose First Line Only from the Align to Grid menu in the Indents and Spacing area of the Paragraph Style Options dialog box.

TIP This forces the first line of a paragraph to align to the grid but allows the other lines in the paragraph to be controlled by the leading **25**.

Baseline Grid

...lso set a custom baseline grid for a ...e. This is especially helpful for for-...margin notes alongside text .

To create a custom grid for a text frame:

1. Select the text frame.

2. Choose **Object > Text Frame Options** and then click Baseline Options. This opens the text frame baseline controls **27**.

3. Check Use Custom Baseline Grid to set the options.

4. Use the Start field to control where the grid should start vertically in the document.

5. Use the Relative To menu to choose between the top of the page or the top margin.

6. Use the Increment Every field to control the space between the gridlines.

7. Use the Color controls to set the color of the grid.

8. Don't forget to set the text to align to the baseline grid.

Document grid

"All the same," said the Scarecrow, "I shall ask for brains instead of a heart; for a fool would not know what to do with a heart if he had one."

"I shall take the heart," returned the Tin Woodman; "for brains do not make one happy, and happiness is the best thing in the world."

Custom frame grid

Is the Scarecrow actualy smart here? Does the Tin Woodman show feeling? What does this tell you?

26 A **custom frame grid** *allows you to have multiple grids in a document.*

27 *The* **Baseline Grid settings** *in the Text Frame Options.*

Baseline Grid

Chapter Two: The Council with the Munchkins

She was awakened by a shock, so sudden and severe that if Dorothy hurt

Chapter Two: The Council with the Munchkins

She was awakened by a shock, so sudden and severe that if Dorothy had not been lying on the soft bed she might have been hurt.

28 *The* **Balance Ragged Lines command** *rearranges text so there is a more equal number of words in the lines.*

Kin
King
Kingd
Kingdom

29 *As you add more letters to an OpenType font, the previous letters change.*

What is OpenType?

OpenType is a type format that was developed by Adobe and Microsoft. OpenType fonts have many advantages over previous type formats. In addition to containing thousands of glyphs, OpenType fonts are also cross-platform. This means you can use the same font on Mac or Windows without any document reflow.

Adobe sells different types of OpenType fonts. "Pro" versions of a font, such as Minion Pro, contain the extended character sets that give you access to fractions, ligatures, and other special effects. "Standard" versions, such as Futura Std, contain only the basic characters.

Balancing Ragged Lines

Another nuance for good typography is to make sure that there are no uneven line breaks, especially in headlines or centered type. InDesign's Balance Ragged Lines command makes this easier **28**.

To balance uneven line breaks:

1. Select the text.

2. Choose Balance Ragged Lines from the Paragraph panel menu.

   or

   Choose Balance Ragged Lines in the Indents and Spacing area of the Paragraph Style Options dialog box.

Using OpenType

Instead of the paltry 256 glyphs (characters) in ordinary fonts, OpenType fonts can have thousands of glyphs. InDesign has special commands that help you get the most out of OpenType fonts. For instance, you can set the commands to automatically swap ordinary characters with special OpenType glyphs.

To set automatic OpenType alternate characters:

1. Select the text.

   TIP OpenType features can be applied to all the text in a document or just part of the text.

2. Choose **Type > Character** to open the Character panel.

3. Choose the options from the OpenType submenu in the Character panel menu. InDesign automatically swaps characters with the alternate glyphs in each category **29**.

You can also manually choose alternate glyphs for each character in the font.

To choose the alternate glyphs:

1. Select the character in the text.
2. Choose **Type > Glyphs** to open the Glyphs panel.
3. Press the triangle next to the selected character in the panel **30**. The alternate glyphs for the selection appear.
4. Choose one of the alternate characters. This replaces the selected text with the alternate character in the Glyphs panel.

You can also set the Glyphs panel to display just certain categories of glyphs.

To view certain categories in the Glyphs panel:

1. Press the Show list in the Glyphs panel.
2. Choose the category of OpenType characters that you want to display **31**.

TIP Not all OpenType fonts contain all the possible glyph features. So the Show list will display different categories depending on the OpenType font chosen.

30 *Press a character or letter that has a triangle to see the alternate glyphs.*

31 *The **Show list** in the Glyphs panel lets you choose to see the categories of specialized glyphs.*

Using OpenType

Open Type Categories

Feature name	Comments	Examples	
All Caps	Changes text to uppercase letters. Also changes punctuation and spacing. Notice how the question mark and hyphens are raised in the OpenType all caps formatting.	Manually typed all caps	¡MAMMA-MEXICO?
		OpenType all caps	¡MAMMA-MEXICO?
Small Caps	Changes lowercase text to small capital letters. More appropriate weight for the letters compared to the fake small caps created electronically.	Electronic small caps	SMSOLUTIONS
		OpenType small caps	SMSOLUTIONS
All Small Caps	Changes all text, including uppercase characters, to small capital letters. Use for acronyms such as FBI, CIA, and PDF. The advantage to this setting is that you do not have to retype uppercase characters to make the conversion.	Without small caps	The FBI and CIA opened the IRS PDF.
		With small caps	The FBI and CIA opened the IRS PDF.
Ligatures	Applies the special letter combinations such as fi and fl. Other ligatures, such as ffi, ffl, and ff may be present in most Adobe Pro OpenType fonts.	No ligatures	difficult flush fish
		With ligatures	difficult flush fish
Discretionary Ligatures	Applies both discretionary ligatures and historical ligatures. These ligatures should be used sparingly as they are not common in contemporary text.	No discretionary ligatures	reaction burst
		With discretionary ligatures	reaction burst
Fractions	Converts numbers around a slash into numerator and denominator characters and changes the slash to a virgule. Settings for Numerator and Denominator also use the fraction glyphs.	Manually styled	3^1/$_2$ 4^3/$_4$
		OpenType formatted	3½ 4¾
Ordinals	Converts the characters to the superscript position. Like fractions, the OpenType version is faster to apply and has a better weight than electronic styling.	Manually styled	1st 2nd 3rd 4th
		OpenType formatted	1st 2nd 3rd 4th
Swash	Substitutes a stylized alternative for the ordinary glyphs. Swashes are usually found in the italic version of a font. They are contextual and are inserted at the beginning or end of a word.	Without swash	Quick Awesome
		With swash	Quick Awesome
Stylistic Sets	Substitutes sets of characters that are applied depending on their context in relationship to other letters. Visible in the Glyphs panel.	Without stylistic set	Huddled
		With stylistic set	Huddled

Open Type Categories

Open Type Categories

Feature name	Comments	Examples	
Contextual Alternates	Substitutes specially designed characters that are applied depending on their context in relationship to other letters.	Without contextual alternates	*bogged who fish stall lodge*
		With contextual alternates	*bogged who fish stall look lodge*
Stylistic Alternates	Created by the type designer, these alternatives are inserted as alternate choices to the selected glyphs.	Original character	$\&$
		Stylistic alternate	$\&$
Superscript/ Superior	Substitutes proper superscript or superior characters for ordinary glyphs. Limited to numbers, punctuation, and a selected set of letters.	Manually styled	x^2 $^{\$}4.00$ 2^e
		OpenType formatted	x^2 $^{\$}4.00$ 2^e
Subscript/Inferior	Like superscript, this substitutes proper subscript characters for ordinary glyphs. Limited to just numbers and punctuation, not letters.	Manually styled	H_2O
		OpenType formatted	H_2O
Slashed Zero	Substitutes a slashed zero for the normal character. Used in scientific and mathematical writing.	No slashed zero	$x-0=y$
		Slashed zero	$x-\emptyset=y$
Figure (number) types	There are four categories of figure types. *Tabular figures* have fixed widths and are used particularly where the numbers need to line up under each other. *Proportional figures* have variable widths. Use these unless it is necessary to line figures up into columns of tabular data. *Lining figures* have a uniform height. Use them with all cap text or for a contemporary look. *Oldstyle figures* have unequal heights. Use them with mixed-case text or when a more traditional look is desired. *Default figure* is the category that the type designer has designated as the default. This is usually tabular lining.	These are the four types of figures:	
		Tabular lining	12: 09/11/2001 34: 07/22/2008
		Tabular oldstyle	12: 09/11/2001 34: 07/22/2008
		Proportional lining	12: 09/11/2001 34: 07/22/2008
		Proportional oldstyle	12: 09/11/2001 34: 07/22/2008

COLOR MANAGEMENT 17

I remember when my family got our first color television set. Back then, there weren't many programs broadcast in color, so a color television was a strange and mysterious thing.

No one in the family knew how to make the pictures look realistic. We jumped up to adjust the image whenever we changed channels. My sister and I spent more time fiddling with the TV controls than watching the shows.

Well, not many people understand how color is managed in desktop publishing. They don't know how to make colors look better or how to control images from different applications. They spend most of their time fiddling with the knobs.

Color management is a very complex subject — far too deep for the scope of this book. This chapter covers only the most basic steps for managing color in InDesign. Fortunately, the controls are similar to those in other Adobe products. So if you've set your color management in Photoshop, you will find the same settings in InDesign.

If you are interested in learning more about color, I suggest *Real World Color Management,* by Bruce Fraser, Fred Bunting, and Chris Murphy, published by Peachpit Press.

Choosing Color Settings

The first step for color management is to set up the color system. Fortunately, Adobe provides predefined color settings that are suitable for many users.

To turn on color management:

1. Choose **Edit > Color Settings**. This opens the Color Settings dialog box **1**.

2. Check Enable Color Management. This opens the color settings controls.

3. Choose one of the predefined settings from the Settings menu **2**:

   • Choose **General Purpose** if you are printing to an office printer.

   • Choose **Prepress** if you are sending files out to a high-end service provider.

   • Choose **Web/Internet** if you will be outputting to the Web.

   • Choose **CMS Off** to minimize the effects of color management. (Color management is never really completely off.)

TIP You may have different settings than those shown here if you are not in North America.

4. Click OK to apply the color settings. In many cases, this is all you need to do to set color management in InDesign.

1 The **Color Settings dialog box** *contains the controls for managing how colors are displayed and printed.*

2 The **Settings menu** *lets you choose one of the predefined color management settings.*

Talk to Your Print Shop

Most designers I know are embarrassed to admit they don't understand color management. It's nothing to be ashamed of. What you need to do is talk to your print shop. Ask them what settings they recommend for color management. And remember, color management also needs to be set in image-creation applications — such as Adobe Illustrator and Adobe Photoshop — that you use to create images placed in InDesign.

The working space applies the default color profiles for RGB and CMYK colors *(see Chapter 5, "Working in Color").*

To set the RGB working space:

◆ Use the RGB menu to choose one of the following RGB display settings **3**:

- **Adobe RGB (1998)** has a large color gamut. Use it if you do print work with a broad range of colors.

- **Apple RGB** reflects the characteristics of the Apple Standard 13-inch monitor. Use for files displayed on Mac OS monitors or for working with older desktop publishing files.

- **ColorMatch RGB** matches the color space of Radius PressView monitors.

- **SRGB IEC61966-2.1** reflects the characteristics of the average PC monitor. It is recommended for Web work, but is too limited for prepress.

- **Monitor RGB** sets the working space to the color profile of your monitor. Use this if your other applications do not support color management.

- **ColorSync RGB** (Mac) matches the RGB space specified in the control panel for Apple ColorSync 3.0 or later.

TIP When the Advanced Mode is chosen, the RGB Working Space menu displays additional options.

To set the CMYK working space:

◆ Use the CMYK menu to choose the CMYK output settings **4**.

TIP Each setting describes the type of ink and paper used in the printing.

3 *The* **Working Space RGB menu** *lets you choose the display options for RGB colors.*

4 *The* **Working Space CMYK menu** *lets you choose the output destination for printing CMYK colors.*

Choosing Color Settings

You can also set what happens when placed images contain different color profiles than the current working spaces.

To set the Color Management Policies:

1. Choose a setting in the RGB and CMYK Color Management Policy menus and **6** as follows:

   - **Off** turns off color management for imported images or documents.

   - **Preserve Embedded Profiles** maintains the profile in the imported image or document.

   - **Preserve Numbers** maintains the actual color values without applying any profiles.

   - **Convert to Working Space** converts placed images and documents to the working spaces you set for the InDesign document.

2. Check Ask When Opening (under Profile Mismatches) to give a choice when opening documents with different profiles **7**.

3. Check Ask When Pasting (under Profile Mismatches) to give a choice when pasting information from documents with different profiles.

4. Check Ask When Opening (under Missing Profiles) to give a choice when pasting information from documents that have no color profiles.

5 *The* RGB **Color Management Policy** menu *lets you choose what to do with different* RGB *color profiles.*

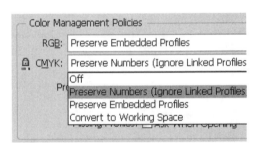

6 *The* CMYK **Color Management Policy** menu *lets you choose what to do with different* CMYK *color profiles.*

7 *The* **Profile Mismatches and Missing Profiles** options *control what happens when different profiles are in the same document.*

Choosing Color Settings

8 *The* **Conversion Options** *are displayed in the Color Settings when the Advanced Mode is checked.*

9 *The* **Engine menu (Win)** *lets you choose the Adobe Color Engine or the Microsoft Image Color Management for color management.*

10 *The* **Engine menu (Mac)** *lets you choose the Adobe Color Engine or the Apple ColorSync or Apple Color Management Module for color management.*

11 *The* **Intent menu** *lets you choose how the final color display should look.*

Black and White Points?

A *white point* is the most extreme highlight in an image. This is the part of the image that should be totally white without any ink. A *black point* is the most extreme black part of an image.

The Conversion Options, in the Advanced Mode, control how objects and color data are converted **8**.

To set the conversion options:

1. Choose one of the settings in the Engine menu **9** and **10**:

   • **Adobe (ACE)** uses the Adobe color management system and color engine. This is the default setting for most preset color configurations.

   • **Apple ColorSync (Mac)** or **Apple CMM (Mac)** uses the color management system provided for Mac OS computers. Unless you have an optional color module installed, there is no difference between the two settings.

   • **Microsoft ICM (Win)** uses the color management system provided for Windows computers.

   TIP Choose Adobe (ACE) if you are working with other Adobe products.

2. Choose one of the settings in the Intent menu **11**:

   • **Perceptual** preserves the relationships between colors in a way that is perceived as natural by the human eye.

   • **Saturation** is suitable for business graphics, where the exact relationship between colors is not as important as having vivid colors.

   • **Relative Colorimetric** is the default rendering intent used by all predefined color management configurations.

   • **Absolute Colorimetric** maintains color accuracy at the expense of preserving relationships between colors.

3. Check Use Black Point Compensation to adjust for differences in black points.

   TIP Adobe strongly recommends you keep the Use Black Point Compensation option selected.

Choosing Color Settings

Saving and Loading Color Settings

One of the things that drives my students crazy is when a color in Adobe InDesign looks different when displayed in Adobe Illustrator or Adobe Photoshop. Fortunately, it is easy to synchronize your Adobe application color settings so the color looks the same.

To save the color settings:

1. Set your color settings as described in the previous section.

2. Click the Save button in the Color Settings dialog box.

3. Name the color settings file (.csf) and save it in the following location :

   • Disk: Users: [User]: Library: Application Support: Adobe: Color: Settings (Mac).

   • Disk: Documents and Settings: [User]: Application Data: Adobe: Color: Settings (Win).

TIP This saves the setting in a location where the other Adobe applications can use the settings file.

Once you have saved the color settings, you can open or load them into InDesign or another Adobe application.

To open the color settings:

1. Click Load in the Color Settings dialog box.

2. Navigate to the Color: Settings folder as described in the previous exercise.

3. Choose the color settings file.

TIP If you have chosen the same color settings for all your Adobe applications, a message appears at the top of the Color Settings dialog box stating that your settings are synchronized .

12 *Use the* **Save Color Settings dialog box** *to save your own color settings file.*

13 *A* **message in the Color Settings dialog box** *lets you know if all your Adobe applications are using the same color settings.*

Saving and Loading Color Settings

Color Management button

14 *The **Adobe Bridge Center** allows you to synchronize color management settings across all the Adobe Creative Suite applications.*

15 *Use the **Suite Color Settings dialog box** to choose the color settings file you want to apply to all the applications.*

If your copy of InDesign is part of the Adobe Creative Suite, you have an additional feature that allows you to easily synchronize all the applications in the suite.

To synchronize color settings using Adobe Bridge:

1. Open Adobe Bridge.

2. Choose **Edit > Creative Suite Color Settings**. This opens the Suite Color Settings dialog box.

   or

   Click the Color Management button in the Adobe Bridge Center **14**. This opens the Suite Color Settings dialog box.

3. Choose the color setting from the list and then click Apply. This synchronizes the color management across the Adobe Creative Suite applications **15**.

TIP If you have chosen the same color settings for all your Adobe applications, a message appears at the top of both the Suite Color Settings and the Color Settings dialog boxes stating that your settings are synchronized.

Saving and Loading Color Settings

Working with Profiles

You can also set profiles and color management for individual imported images.

To control a placed image's color management:

1. If the graphic has already been placed into the layout, select it, and then choose **Object > Image Color Settings** to open the Image Color Settings dialog box .

   or

   If you're about to import the graphic, click the Color tab of the Image Import Options dialog box. This displays the Profile and Rendering Intent menus .

2. Use the Profile menu to choose the source profile to apply to the graphic.

3. Use the Rendering Intent menu to choose a rendering intent.

16 *The* **Image Color Settings dialog box** *allows you to assign a specific profile and rendering intent to an imported image.*

17 *The* **Color tab in the Image Import Options dialog box** *allows you to assign a specific profile and rendering intent to an image that is about to be imported.*

(side margin) **Working with Profiles**

INTERACTIVE PDF 18

At the risk of sounding like an old codger, I can remember when a page-layout program only laid out print files. The idea of creating "push buttons" that sent you flying to other pages — or even other documents — was totally unfathomable. After all, how was someone supposed to press on a weather summary on the front page of a newspaper to jump to the full weather map on the last page?

So it is with some amazement that I write this chapter. Page layout no longer refers to just printed pages. InDesign has a wealth of features that let you create interactive elements for electronic documents.

These interactive features may be simple links that let readers move from one page to another. They may be hyperlinks to Web pages. They may also be special bookmarks that can be used as navigational tools. They may even be rollover buttons that can play movies and sounds in a PDF document.

Of course, if you have no interest whatsoever in creating these types of interactive elements, feel free to skip this chapter entirely. Who cares if this is the future of publishing!

Types of Interactive Elements

There are three different types of interactive elements you can add to InDesign documents: Hyperlinks, Bookmarks, and Buttons. Each has its own particular uses, but some of the features may overlap. Before you start work, decide which type of interactive element is right for you.

Feature	Description	Advantages	Limitations
Hyperlink	Adds a hotspot area to text or objects that is linked to other parts of the document, other documents, or Web pages.	Can be applied directly to the text inside a story. Can be created automatically using the Table of Contents or Indexing feature.	Provides only very primitive visual indications of the linked area.
Bookmark	Adds a navigational element that is visible in the Adobe Reader Bookmark pane.	The Bookmark pane is visible at all times in the document. Can be created automatically using the Table of Contents feature.	Requires some education to teach the reader how to use the Bookmark pane in the Reader. Is not directly on the document page. No special visual indication in the document.
Button	Adds a hotspot area that can contain text or graphics. This hotspot can be set to invoke a wide variety of behaviors including navigation as well as movie or audio playback.	Offers the most navigational and design choices.	Buttons can't be created automatically from text.

Hyperlinks panel menu

New Hyperlink icon

1 *The* **Hyperlinks panel** *is used to define both the destinations and the hyperlinks.*

2 *The* **New Hyperlink Destination dialog box** *lets you set a page destination.*

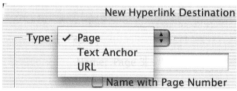

3 *The* **Type menu** *lets you choose the type of hyperlink destination.*

Which Comes First, Source or Destination?

Maybe it's years of working in HTML or JavaScript, but the first time I tried to create hyperlinks in InDesign, I got all fouled up. I started by trying to define a source for the hyperlink — the item that you click — and then setting its destination — the place where the link sends you.

InDesign doesn't work this way. You must set the destination first, and then set the source. I know it seems backward, but that's the way it must be done.

Defining Hyperlinks

A hyperlink is an area of a page that can be clicked to send the reader to a new page, open a new document, move to a Web page, or send an e-mail message. There are two parts to creating a hyperlink. The *source* is the object or text that you click to trigger the hyperlink. The *destination* is the page or Web link you go to.

TIP You must define a destination first, before you define the source.

To choose the type of hyperlink:

1. Choose **Window > Interactive > Hyperlinks**. This opens the Hyperlinks panel **1**.

2. Choose New Hyperlink Destination from the Hyperlinks panel menu. This opens the New Hyperlink Destination dialog box **2**.

3. Choose the type of hyperlink from the Type menu as follows **3**:

   - **Page** creates a page destination that links to a specific page in the document. This is the only type of hyperlink that lets you set a magnification for the link.

   - **Text Anchor** creates a link to a selected area of text. This option is only available if you have selected text.

   - URL lets you link to an Internet page.

Defining Hyperlinks

A *page destination* specifies the page and the magnification to use when you move to the link.

To create a page destination:

1. Choose New Hyperlink Destination in the Hyperlinks panel menu to open the New Hyperlink Destination dialog box.

2. Choose Page from the Type menu. This opens the settings for the page destination .

3. Use the Page controls to enter the page number that you want to jump to.

4. If desired, use the Name field to enter a descriptive name for the page.

    or

    Check the Name with Page Number option to automatically name the destination with its page number and whatever Zoom setting has been chosen.

5. Choose the Zoom settings as follows 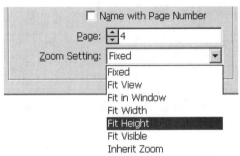:

    - **Fixed** displays the page as it was when the link was created.

    - **Fit View** displays the visible portion of the page.

    - **Fit in Window** displays the entire page in the document window.

    - **Fit Width** or **Fit Height** displays the width or height of the page.

    - **Fit Visible** displays the areas that contain text or graphics.

    - **Inherit Zoom** displays the same magnification that was active when the link was clicked.

6. Click OK to create the destination.

TIP Don't worry that you don't see your destination listed in the Hyperlinks panel. Destinations aren't shown there. Destinations are shown when you define the hyperlink source.

The New Hyperlink Destination dialog box set for a **Page destination**.

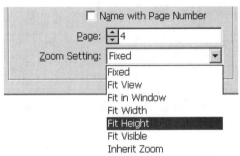

The **Zoom Setting menu** *controls the magnification of the destination page.*

Defining Hyperlinks

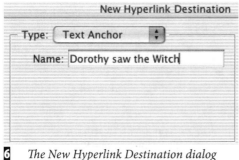

New Hyperlink Destination

Type: Text Anchor

Name: Dorothy saw the Witch

Type: URL

Name: Vectorbabe

URL: http://www.vectorbabe.com

6 *The New Hyperlink Destination dialog box set for a* **Text Anchor destination**.

The second type of hyperlink is a text anchor. A text anchor destination allows you to link to a specific area of text on a page.

To create a text anchor destination:

1. Highlight the text that you want as the destination.

2. Choose New Hyperlink Destination in the Hyperlinks panel menu. This opens the New Hyperlink Destination dialog box.

3. Choose Text Anchor from the Type menu **6**.

4. Use the default name, which comes from the selected text.

   or

   Enter a name for the destination.

The third type of hyperlink is a URL (uniform resource locator). These are the links that can be used to open Web pages, send e-mail, or transfer files.

To create a URL destination:

1. Choose New Hyperlink Destination in the Hyperlinks panel menu to open the New Hyperlink Destination dialog box.

2. Choose URL from the Type menu **7**.

3. Enter a name for the destination.

4. Enter the URL information.

Defining Hyperlinks

You can use the Hyperlink Destination Options dialog box to edit the destinations that you create for the document. This is also the place where you can see which destinations have been defined for your document.

To edit a destination:

1. Choose Hyperlink Destination Options in the Hyperlinks panel menu to open the dialog box.

2. Choose a previously defined destination from the Destination menu.

3. Click the Edit button 8. The controls for the destination become active.

TIP These controls change depending on the type of destination chosen.

4. Make whatever changes you want to the destination.

   or

   Click the Delete button to delete the destination from the document.

   or

   Click the Delete All button to delete all the destinations from the document.

TIP If you are editing a Text Anchor destination, you can change the text destination by selecting Set to Current Text Insertion Point.

8 *Use the* **Hyperlink Destination Options dialog box** *to edit the destinations in a document.*

Defining Hyperlinks

9 *The* **New Hyperlink dialog box** *lets you link to destinations as well as set the appearance of the hotspot area.*

Once you have set the hyperlink destinations, you can then create the hyperlink sources that link to those destinations.

To create a hyperlink from an existing destination:

1. Select the text or graphic that you want to be the hotspot or trigger area for the link.

2. Click the New Hyperlink button in the Hyperlinks panel.

   or

   Choose New Hyperlink from the Hyperlinks panel menu. The New Hyperlink dialog box appears **9**.

3. Use the Name field to name the hyperlink. This is the name that appears in the Hyperlinks panel.

4. Set the hyperlink destination as described later in this chapter.

5. Set the Appearance as described later in this chapter.

6. Click OK to create the hyperlink. The link appears in the Hyperlinks panel.

Defining Hyperlinks

To choose a page destination:

1. In the New Hyperlink dialog box, choose Page from the Type menu. This opens the Page Destination area .

2. Use the Document menu to choose the destination document. This adds any destinations that were defined in that document to the Name menu.

3. Choose a previously defined page destination from the Name menu .

Of course, it's possible to create a hyperlink without having previously defined a page destination.

To create an unnamed page destination:

1. In the New Hyperlink dialog box, choose Page from the Type menu. This opens the Page Destination area.

2. Choose [Unnamed] from the Name menu. This allows you to define an unnamed destination.

3. Use the Page controls to set the page number.

4. Set the Zoom Setting for Hyperlinks as described earlier in this chapter.

TIP The term [Unnamed] only applies to the destination. The hyperlink still appears in the Hyperlinks panel .

To choose a text anchor destination:

1. In the New Hyperlink dialog box, choose Text Anchor from the Type menu.

2. Use the Document menu to choose the destination document. This adds any destinations that were defined in that document to the Name menu.

3. Choose a previously defined text anchor destination from the Name menu .

10 *The* **Page Destination area** *of the New Hyperlink dialog box lets you set the destinations for hyperlinks.*

11 *The* **Name menu** *lets you choose previously defined page destinations for a hyperlink.*

12 *Hyperlinks appear in the Hyperlinks panel. Icons show the type of hyperlink.*

13 *The* **Name menu** *lets you choose a previously defined text anchor as a destination for a hyperlink.*

14 *The* **URL Destination area** *of the New Hyperlink dialog box lets you set the destinations for URL hyperlinks.*

15 *The* **Name menu** *lets you choose previously defined URL destinations for a hyperlink.*

16 *The* **URL Destination area** *lets you create an unnamed destination.*

To choose a previously defined URL destination:

1. In the New Hyperlink dialog box, choose URL from the Type menu. This opens the URL Destination area **14**.

2. Use the Document list to choose the destination document. This adds any destinations that were defined in that document to the Name menu.

3. Choose a previously defined URL destination from the Name menu **15**.

You can easily create a URL destination without having previously defined a URL destination.

To create an unnamed URL destination:

1. In the New Hyperlink dialog box, choose URL from the Type menu. This opens the URL Destination area **16**.

2. Choose [Unnamed] from the Name menu. This allows you to define an unnamed destination.

3. Enter the URL in the URL field.

TIP The term [Unnamed] only applies to the destination. The hyperlink itself still has the name you enter at the top of the New Hyperlink dialog box.

TIP You can also create a URL hyperlink by highlighting a URL contained in the text and choosing New Hyperlink from URL in the Hyperlinks panel menu. This adds the hyperlink to the panel and automatically sets the destination as the highlighted URL text.

Defining Hyperlinks

Defining Hyperlinks

To choose the appearance of a hyperlink:

1. Use the Type menu in the Appearance area to choose a setting for the visibility of the rectangle around the hotspot .

   - **Visible Rectangle** creates a rectangular area that can be seen.

   - **Invisible Rectangle** creates a hotspot area that is not shown.

2. Use the Highlight menu to choose the appearance of the hotspot area when clicked **18**:

   - **None** creates no highlight on the area.

   - **Invert** creates the effect of inverting the colors of the hotspot area.

   - **Outline** creates an outline rectangle around the hotspot area.

   - **Inset** creates the effect of a 3D cutout in the hotspot area.

3. Use the Width menu to choose the thickness of the visible rectangle **19**:

   - **Thin** is the most tasteful setting.

   - **Medium** is a more obvious setting.

   - **Thick** is really too ugly to use.

4. Use the Style menu to choose the type of line for the visible rectangle **20**:

   - **Solid** is the most tasteful setting.

   - **Dashed** doesn't look as nice.

5. Choose a color from the Color menu.

17 *The* **Appearance area** *of the New Hyperlink dialog box lets you set how hyperlinks are displayed in the document.*

18 *Examples of the three* **Highlight effects** *applied to links.*

19 *Examples of the three* **Width settings** *applied to links.*

20 *Examples of the* **Style settings** *applied to links.*

21 *The* **Hyperlink Options dialog box** *lets you edit the settings for hyperlinks.*

Tips for Hyperlinks

Hyperlinks don't have to be ordinary text or plain frames. You can use placed images, text inside tables, or even inline graphics as the source objects for hyperlinks.

If you use text as the source object for a hyperlink, you may not want to display the clunky rectangle as the link indicator. Instead, consider using an underline with colored text (applied as a character style), to indicate where the hyperlink is located. This changes the link so it is more similar to links in Web pages.

Finally, you can automate some of the process of creating hyperlinks by applying the source object to a master page. The hyperlink can then be visible on all the pages based on that master page.

As you work, you can edit the settings for the hyperlink source.

To edit hyperlinks:

1. Double-click the hyperlink entry in the Hyperlinks panel.

   or

   Choose Hyperlink Options in the Hyperlinks panel menu. This opens the Hyperlink Options dialog box **21**.

2. Make changes in the Hyperlink Options dialog box.

Once you have created a hyperlink, you can change or reset the text selection or frame that was used as the source object.

To reset the hyperlink source:

1. Highlight the text or select the frame that you want to be the new hyperlink source.

2. In the Hyperlinks panel, select the hyperlink that you want to change.

3. Choose Reset Hyperlink from the Hyperlinks panel menu. The original source object is changed to the new selection.

If you have named an external document as a destination, you may need to update the hyperlink to that external document. For instance, if the page name or location has changed, the hyperlink needs to be updated.

To update the hyperlink to an external document:

1. Select the Hyperlink in the Hyperlinks panel.

2. Choose Update Hyperlink from the Hyperlinks panel menu.

3. Choose Reset Hyperlink from the Hyperlinks panel menu.

TIP If the external document is closed, hold the Opt/Alt key to open the document.

Defining Hyperlinks

Working with Hyperlinks

Once you have set up your destinations and hyperlinks, you can use the Hyperlinks panel to navigate through the document. This lets you easily move to specific locations in your InDesign document.

To move to a hyperlink:

1. Select the hyperlink in the Hyperlinks panel .

2. Choose Go to Source from the Hyperlinks panel menu.

   or

   Click the Go to Source icon in the Hyperlinks panel.

To move to a hyperlink destination:

1. Select the hyperlink in the Hyperlinks panel.

2. Choose Go to Destination from the Hyperlinks panel menu.

   or

   Click the Go to Destination icon in the Hyperlinks panel.

TIP If the destination is a URL, the default Web browser will be launched.

To delete a hyperlink destination:

1. Select the hyperlink in the Hyperlinks panel.

2. Choose Delete Hyperlink from the Hyperlinks panel menu.

   or

   Click the Delete Hyperlink icon in the Hyperlinks panel.

Go to source   Go to destination

Delete hyperlink

22 *You can use the* **Hyperlinks panel** *to navigate through the document.*

Automatic Hyperlinks

If it seems too much work to create manual hyperlinks, remember that you automatically create hyperlinks when you use the Table of Contents or Index feature.

The manual hyperlinks are best used for those instances when you need to add just a few links to a document. For example, you might want to add a URL address to a sales brochure or a page link to a small document.

Exporting and Testing Hyperlinks

You must export the InDesign file as a PDF in order to test your hyperlinks *(see Chapter 19, "Output," for how to export as a PDF)*. Also, you must remember to check the option to include hyperlinks in order to make them active in the PDF.

Working with Hyperlinks

The **Bookmarks** pane *in Acrobat displays the bookmarks created in InDesign.*

Page bookmark
Text bookmark
New bookmark
Delete bookmark

The **Bookmarks panel** *holds the bookmarks created for the document.*

Working with Bookmarks

Bookmarks provide a different way to navigate within a document. Instead of elements on the page, bookmarks are displayed in the Acrobat or Reader Bookmark pane . The reader clicks each bookmark to move to that position in the document. One of the advantages to using bookmarks is that the bookmark pane can be always visible next to the area being read.

To create a bookmark:

1. Choose **Window > Interactive > Bookmark** to open the Bookmarks panel .

2. Do one of the following to create the destination for the bookmark:

   • Place the insertion point at a point within the text. This creates a text bookmark.

   • Select the text. This creates a text bookmark named with the selected text.

   • Select a frame or graphic. This creates a page bookmark.

   • Double-click a page in the Pages panel. This creates a page bookmark.

3. Click the New Bookmark icon in the Bookmarks panel.

   or

   Choose New Bookmark from the Bookmarks panel menu. The bookmark is added to the Bookmarks panel.

TIP Icons show the difference between text and page bookmarks, although there are no such differences in Acrobat.

TIP If you already have bookmarks in the Bookmarks panel, the new bookmark is created directly under whichever bookmark is selected in the panel.

Working with Bookmarks

New bookmarks are created with the name Bookmark 1, Bookmark 2, and so on. You can rename the bookmark with a more descriptive name to help readers know what is located there.

To rename a bookmark:

1. Select the bookmark in the Bookmarks panel.

2. Choose Rename Bookmark from the Bookmarks panel menu. This opens the Rename Bookmark dialog box 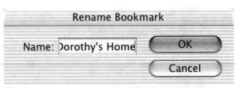.

3. Enter a new name in the field and click OK.

You can also rename a bookmark directly in the list area of the Bookmarks panel.

To rename a bookmark in the list area:

1. Click once to select the bookmark in the Bookmarks panel.

2. Click again to open the field that contains the bookmark name 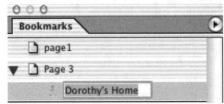.

3. Type the new name.

4. Press Return/Enter or click a different bookmark to apply the new name.

You can also delete bookmarks you no longer want in the document.

To delete a bookmark:

1. Select the bookmark in the Bookmarks panel.

2. Choose Delete Bookmark from the Bookmarks panel menu.

   or

   Click the Delete Bookmark icon in the Bookmarks panel.

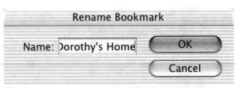

25 *Use the* **Rename Bookmark dialog box** *to change the bookmark names.*

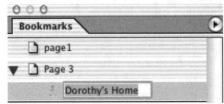

26 **Click the bookmark name** *to type a new name directly in the Bookmarks panel.*

Working with Bookmarks

Destination indicator

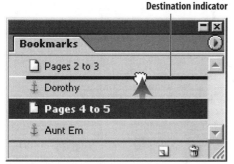

27 *Drag the bookmark up to* **move it to a new position** *in the Bookmarks panel.*

Name highlighted

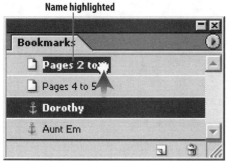

28 *Drag the bookmark onto the name to* **nest it under another bookmark.**

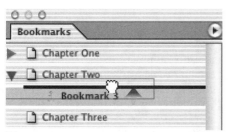

29 *Drag the bookmark up until you see the black line to* **unnest it from a bookmark.**

Bookmarks don't have to appear in the order that you create them. You can move important bookmarks up to the top of the list, even if they refer to pages that are at the end of your document.

To move bookmarks to new positions:

1. Drag the bookmark up or down the list to the new position.

2. When you see a black line appear, release the mouse button. The bookmark moves to the new position **27**.

TIP Use the Sort Bookmarks command to rearrange the bookmarks into the order they occur in the document.

You can also *nest*, or move bookmarks so they are contained within others. The top bookmark is called the *parent*; the nested bookmark is called the *child*. This allows you to have a very long bookmark list that can be expanded as necessary.

To nest bookmarks:

1. Drag the bookmark you want to nest onto the name of the parent bookmark.

2. When the name is highlighted, release the mouse **28**. The child bookmark is indented under the parent. A triangle controller appears that lets you open or close the parent bookmark.

TIP When you delete a bookmark, you also delete any bookmarks that are nested within that bookmark.

TIP You can continue to nest bookmarks through as many levels as you want.

To unnest bookmarks:

1. Drag the child bookmark out from the parent so that the black line is no longer indented below the parent bookmark **29**.

2. Release the mouse button. The child bookmark is no longer nested.

Working with Bookmarks

Adding Sounds

Despite the mind-bending concept of adding sound to a page layout, it's actually very simple to add sounds to an InDesign document. Just remember, you won't actually play the sound in InDesign. The sound is played as part of a PDF, when repurposed as part of an XML document.

To add a sound to a document:

1. Choose **File > Place** and then choose the sound file you want to import. The cursor changes into the Sound Clip cursor .

2. Click the Sound Clip cursor on the document. This adds a sound clip object to the document .

TIP The sound clip is displayed with an image that Adobe provides as the sound poster. This file is called *StandardSoundPoster.jpg* and is in InDesign application folder: Presets: Images. This file can be swapped for any other image you want to use.

You can also add an empty sound clip that can be filled with a sound at some other time.

To add an empty sound clip:

1. Draw a frame.

2. Choose **Object > Interactive > Sound Options**. This opens the Sound Options dialog box .

3. Enter a name in the Name field and click OK. The frame has been converted to an empty sound clip.

 The **Sound Clip cursor** *indicates you are importing a sound file.*

Sound file name
Sound icon

A **Sound Clip object** *created by clicking the Sound Clip cursor.*

 A **Sound Options dialog box** *for an empty sound clip. Notice there is no file specified under Options.*

Sound and Video Requirements

InDesign supports the same media file types as Adobe Acrobat. This means that you can import any sound or video file that can be played by Apple QuickTime, Flash Player, Windows Built-In Player, and Windows Media Player.

On the Mac, QuickTime plays all the media files. So all you need is QuickTime 6 or later. On Windows, you need QuickTime as well as the other players.

Adding Sounds

33 *You can set a* **name and description for a sound** *in the Sound Options dialog box.*

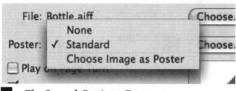

34 *The* **Sound Options Poster menu** *lets you choose the image that is displayed in a sound clip.*

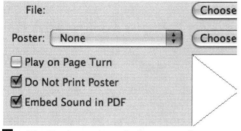

35 *The* **Options controls** *for a sound in the Sound Options dialog box.*

If you have an empty sound clip, you use the Sound Options dialog box to fill it with a sound and set the other sound properties.

TIP You can also edit a filled sound clip by modifying the settings in the Sound Options dialog box.

To set the sound options:

1. Open the Sound Options dialog box by double-clicking the sound clip.

   or

   Select the sound clip and choose **Object > Interactive > Sound Options**.

2. Enter a name for the sound clip in the Name field **33**.

3. If desired, enter a description that can be read by hearing-impaired users.

4. Use the Choose button to add a sound to the sound clip or to change the sound in the clip.

5. Use the Poster menu to choose an image that will be used to show where the sound is in the document **34**:

   - **None** leaves the sound clip frame empty.

   - **Standard** uses the standard icon **34**.

   - **Choose Image as Poster** lets you import a custom image to use as the sound poster.

6. Use the Choose button to choose the custom image **35**.

7. Check Play on Page Turn to have the sound automatically play when the page is opened **35**.

8. Check Do Not Print Poster to prevent the poster image from printing **35**.

9. Check Embed Sound in PDF to add the sound file to the PDF. If this is unchecked, you will have to make sure the sound file is kept with the PDF document **35**.

Adding Sounds

Adding Movies

Movies can be easily added to an InDesign document. Just remember, you won't actually play the movie in InDesign. The movie is played as part of a PDF, when repurposed as part of an XML document, or when packaged for a GoLive Web page. Consider what it would be like if this book came as a PDF. Instead of the static images, you would see little movies that showed how things work.

To add a movie to a document:

1. Choose **File** > **Place** and then choose the movie file you want to import. The cursor changes into the Movie Clip cursor .

2. Click the movie cursor on the document . This adds a Movie Clip object to the document.

TIP The movie clip displays the name of the movie and the Movie Clip icon.

TIP The movie clip is displayed with the default poster image that was set for the movie when it was created.

The **Movie Clip cursor** *indicates that you are importing a sound file.*

Movie icon

Movie name

A **Movie Clip object** *appears when you click to import a movie.*

Linking Versus Embedding Media Clips

Media clips such as movies and sound files can be linked to the PDF or embedded in the document. You can choose either one, but be aware of the limitations of each method.

Embedding a media clip adds to the size of the PDF. In the case of movies, this can add greatly to the final size of the file. If you embed a movie clip, only those viewers with Acrobat 6 or 7, or Adobe Reader will be able to view the movie. Users with earlier versions of the software will have to upgrade in order to view your documents correctly.

Linking to a media clip keeps the file size down, but then you must remember to keep the media clip with the PDF or it will not play properly.

Also, if you link to a media clip, it resides outside the PDF document. This can cause problems if you distribute your files on CD-ROM. Someone can copy the movie to use for their own purposes. If you don't want people to be able to use your media for their own projects, you can embed the media clip to prevent them from easily snatching the sound or movie to use in their own work.

You can control whether media clips are linked or embedded in the Sound or Movie Options dialog boxes, or when you export the PDF.

---

38 *The* **Movie Options dialog box** *for an empty movie clip frame.*

39 *Use the Movie Options dialog box to set the* **Name and Description** *for a movie.*

You can also add an empty movie clip that can be filled with a movie at some other time or used as the placeholder for a movie connected via a URL.

To add an empty movie clip:

1. Draw a frame.

2. Choose **Object** > **Interactive** > **Movie Options**. This opens the Movie Options dialog box.

3. Enter a name in the Movie Options dialog box and click OK. The frame holds an empty movie clip **38**.

If you have an empty movie clip, you use the Movie Options dialog box to fill it with a movie and set the other movie properties.

TIP You can also edit a filled movie clip by modifying the settings in the Movie Options dialog box.

To set the name and movie description:

1. Open the Movie Options dialog box by double-clicking the movie clip.

   or

   Select the movie clip and choose **Object** > **Interactive** > **Movie Options**.

2. Enter a name for the movie clip in the Name field **39**.

TIP When you fill a movie clip, it uses the name of the actual movie file by default. You can rename it in the Movie Options dialog box.

3. If desired, enter a description to help identify the movie **39**. This description is used if the movie cannot be played or for visually impaired users who use screen readers to hear the description of the file.

Adding Movies

The movie source is the movie clip that will be played. You have several options for how to choose the movie source .

To add a movie to the document movie clip:

1. In the Movie Options dialog box, click Choose a File.

2. Click the Choose button to navigate to find the movie you want to add to the document.

3. Click Embed Movie in PDF to add the movie to the exported PDF.

You can also play streaming media in your PDF document. This avoids all problems with file sizes. However, it does mean that an Internet connection must be available when the movie is played.

To choose a URL connection for a movie:

1. Create an empty movie frame and then open the Movie Options dialog box.

2. In the Movie Options dialog box, click Specify a URL .

3. Type the URL where the movie can be accessed.

4. If you have an active Internet connection, click Verify URL and Movie Size to make sure the settings are correct.

40 *The* **Source controls** *set to play a local file within the document.*

41 *The* **Source controls** *set to play a URL-based movie within the document.*

*(sidebar)* Adding Movies

Use the **Poster menu** to choose the image that is displayed on the static page.

Use the **Choose Movie Frame as Poster dialog box** to choose the frame you want to add as the movie poster.

Use the **Mode menu** to choose how often the movie plays.

Movie Display Options

You can also set the poster options for the movie. This allows you to set an image that fills the space in the frame for the movie clip.

To set the movie poster options:

◆ In the Movie Options dialog box, choose one of the following from the Poster menu :

- **None** sets no poster for the movie.

- **Standard** uses the image from the StandardMoviePoster.jpg file in InDesign application folder: Presets: Images. This file can be swapped for any other image you want to use.

- **Default Poster** uses the poster image that was created when the movie was edited.

- **Choose Image as Poster** lets you navigate to choose an image to use as the poster.

- **Choose Movie Frame as Poster** opens a dialog box that lets you advance through the movie to choose the poster . When this option is chosen, the listing **Frame from Movie** is checked in the menu.

You can also set the options for how often the movie plays.

To set the play options for the movie:

◆ In the Movie Options dialog box, choose one of the following from the Mode menu :

- **Play Once Then Stop** plays the movie a single time.

- **Play Once Stay Open** plays the movie, then leaves the movie player open to play again.

- **Repeat Play** sets the movie to play over and over in a loop.

You can also set the rest of the options for how the movie plays .

To set the movie display options:

1. Check Play on Page Turn to have the movie automatically play when the page is opened.

TIP A movie or sound clip may take a moment to load before it starts playing.

TIP The automatic page turn isn't the only way to play movies. A movie can be played by clicking the movie object in the PDF page. Also, you can create button behaviors that play movies.

2. Check Show Controller During Play to display the user controls that let you start, stop, rewind, forward, and change the sound of the movie .

3. Check Floating Window to display the movie in a separate window that appears above the Acrobat document.

4. If you check Floating Window, use the Size menu to set the dimensions of the movie window .

TIP The size options for a floating window movie are listed in multiples of the original movie size. 1/2x means one-half times the size of the original. 3x means three times the size of the original. Max means the maximum size to fit the monitor.

TIP A movie that is nonfloating is displayed at the size that it was originally created.

5. If you check Floating Window, use the Position menu to set where the movie plays in relation to the Acrobat document .

45 *The settings at the bottom of the Movie Options dialog box that* **control how the movie plays.**

46 *The* **Controller** *is displayed at the bottom of the movie.*

47 *Use the* **Size menu** *to set the size of a movie that plays in a floating window.*

48 *Use the* **Position menu** *to choose where a movie that plays in a floating window is displayed.*

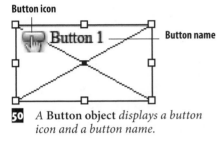

The Button tool in the Tools panel.

Button icon

Button name

A Button object displays a button icon and a button name.

You can use the numerical controls in the Button dialog box to set the size of a button.

An example of how a button can contain text or an image.

Creating Buttons

Buttons go much further than links. Links let you move to destinations or open Web pages. Buttons contain the code that can send you to destinations, flip pages, open Web pages, play movies, show and hide other buttons, and other tricks. The first thing you want to do is create a button and assign a simple action.

To create a button manually:

1. Select the Button tool in the Tools panel ⁴⁹.
2. Drag across the page to create the button object. The button appears on the page with a button icon and name ⁵⁰.

TIP The entire frame is considered the button, not just the little button icon in the frame.

TIP Buttons are drawn like any other object. Use all the same modifier keys and techniques that you use when drawing objects. *(See Chapter 4, "Working with Objects," for more information on drawing objects.)*

To create a button numerically:

1. Select the Button tool in the Tools panel.
2. Click with the Button tool on the page. This opens the Button dialog box ⁵¹.
3. Enter the width and height for the button.

You can also convert any existing object into a button. This makes it easy to turn images or text into buttons ⁵².

To convert an object into a button:

1. Select the object that you want to make into a button.
2. Choose **Object > Interactive > Convert to Button**. The button icon and name appear inside the converted object.

Creating Buttons

You can also add content, such as text or images, to existing buttons.

To type text in a button:

1. Move the Text tool over the button. The cursor changes to curved edges 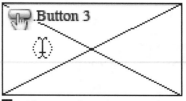. This indicates that text can be added to the button.

2. Click the Text tool. A blinking insertion point indicates that you can type text in the button.

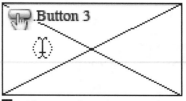

53 *The* **curved text cursor** *indicates that you can click to add text to a button.*

To import text into a button:

1. Select the button.

2. Choose **File > Place** and select the text file you want to import. The text flows into the button **54**.

TIP The text inside a button is in a separate text frame that has been pasted into the button frame. Use the Direct Selection tool to access the text frame.

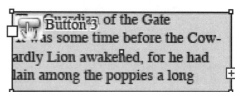

54 *Text can be imported into a button. The overflow symbol lets you flow the text out to another text frame.*

To add an image to a button:

1. Select the button.

2. Choose **File > Place** and select the image file you want to import. The image appears inside the button **55**.

TIP You can also click with a loaded cursor to add an image to a button.

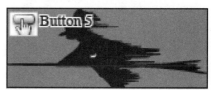

55 *An image can be imported into a button.*

Creating Buttons

56 *The **Button Options dialog box** set to the General control.*

57 *Enter a description in the General Button Options that the viewer can see while holding the cursor over the button in the PDF viewer.*

58 *The **Visibility in PDF menu** in the Button Options dialog box.*

General Button Properties

Once you have created a button, you can set its properties. These are divided into two sections. General properties let you name the button and control how it is viewed in the PDF. The other section is the Behavior properties, which let you apply actions to the button.

To set the General controls of the Button Options:

1. Double-click the button to open the Button Options dialog box **56**.

   or

   Select the button and choose **Object** > **Interactive** > **Button Options**.

TIP If you have text in the button, you'll need to use the Object menu command to open it. Otherwise, you'll place an insertion point in the button's text.

2. Click the General control.

3. Choose a name for the button or leave the default name in place.

4. Enter a description for the button. This description is visible when the mouse passes over the button in Acrobat. It is also used as the alternate text heard by visually impaired users **57**.

5. Choose one of the following from the Visibility in PDF menu **58**:

   • **Visible** displays the button. This is the most common setting.

   • **Hidden** hides the button. This setting can be overridden by the Show/Hide Fields behavior.

   • **Visible but Doesn't Print** allows the button to be seen but keeps it from cluttering up any printouts of the page.

   • **Hidden but Printable** allows you to add information to a printout without cluttering up your onscreen page.

General Button Properties

Setting the Button States

Part of the fun of using interactive buttons in PDF documents is that you can make the buttons change their appearance when the viewer passes the mouse over them or clicks the button. Each different appearance for the button is called a button *state*. InDesign lets you add states and control their appearance.

To add button states:

1. If it's not already open, choose **Window** > **Interactive** > **States** to open the States panel **59**.

TIP You need to choose Panel Options from the States panel menu and change the Thumbnail Size to see the preview of the states.

2. Select the button. Unless you have already modified it, only the Up state is listed in the States panel.

3. Click the New State icon to add the Rollover state.

   or

   Choose New State from the States panel menu.

4. Click the New State icon again to add the Down state.

TIP After you add the Down state, the New State icon is unavailable, as there are no other states you can add.

To delete button states:

1. Select the state you want to delete.

2. Click the Delete State icon.

   or

   Choose Delete State from the States panel menu.

TIP You cannot delete the Up state.

TIP Instead of deleting states, you may want to use the Enable State setting.

New state

Delete state

59 *Use the* **States panel** *to add new states to the button display.*

Understanding the States

The three button states refer to the appearance of the button in relation to the mouse:

- *Up* refers to the state when the mouse cursor is not near the button. This is also the appearance when the user releases the mouse after clicking the button. Some programs may call this the *Normal* state.

- *Rollover* refers to the state when the mouse cursor passes over the boundaries of the button. Some programs call this the *Over* state.

- *Down* refers to the state when the cursor has been positioned over the button and the mouse button has been pressed.

Other programs may have additional states for their buttons, but Acrobat stops at three.

Setting the Button States

Enabled state

Disabled state

60 *The check marks next to the state names indicate if the state is* **enabled or disabled.**

61 *The* **State Options dialog box** *lets you convert states or change their enable setting.*

Instead of deleting states, which tosses out their content, it may be easier to change whether or not the state is exported with the PDF. This is called *disabling* the state.

To enable a state:

◆ Click the checkbox next to the name of the state **60**. If the check mark is visible, it means the state is enabled and will export with the PDF.

or

Choose State Options and check Enable State in the State Options dialog box.

To disable a state:

◆ Click the checkbox next to the name of the state. If the check mark is not visible, it means the state is disabled and will not export with the PDF.

or

Choose State Options and uncheck Enable State in the State Options dialog box **61**.

If you have only a Down state or a Rollover state, you can turn one type of state into another.

To convert a state:

1. Select the state you want to convert.

2. Choose State Options from the States panel menu.

3. Use the State menu to change the Down state to Rollover or vice versa.

Setting the Button States

One of the reasons you want to create button states is so that the button changes appearance as the mouse cursor passes over or clicks the button. There are two ways to accomplish this. The first way is to use imported artwork to change the appearance of each state. The second way is to modify the art inside the button using InDesign's effects.

To create new states using imported artwork:

1. Create a button. The Up state is automatically selected.

2. Click the Place Content into Selected State icon **62**. This opens the dialog box that lets you add imported artwork into the Up state.

3. Click the New State icon. This creates a Rollover state that contains the same artwork as the Up state.

4. With the Rollover state selected, click the Place Content into Selected State icon. This changes the artwork in the Rollover state **63**.

   or

   Choose Place Content into State from the States panel menu.

5. Click the New State icon to create the Down state.

6. With the Down state selected, click the Place Content into Selected State icon. This changes the artwork in the Down state **63**.

Setting the Button States

Place content into selected state

Delete content of selected state

62 *Use the* **States panel** *to change the artwork in button states.*

63 *You can change the artwork from one state to another.*

64 *Each one of the states in this button was modified by selecting the text inside the button and making changes.*

You can use the commands to place content at any time to modify the appearance of a button state.

To edit button states using imported artwork:

1. Select the button state you want to modify.

2. Click the Place Content into Selected State icon to import new artwork into the button state.

The second way to change the appearance of a button is to directly select the object inside the button frame.

To change a button state by selecting the object:

1. Select the button you want to modify.

2. Select the state, in the States panel, that you want to modify.

3. Use the Direct Selection tool to select the object inside the button frame.

TIP You will know you're working on the object inside the button when the states disappear from the States panel.

4. Use any of InDesign's styling features to add a fill, stroke, or effect to the object **64**.

TIP You can also use the **File > Place** command to add text or an image to the object inside the button.

You can also delete the artwork from any state.

To delete the content from a button state:

1. Select the state.

2. Click the Delete Content of Selected State icon. This deletes all the original artwork as well as any effects that you have applied to the state.

   or

   Choose Delete Content from State from the States panel menu.

Setting the Button States

You don't have to work too hard to create different appearances for the button states. Adobe has created three appearance themes that you can instantly apply to buttons. The themes apply different looks to each of the button states.

To apply the appearances to buttons:

1. Select the button.

2. Choose one of the themes from the Appearance menu in the States panel :

   • **Bevel** colors the inside of the button and applies a gradient stroke around the edge of the object, creating the look of a beveled rectangle 66.

   • **Drop Shadow** colors the inside of the button and applies a drop shadow to the area inside the button frame 66.

   • **Glow** applies a multi-colored gradient to the object inside the button 66.

TIP The themes delete any imported images or custom content that was applied to the button states, and they apply their own styled content.

TIP The appearance themes will delete any nonrectangular shapes from the button.

You can modify the appearance themes that you apply to buttons.

To modify the button themes:

1. Select the button state.

2. Use the Direct Selection tool to select the object inside the button.

3. Use any of the style techniques to change the appearance of the theme 67.

65 *Use the* **Appearance menu** *in the States panel to apply preset themes to button states.*

66 *The* **appearance themes** *for the button states.*

67 *Use the Direct Selection tool to* **customize the appearance of a button state.** *Here the Down state of the Drop Shadow theme has been modified by changing the gradient and drop shadow effect.*

Setting the Button States

68 *The* **Behaviors section** *of the Button Options dialog box.*

69 *The* **Events menu** *lets you set which mouse trigger applies the behavior.*

70 *The* **Behavior menu** *lets you set which behavior is applied to the button.*

71 *The* **behavior list** *shows the events and behaviors that have been applied to the button.*

Applying Behaviors

A button without a behavior is like a light switch that is not connected to a lamp. You can press the button all you want, but nothing changes on the page. Behaviors let your buttons move pages, play movies, or change the appearance of the PDF page.

To apply a behavior to a button:

1. Select the button.
2. Open the Button Options dialog box.
3. Select the Behaviors control in the Button Options **68**.
4. Choose the mouse event that will apply the behavior **69**:
   - **Mouse Up** applies the behavior when the mouse button is released after a click.
   - **Mouse Down** applies the behavior as the mouse button is pressed down.
   - **Mouse Enter** applies the behavior when the mouse cursor is moved over the button.
   - **Mouse Exit** applies the behavior when the mouse cursor is moved away from the button.
   - **On Focus** applies the behavior when the button is prompted by tabbing through the fields.
   - **On Blur** applies the behavior when tabbing takes the focus off the button.
5. Choose the behavior from the Behavior menu **70**.
6. Depending on the behavior, set any additional controls for the behavior.
7. Click the Add button in the Behaviors panel. The event and behavior appear in the list on the left of the dialog box **71**.
8. If desired, you can apply additional behaviors to the button.

Applying Behaviors

Button Behaviors

Use this chart as a guide to how to apply button behaviors.

Behavior name	What it does	Settings
Close	Closes the document.	None
Exit	Exits (quits) the application that displays the PDF document, such as Adobe Reader.	None
Go To Anchor	Moves to a predefined destination that can be a text anchor, page, or bookmark. Lets you choose the document, the destination, and the zoom command.	Document: Chapter one... Choose... / Anchor: Page 1 Page / Zoom: Inherit Zoom
Go To First Page	Moves to the first page of the document. Lets you choose the zoom command.	Zoom: Inherit Zoom
Go To Last Page	Moves to the last page of the document. Lets you choose the zoom command.	Zoom: Inherit Zoom
Go To Next Page	Moves to the next page of the document. Lets you choose the zoom command.	Zoom: Inherit Zoom
Go To Next View	Only available when the Go To Previous View command was active. Then the command moves forward through the views.	None
Go To Previous Page	Moves to the previous page of the document. Lets you choose the zoom command.	Zoom: Inherit Zoom
Go To Previous View	Moves to whatever document, page, or zoom view was previously chosen.	None
Go To URL	Opens a Web page or Web command. Lets you type in the URL.	URL: http://

Behavior name	What it does	Settings
Movie	Controls the play of a movie. Lets you specify the movie and set the play controls.	Movie: [▼] Play Options: [Play ▼] Play / Stop / Pause / Resume
Open File	Opens an external file, which does not have to be a PDF document. Viewer must have the application that created the file. You must specify the full path to open the file.	Select File: [ ] Browse...
Show/Hide Fields	Displays the fields in the document and lets you set them to be hidden or visible by the action of the button.	Trigger 4 / Sunset 4 / Trigger 5 / Button 1 Show All / Hide All / Clear All
Sound	Controls the play of a sound clip. Lets you specify the sound and set the play controls.	Sound: [▼] Play Options: [Play ▼] Play / Stop / Pause / Resume
View Zoom	Lets you change the level of zoom as well as change the layout options such as Continuous and Continuous-Facing.	Zoom: [Full Screen ▼] Full Screen / Zoom In / Zoom Out / Fit In Window / Actual Size / Fit Width / Fit Visible / Reflow / Single Page / Continuous / Continuous-Facing / Rotate Clockwise / Rotate Counterclockwise Add

Button Behaviors

Modifying Behaviors

The most sophisticated buttons are those that apply multiple behaviors. You can apply multiple behaviors to the same mouse event or to separate mouse events.

To apply multiple behaviors to a button:

1. Select the button and open the Button Options dialog box.

2. Select the Behaviors tab.

3. Choose the event and behavior settings and then click the Add button. The behavior appears in the list on the left side of the dialog box.

4. Choose an additional event and behavior settings, and click the Add button.

TIP If the behavior uses the same event as the first, it appears nested under the event name. If the behavior uses a different event, it appears under that event name .

To edit existing behaviors:

1. Choose the behavior in the behavior list that you want to edit.

2. Make whatever changes you want to the behavior settings.

3. Click the Update button.

TIP The Update button replaces the Add button when you edit existing behaviors.

To change the position of a behavior:

◆ Drag the behavior up or down in the behaviors list . The behaviors are applied in the order that they appear in the list.

To change the event associated with a behavior:

◆ Drag the behavior from one event to another in the behaviors list.

Multiple behaviors *appear in the behaviors list.*

You can **drag a behavior** *to a new position or to a different event.*

Modifying Behaviors

74 *The* **Delete Button** *lets you delete behaviors or events from the behaviors list.*

75 *Click the checkbox next to a behavior or an event to* **deactivate the behavior or event**.

You may have applied a behavior that you no longer want applied to the button. Fortunately, you can delete behaviors from the button.

To delete a behavior:

1. Select the behavior in the behaviors list that you want to delete.

2. Click the Delete button. The behavior will be deleted from the behaviors list **74**.

TIP If that behavior was the only one listed for the event, the event will also be deleted from the list.

Instead of deleting behaviors that you have so carefully defined, you can deactivate them so they are still in the behaviors list but don't get applied to the final PDF. You can also deactivate all the behaviors under a mouse event.

To deactivate a behavior or mouse event:

1. Select the behavior or the mouse event in the behaviors list.

2. Click the checkbox next to the behavior or the event **75**. This deactivates the behavior or event from the exported PDF.

Modifying Behaviors

Exporting Interactive PDFs

There are a few settings you must be aware of when exporting interactive and multimedia PDFs from InDesign. *(See Chapter 20, "Exporting," for the complete instructions on exporting PDF files from InDesign.)*

To set the interactive/multimedia export controls:

1. Choose **File** > **Export** and then choose Adobe PDF for the format.

2. Name the file and click the Save button. This opens the Export Adobe PDF dialog box.

3. Check Bookmarks, Hyperlinks, and Interactive Elements to make sure they are part of the final PDF document **76**.

TIP If you want to embed a movie clip within the file, you must save the document as Acrobat 6 (PDF 1.5) or higher **77**.

4. Use the Multimedia menu to use or override the object embed settings **77**.

76 *Remember to include* **Bookmarks, Hyperlinks, and Interactive Elements** *when you export the PDF document.*

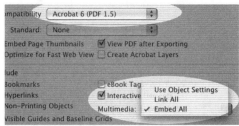

77 *You must save the file as Acrobat 6 (PDF 1.5) or higher in order to be able to embed all media clips in the exported PDF.*

OUTPUT 19

Several years ago the title of this chapter would have been "Printing." That was what you did with page-layout documents: You printed them using a desktop printer. Today, however, there are many more choices for publishing your InDesign documents.

Most InDesign files are created as part of the professional prepress process. *(For more information on professional printing, see* The Non-Designer's Scan and Print Book, *by Sandee Cohen and Robin Williams, published by Peachpit Press.)* You need to know more than just how to print to a desktop printer. You need to know how to make sure your document has been set up correctly. You need to know what files are necessary to send to a print shop.

So this chapter is now called "Output." Output refers to preparing documents and printing them — either with an ordinary desktop printer or with a high-end printing device such as an imagesetter.

Printing a Document

When a document is printed, many different instructions are sent to the printing machine. You need to set those instructions correctly.

TIP Adobe recommends using only the controls inside the InDesign Print dialog box — not the Page Setup (Mac) dialog box or the Printer Properties (Win) dialog box.

To print a document:

1. Choose **File > Print**. This opens the Print dialog box .

2. Click each of the categories ▇ on the left side of the dialog box to set the options as described in the chart on the following page.

TIP You do not need to set all the controls every time you print unless you need to change a specific setting.

3. Click the Print button to print the document according to the settings.

Before you print a document, you may want to set some objects (such as private notes or alternate designs) to not print.

To set elements to not print:

◆ Select the object and turn on Nonprinting in the Attributes panel.

or

Turn off the visibility of the layer in the document. This suppresses the printing for all objects on the layer.

▇ *The* **Print dialog box** *contains all the settings for printing documents.*

▇ *Click each of the categories to display those settings in the Print dialog box.*

Printing a Document

3 *The* **Printer list** *lets you choose the printer to print a document.*

4 *The* **Copies and Pages area** *of the General controls for printing.*

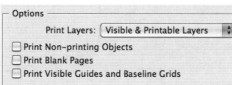

5 *The* **Print Layers menu** *in the Options area of the General controls for printing.*

6 *The* **Options area** *of the General controls for printing.*

Setting the General Print Options

If you are printing to a desktop printer, the options in the General category may be all you need to set to print a document.

To choose the printer:

◆ Choose the printer from the Printer menu at the top of the dialog box **3**.

To control the copies:

1. Set the number of copies in the Copies field **4**.

2. Choose Collate to print multiple copies organized as complete sets.

3. Choose Reverse Order to print the copies back to front.

To control the pages:

1. Choose All to print all the pages **4**.

   or

   Choose Range. Use a hyphen to specify a range of pages. Use a comma to specify individual pages.

2. Choose Collate to print copies as sets.

3. Use the Sequence menu to choose All Pages, Even Pages, or Odd Pages.

4. Check Spreads to print spreads together.

5. Choose Print Master Pages to print any master pages in the document.

To set the general options:

1. Choose which layers to print **5**.

2. Check Print Non-printing Objects to print objects set to not print **6**.

3. Check Print Blank Pages to print pages that have no visible items.

4. Check Print Visible Guides and Baseline Grids to print the guides and grids.

Choosing the Setup Controls

The Setup options contain the controls to set the paper size and orientation.

To set the paper size and orientation:

1. Use the Paper Size menu to choose the size of the paper on which to print the document .

TIP This menu changes depending on the type of printer chosen.

2. Click one of the Orientation buttons. This changes the rotation of the document on the printed page.

To choose the setup options:

1. Set the Scale amount for either Height or Width to change the size of the printed document on the paper .

2. Click the Scale to Fit button to have the document automatically resized to fit the chosen paper size.

3. Use the Page Position menu to choose where to position the document on the printed page .

4. Check Thumbnails to print small versions of the pages on a single page.

5. If you have chosen Thumbnails, use the Thumbnails menu to choose how many pages are printed on each page .

TIP See the next exercises for information on how to use the Tile controls.

7 The **Paper Size and Orientation controls** *in the Setup category of the Print dialog box.*

8 The **Options controls** *in the Setup category of the Print dialog box.*

9 The **Page Position menu** *in the Setup category of the Print dialog box.*

10 The **Thumbnails menu** *in the Setup category of the Print dialog box.*

11 *The* **Tile menu** *in the Setup category of the Print dialog box.*

Printed area

Nonprinted area

Overlap area

12 *The Preview area set to* **Auto tile.**

Printed area

Overlap area

13 *The Preview area set to* **Auto Justified tile.**

Tiling Pages

If your document is larger than the paper in the printer, you can print portions of the document on different pages. You can then assemble the pages together. This is called *tiling*. Auto tiling automatically divides the page into smaller segments.

To set automatic tiling:

1. Check Tile in the Setup category of the Print dialog box.

2. Choose Auto from the Tiling menu **11**.

3. Set the amount in the Overlap field. This controls how much of one page is repeated on the tile for a second section of the page.

TIP The Preview area in the lower left portion of the Print dialog box shows how the page will be tiled **12**.

Auto justified tiling divides the pages so that the right edge of the document lies on the right side of a printed page and the bottom edge of the document lies on the bottom edge of a printed page **13**.

TIP The Auto setting ensures that there is no white space on the right side and bottom of the tiled pages.

To set auto justified tiling:

1. Check Tile in the Setup category of the Print dialog box.

2. Choose Auto Justified from the Tiling menu.

Tiling Pages

You can also tile pages manually. This lets you make sure that the edge of the paper does not cut across an important portion of the document.

To set manual tiling:

1. Use the zero-point crosshairs on the ruler to set the upper-left corner of the area you want to print . (See Chapter 2, "Document Setup," for more information on setting the zero point of the ruler.)

2. Choose **File > Print**.

3. Click the Setup category of the Print dialog box.

4. Choose Manual from the Tiling menu.

TIP The Preview area of the Print dialog box shows the area that will be printed **15**.

5. Click Print to print that one page.

6. Reposition the zero-point crosshairs to set a new area to be printed.

7. Follow steps 2 through 5 to define and print the second tile.

8. Repeat the process until the entire page has been printed.

14 Move the zero-point crosshairs *to set the area to print as a tile on one page.*

Printed area

Nonprinted area

15 *The Preview area set to* **Manual tile**.

Tiling Pages

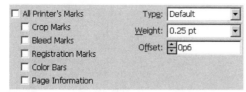

16 *The **Marks settings** in the Marks and Bleed category of the Print dialog box.*

17 *The **page marks and information** as they appear on the printed page.*

Setting Marks and Bleed

You can also add information that shows where the page is to be trimmed, the document name, and so on. This information is sometimes called printer's marks or page marks.

To set the page marks:

1. Check All Printer's Marks to turn on all the marks, or use the checkboxes to set each one individually **16** and **17**.

   - **Crop Marks** indicates where the page should be trimmed.

   - **Bleed Marks** shows how far outside the crop marks you must put graphics so that they are trimmed correctly.

   - **Registration Marks** adds crosshair targets that are used to line up pieces of film.

   - **Color Bars** provides boxes that display the colors used in the document as well as the tint bars that can be used to calibrate the printing press for correct tints of colors.

   - **Page Information** prints the name of the file, the page number, and the time the document was printed.

2. Use the Type menu to choose a custom set of marks such as those used in Japanese printing.

3. Enter an amount in the Weight menu for the thickness of the crop marks.

4. Enter an amount in the Offset field to determine how far away from the trim the page marks should be positioned.

You can also control the bleed, or the area that allows objects that extend off the page to print **18**.

— **Bleed area**

To set the bleed area:

◆ To use the bleed set in the Document Setup dialog box, check Use Document Bleed Settings **19**.

or

Deselect Use Document Bleed settings and then set the custom amounts for the bleed around each side of the page **20**.

TIP These custom bleed controls make it easy for print shops to set a uniform bleed as part of a print preset.

If you have set a slug for the document, you can choose whether that slug area prints or not.

To set the slug area:

◆ To print items in the slug area, check Include Slug Area.

18 *An example of an object that bleeds off a page.*

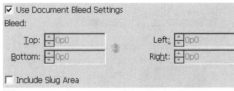

19 *Check the option for **Use Document Bleed Setup** to have the bleed use the same settings as in the Document Setup dialog box.*

20 *The **Bleed controls** allow you to define a custom bleed in the Print dialog box.*

Why Do We Need To Bleed?

Why do you need to position objects so they bleed off the page layout? The reason is that the machines that trim books and pages don't always cut perfectly. Take a look at the thumbtabs on the sides of this book. If you flip from page to page, you will see that the gray area isn't always the same size. That's because when the paper for the book is trimmed, some of the pages are cut slightly different from the others. (Yes, I know this will happen, even before the book is printed.)

So instead of trusting that the trim position is always perfect, I set a bleed by extending the gray area outside the edge of the page. That way I don't have to worry if the trim is slightly off. I know that the gray area will still be visible outside the trim.

Unless your print shop is trying to trim pages in the middle of an earthquake, you shouldn't need more than a quarter-inch bleed. However, if you are in doubt, ask your print shop for the size they would like for a bleed.

---

21 *The Color menu in the Output category of the Print dialog box.*

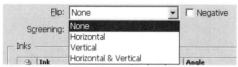

22 *The Flip menu in the Output category of the Print dialog box.*

Original	Horizontal	Vertical	Horizontal & Vertical

23 *Examples of how the Flip menu changes the readability of a document.*

What Does RIP Stand For?

You may hear people use the term RIP when they talk about printing. RIP stands for *raster image processing*.

RIP is simply a fancy term for what happens when a file is processed for output by a high-resolution imagesetter. In addition, RIP also refers to the device that does the processing.

Setting the Output Controls

You may need to set the color controls to choose how color documents are printed.

To control how colors are printed:

1. Choose one of the following from the Color menu **21**:

   - **Composite Leave Unchanged** prints without converting colors to either RGB or CMYK.

   - **Composite Gray** prints all the colors as a gray image. Use this when printing on one-color laser printers.

   - **Composite RGB** prints all the colors as an RGB image. Use this when printing on RGB ink-jet printers.

   - **Composite CMYK** prints all the colors as a CMYK image. Use this when printing on PostScript CMYK printers.

   - **Separations** prints all the colors onto separate plates or pages.

   - **In-RIP Separations** prints all the colors onto separate plates using the separation controls in the RIP.

2. If you choose one of the composite settings, you can check Text as Black.

TIP The Text as Black command is helpful if you have color text that you want to be more readable when printed on a one-color printer.

3. Use the Flip menu if you need to flip the orientation of the page **22** and **23**.

4. Check the Negative box in the Output category of the Print dialog box.

TIP These last two options are not commonly used for desktop printers, but are used by print shops when they create film separations.

You can also change the screen frequency and angle of halftones in the image.

To change the screen settings:

1. Use the Screening menu to set the frequency and angle for the screen applied to images 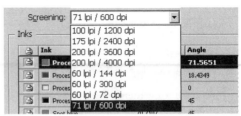.

2. Select a color in the Inks area and then use the Frequency and Angle fields 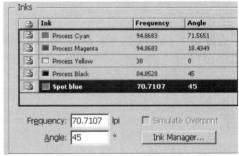.

TIP Always talk to your Print Service Provider for the correct settings.

Trapping refers to the various techniques that are used to compensate for the misregistration of printing plates. However, if you don't understand trapping, you should consult with the service bureau that will print your file before you set the trapping.

To turn on basic trapping:

◆ Choose Application Built-In or Adobe In-RIP from the Trapping menu .

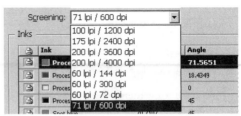

24 *The Screening menu in the Output category of the Print dialog box.*

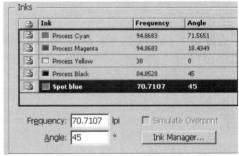

25 *The Frequency and Angle fields in the Output category of the Print dialog box.*

26 *The Trapping menu in the Output category of the Print dialog box.*

27 *Use the* **View menu** *in the Separations Preview panel to turn on the separations preview.*

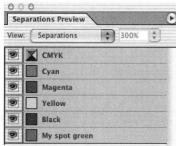

28 *The* **colors in the document** *are displayed in the Separations Preview panel.*

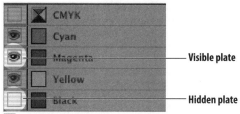

29 *Click the* **Show/Hide icons** *in the Separations Preview panel to change the display of the colors on the page.*

Working with Separations Preview

When a document is printed with more than one color, each color is called a plate. Printing the different colors onto separate plates is called making separations. You use the Separations Preview panel to view the different color plates onscreen. This makes it possible to gauge how a document will look on press.

To turn on separations preview:

1. Choose **Window > Output > Separations Preview**. The Separations Preview panel appears.

2. Choose Separations from the View menu **27**. This displays the controls for the colors in the document **28**.

3. Click each Show/Hide icon next to the color name to change the display of the colors on the page **29**.

TIP Click the Show/Hide icon next to the CMYK listing to show or hide all those plates together.

My Favorite Childhood Book

One of my favorite books I had as a kid was a *World Book Encyclopedia* that had acetate pages that you could flip to see how colors built up to a full-color image. (It's true! At the age of 13 I was into page production and color separations.)

When I worked in advertising we called these color breakdowns *prog proofs* (for progressive proofs). But during many years of working with computer graphics, we had no way to see how colors combine on the page. The best we could do was print color on individual laser prints and then hold them up to the window to see how the colors would separate.

With InDesign, I am thrilled to use the Separations Preview — an electronic version of my *World Book* acetate pages. Instead of flipping pages, I click ink colors on and off. I can spend hours doing it. It makes me feel like a kid again!

The Separations Preview panel also lets you view the total amount of ink for each plate.

To view the inks for each plate:

1. Choose Separations from the View menu.
2. Move the cursor around the page. The ink percentages appear next to the name of each color 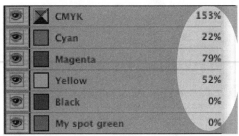.

Separations Preview also shows you the areas of the page that exceed a certain ink limit. For instance, many print shops will request that you not define colors totaling more than 300% of all the inks combined. The Ink Limit setting lets you see if there are any areas that exceed this limit.

To check the ink limit:

1. Select Ink Limit from the View menu in the Separations Preview panel.
2. Use the amount menu to set the ink limit amount **31**.

TIP When you switch to the Ink Limit view, the document preview changes to a grayscale image. Any areas that exceed the ink limit are shown in red. The deeper the red, the more the color is over the ink limit.

TIP You can also enter your own custom amount in the Ink Limit field.

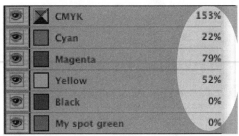

30 *The Separations Preview displays the* **ink percentages next to each color plate***.*

31 *Use the* **Ink Limit controls** *to check the total ink applied in areas of the layout.*

Ink does print

Ink does not print

32 *The* **printer icon next to an ink color** *indicates whether that ink will print or not.*

Color Separations and Ink Manager

The Inks area of the Output category also lets you control how the inks are separated and printed.

To set the inks to be printed:

◆ Click the printer icon next to the name of each color. Each click changes how the ink will print as follows **32**:

- If the icon is visible, the color will print.
- If the icon is not visible, the color does not print.

Sometimes you find yourself with a document that contains spot colors that should be process colors. The Ink Manager lets you convert the spot colors to process inks.

33 *The* **Ink Manager dialog box** *gives you control over how inks are separated or printed.*

To convert spot colors to process:

1. Open the Ink Manager by clicking the Ink Manager button in the Output area of the Print dialog box **33**.

TIP You can also open the Ink Manager from the Swatches panel menu or the Separations Preview panel menu.

2. Click the color icon next to the name of each color. Each click changes how the ink will print as follows **34**:

- A CMYK symbol indicates that the color will separate as a process color.
- A spot color symbol indicates that the color will separate on its own plate.

3. Click the All Spots to Process option to convert all spot colors to process.

4. If desired, check Use Standard Lab Values for Spots. This converts the spot colors to process using their built-in Lab color values.

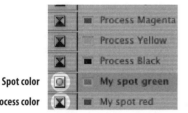

Spot color

Process color

34 *Click the* **color icons** *in the Ink Manager to convert spot colors to process.*

Color Separations and Ink Manager

When you import artwork that contains spot colors, those spot colors are added to the document and the Swatches panel. There are no problems if the imported colors are named exactly the same as existing colors. But if the name of the imported color differs from the color you have defined, you can wind up with two separate color plates instead of one . Thankfully, InDesign lets you map one color to be an alias of another.

To map one color to be the alias of another:

1. Select the color you want to change in the Ink Manager.

2. Use the Ink Alias menu to choose a different color to map to the selected one 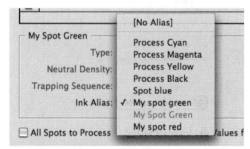. The color is listed in the Ink Manager as mapped to the other color 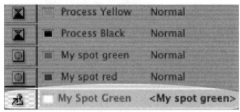.

TIP You can map the selected color to a spot or process color.

TIP Colors that are mapped to another color are not listed in the Inks area of the Output category. They are also not listed in the Separations Preview panel.

35 *An example of how names typed in different cases can create* **too many spot colors** *in a document.*

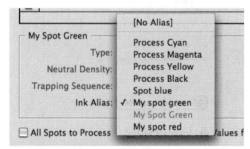

36 *Use the* **Ink Alias menu** *to have one color map to a different one.*

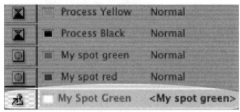

37 *An example of how* **one color is used as the alias** *for another.*

38 *Use the* **Send Data menu** *in the Graphics category to control how images are printed.*

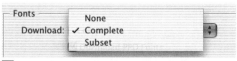

39 *Use the* **Download menu** *in the Graphics category to control how much of a font is sent to the printer.*

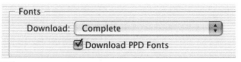

40 *Choose* **Download PPD Fonts** *to send printer fonts as part of the print information.*

Setting the Color Management Options

Rather than go into details of color management, it is better for me to recommend that you ask your print shop how to set the color management options.

Not only is the field of color management way beyond the scope of this book, it's probably way beyond what you want to read in this book.

Suffice it to say there is no "QuickStart" for color management. It's a deep topic and deserves much more than a section in my book. See *Real World Color Management* by Bruce Fraser, Chris Murphy, and Fred Bunting (Peachpit Press) for the best information on the topic.

Setting the Graphics Options

The Graphics options control how much information is sent to the printer. You can control the data that is sent for placed images.

To control the data sent for images:

◆ Choose one of the following from the Images Send Data menu **38**:

- **All** sends all the information for the image. This is the slowest setting.

- **Optimized Subsampling** sends only the amount of information necessary for the chosen output device. Use this option if you're proofing high-resolution images on a desktop printer.

- **Proxy** sends only a 72-ppi version of the image.

- **None** replaces the image with crosshairs within the frame. Use this option when you want to proof only the text in the file.

You can also control how much of the font information is sent to the printer.

To control the font information sent for printing:

1. Choose one of the following from the Download menu **39**:

- **None** sends no font information, only a reference to the font. Do not use this option unless you understand how to replace the reference in the PostScript data stream.

- **Complete** sends the entire set of glyphs for the font. This is the longest option.

- **Subset** sends only those glyphs used in the document.

2. Choose Download PPD Fonts to send all fonts, even if they have been installed on the printer **40**. This option is helpful if you use a variation of the fonts installed on the printer.

Setting the Advanced Options

The Advanced category lets you set the options for OPI and choose a transparency preset. *OPI* stands for *Open Prepress Interface*. The OPI controls are used when files are sent to Scitex and Kodak prepress systems.

To set the OPI controls:

1. In the OPI area, click the OPI Image Replacement checkbox **41**.

2. Choose which types of images should be replaced during an OPI workflow. (An OPI workflow uses low-resolution images for the layout and swaps them with high-resolution images just before printing.)

When you use any of the transparency features, InDesign needs to flatten or convert those effects into vector and raster images as they are sent for output. The Transparency Flattener section of the Advanced category controls how InDesign flattens the image.

To set the flattener preset:

1. Use the Preset menu to choose one of the flattener settings **42**.

2. If you have used the Pages panel to flatten individual spreads, you can check Ignore Spread Overrides to override that setting. This means that the setting you choose in this dialog box will be used no matter what flattener settings you have applied to the individual pages.

41 *Set the* **OPI Image Replacement** *options to control how images are handled during prepress.*

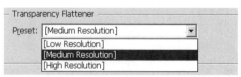

42 *Use the* **Preset menu** *in the Transparency Flattener area to set the resolution for converting transparency effects into rasterized images.*

43 *The* **Transparency Flattener Presets** **dialog box** *lets you define new presets for handling transparency effects.*

44 *The* **Transparency Flattener Preset** **Options dialog box** *contains the settings for a custom transparency flattener preset.*

45 *The* **Options area** *in the Transparency Flattener Preset Options dialog box.*

Flattener Presets and Preview

The transparency flattener presets control how the transparency effects, drop shadows, and feathers are handled during output.

To create a transparency flattener preset:

1. Choose **Edit > Transparency Flattener Presets**. This opens the Transparency Flattener Presets dialog box **43**.

2. Click the New button. The Transparency Flattener Preset Options dialog box appears **44**.

3. Use the Name field to name the preset.

4. In the Options area, move the Raster/ Vector Balance slider to create more vector or more rasterized artwork **45**.

5. Set an output resolution in the Line Art and Text Resolution field.

TIP A setting of 300 dpi is sufficient for most output.

6. Set an output resolution for gradient objects in the Gradient and Mesh Resolution field.

TIP A setting of 150 dpi is sufficient for most gradients.

7. Check Convert All Text to Outlines to convert the text to paths.

TIP If this box is not checked, only transparent portions of the text may be converted to outlines. This option makes the text width consistent.

8. If you have strokes that pass through different transparencies, you may want to choose Convert All Strokes to Outlines to convert the strokes to filled paths.

9. Check Clip Complex Regions to ensure that any differences in raster and vector objects always fall along existing paths.

TIP This can result in complex clipping paths, which may not print on some devices.

Flattener Presets and Preview

To edit a transparency flattener preset:

1. Choose the preset you want to edit.

TIP The three default presets, surrounded by brackets, cannot be edited 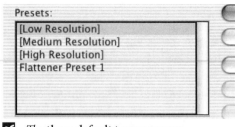.

2. Click the Edit button.

3. Edit the preset in the Transparency Flattener Presets dialog box.

TIP The Preset Settings area displays a readout of the settings for each preset .

To delete transparency flattener presets:

1. Choose the presets you want to delete.

TIP The three default presets, surrounded by brackets, cannot be deleted 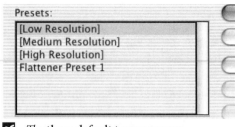.

TIP Use the Shift key to select multiple adjacent presets. Use the Cmd/Ctrl key to select multiple nonadjacent presets.

2. Click the Delete button.

You can also save transparency flattener presets to share among others. Once saved, the presets can then be loaded onto other machines.

To save a transparency flattener preset:

1. Choose the presets you want to save.

TIP Use the Shift key to select multiple adjacent presets. Use the Cmd/Ctrl key to select multiple nonadjacent presets.

2. Click the Save button.

3. Name the file.

To load a transparency flattener preset:

1. Click the Load button.

2. Navigate to find the file that contains the presets.

3. Click Open. The presets appear in the Transparency Flattener Presets dialog box.

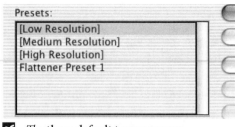

46 *The* **three default transparency flattener presets** *in brackets cannot be edited or deleted.*

47 *The* **Preset Settings area** *displays a readout of the settings for a particular transparency flattener preset.*

Flattener Presets and Preview

48 *The* **Custom Spread Flattener Settings** **dialog box** *lets you apply different flattener controls to a specific spread.*

A Short Course in Flattening

You may feel a little overwhelmed by all the controls for flattening transparency. Don't panic: Most of the flattening options are best set by the print house that will output your files.

However, there are some simple rules that can make it easier to get successful results when flattening artwork.

Unless you absolutely want text to be part of a transparency effect, keep your text above any transparency effects. For instance, instead of putting text underneath a drop shadow, move it above. If the text is black, you won't see any difference in the final output. If it's a color, set it to overprint.

Try to avoid overlapping two gradients with transparency effects. That combination creates objects that are much too complex.

Run tests. The first time I used transparency and blend modes, I sent ten sample pages to my publisher, who had them output at the print shop. We looked to make sure none of the text had changed and there were no problems with the images. It saved us a lot of worry when the book went to press.

You can apply a flattener preset to the document in the Advanced category of the Print dialog box. However, you may have one page that requires special flattener controls. InDesign lets you apply flattener presets to each specific spread.

TIP Flattening must be handled on a per spread, not per page, basis.

To apply a flattener preset to an individual spread:

1. Move to the spread.

2. In the Pages panel menu, choose one of the following from the Spread Flattening menu:

   • **Default** leaves the spread flattening at whatever setting is applied to the document.

   • **None (Ignore Transparency)** prints the spread without any transparency effect. This setting is useful for print shops that need to troubleshoot during output.

   • **Custom** opens the Custom Spread Flattener Settings dialog box. These settings are identical to ones in the Transparency Flattener Preset Options dialog box **48**.

Instead of waiting for your file to be printed, you can preview how the flattening will occur with the Flattener Preview panel.

To preview the flattener settings:

1. Choose **Window** > **Output** > **Flattener Preview**. This opens the Flattener Preview panel .

2. Choose one of the options from the Highlight menu . This controls which objects will be displayed in the flattener preview.

3. Use the Preset menu to choose which flattener preset is used to control the flattener preview.

4. Click the Refresh button to update the screen preview. The page displays the highlighted objects in red against other grayscale objects .

   or

   Check Auto Refresh Highlight to have the screen update automatically.

5. Check Ignore Spread Overrides to use only the setting in the Preset menu.

6. If you want, click the Apply Settings to Print button to apply the settings to the Advanced category of the Print dialog box.

TIP You can open the Transparency Flattener Presets dialog box using the Flattener Preview panel menu.

49 *The* **Flattener Preview panel** *lets you see the effects of the flattener presets on your document.*

50 *Use the* **Highlight menu** *to choose which objects will be displayed in the flattener preview.*

Text below shadow   Text above shadow

51 *The* **Flattener preview highlights** *the objects affected by transparency. Here the text below the shadow is highlighted while the text above the shadow is not.*

Transparency Resources

This book can hardly cover all the aspects of setting transparency and flattening. For more information see the InDesign online Help pages.

Also, download the document *Getting Started with Transparency using Adobe Creative Suite Software* on the Adobe Web site.

Finally, if you are a service provider, you should look at the Print Service Provider Resources page of the Adobe Solutions Network (ASN).

Flattener Presets and Preview

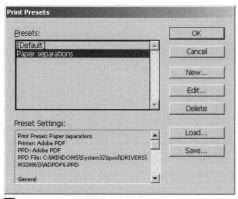

52 *Click the* **Save Preset button** *to save the current Print settings as a print preset.*

53 *Use the* **Save Preset dialog box** *to name your own printer preset.*

54 *A saved preset can be applied using the* **Print Preset menu** *at the top of the Print dialog box.*

55 *Saved presets are listed in the* **Print Presets dialog box***.*

Working with Print Presets

With all the areas in the Print dialog box, you wouldn't want to have to set all the controls each time you have a new document. InDesign lets you save the print settings so you can easily apply them later.

To save a print preset:

1. Set all the categories in the Print dialog box to the settings you want to save.

2. Click the Save Preset button at the bottom of the Print dialog box **52**. This opens the Save Preset dialog box **53**.

3. Enter a name for the preset.

4. Click OK. This saves the preset.

To apply a print preset:

◆ Choose a saved preset from the Print Preset menu at the top of the Print dialog box **54**.

You don't need to go through the Print dialog box to create and save a print preset.

To define a printer preset:

1. Choose **File > Print Presets > Define**. The Print Presets dialog box appears **55**.

2. Click the New button to define a new preset. This opens a version of the Print dialog box that lets you set the various print categories.

   or

   Click the Edit button to make changes to the selected print preset.

To delete a printer preset:

1. Select the presets you want to delete in the Print Presets dialog box.

2. Click the Delete button.

One of the benefits of working with printer presets is that you can export them so others can print documents with the same settings.

To export printer presets:

1. In the Print Presets dialog box, select the presets you want to export.

TIP Use the Shift key to select adjacent multiple presets. Use the Cmd/Ctrl key to select nonadjacent multiple presets.

2. Click Save. A dialog box appears where you can name the document that contains the exported presets.

Your service bureau can provide you with printer presets that you can import to use for printing or packaging documents.

To import printer presets:

1. In the Print Presets dialog box, click Load.

2. Use the dialog box to select the document that contains the presets exported from another machine.

3. Click OK. The presets appear in the Print Presets dialog box.

Creating a Print Summary

With all the settings in the Print dialog box, you may want to keep track of how a document has been printed. The Summary area gives you a report of all the print settings.

To use the Summary area:

♦ Scroll through the summary area to see all the settings applied to a print job **56**.

   or

   Click the Save Summary button to save a text file listing all the print settings.

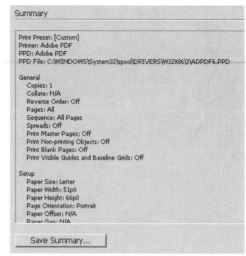

56 *Use the* **Summary area** *to see all the print settings applied to a document.*

57 The **Print Booklet dialog box** *lets you create printer's spreads.*

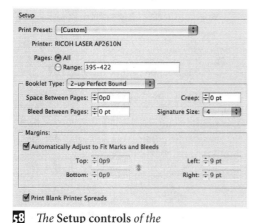

58 The **Setup controls** *of the Print Booklet dialog box.*

59 The **Print Preset menu** *lets you choose which print preset should be used.*

Creating Printer's Spreads

When you work on an InDesign document, you view the pages in what are called *reader's spreads.* However, when documents are printed, they need to be arranged in what are called *printer's spreads.* (This is also called *imposing* pages in position.)

For example, in an 8-page brochure, page one would be paired up with page eight. Page two would be next to page seven. Manually creating printer's spreads is a nightmare. Fortunately, you can easily arrange your document into printer's spreads using the Print Booklet command.

To impose a document into printer's spreads:

1. Choose **File > Print Booklet**. The Print Booklet dialog box appears **57**.

2. Click the Setup category. The Setup controls appear **58**.

3. Choose a print preset from the Print Preset menu **59**. If you have no preset available, choose [Current Document Settings] to use whatever printer is chosen in your Print dialog box.

TIP This setting allows you to choose the Adobe PDF printer to impose as a PDF file.

4. Use the Pages control to choose which pages should be imposed.

5. Choose the Booklet Type and Margins controls as explained in the following exercises.

Creating Printer's Spreads

There are different types of booklets. Each one requires separate controls. If you are unsure of which type of booklet you are creating, ask your print shop.

TIP Check with your printer for the correct settings for all of these controls.

To set the type of booklet:

1. Choose the orientation and binding for the booklet from the Booklet Type menu .

2. Depending on the orientation and binding, you may need to set any or all of the following controls:

   • **Space Between Pages** is the amount of space between the pages.

   • **Bleed Between Pages** is the amount of space added around the pages.

   • **Creep** is an adjustment for the thickness of the pages as they are folded.

   • **Signature size** is how many pages are bound together.

You also need to set the margins for the pages that are imposed.

To set the margins:

Choose Automatically Adjust to Fit Marks and Bleeds 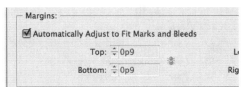 to set the amount necessary to fit any printer's marks and bleeds on the original layout.

or

Deselect that option and manually set the margins.

To print blank spreads:

◆ Choose Print Blank Printer Spreads to include those spreads that don't contain any items on the pages.

60 *The* **Booklet Type menu** *of the* Print Booklet dialog box.

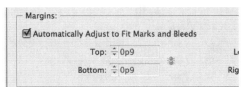

61 *Choose* **Automatically Adjust to Fit Marks and Bleeds** *to set the booklet margins automatically.*

Please! Think Before You Impose!

At least once a month I read about someone who thinks they need to send printer spreads in to their service bureau before their job (brochure, book, pamphlet, or other document) can be printed.

This is not a safe road to go down. Creating printer spreads is not something the average designer is trained to do. Even I wouldn't have the foggiest idea of how to make the settings for my jobs. There are too many variables.

I have no idea what the signature size is going to be or how many pages will be imposed together.

Even worse, I don't know what to choose for the creep size as I don't know how thick the folds in my paper will be.

Having said that, if all you want to do is set up a job to be run on your office printing machine, or send the job to the local copy shop for a simple booklet, then the Print Booklet command is perfect for you!

Creating Printer's Spreads

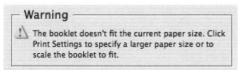 *The **Preview window** of the Print Booklet dialog box shows how the pages will be imposed.*

 *Use the **page controls** to scroll through previews of the imposed pages.*

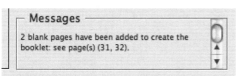 *The **Messages area** of the Print Booklet dialog box gives you information about the imposed document.*

*The **Warning area** of the Print Booklet dialog box alerts you to any problems that may occur in the imposed document.*

You can gauge if you're setting things up correctly by checking the Preview in the Print Booklet dialog box.

To preview the imposed pages:

1. Choose Preview from the Print Booklet dialog box. The pages as they will be imposed appear in the preview window 62.

2. Use the page controls to scroll through a preview of all the imposed pages 63.

3. Check the Messages area to see if there is any information that you should know about regarding the imposition 64.

4. Check the Warning area to see if there are alerts for any problems in the final imposed document 65.

You can also see a summary of all the settings for an imposed document.

To see the summary of the imposed settings:

◆ Choose Summary from the Print Booklet dialog box. The summary appears.

Creating Printer's Spreads

Creating PostScript Files

Instead of sending the InDesign document to a service bureau, you can create a Post-Script file that contains all the information necessary to print the file. (This is sometimes called *printing to disk*.) A standard PostScript file contains all the information necessary to print the file as well as the specific information about the printer.

66 *Choose* **PostScript® File** *from the Printer menu to create a file that contains all the information necessary to print the document.*

To create a standard PostScript file:

1. Choose **File** > **Print**.

2. Choose PostScript® File from the Printer menu **66**.

3. Choose the type of printer that will print the file.

4. Set all the options in the print categories in the Print dialog box.

TIP Check with the service bureau that will print your file for the correct options.

5. Choose a name and location for the file.

6. Click Save.

67 *Choose* **Device Independent** *from the PPD menu to create a PostScript file that can be printed to any printer.*

A device-independent PostScript file does not contain any information about the type of printer or output device.

TIP This lets you create a PostScript file even if you don't know the type of printer that your document will be printed on.

To create a device-independent PostScript file:

1. Choose **File** > **Print**.

2. Choose Device Independent from the PPD menu **67**.

3. Follow steps 3 through 6 in the previous exercise.

68 *The* **Preflight dialog box** *lets you choose each of the categories for the various aspects of printing a document.*

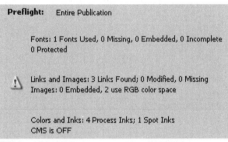

69 *The* **Summary area** *of the Preflight dialog box gives you an overview of the categories checked during a preflight.*

70 *The* **preflight categories** *let you see the details of the preflight report.*

Creating a Preflight Report

When you create an InDesign document, you have two jobs: designer and production manager. As the production manager, you need to know if there could be any problems printing your job. Fortunately, InDesign has a built-in preflight utility that checks all the elements in your document to make sure they print correctly. (The name comes from the list that airline pilots complete before they take off.)

To run the preflight utility:

1. Choose **File > Preflight**. InDesign takes a moment to check all the elements of the document and then opens the Preflight dialog box **68**.

2. Review the information in the Preflight Summary **69**.

   TIP Any potential printing problems are flagged with an alert symbol in the Preflight Summary.

3. Click each of the categories in the Preflight dialog box **70**. *(See the following exercises for details on these categories.)*

4. Click the Report button to create a report of the preflight status.

   or

   Click the Package button to copy all the necessary files into a folder that you choose before you print the document.

   TIP The Package button is the same as the Package command located on the File menu.

   TIP You can open the preflight report in a text editor.

Your service bureau may ask you to use only Type 1 fonts. The Fonts area lets you make sure that you have used the correct fonts and that they are correctly installed.

To review the fonts information:

1. Choose Fonts from the categories on the left of the Preflight dialog box. This opens the Fonts area, which shows the type of font and whether it is installed in the system 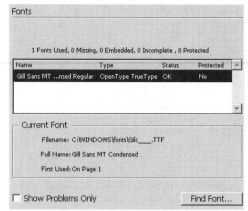.

2. If you want to replace a nonstandard or missing font, click the Find Font button. This opens the Find Font dialog box that lets you replace fonts.

You also want to make sure that placed graphics are in the correct format and that they aren't missing or modified.

To review the Links information:

1. Choose Links and Images from the categories on the left of the Preflight dialog box. This opens the Links area, which shows the placed images .

2. Choose the modified or missing image.

3. If the image is modified, click the Update button.

   or

   If the image is missing, click the Relink button. This opens the Find dialog box.

4. Navigate to choose the missing image.

5. Click the Repair All button to have InDesign update all modified images or open the dialog box for all missing images.

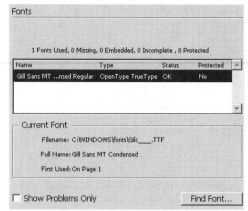

71 *The* **Fonts area of the Preflight dialog box** *shows you the status of the fonts used in a document.*

72 *The* **Links and Images area of the Preflight dialog box** *shows you the status of the placed images in the document.*

Creating a Preflight Report

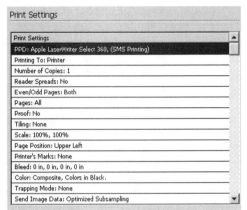

73 *The* **Colors and Inks area** *of the Preflight dialog box shows the process and spot color plates in the document.*

Print Settings

74 *The* **Print Settings area** *of the Preflight dialog box shows you the current print settings applied to the document.*

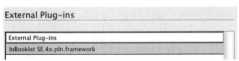

75 *The* **External Plug-ins area** *of the Preflight dialog box shows any third-party plug-ins that have been installed.*

You should also check the colors and inks to make sure that the right number of colors print.

To review the Colors and Inks information:

◆ Choose Colors and Inks from the categories on the left of the Preflight dialog box. This shows the colors used within the document **73**.

You can also look at the Print Settings for a complete list of all the print settings currently applied to the document.

To review the Print Settings information:

◆ Choose Print Settings from the categories on the left of the Preflight dialog box. This shows the print settings applied to the document **74**.

You can also look to see if any external plug-ins were used in creating the document. You may need to alert your print shop that these plug-ins are necessary for outputting the document.

TIP You don't need to worry about the plug-ins unless you have installed any special third-party plug-ins.

To review the external plug-ins information:

◆ Choose External Plug-ins from the categories on the left of the Preflight dialog box. This shows any third-party plug-ins that have been installed **75**.

Creating a Preflight Report

Packaging a Document

A package contains everything necessary to print a document. Instead of manually collecting the files, you can let the Package command assemble the files for you.

To package files for printing:

1. Choose **Fire>Package**. InDesign looks through the document and then opens the Printing Instructions dialog box .

2. Fill out the contact and file information.

3. Click Continue. This opens the Create Package Folder dialog box .

4. Name the folder that will hold the files.

5. Check the following options for the package:

   • **Copy Fonts (except CJK)** copies the fonts used in the document except double-byte fonts such as those for Chinese, Japanese, and Korean languages.

   • **Copy Linked Graphics** copies placed images that are not embedded in the file.

   • **Update Graphic Links in Package** automatically updates any modified graphics.

   • **Use Document Hyphenation Exceptions Only** limits the hyphenation exceptions to only those added to the document.

   • **Include Fonts and Links from Hidden Document Layers** adds the fonts and graphics from layers that are not visible.

   • **View Report** launches a text editor to open the report created with the document.

6. Click Save to assemble all the necessary files in the folder.

76 *The* **Printing Instructions dialog box** *lets you create a text file with contact information and instructions about the document package.*

77 *The* **Create Package Folder dialog box** *lets you choose which items should be included in the package folder.*

EXPORTING 20

Printing your document on paper is not the only way in which your InDesign files can be published. Exporting gives you many options for publishing documents.

For instance, you might want clients to read your document electronically — even if they don't have the InDesign application. Or you might want to take a design that you created with InDesign and use it as the graphic in another page-layout program. Or you may want to turn your InDesign document into Web pages. You may even want to display your InDesign pages on mobile phones!

When you convert your InDesign files into other formats, you use the export features of the program. Using the export command lets you change InDesign documents into other types of publications such as portable document format (PDF) files or Web hypertext markup language (XHTML) pages.

Setting the Export File Options

InDesign gives you many export options. In each case you choose a file format, name the file, and save it to a location.

To choose a file format:

1. Choose **File > Export**. The Export dialog box appears █.

TIP You won't see the options for exporting text unless your insertion point is inside a text frame.

1 *The* **options for exporting** *InDesign documents.*

2. Give the file a name and set the location.

3. Choose one of the following formats from the Save as Type (Win) or Format (Mac) menu:

Adobe InDesign Tagged Text	Creates a text file formatted with codes.
Adobe PDF	Creates an Acrobat file.
EPS	Creates a file that can be placed as a graphic. This format is rarely needed today.
InCopy CS Document and InCopy Document	Creates text files that can be opened using InCopy.
InDesign Interchange	Creates a special format that can be used for converting InDesign CS3 documents so they can be opened by the InDesign CS2 application.
JPEG	Converts the page or selected elements into a raster image that can be used in a Web page.
Rich Text Format	Exports selected text with formatting that can be read by most word processing applications.
SVG and SVG Compressed	Creates scalable vector graphics that can be viewed on the World Wide Web.
Text Only	Exports selected text without any formatting.
XML	Creates text formatted with the Extensible Markup Language that offers customizable definitions and tags. *(Working with* XML *is beyond the scope of this book. I recommend* Real World Adobe InDesign CS3, *by David Blatner and Olav Martin Kvern, for their expertise on this topic.)*

4. Click Save. This opens the options dialog box for each format.

TIP InDesign also remembers the last export format you chose each time you choose Export.

2 *The Export PDF* **categories list.**

3 *The* **General category** *of the Export PDF dialog box.*

4 *The* **Compatibility menu** *lets you choose which PDF version you export.*

5 *The* **Standard menu** *lets you apply an ISO printing standard for PDF documents.*

Creating PDF Files

You can convert your InDesign files into PDF documents so that others can read them — even if they do not have the InDesign application.

To set the PDF export options:

1. Click each of the categories on the left side of the dialog box **2** to display the options.

TIP You do not need to set all the controls every time you print unless you need to change a specific setting.

2. Click the Export button to create the PDF file.

Setting the PDF General Controls

These are the various areas in the General category for exporting as a PDF **3**.

To set the PDF version and standard:

1. Use the Compatibility menu to choose which version of PDF files you want to save **4**.

TIP Higher versions allow you to save a PDF with more options.

2. Use the Standard menu to choose one of these five recognized ISO (International Organization for Standardization) standards for PDF/X files **5**:

TIP Check with your print shop or publication for which PDF/X file they require.

Creating PDF Files; Setting PDF General Controls

To specify which pages to export:

1. In the Pages area, select All to export all the pages in the document .

   or

   Select Range to enter specific pages.

TIP Use the hyphen to select a range of pages such as *4–9*, or use commas to enter individual pages such as *3, 8*.

2. Check Spreads to keep pages that are within spreads together in the Acrobat file.

To set the general options:

1. Choose one of the following from the Options area in the General category **7**:

   • **Embed Page Thumbnails** adds a thumbnail image for each page. It is not necessary for Acrobat 5 and higher.

   • **Optimize for Fast Web View** prepares for downloading from Web servers.

   • **Create Tagged PDF** adds tags that allow the PDF to be read by screen readers.

   • **View PDF after Exporting** opens the finished Adobe PDF file in Acrobat.

   • **Create Acrobat Layers** is available for PDF 1.5 and higher. It converts the InDesign layers into Acrobat layers.

2. Choose which layers to include from the Export Layers list **7**.

6 *The* **Pages area** *in the General category of the Export PDF dialog box.*

7 *The* **Options controls** *in the General category of the Export PDF dialog box.*

ISO Standards?

The ISO (International Organization for Standardization) has created standards for PDF documents. When you use these standards you are choosing settings that are relied on as working properly for many publishers. This eliminates many of the color, font, and trapping variables that may create printing problems.

You may be asked to use a PDF/X standard if you are creating PDF documents that will be placed in magazines or newspapers.

Setting the PDF General Controls

8 *The* **Include settings** *in the General category of the Export PDF dialog box.*

9 *The* **Multimedia menu** *in the General category of the Export PDF dialog box.*

Talk to Your Service Bureau

If you create PDF files for onscreen viewing or to be downloaded from the Web, you can use the compression settings to reduce the file size.

However, if you create PDF files to be output by a service bureau for print work, you should not apply too much downsampling or compression.

Ask your service bureau for the correct settings. Better yet, ask them to create a PDF preset that you can load onto your machine.

To control what to include in the PDF:

◆ Choose one of the following from the Include area in the General category **8**:

- **Bookmarks** creates bookmarks for table of contents entries, preserving the TOC levels.
- **Hyperlinks** creates Acrobat hyperlinks from InDesign hyperlinks, table of contents entries, and index entries.
- **Visible Guides and Grids** exports the guides and grids currently visible in the document.
- **Non-Printing Objects** exports objects that have the nonprinting option applied.
- **Interactive Elements** exports InDesign's buttons as interactive PDF elements.

If you have movie or sound clips in the document, you can choose whether those files should be linked or embedded in the PDF document.

To set the multimedia embedding options:

1. Check the option for Interactive Elements. This activates the Multimedia menu.

2. Choose one of the following from the Multimedia menu in the General category **9**:

- **Use Object Settings** embeds or links the movie or sound clip according to the settings applied to each media clip.
- **Link All** overrides any object setting and links all media clips to the PDF. Both the PDF and the media files must be kept together for the media to play properly.
- **Embed All** overrides any object setting and embeds all media clips in the PDF.

Setting the PDF General Controls

Setting the PDF Compression Options

One of the benefits of creating PDF files is that they can be compressed to take up less space. You use the same controls for compressing color and grayscale bitmap images .

To set the color and grayscale downsampling:

1. Choose one of the following from the Sampling menu 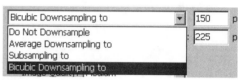:

   - **Do Not Downsample** does not throw away any pixel information. Use this to maintain all information in the image.

   - **Average Downsampling to** averages the pixels in a sample area.

   - **Subsampling to** reduces processing time compared to downsampling, but creates images that are less smooth.

   - **Bicubic downsampling to** is the slowest but most precise method, resulting in the smoothest tonal gradations.

2. When you have set a downsampling method, enter an amount in the resolution field .

TIP For print work this setting is usually 1.5 times the line screen of the printing press.

TIP For onscreen viewing this setting is usually 72 pixels per inch.

3. Enter an amount in the field for images above a certain resolution .

TIP This helps you downsample only high-resolution images without losing information in lower-resolution images.

10 *The* **compression controls** *in the Export PDF dialog box for color and grayscale bitmap images.*

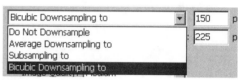

11 *The* **Sampling menu** *for color and grayscale bitmap images.*

12 *The* **Resolution fields** *for color and grayscale bitmap images.*

13 *The* **Compression menu** *for color and grayscale bitmap images.*

14 *The* **Image Quality menu** *for color and grayscale bitmap images.*

15 *The* **compression controls** *for monochrome images.*

16 *The* **Sampling menu** *for monochrome images.*

To set the color and grayscale compression:

1. Choose one of the following from the Compression menu **13**:

   - **None** applies no compression.

   - **Automatic (JPEG)** lets InDesign automatically determine the best quality for color and grayscale images.

   - Use **JPEG** for images with tonal changes.

   - Use **ZIP** for images with large areas of flat color.

   - Use **JPEG 2000** for tonal images for Acrobat 6 or higher.

   - Use **Automatic (JPEG 2000)** for color and grayscale images for Acrobat 6 or higher.

2. Choose an Image Quality setting **14**:

   - Maximum sets the least amount of compression.

   - Minimum sets the most.

There are different compression options for monochrome bitmap images (such as 1-bit scanned art) **15**.

To set the monochrome bitmap downsampling:

◆ Choose one of the following from the Sampling menu **16**:

   - **Do Not Downsample** does not throw away any pixel information. Use this setting if you want to maintain all the information in the image.

   - **Average Downsampling to** averages the pixels in a sample area.

   - **Subsampling to** is faster than down-sampling, but creates images that are less smooth.

   - **Bicubic downsampling to** is the slowest but most precise method, resulting in the smoothest tonal gradations.

Setting the PDF Compression Options

To set the monochrome bitmap resolution:

1. When you have set a downsampling method, enter an amount in the resolution field .

TIP For print work, this setting is usually the resolution of the output device with a limit of 1500 dots per inch.

2. Enter an amount in the field for images above a certain resolution .

TIP This helps you downsample only high-resolution images without losing information in lower-resolution images.

To set the compression for monochrome images:

1. Choose one of the following from the Compression menu :

   - **None** applies no compression to the image.

   - CCITT **Group 3** is similar to the compression used for faxes.

   - CCITT **Group 4** is a general-purpose method that produces good results for most monochromatic images.

   - ZIP works well for black-and-white images that contain repeating patterns.

   - **Run Length** produces the best results for images that contain large areas of solid black or white.

2. Check Compress Text and Line Art to further reduce the size of the file.

3. Check Crop Image Data to Frames to delete the image outside the frame.

17 *The resolution fields for monochrome images.*

18 *The Compression menu for monochrome images.*

Setting the Marks and Bleeds PDF Options

The options for setting the Marks and Bleeds category for PDF documents are the same as the options when you print the file. *See Chapter 19, "Output," for how to work with those settings.*

(side tab) **Setting the PDF Compression Options**

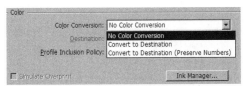

19 *The* **Color Conversion menu** *allows you to control how colors in a PDF are handled.*

20 *The* **Profile Inclusion Policy menu** *controls how color management profiles are handled.*

More Info on Color Profiles

If you are interested in learning more about color profiles, you should visit www.color. org. This is the home of the International Color Consortium. From their Web site:

The International Color Consortium was established in 1993 by eight industry vendors for the purpose of creating, promoting and encouraging the standardization and evolution of an open, vendor-neutral, cross-platform color management system architecture and components. The outcome of this cooperation was the development of the ICC profile specification.

The intent of the International Color Consortium (R) profile format is to provide a cross-platform device profile format. Device profiles can be used to translate color data created on one device into another device's native color space.

Setting the Output PDF Options

The Output category contains the controls for how color is handled as well as the PDF/X settings.

To set the color controls:

1. Choose one of the following from the Color Conversion menu **19**:

   - **No Color Conversion** does not convert the colors in the document.

   - **Convert to Destination** converts all colors to the destination profile.

   - **Convert to Destination (Preserve Numbers)** converts colors to the destination profile only if the embedded profiles differ.

2. Choose a profile for the type of output device from the Destination menu. This is typically the type of printing machine that will handled the file.

3. Choose one of the following from the Profile Inclusion Policy menu to control how the color profiles are handled in the document **20**.

   - **Don't Include Profiles** removes all color management from the document.

   - **Include All Profiles** creates a color-managed document.

   - **Include Tagged Source Profiles** is used if you only output to specially calibrated output devices.

   - **Include All RGB and Tagged Source CMYK Profiles** is used to calibrate both RGB and CMYK images.

4. Check Simulate Overprint to show onscreen a representation of how overprinting will look when printed.

5. Click the Ink Manager button to control how process and spot colors are handled.

If you have chosen a PDF/X standard, you can control the output profiles for the document.

To set the PDF/X profile controls:

1. Use the Output Intent Profile Name menu to select the profile that matches how the document will be printed 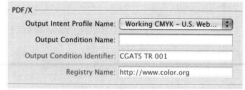.

2. If desired, enter an optional description of how the file will be output in the Output Condition Name field. This information is then stored in the PDF/X file.

3. If desired, enter the registration name for the output condition in the Output Condition Identifier field. This field is automatically filled in when you choose one of the standard output profiles.

4. If desired, enter the URL in the Registry Name field where the output information is stored. This field is automatically filled in when you choose one of the standard output profiles.

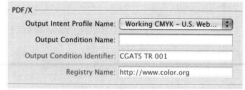

The **PDF/X** area *controls the profiles for* PDF/X *files.*

Setting the Output PDF Options

Subsetting Fonts?

One reason why PDFs became popular is you don't have to worry about someone having particular fonts in order to view the file. You can *embed* the entire font or you can *subset* only a portion.

If you embed the entire font, you add to the file size, but you allow anyone who has the font to make changes to the text. If you subset the font, it makes a smaller file, but it also means that the person on the other end won't be able to make changes to the text.

The default setting of 100% means that only a subset of the font will be embedded unless you have used every single character in the font. If you lower the threshold to, let's say 35%, InDesign embeds only the characters used in the document up to a maximum of 35% of the characters. If you use more than 35% of the characters, InDesign embeds all the characters in the font.

There is no option to embed the entire font per se, but if you set the amount to 1% then you will most likely embed all the characters in the font.

Subset fonts when percent of characters used is less than: 100%

onts with appropriate permission bits will be embedded.

22 *The* **Subset fonts when percent of characters used is less than** field *in the Advanced area of the Export* PDF *dialog box.*

Job Definition Format (JDF)

☐ Create JDF File Using Acrobat

ⓘ Requires Adobe Acrobat 7.0 Professional to be installed. Checking this option au deselects the "Spreads" option in the General panel.

23 *The* **Job Definition Format (**JDF**)** option *in the Advanced area of the Export* PDF *dialog box.*

What's a Job Definition Format File?

A Job Definition Format (JDF) file describes the intent of the final output of a file. These specifications are used to produce the final printed piece. This file can specify the paper and ink, production quantities, and customer information.

The JDF file and associated PDF files travel together as part of the JDF workflow, from JDF device to JDF device. When the JDF file is submitted to production, the information it contains is used to define the processes for print production.

Setting the Advanced PDF Options

The Advanced category contains the controls for handling colors and fonts, and for setting the transparency flattener options.

TIP The OPI controls are the same as the ones in the Print dialog box.

TIP The Transparency Flattener controls are the same as the ones in the Print dialog box.

To control how much of a font is embedded:

◆ Enter an amount in the Subset Fonts field for the threshold amount **22**. That threshold determines at what point all the characters of the font will be embedded.

To add a Job Definition Format to the file:

◆ Select the option to Create JDF File Using Acrobat **23**. This adds Job Definition Format (JDF) information to the PDF document.

TIP You must have Acrobat 7 Professional or higher installed in order to add the JDF information to the file.

Setting the Advanced PDF Options

Setting the Security PDF Options

You can also set security options for PDF files to restrict who can open the file or to limit what they can do to it.

The Document Open Password area allows you to set the password that readers must enter in order to open the file.

To set the document password:

1. Check Require a Password to Open This Document .

2. Type a password in the Document Open Password field.

The Permissions area sets up what edits and modifications people can make to the PDF once they have opened it. The Permissions password is needed in order to change the settings in the Permissions area.

To set the permissions password:

1. Check Use a Password to Restrict Printing, Editing, and Other Tasks 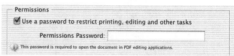.

2. Type a password in the Permissions Password field.

TIP This can't be the same as the Document Open Password.

To set the printing permission:

◆ Choose one of the following from the Printing Allowed menu 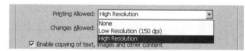:

- **None** turns off all printing from the document.

- **Low Resolution (150 dpi)** prints only low-resolution versions of the images.

- **High Resolution** prints the full resolution of the images.

24 The **Document Open Password area** *of the Security category of the Export PDF dialog box.*

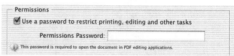

25 The **Permissions area** *of the Security category of the Export PDF dialog box.*

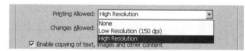

26 The **Printing Allowed menu** *of the Security category of the Export PDF dialog box.*

27 *The* **Changes Allowed menu** *of the Security category of the Export PDF dialog box.*

28 *The other permissions you can set in the Security category of the Export PDF dialog box.*

Limits of Security

Even when you set security options, there are some additional things to remember.

First, if you e-mail a PDF document, send the password in separate e-mail. That makes it less likely that the password will be found if your e-mail is hijacked.

Next, passwords are case-sensitive. Use a combination of uppercase and lowercase letters as well as numbers to make the password more secure. Don't use ordinary words as passwords.

Finally, if you feel that you would lose your entire livelihood if the PDF were to fall into the wrong hands, then don't distribute it as a PDF. There are plenty of people who take it as a challenge to break into password-protected PDF documents.

To set the changes that are allowed:

1. Choose one of the following from the Changes Allowed menu **27**:

   • **None** allows no changes whatsoever.

   • **Inserting, deleting and rotating pages** allows the user only to add, remove, or change the position of pages in the document. It does not allow changing the content of the pages.

   • **Filling in form fields and signing** allows changes to form fields or applying a security signature to the document.

   • **Commenting, filling in form fields, and signing** allows adding comments, changing form fields, or applying a security signature to the document.

   • **Any except extracting pages** allows all changes except removing pages from the document.

2. Check any of the following as desired **28**:

   • **Enable copying of text, images and other content.**

   • **Enable text access of screen reader devices for the visually impaired.**

   • **Enable plaintext metadata.**

Working with PDF Presets

Just as you can create printer presets for printing documents, you can also create PDF presets that contain settings for generating different types of PDF documents. For example, you may want to post a PDF file on the Web or send the file to a print shop for output.

To save the current PDF settings as a PDF preset:

1. Set the options in the Export PDF dialog box.

2. Click the Save Preset button **29**. This opens the Save Preset dialog box **30**.

3. Enter a name for the preset and click OK. The new preset appears at the top of the Export PDF dialog box.

Once you have saved a preset, you can easily apply it.

To apply a PDF preset:

◆ Choose a saved preset from the Preset menu at the top of the Export Adobe PDF dialog box **31**.

   or

   Choose **File > Adobe PDF Presets > Define** and then pick the preset listed in the menu.

You can also define PDF presets without going through the Export PDF dialog box.

To create a PDF preset:

1. Choose **File > Adobe PDF Presets** to open the Adobe PDF Presets dialog box **32**.

2. Click New. This opens the New PDF Export Preset dialog box.

3. Name the preset.

4. Choose each of the categories and set them as described earlier in this chapter.

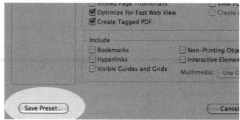

29 Click the Save Preset button *to create a preset based on the current settings in the Export Adobe PDF dialog box.*

30 *Enter a name for a PDF preset in the* Save Preset dialog box.

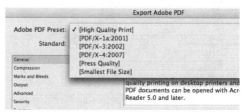

31 *Choose a preset to apply to a PDF from the* Preset menu *in the Export PDF dialog box.*

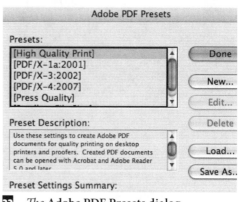

32 *The* Adobe PDF Presets dialog box *displays the PDF presets that ship with InDesign.*

A custom **PDF** *preset, listed without brackets, can be edited, deleted, exported, or imported.*

To edit a PDF preset:

1. Select the custom preset you want to edit in the Adobe PDF Presets dialog box .

2. Click the Edit button. This opens the Edit PDF Export Preset dialog box.

TIP There is no difference between the New PDF dialog box and the Edit PDF dialog box except the name in the title bar.

3. Choose each of the categories and make changes as described earlier in this section.

To delete a PDF preset:

1. Select the preset you want to delete in the Adobe PDF Presets dialog box .

TIP Use the Shift key to select multiple adjacent presets.

TIP Use the Cmd/Ctrl key to select multiple nonadjacent presets.

2. Click the Delete button.

3. Click OK to confirm your choice.

To export PDF presets:

1. In the Adobe PDF Presets dialog box, select the presets you want to export .

TIP Use the Shift key to select multiple adjacent presets.

TIP Use the Cmd/Ctrl key to select multiple nonadjacent presets.

2. Click the Save As button. This creates a file that contains the exported presets.

To import PDF presets:

1. Click the Load button in the Adobe PDF Presets dialog box .

2. Use the dialog box to select the document that contains the presets exported from another machine.

3. Click OK. The presets appear in the Adobe PDF Presets dialog box.

Working with PDF Presets

Creating EPS Files

You might create a special shape or design in InDesign that you would like to use in another layout program. Export the file as an EPS, or Encapsulated PostScript, file so that you can use it in other applications.

To create an EPS file:

◆ Click the General tab in the Export EPS dialog box to display the pages, bleed, and general controls 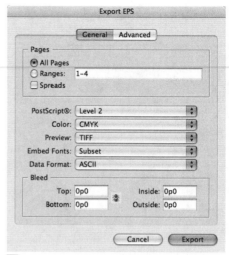.

or

Click the Advanced tab to display the production controls . These are the same as the graphic options for printing

To set the EPS pages options:

1. In the General area, choose All Pages to export all the pages in the document as EPS files.

TIP Each page is exported as its own EPS file.

or

Choose Ranges and enter the numbers of the pages you want to export.

2. Check Spreads to export spreads as a single EPS file.

The PostScript level sets the complexity of the instructions that are sent to the printer.

To set the EPS PostScript level:

◆ In the General area, use the PostScript menu to choose the following:
   • **Level 2** is used with older printers.
   • **Level 3** is used with newer printers. Use Level 3 only if you know the printer can handle Level 3 PostScript.

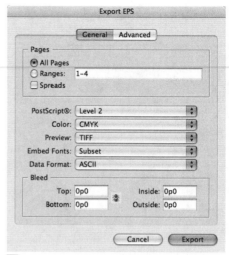

34 *The* **Export EPS dialog box** *lets you create an EPS file that can be placed in other programs.*

35 *The* **Advanced section** *in the Export EPS dialog box contains production controls for creating an EPS file.*

Creating EPS Files

36 *Use the **PostScript menu** in the Export EPS dialog box to set the type of printing instructions.*

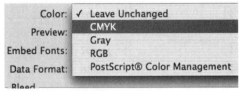

37 *Use the **Color menu** in the Export EPS dialog box to control the colors in the file.*

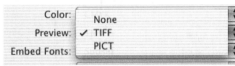

38 *Use the **Preview menu** in the Export EPS dialog box to give a preview to the image.*

39 *Use the **Embed Fonts menu** in the Export EPS dialog box to control how many characters in a font are added to the EPS file.*

Using EPS Files?

EPS is an archaic format that is hardly used today. Most of today's layout programs import PDF files.

The only time I suggest using the EPS format is if you are placing images in older programs that can't import PDF files.

To set the EPS colors:

◆ In the General area, use the Color menu to choose one of the following options **37**:

- **CMYK** forces the colors to CMYK. Use this setting for process separations.

- **Gray** converts the colors to their grayscale values. Use this to limit the colors to a black plate.

- **RGB** converts the colors to the RGB color space. Use this for onscreen presentation programs.

- **PostScript® Color Management** lets a PostScript printer use its own in-RIP separations to control the color.

To set the EPS preview:

◆ In the General area, use the Preview menu to choose one of the following **38**:

- **None** adds no preview to the file.

- **TIFF** creates a preview that is visible on both the Mac and Windows platforms.

- **PICT** (Mac only) creates a preview that is visible on the Mac only.

Just as you can embed fonts in a PDF file, you can also embed fonts in an EPS file.

To embed fonts in the EPS file:

◆ In the General area, use the Embed Fonts menu to choose one of the following options **39**:

- **None** does not embed any fonts in the file.

- **Complete** includes all the characters in the fonts.

- **Subset** includes only the characters you have used in the file.

Creating EPS Files

EPS files need to be formatted with a specific type of data.

To set the data format of the EPS file:

◆ In the General area, use the Data Format menu to choose one of the following options :

- **Binary** is acceptable for most instances.

- **ASCII** is used for a PC network that requires ASCII data.

TIP Choose Binary. If you have trouble printing, then switch to ASCII.

Just as you can add a bleed area when printing a document, you can add a bleed to an EPS file.

To set the size of a bleed:

◆ In the General area, use the Bleed fields to create a bleed area .

InDesign Interchange Format

The InDesign Interchange Format creates an InDesign Interchange Format file (INX). This INX file can then be opened using InDesign CS2.

To open CS3 files using InDesign CS2:

1. Choose **File > Export** to open the Export dialog box.

2. Choose InDesign Interchange from the Format (Mac) or Save as Type (Windows) menu.

3. Name the INX file and click Save.

4. In InDesign CS2, choose **File > Open** and navigate to open the INX file. The INX file is converted into an InDesign CS2 file.

TIP There are no further controls for the Interchange format.

40 *Use the* **Data Format menu** *in the Export EPS dialog box to specify the formatting language of the EPS file.*

41 *Set the size of the bleed in the* **Bleed fields** *in the Export EPS dialog box.*

Using INX files?

Yes, you can save an InDesign document as an INX file and then have someone with InDesign CS2 open the file. But there are quite a few things to remember:

- If the CS3 file uses features such as repeating nested styles, which aren't available in InDesign CS2, those features will change.

- Don't use the INX file as a permanent workflow. This means don't expect to send files back and forth between two designers. Something is going to get lost in the translation.

- Never, never, never send an INX file to a print shop to have them open it in the older version of InDesign. This is a recipe for disaster.

Make sure the InDesign CS2 application has all the latest patches. CS2 can't open INX files without the proper updates.

You can also save a CS3 file as an INX file and then re-open it in CS3. This can sometimes fix problems with the file. But watch out: I've seen some settings get mixed up when the INX file is converted back into an InDesign file.

Creating EPS Files; InDesign Interchange Format

42 *Use the* **Export JPEG dialog box** *to convert an InDesign document into a JPEG file.*

43 *The* **Image Quality menu** *controls the size and the quality of JPEG images.*

44 *The* **Format menu** *controls how JPEG images are revealed.*

Setting the JPEG Options

You might want to convert an InDesign document into a JPEG file that can be posted on the Web. This can be done using the Export JPEG dialog box **42**.

To set the area or page to be converted:

1. Use the Export area in the Export JPEG dialog box to choose one of the following:

    - **Selection** exports just the selected items as the JPEG. (The selection must be made before you choose **File > Export**.)

    - **Range** exports a range of pages as individual JPEG files.

    - **All** exports all the pages as individual JPEG files.

2. If you are exporting pages, you can select Spreads to export both pages in the spread to a single JPEG file **42**.

You can also control the quality of the JPEG image and how it is displayed in the browser.

To set the JPEG quality and display:

1. Use the Export JPEG dialog box's Image Quality menu to choose the quality of the JPEG image **43**.

TIP The higher the quality, the larger the final file size.

2. Choose a Format Method as follows **44**:

    - **Progressive** creates an image that appears gradually on the page.

    - **Baseline** creates an image that appears all at once, after the entire image has been downloaded.

3. Choose a resolution option.

TIP Use 72 PPI for Web images. Use higher resolutions for print images.

Setting the JPEG Options

Exporting SVG Files

InDesign also lets you export documents in SVG (scalable vector graphics) format, which can be viewed on the Web. This format is also being used as the file format for graphics on mobile phones.

To set the basic SVG options:

1. Choose SVG or SVG Compressed from the Save as File Type (Win) or Format (Mac) menu. The SVG Options dialog box appears .

2. Click the More Options button to see the complete set of controls for exporting SVG files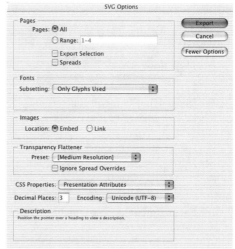

You can choose which pages or even which selected objects are exported as an SVG file.

To set the area or pages to be converted:

1. In the Pages area, select All to export all the pages in the document 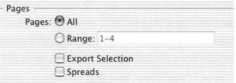.

   or

   Select Range to enter specific pages.

2. If you have any objects selected, you can check Export Selection to convert just those objects into an SVG file.

3. Check Spreads to keep pages that are within spreads together in the SVG file.

45 *The* **SVG Options dialog box** *contains the controls for creating SVG and SVG Compressed files.*

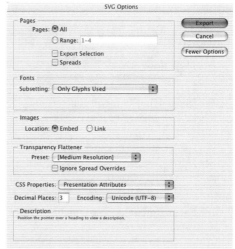

46 *The* **More Options for the SVG Options dialog box** *contains additional controls for creating SVG and SVG Compressed files.*

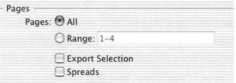

47 *The* **Pages options** *in the SVG Options dialog box let you control which pages are exported into SVG files.*

Exporting SVG Files

48 *The* **Fonts Subsetting menu** *lets you choose how much of a font is embedded in an SVG file.*

49 *The* **Images Location controls** *let you choose to embed or link images in the SVG file.*

SVG files can be changed using database publishing. You may want to embed fonts so that there are characters available for the new text.

To set the fonts for an SVG file:

◆ In the Fonts area, use the Subsetting menu to choose one of the following **48**:

- **None (Use System Fonts)** does not embed any characters in the file.

- **Only Glyphs Used** embeds only the characters in the file. This may limit the ability to edit the text later.

- **Common English** embeds all the characters in English documents.

- **Common English & Glyphs Used** adds any non-English characters used in the document as well as the Common English characters.

- **Common Roman** embeds characters used in Roman language documents.

- **Common Roman & Glyphs Used** adds characters used to Common Roman.

- **All Glyphs** uses all characters in a font, such as characters in Japanese fonts.

You can also control how placed images are embedded within an SVG file.

To set the images for an SVG file:

◆ In the Images area, choose Embed to add the image into the SVG file **49**.

or

Choose Link to have the image exist outside the SVG file.

TIP Use the Link setting if you have many SVG files that use the same image.

Exporting SVG Files

The More Options button provides additional controls **46**. The Transparency Flattener section is identical to the controls in the Print dialog box. You can also control the css (Cascading Style Sheets) properties.

To set the css properties:

◆ Choose one of the attributes settings from the css Properties menu **50**:

You can also set how precisely the curves are drawn for vector shapes in the svg file.

To set the decimal precision:

◆ Enter a value of 1 to 7 in the Decimal Places field to set how precisely the curves should be drawn.

TIP The highest value results in a larger file size but creates the best image quality.

You can choose the encoding for the character set in the svg file.

TIP Ask your Web designer which encoding is preferred.

To set the encoding:

◆ Choose one of the encoding settings from the Encoding menu **51**.

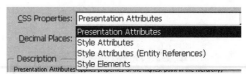

50 *The* **css Properties** *let you choose properties of cascading style sheets.*

51 *From the* **Encoding menu** *choose how the characters should be encoded.*

Working with InCopy

In addition to exporting stories as text files, you can also export them for use with Adobe InCopy. InCopy is the word processing and editing program that works in tandem with InDesign.

A designer lays out InDesign pages and then exports them to InCopy. A writer or editor can work on the text for those pages. The designer doesn't have to worry that the writer will inadvertently move something or change the layout. And the writer has many more word processing tools than are available in InDesign.

For instance, InCopy lets you edit text using automation text macros and a built-in thesaurus. You can even track changes using electronic notes.

If you are using InCopy, you will find many of its commands and tools very similar to the ones described in this book. There are other commands, however, that are unique to InCopy.

There are two ways to purchase InCopy. If you are a small company with just a few designers and editors, you can purchase InCopy directly from Adobe. If you are a large organization, you should consider using a systems integration specialist to configure InDesign and InCopy specifically for your needs. See the Adobe Web site (www.adobe.com) for more information.

Exporting Text

You may find it necessary to export text from InDesign. For instance, you may want to send the text to someone who works with Microsoft Word. You can send them a text file by exporting the text.

To export text:

1. Place an insertion point inside the frame that contains the text. All the text within that story will be exported.

TIP Select an area of text to export only that portion of the text.

2. Choose **File > Export.** This opens the Export dialog box.

3. Choose a text export format:
   - **Rich Text Format** keeps all the styles and text formatting. This format can be opened by most word processors, especially Microsoft Word.
   - **Text Only** exports only the characters of the text and discards any styles and text formatting. Use this option only if you want to strip out the text formatting or if the application you are working with does not support the Rich Text Format.
   - **Adobe InDesign Tagged Text** format exports the text with special codes for local character formatting and styles.

4. Name the file and choose a destination.

5. Click Save to export the file.

Exporting Text

Exporting Cross-Media Files

One of the most frustrating areas of desktop publishing is how to convert print layouts, such as InDesign documents, into other formats that can be used on the Web as well as in other InDesign layouts. XML stands for the Extensible Markup Language. When you convert documents into XML files, you can then open them in other programs such as Dreamweaver.

While a complete rundown of the XML and cross-media properties is way beyond this book, here are the basics on how to create XML and XHTML cross-media files.

To export as XML or cross-media files:

◆ Choose **File** > **Cross-media Export** and then choose one of the following:

- **XML** for use in other InDesign files or Web applications. This opens the Export XML dialog box **52**.

- **XHTML/Dreamweaver** for use in Dreamweaver Web pages. This opens the XHTML Export Options dialog box **53**.

- **XHTML/Digital Editions** for posting files as Adobe Digital Editions Web pages. This opens the XHTML/Digital Editions dialog box **54**.

52 *The* **Export XML** *dialog box lets you create files for Web applications and other InDesign layouts.*

53 *The* **XHTML Export Options** *are used for exporting InDesign layouts into Dreamweaver Web pages.*

54 *The* **XHTML/Digital Editions Export Options dialog box** *is used for converting InDesign layouts into Adobe Digital Editions Web pages.*

CUSTOMIZING 21

Working with computer software is a personal thing. I'm always impressed with how emotional my students are (maybe *too* emotional) about how their software should work. One student tells me she hates the way a certain feature works; yet another insists it's his favorite thing in the entire program.

The InDesign team recognizes that some people want the program to work one way, and others want it exactly the opposite. That's why there are many ways to customize the program.

You can change the keyboard shortcuts so that they are similar to other software you use. You can modify the settings for the display of images and onscreen elements. You can control how text wraps around other objects. You can even throw away all your own customized settings and start back at the out-of-the-box settings.

It's all your choice.

Modifying Keyboard Shortcuts

Keyboard shortcuts are the fastest way to invoke program commands. However, if you are used to working with other programs, your fingers may be trained to use those other shortcuts. You may also want to assign a shortcut to a command that doesn't have a shortcut. InDesign lets you change the keyboard shortcuts to keystrokes that match your preferences.

InDesign ships with three sets of shortcuts. The default set is the one that the Adobe engineers created. This set uses most of the shortcuts found in Adobe products such as Adobe Illustrator or Adobe Photoshop. The second set contains the shortcuts used in PageMaker 7.0. The third set contains the shortcuts used in QuarkXPress 4.0.

To change the shortcut set:

1. Choose **Edit > Keyboard Shortcuts**. The Keyboard Shortcuts dialog box appears 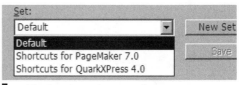.

2. Choose one of the shortcuts from the Set menu .

3. Click OK. The new shortcuts appear in the menus .

TIP Some keyboard shortcuts are "hard-wired" to the program and do not change to match the keystrokes in PageMaker or QuarkXPress. For instance, the Zoom tool does not change to the XPress Control key (Mac) or Ctrl-Spacebar (Win) shortcuts.

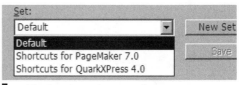

1. The **Keyboard Shortcuts dialog box** *lets you change the shortcuts used for commands, tools, and panels.*

2. The **Set menu** *lets you choose a set of keyboard preferences.*

Default set active

QuarkXPress 4.0 set active

3. *You can switch the InDesign default shortcuts to the set for other applications.*

4 *The* **New Set dialog box** *lets you name a new shortcut set and choose which set it should be based on.*

Creating Your Own Keyboard Shortcuts

I use quite a few different programs from many different software companies. I've taught QuarkXPress for more than 17 years. I work with both Adobe Illustrator and Acrobat. I also know Adobe Photoshop and Adobe Fireworks. And I use InDesign to lay out all my books.

With all those programs in my head, I find it easier to teach my fingers just one set of shortcuts. That's InDesign because I use it the most.

I don't change InDesign's keyboard shortcuts to follow all those other programs. I find it easier to concentrate on learning InDesign's shortcuts. It's the primary program I use when working on a book — so I'd rather remember its shortcuts.

If you work with other programs such as Macromedia FreeHand, you may want to create your own shortcut set to match it.

To create a new shortcut set:

1. Choose **Edit > Keyboard Shortcuts**.

2. Choose New Set. This opens the New Set dialog box **4**.

3. Enter a name for the set.

4. Choose a set that the new set will be based on.

TIP A set must be based on another set so that it starts with some shortcuts. However, if you later change something in the original set, the one that was based on it does not change.

5. Click OK. You can now edit the set as described on the next page.

If you want a list of keyboard shortcuts to print out and post next to your computer, you can create a file with all the shortcuts.

To create a list of the keyboard shortcuts:

1. Choose **Edit > Keyboard Shortcuts**.

2. Use the menu to choose the set.

3. Click the Show Set button. This opens the list of shortcuts in Notepad (Win) or TextEdit (Mac).

4. Print the text file.

TIP I can't always remember where a specific shortcut is located. So I create the text file of shortcuts and then use the text editor Find command to search for the location of the shortcut.

Modifying Keyboard Shortcuts

Modifying Keyboard Shortcuts

You can change the shortcut applied to a command. However, not all commands have shortcuts assigned to them. So you can also assign a shortcut to commands.

To change or assign a shortcut:

1. Choose a shortcut set in the Keyboard Shortcuts dialog box.

   or

   Create a new set.

2. Use the Product Area menu to choose the part of the program that contains the command to which you want to assign a shortcut 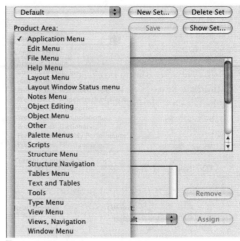.

3. Choose a command from the list under the Product Area menu 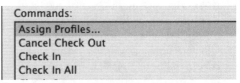.

4. Use the Context menu to choose in what portion of the program the keystroke will work .

5. Click inside the New Shortcut field to make that field active.

6. Press the keys on the keyboard that you want to assign to invoke the command.

TIP If the keystroke is already assigned to another command, the command that uses the shortcut is listed in the Currently Assigned To area .

7. Change the keys if necessary by selecting them and typing a new combination.

   or

   Click Assign to apply the new shortcut.

8. Click Save to save the set as modified.

To delete a set:

1. Use the Set menu to choose the set you want to delete.

2. Click the Delete Set button.

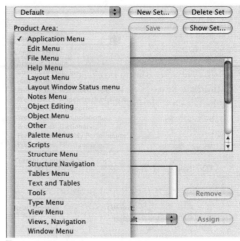

5   *The **Product Area menu** lets you choose which parts of the program you want to change.*

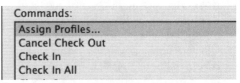

6   *The **Commands field** contains a list of the commands available for a specific product area.*

7   *The **Context menu** lets you choose in which context a keyboard shortcut is applied.*

8   *The **Currently Assigned to area** shows what command a keystroke is assigned to.*

9 The **Menu Customization dialog box** *lets you modify the appearance of menu commands.*

10 The **Category list** *lets you choose between the Application menus or the Context & Panel menus.*

11 *Click the* **Visibility icon** *to change the menu display. When the icon is hidden, the menu command does not show.*

12 *Use the* **Color menu** *to highlight a command with a color in the menu.*

Modifying the Menu Commands

You may feel that the menus in InDesign are too long for you to easily find the command you want to choose. Or you would like one menu command to stand out from the others. You can easily customize the menus to highlight or hide certain commands

To highlight menu commands:

1. Choose **Edit** > **Menus**. This opens the Menu Customization dialog box **9**.

2. Use the Category list to choose the Applications menus or the Context & Panel menus **10**.

3. Click the command you wish to customize.

4. Click the visibility icon to cause the command to be hidden or visible in the menu **11**.

5. Use the Color menu to choose a background color to highlight the command in the menu **12**.

6. Use the Save or Save As buttons to save the custom set of menus.

As you are working, you may want to invoke a command that has been hidden. Rather than turn off the custom menu configuration, you can temporarily restore the command.

To restore a hidden command to a menu:

1. Click the menu that ordinarily contains the command.

2. Choose Show All Menu Items from the bottom of the menu. This temporarily restores all hidden commands to that menu.

Modifying the Menu Commands

Choosing the Preferences Categories

InDesign has 17 categories that let you customize how the program works.

TIP Change the preferences with no document open to create the defaults for all new documents.

To choose a preference category:

1. Choose **Edit** > **Preferences** > **[category]** (**Win**). This opens the Preferences dialog box .

   or

   Choose **InDesign** > **Preferences** > **[category]** (**Mac**).

2. Click the categories on the left side of the dialog box to open a new category.

General Preferences Controls

The General category lets you control several types of preferences .

If you have several sections in the same document, they could all have a page number of 1. The page numbering preferences change how the page numbers are displayed.

To set the page number preferences:

◆ Choose one of the following from the Page Numbering View menu 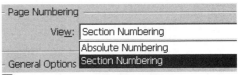:

   • **Absolute Numbering** uses the physical placement number of the page in the document **16**.

   • **Section Numbering** uses the numbers set from the section options **16**.

13 *The* **Preferences dialog box.**

14 *The* **General settings** *of the Preferences dialog box.*

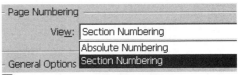

15 *The* **Page Numbering View menu** *lets you choose the section numbers or absolute numbers.*

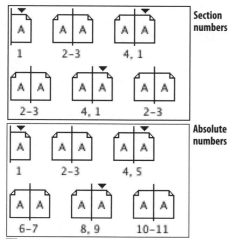

Section numbers

Absolute numbers

16 *The difference in the Pages panel between using absolute numbers and section numbers. The black triangles indicate the start of a new section.*

17 *The **Font Downloading and Embedding** lets you control if fonts are embedding or subset.*

Reset All Warning Dialogs

18 *Click the **Reset All Warning Dialogs** to bring back those annoying alert messages when you perform certain actions.*

To set the scaling preferences:

◆ Choose one of the following from the When Scaling area:

- **Apply to Content** scales text so that the point size changes.
- **Adjust Scaling Percentage** scales text so that the original point size is displayed with the new size in parenthesis.

To set the script preferences:

◆ Deselect Enable Attached Scripts to protect your computer from JavaScripts that are invoked from menu items.

The Font Downloading and Embedding section controls the threshold below which a font is subset.

To choose the threshold for font subsetting:

◆ Enter an amount in the Always Subset Fonts With Glyph Counts Greater Than field **17**.

TIP A number such as 2000 ensures that fonts with large character sets are always subset, creating smaller files. But custom fonts with only one or two characters are set in their entirety.

Every once in a while you may see a dialog box that warns you about doing something. These alerts have boxes you can check so you never see the warning again. If you've turned them off, you can reset them all to turn back on.

To reset the warning dialog boxes:

◆ Click the Reset All Warning Dialogs button at the bottom of the General preferences **18**. An alert box informs you that you will now see the warnings.

General Preferences Controls

Interface Preferences

The Interface preferences control how some aspects of the program appear .

To change the display of the Tools panel:

◆ Use the Floating Tools Panel menu to choose how the Tools panel is displayed ⓶⓪:

TIP You can also change the shape of the Tools panel by clicking the icon in the Tools panel title bar *when it is not docked.*

Tool Tips are notes that appear when you pause the cursor over an onscreen element ②①.

To control the tool tips:

◆ Use the Tool Tips menu to choose one of the following:

- **Normal** waits a moment before displaying the tip.
- **None** turns off the display of the tips.
- **Fast** displays the tips almost immediately after the cursor pauses over the tool or feature.

To change the place cursor preview:

◆ Deselect the option to show Thumbnails on Place to see only the cursor, and not the preview, for placed text and images.

To change how docked panels collapse:

◆ Select Auto-Collapse Icon Panels to cause selected docked panels to close when you move back to the document.

⓳ *The* **Interface settings** *of the Preferences dialog box.*

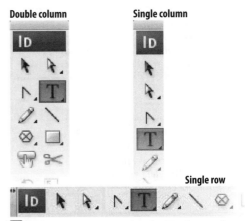

⓴ *The* **arrangements for the Tools panel.**

㉑ *An example of a* **tool tip** *that appears when you pause over an interface element.*

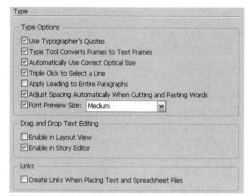

22 *The* **Type settings** *of the Preferences dialog box.*

"The Wizard of Oz" Off
"The Wizard of Oz" On

23 *An example of using* **typographer's quotes**.

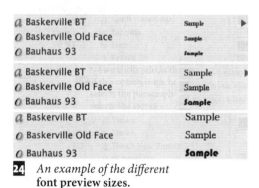

24 *An example of the different* **font preview sizes.**

Type Preferences

Use the Type Preferences controls for working with text **22**.

To set the type options preferences:

1. Use Typographer's Quotes automatically changes typewriter quotes into the proper curly quote characters **23**.

2. Type Tools Converts Frames to Text Frames lets you double-click inside a frame to change from the Selection tools to the Type tool.

3. Automatically Use Correct Optical Size sets the correct value for the optical size of Multiple Master fonts.

4. Triple Click to Select a Line does the following:

   - Three clicks selects a line.
   - Four clicks selects a paragraph.
   - Five clicks selects the story.

   TIP If this option is unchecked, three clicks selects the paragraph and four clicks selects the story.

5. Apply Leading to Entire Paragraphs lets InDesign work more like QuarkXPress.

6. Adjust Spacing Automatically When Cutting and Pasting Words avoids adding two spaces when pasting text from one position to another.

7. Font Preview Size lets you choose the size of the preview of fonts in the Type menu. Larger previews take longer to display **24**.

   TIP Deselect this option to turn the font preview off. This helps the Font menu display faster.

You can also control whether or not drag-and-drop text is activated.

To turn on drag-and-drop text:

1. Select Enable in Layout View to have drag-and-drop text active when working within frames on the pages.

2. Select Enable in Story Editor to have drag-and-drop text active when working within the Story Editor.

TIP I love drag-and-drop text, so I have mine turned on for both views. But most designers keep it off in the layout view so they don't inadvertently drag text to new positions.

The early versions of InDesign automatically linked text and spreadsheet documents back to their original file. Now, a preference controls whether placed text files are automatically linked to their source.

To choose if text files are linked or embedded:

◆ Click the option Create Links When Placing Text and Spreadsheet Files to link those styles back to the original files **25**. If you make changes to the word processor or spreadsheet file, those changes will automatically update in InDesign.

TIP All local formatting you have applied will be discarded when the text is updated.

25 *A placed text file shows in the Links panel when the links to external files and spreadsheets is turned on.*

A Suggestion for an Editorial Workflow

Many people I know want to turn on the option to create links when placing text and spreadsheet files because they need editors to make changes to their document.

The problem with that workflow is that any formatting applied to the text in InDesign will be lost when the text is updated.

A better solution would be to work with InCopy, which allows InDesign stories to be edited without InDesign running. Then, the text can be updated in InDesign without losing any formatting.

Type Preferences

26 *The **Advanced Type** settings of the Preferences dialog box.*

27 *The **non-Latin input controls** for the Macintosh and Windows operating systems.*

Advanced Type Preferences

Don't let the term "Advanced Type" throw you off. These are settings that you may want to change depending on the typefaces you work with.

The Character Settings control the size and position of superscript, subscript, and small cap characters **26**.

To set the Character Settings preferences:

1. Enter amounts in the Size fields to control the size of the characters.

2. Enter amounts in the Position fields to control how far above or below the baseline the characters are positioned.

TIP The percentage amount is based on the total space between the two lines.

A non-Latin typeface is one that uses 2-byte and 4-byte characters. Japanese, Korean, and Chinese are examples of non-Latin typefaces. If you work with non-Latin typefaces, you may need to use features in the operating system to enter characters instead of the keyboard **27**.

To use the operating system to enter non-Latin text:

◆ Click the option Use Inline Input For Non-Latin Text to allow you to input text using the electronic keyboards built into the computer operating system.

Advanced Type Preferences

Composition Preferences

The Highlight settings let you control which parts of the text are highlighted to indicate composition or typographic violations or substitutions **28**.

To set the highlight options:

◆ Set the Highlight options as follows **29**:

- **Keep Violations** displays lines that have been broken in violation of the Keep With settings that you chose for the paragraph options.

- **H&J Violations** highlights those areas that violate the hyphenation or justification controls.

TIP H&J Violations occur when InDesign has no other way to set the text except to break the H&J controls.

- **Custom Tracking/Kerning** highlights the text with tracking or kerning applied to it.

- **Substituted Fonts** highlights characters that are substituted for a font that is not installed in the computer system.

TIP This is the famous pink highlight for a missing font that many people see when they import text or change typefaces.

TIP If the shape of the uninstalled font exists in the Adobe Type Manager database, the shape of the font is approximated. If not, a default font is used.

- **Substituted Glyphs** highlights Open Type characters that have been substituted with alternate glyphs.

28 *The* **Composition settings** *of the Preferences dialog box.*

low bricks one by one. She started slowly at first, but then started to walk faster

29 *An example of text with a* **highlight** *applied.*

30 *The effect of setting the* **Justify Text Next to an Object**.

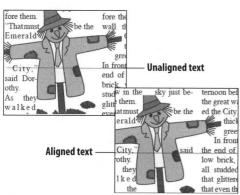

Unaligned text

Aligned text

31 *When* **Skip By Leading** *is turned off, the text does not line up across columns. When it is turned on, the text does line up.*

You can also control the effect of the Text Wrap settings and how text wraps around objects.

To set the text wrap options:

◆ Choose one of the following from the Text Wrap options:

- **Justify Text Next to an Object** forces text next to an object to be justified if it wraps around an object inside the frame **30**.

- **Skip by Leading** forces text that has wrapped around an object to move to the next available leading increment. This avoids problems where text may not line up across columns or frames **31**.

- **Text Wrap Only Affects Text Beneath** causes InDesign text wrap to work only on text below the object, rather than text above and below the object.

TIP Some designers turn this on because they want InDesign to work more similarly to QuarkXPress. Don't do it! You're only limiting yourself from some of the more interesting effects that InDesign offers.

Composition Preferences

Units & Increments Preferences

Units and Increments refer to the units of measurements and how much things change when you apply keyboard shortcuts .

To set the ruler units:

1. Use the Origin menu to select one of the following :

   - **Spread** sets the horizontal ruler to stretch across the pages in a spread.

   - **Page** sets the horizontal ruler to reset for each individual page in a spread.

   - **Spine** sets the horizontal ruler to stretch across the spine of the document.

2. Use the Horizontal and Vertical menus to select the unit of measurement for each of the rulers .

   or

   Set an amount, in points, for a custom unit of measurement.

To set the number of points per inch:

- Use the Points/Inch field to choose between the PostScript or the Traditional numbers of points per inch 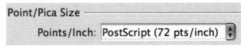.

The keyboard increments control how much the objects move or the text changes.

To set the keyboard increments:

- Enter an amount in the fields as follows:

   - **Cursor Key** lets you choose the amount that the arrow keys move objects.

   - **Size/Leading** controls the amount that the type size and leading change.

   - **Baseline Shift** lets you set the amount that the baseline shift changes.

   - **Kerning** controls the amount that the kerning changes.

32 *The* **Units & Increments settings** *of the Preferences dialog box.*

33 *The* **Origin menu** *lets you choose how the rulers stretch across the page.*

34 *The* **units of measurement** *for the horizontal and vertical rulers.*

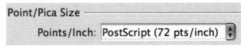

35 *Use the* **Points/Inch field** *to choose between the PostScript measurement for points per inch or the Traditional measurement.*

36 *The **Grids settings** of the Preferences dialog box.*

37 *An example of setting the **Grids in Back option** in the Grids category.*

Grids Preferences

Designers just love to set up lines that stretch up and down and across their pages to help keep text and graphics lined up correctly. The Grids preferences control those lines **36**.

To set the baseline grid options:

1. Use the Color menu to choose a color for the baseline grid.

2. Use the Start field to position where the grid should start on the page.

3. Use the Relative To menu to position the start of the grid relative to the top of the page or the top margin.

4. Use the Increment Every field to set the distance between the lines of the grid.

5. Use the View Threshold field to set the lowest magnification at which the grid is visible.

TIP Set this for something like 75% to make it easier to see the entire page when you zoom out.

To set the document grid preferences:

1. Use the Color menu to choose a color for the document grid.

2. Enter a value for the Horizontal and Vertical fields as follows:

   • **Gridline Every** sets the distance between the major lines of the grid.

   • **Subdivisions** sets the number of secondary lines of the grid.

To set the positioning of the grids:

◆ Check Grids in Back to position the grids behind graphics and text **37**.

Grids Preferences

Guides & Pasteboard Preferences

You can customize the appearance and size of your ruler guides and the pasteboard.

The Color area is a rainbow of choices for how to color onscreen guides and areas .

To set the onscreen elements colors:

◆ Use the menus to set the colors for each of the following:

- **Margins** sets the color of the guides created by the margins settings.

- **Columns** sets the color of the guides created by the column setting.

- **Bleed** sets the color of the guide around the bleed area.

- **Slug** sets the color of the guide around the slug area.

- **Preview Background** sets the color of the area that surrounds the page in the preview mode.

To set the Guide Options:

1. Use the Snap to Zone field to set how close the objects should be when they snap to guides. This amount is set in pixels.

2. Check Guides in Back to hide the guides when they appear behind objects.

To set the Pasteboard Options:

◆ Enter an amount in the Minimum Vertical Offset field to increase or decrease the amount of pasteboard space above and below the page **39**.

38 *The **Guides & Pasteboard settings** in the Preferences dialog box.*

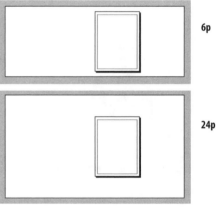

6p

24p

39 *The effect of increasing the minimum vertical offset.*

40 The **Dictionary settings** *in the Preferences dialog box.*

Double quote choices

Single quote choices

41 The **Quote menus** *in the Dictionary preferences.*

Dictionary Preferences

The Dictionary preferences work with whichever languages and dictionaries are used for InDesign documents **40**.

The Language setting is used to choose which language dictionary should be used to check whether words are correctly spelled. Consider that the word *cinema* is correctly spelled if English is the chosen language. However, the word is incorrectly spelled if French is chosen as the language. In that case the word should be *cinéma*.

To set the language options:

1. Use the Language menu to set the default language.

2. If you have installed special hyphenation preferences, choose a preference from the Hyphenation menu.

3. If you have installed special spelling preferences, choose a preference from the Spelling menu.

4. Use the Double Quotes menu to choose the characters for double quotation marks **41**.

5. Use the Single Quotes menu to choose the characters for single quotation marks **41**.

TIP The Quotes menus list the marks used for different languages, such as Spanish and French. Or you can enter your own characters in the field.

Dictionary Preferences

Sharing Dictionaries

You may want to create a single dictionary that everyone in your workgroup can share. When a user dictionary is stored on a server, the first user to load the dictionary locks the file; all subsequent users see that the dictionary is locked. Files can also be locked through the operating system, which makes the file read-only. If you share a user dictionary over the network server, you may want to lock the file so that it's read-only for all users, allowing only the administrator to add words.

You use the dictionary management tools to create, link to, add, and delete new user dictionaries. This allows you to create several dictionaries for InDesign.

To create a new user dictionary:

1. Click the New Dictionary button in the Dictionary preferences .

2. Name and save the dictionary file (.udc) to a location. The new dictionary appears in the Dictionary list 43.

You don't have to create your own new dictionary. You can use the dictionary management tools to add someone else's dictionary to your version of InDesign.

To add a dictionary:

1. Click the Add Dictionary button in the Dictionary preferences.

2. Navigate to select the new dictionary. The dictionary appears in the Dictionary list.

To delete a dictionary:

1. Select the dictionary that you want to delete in the Dictionary list.

2. Click the Delete Dictionary button in the Dictionary preferences.

To relink a dictionary:

1. Select the dictionary that has a missing or modified icon next to its name in the Dictionary list 44.

2. Click the Relink Dictionary button in the Dictionary preferences.

3. Navigate to find the missing dictionary.

New Dictionary   Delete Dictionary
Relink Dictionary   Add Dictionary

42 *The* **Dictionary buttons** *in the Dictionary preferences.*

43 *The* **Dictionary list** *displays the list of dictionaries installed in the Dictionary preferences.*

44 *The* **Missing icon in the Dictionary list** *indicates that you need to relink to the dictionary.*

Dictionary Preferences

45 *The* **Compose Using menu** *in the Dictionary category.*

46 *The* **User Dictionary options** *determine what happens to hyphenation exceptions.*

The hyphenation exceptions let you choose to apply the hyphenations created by editing the Dictionary or those built into the application.

To set the hyphenation exceptions:

◆ Choose one of the following from the Compose Using menu **45**:

- **User Dictionary** uses only the hyphenation exceptions set by editing the Dictionary.

- **Document** uses the hyphenation exceptions list stored inside the document. *(See the next exercise for how to add the user dictionary hyphenation exceptions to a document.)*

- **User Dictionary and Document** merges the exceptions in both the document and the user dictionary. This is the default setting.

The User Dictionary options let you merge hyphenation exceptions into a document and create new hyphenation exceptions that affect the document **46**.

To set the user dictionary preferences:

1. Merge User Dictionary into Document adds the hyphenation exceptions in the user dictionary to the document. This is on by default.

TIP This is especially useful if you send the native InDesign document to a service bureau for output.

2. Recompose All Stories When Modified applies the new exceptions in the user dictionary to all the stories in the document.

Dictionary Preferences

Spelling Preferences

The Find section of the Spelling preferences controls what types of problems the spelling checker flags during a spelling check .

To set the Find options for Spelling:

1. Select Misspelled Words to find words that are not known in the spelling dictionary.

2. Select Repeated Words to find instances of words that are repeated, such as "the the spelling checker."

3. Select Uncapitalized Words to find words that are listed in the dictionary as capitalized. For instance, proper names of countries are capitalized in the dictionary.

4. Select Uncapitalized Sentences to flag uncapitalized words that begin sentences.

Dynamic spelling highlights errors right on your page. If you want to work with dynamic spelling, you have a choice as to which colors the errors are underlined with.

To set the Dynamic Spelling options:

1. Select Enable Dynamic Spelling in the Spelling preferences .

2. Use the Underline Color menus to specify the color used to highlight misspelled words, repeated words, uncapitalized words, and uncapitalized sentences.

47 *The* **Spelling settings** *in the Preferences dialog box.*

48 *Use the* **Dynamic Spelling controls** *to turn on dynamic spelling and specify colors for each of the error categories.*

Spelling Preferences

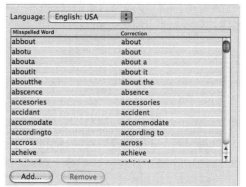

49 *The* **Autocorrect settings** *in the Preferences dialog box.*

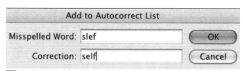

50 *Use the* **Autocorrect Options controls** *to turn on autocorrection for word errors and for capitalization errors.*

51 *The* **Add to Autocorrect List dialog box** *lets you enter the mispelling for a word and its correction.*

Autocorrect Preferences

The Autocorrect preferences not only turn on the Autocorrect feature, they allow you to add or remove those words that you want to have automatically corrected.

To turn on Autocorrection:

1. Choose Enable Autocorrect to turn on the basic correction for words **49**.

2. Choose Autocorrect Capitalization Errors to also automatically correct errors in uppercase and lowercase words.

The Autocorrect list contains the words that are commonly mistyped. In addition to the words the Adobe engineers felt you would mistype, you can easily add your own.

To add words to the Autocorrect list:

1. Use the Language menu to choose the language for the autocorrection.

2. Click the Add button at the bottom of the Autocorrect Preferences **50**. This opens the Add to Autocorrect List dialog box **51**.

3. Type the typical misspelling in the Misspelled Word field.

4. Type the correct spelling in the Correction field.

5. Click OK to add the word to the list.

To delete words from the Autocorrect list:

1. Select the word in the list that you want to delete.

2. Click the Remove button.

Autocorrect Preferences

Notes Preferences

Notes are primarily used in an InDesign/
InCopy workflow. The Notes preferences
control how the notes appear in the InDesign
or InCopy stories .

To set the Notes options:

1. Use the Notes Color list to set a color for
   the user. This color should be unique.

2. Select Show Note Tooltips to display the
   text for the note when the user hovers
   over the note display 🔢.

You can also set the preferences for how
notes are handled when working in the Story
Editor.

To set the options for notes in the Story Editor:

◆ Check the following as desired:

   • **Include Note Content when Checking
     Spelling** to apply a spelling check to the
     note text.

   • **Include Note Content in Find/Change
     Operations** to include the note text in
     the results of a Find/Change routine.

To set the background color for the note:

◆ Use the In Background Color list to
   choose a color for the area behind the
   note when viewed in the Story Editor 🔢.

🔢 *The* **Notes settings** *in the
Preferences dialog box.*

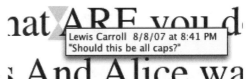

🔢 *A* **note tooltip** *that is revealed when
the cursor pauses over the note.*

🔢 *The* **note background color** *as
displayed in the Story Editor.*

Notes Preferences

55 *The **Story Editor Display** settings of the Preferences dialog box.*

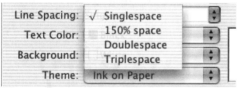

56 *The **Line Spacing menu** of the Story Editor preferences controls the space between the lines of text.*

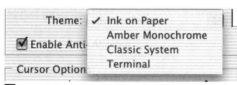

57 *The **Theme menu** lets you quickly change the text and background colors.*

58 *The **Cursor Options** change the display of the cursor within the text.*

Story Editor Display Preferences

If you work in the Story Editor, you can choose the preferences for its display **55**.

TIP None of these settings affect the appearance of the text in the layout.

To set the preferences for text display:

1. Use the Font menu to set the typeface.

2. Use the point size menu to set the size.

3. Use the Line Spacing menu to choose the leading between the lines **56**.

4. Use the Text Color menu to set the color of the text.

5. Use the Background menu to set the color of the Story Editor window background.

   or

   Use the Theme menu to select a preset text and background color scheme **57**.

6. Choose Enable Anti-Aliasing to soften the edges of the text.

7. If you choose Enable Anti-Aliasing, choose an anti-aliasing Type option.

   - **Default** is the typical anti-aliasing.

   - **LCD Optimized** works best on light-colored backgrounds with black text.

   - **Soft** produces a lighter, fuzzier appearance than Default.

You can also change how the cursor, or insertion point, is displayed within the Story Editor. This is helpful for those who are used to editing text on mainframe terminals.

To set the preferences for cursor display:

1. Choose **Edit** > **Preferences** > **Story Editor Display** (Win) or **InDesign** > **Preferences** > **Story Editor Display** (Mac).

2. Choose one of the Cursor Options **58**.

3. Select Blink to make the cursor turn on and off within the text.

Story Editor Display Preferences

Display Performance Preferences

The default view is the view that is used when documents are first opened.

To set the default view:

1. Use the Default View settings menu to choose which of the display performance settings is automatically applied to new documents .

2. Check Preserve Object-level Display Settings to maintain any individual settings applied to graphics.

The Adjust View Settings control how images appear onscreen for each of the three view choices.

To choose the options for Adjust View Settings:

1. Choose one of the options from the Adjust View Settings menu.

2. Drag the slider controls to set the quality for raster images, vector graphics, and the transparency effects.

3. Repeat for the other two view settings.

TIP It takes longer for the screen to redraw if you choose the highest quality previews.

Anti-aliasing is the term used to described the soft edge applied to either text or graphics.

To control the anti-aliasing of text and graphics:

◆ Check Enable Anti-Aliasing to add a soft edge to the type and graphics displayed on the monitor **60**.

59 *The* **Display Performance settings** *in the Preferences dialog box.*

Dorothy On
Dorothy Off

60 *The effect of applying* **anti-aliasing** *to type.*

Display Performance Preferences

On

Off

The Wizard of Oz by
L. Frank Baum

61 *The effect of applying* **greeking** *to type.*

Left position | Middle position | Right position

Which
Witch?

Which
Witch?

62 *The appearance of text and images for each of the Hand Tool slider settings.*

Greeking is the term used to describe the gray band that is substituted for text characters **61**.

To set text to be greeked:

◆ Enter an amount in the Greek Type Below field. This sets the size below which the text characters will be replaced with gray bands onscreen.

When you use the Hand tool to scroll around a document, InDesign needs to determine how text and images that were not originally in the window appear when you move them into view. You use the Hand Tool preferences to control how the images appear or how fast you can move while scrolling.

To set the scrolling preferences:

◆ Drag the Hand Tool slider to one of the following:

- The left position greeks both text and images. This is the fastest setting but it loses the appearance of the page as text and images come into view **62**.

- The middle position greeks images but maintains text visibility **62**.

- The right position turns off all greeking of text and images. This is the slowest setting but it maintains the appearance of the page as text and images come into view **62**.

Display Performance Preferences

Appearance of Black Preferences

As many designers have discovered, when a color-corrected black is displayed on a computer screen, 100% black ink winds up looking very washed out. The Appearance of Black preferences allow you to choose how 100% black ink is displayed and printed 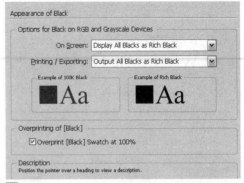.

To control the appearance of black on screen:

◆ Choose one of the following from the On Screen menu:

- **Display All Blacks Accurately** displays 100%K as dark gray. This setting allows you to see the difference between pure black and rich black.

- **Display All Blacks As Rich Black** displays 100%K as jet black (RGB=000). This setting makes pure black and rich black appear the same on-screen.

You can also control how 100%K appears when printing to a non-PostScript desktop printer or exporting to an RGB format. This helps control the appearance of blacks in PDF and JPEG files.

To control the appearance of black when printing or exporting to an RGB format:

◆ Choose one of the following from the Printing/Exporting menu:

- **Output All Blacks Accurately** outputs 100%K using the color numbers in the document. This setting allows you to see the difference between pure black and rich black in the finished document.

- **Output All Blacks As Rich Black** outputs 100%K as jet black. This setting makes pure black and rich black appear the same.

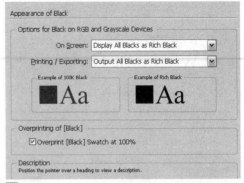

63 *The* **Appearance of Black settings** *in the Preferences dialog box.*

64 *The* **File Handling settings** *in the Preferences dialog box.*

65 *The* **Preview Size menu** *lets you choose the size for the preview image that is saved with the file.*

Working with Previews

You may not see a document preview if you open the file using the Macintosh Finder or Windows Explorer. That's why I recommend using Adobe Bridge to open InDesign documents.

If you save a document with a preview, you will only see a preview of the first spread. However, you will be able to see a preview of all the pages of a template.

File Handling Preferences

If InDesign crashes or the computer is shut down before you can save the InDesign documents, a file is created that contains the recovered document. The Document Recovery Data area lets you choose where that recovered document is located.

TIP Although most people will use the same drive that contains the application, this option lets you specify a folder on a drive that has more space than the one that contains the InDesign application folder.

To set the temporary folder:

1. Click the Browse (Win) or Choose (Mac) button in the Document Recovery Data area **64**.

2. Use the dialog box to choose the location of the recovered documents.

The Saving InDesign Files area lets you add a thumbnail preview to the file. You can also control the size of the preview.

TIP Extra-large previews make it possible to read text in the document. Medium and small previews usually greek all text.

To create a preview with saved documents:

1. In the Saving InDesign Files area, choose Always Save Preview Images with Documents.

TIP You can change the preview option in the Save As dialog box.

2. Choose one of the sizes from the Preview Size menu **65**.

TIP Larger previews increase the file size and the time it takes to save the document.

File Handling Preferences

You can control the position where snippets appear when you drag them onto a page.

To control the location of snippets:

◆ Check the Snippet Import options as follows:

- **Position at Original Location** places the snippet at its original coordinates. This may cause a snippet from a right-hand page to appear on the pasteboard of a left-hand page.

- **Position at Cursor Location** ignores the original coordinates and places the snippet where the mouse is released on the page.

If you work in a collaborative setting, you may want to use the Adobe Version Cue software to help coordinate the workflow.

To turn Version Cue on or off:

1. Select or deselect Enable Version Cue in the Version Cue area.

2. Restart InDesign.

Using Version Cue?

Version Cue is a separate application that tracks changes to a file as you work on it. With Version Cue you can check to make sure you are working on the latest version of an image, a story, or the InDesign file.

You access Version Cue features by way of the Adobe dialog box or through Adobe Bridge, depending on whether you are using Version Cue-enabled software and whether or not you have installed a Creative Suite software set (for example, Adobe Creative Suite 3 Design Premium).

One of my favorite features of Version Cue is the ability to automatically create PDF files and distribute them to a work group.

File Handling Preferences

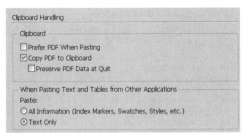

66 *The* **Clipboard Handling settings** *in the Preferences dialog box.*

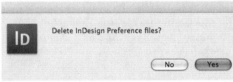

67 *The* **Delete InDesign Preference dialog box** *lets you start from scratch with factory-fresh default settings.*

Clipboard Handling

You may need to change the options for what type of information is included in the clipboard **66**.

To set the clipboard format:

◆ Check the Clipboard options as follows:

- **Prefer PDF When Pasting** adds graphics as self-contained PDF files that retain effects.

- **Copy PDF to Clipboard** copies data as PDF files. Select this in order to paste paths into Illustrator or Photoshop.

- **Preserve PDF Data at Quit** maintains any copied PDF information on the clipboard for use in other applications.

To set the attributes for pasting text:

◆ Check When Pasting Text and Tables from Other Applications as follows:

- **All Information** maintains formatting.

- **Text Only** strips out all formatting.

Trashing Preferences

Sometimes InDesign may start to act strangely. This may mean that the files that hold all your preferences and settings have become corrupt. In that case you need to trash those files and let InDesign start over with the factory settings.

To restore all preferences and default settings:

1. As you launch InDesign, immediately press Ctrl-Alt-Shift (Win) or Cmd-Opt-Shift-Control (Mac).

2. Click Yes when asked if you want to delete your preference files **67**.

Clipboard Handling; Trashing Preferences

Configuring Plug-Ins

InDesign uses a large set of plug-ins as its core set of commands and features. You may want to control which plug-ins are loaded each time you launch the program.

To select the plug-ins set:

1. Choose **InDesign > Configure Plug-ins** (Mac) or **Help > Configure Plug-ins** (Win) to open the Configure Plug-ins dialog box 68:

2. Choose a set from the Set menu 69.

To modify a plug-in set:

1. Select the plug-in set.

2. If the set is one of the default sets, choose Duplicate to make a copy of the set.

3. Click the checkbox column to the left of the name to enable or disable the plug-in from the set.

4. Use the Display checkboxes to see the types of plug-ins.

To see the information about a plug-in:

◆ Click the Show Info button in the Configure Plug-ins dialog box to open the Plug-in Information dialog box.

68 *The* **Configure Plug-ins dialog box** *is where you can control which plug-ins get loaded when you launch InDesign.*

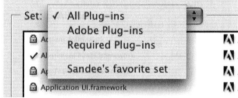

69 *The three* **default plug-ins sets** *cannot be modified. Custom plug-ins sets are shown at the bottom of the Sets menu.*

INDEX

A

Acrobat layers, 294
Add Anchor Point tool, 14, 184, 190
Add Bullets dialog box, 353
Adobe Bridge Center, 417
Adobe InDesign Tags Import
  Options dialog box, 359
Adobe Paragraph Composer, 397
Adobe PDF Presets dialog box, 498–499
Advanced Type preferences, 519
alignment
  cells, 312
  cell text, 328
  object, 103
  optical margin, 396
  paragraph, 65
  stroke, 152
  tab, 305
  text on a path, 238
  text to baseline grid, 405
alignment character, 307
Align panel, 103–105
  alignment icons, 103
  Alignment menu, 103
  defined, 2
  distribute icons, 104
  distribute space icons, 104
  illustrated, 2
  opening, 103
  Use Spacing option, 105
alpha channels
  applying to images, 224
  as clipping paths, 221
Anchored Object Options dialog box, 248
anchored objects, 243–248
  above the line options, 246
  creating, 244
  custom, options, 247
  options, 244
  position setting, 245

as rectangles, 244
releasing, 248
settings, editing, 248
use tips, 248
anchor points
  adding, 184
  defined, 178
  deleting, 184, 189
  modifying, 185
  moving, 182
  selecting, 182
angle measurements, 111
ANPA Color, 131
anti-aliasing, 532
Apply Master dialog box, 269
arrange commands, 102
arrowheads, 160
artwork. See graphics
ASCII text, 258
  defined, 258
  options, setting, 261
Assignments panel, 2
Attributes panel
  defined, 2
  illustrated, 2, 142
  Nonprinting option, 456
  opening, 142
Autocorrect preferences, 529
autoflow cursors, 265
automation, 339–364
  bullets and numbering, 352–354
  Find/Change, 344–350
  Find Font, 360
  footnotes, 355–357
  lines together, 361
  scripts, 364
  spell checking, 340–343
  Story Editor, 351
  tagged text, 358–359

B

H